Dublin

Fionn Davenport
Tom Smallman
Pat Yale
Tony Wheeler

LONELY PLANET PUBLICATIONS
Melbourne • Oakland • London • Paris

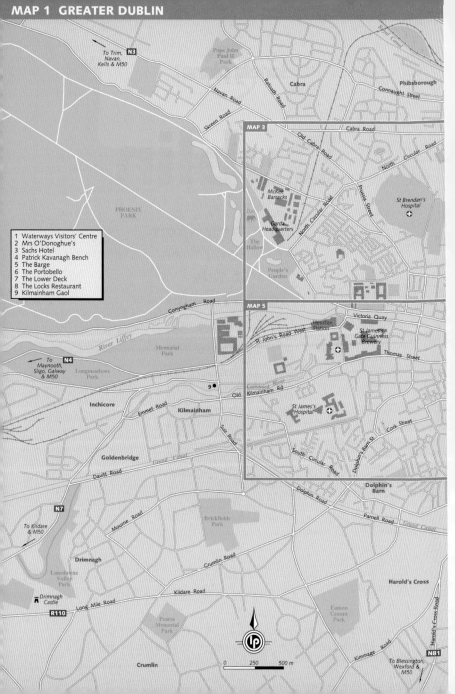

MAP 1 GREATER DUBLIN

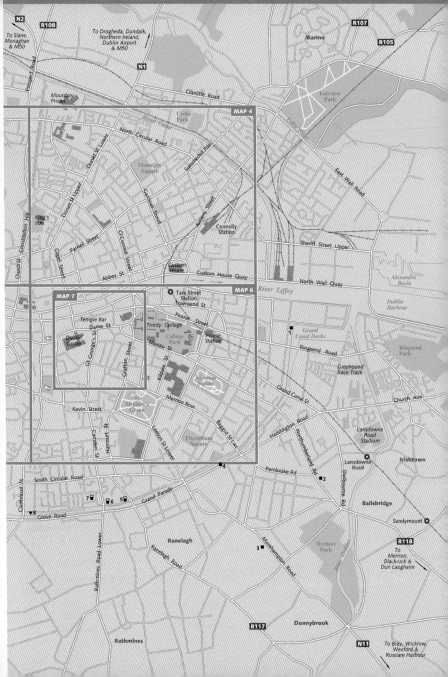

Dublin
3rd edition – June 1999
First published – June 1993

Published by
Lonely Planet Publications Pty Ltd A.C.N. 005 607 983
192 Burwood Rd, Hawthorn, Victoria 3122, Australia

Lonely Planet Offices
Australia PO Box 617, Hawthorn, Victoria 3122
USA 150 Linden St, Oakland, CA 94607
UK 10a Spring Place, London NW5 3BH
France 1 rue du Dahomey, 75011 Paris

Photographs
Many of the images in this guide are available for licensing from
Lonely Planet Images.
email: lpi@lonelyplanet.com.au

Front cover photograph
Out and about in Temple Bar (Doug McKinlay)

ISBN 0 86442 610 0

text & maps © Lonely Planet 1999
photos © photographers as indicated 1999

Printed by Colorcraft Ltd, Hong Kong

Contents – Text

THE AUTHORS   **3**

THIS BOOK   **5**

FOREWORD   **6**

INTRODUCTION   **9**

FACTS ABOUT DUBLIN   **11**

History 11	Economy 18	Religion 27
Geography 16	Population & People 19	Language 27
Climate 17	Education 19	**Dublin's Architecture &**
Ecology & Environment 17	Arts 20	**Architects 29**
Government & Politics 17	Society & Conduct 26	

FACTS FOR THE VISITOR   **36**

When to Go 36	Internet Resources 46	Disabled Travellers 51
Orientation 36	Books 47	Senior Travellers 51
Tourist Offices 37	Photography & Video 48	Dublin for Children 51
Documents 37	Time 48	Dangers & Annoyances 55
Embassies & Consulates 38	Electricity 48	Emergencies 56
Customs 39	Health 49	Business Hours 56
Money 39	Women Travellers 50	Special Events 57
Post & Communications 44	Gay & Lesbian Travellers 51	Doing Business 60

GETTING THERE & AWAY   **61**

Air 61	Bus & Train Discount Deals 67	Organised Tours 68
Bus 66	Ferry 67	Warning 68
Train 66	Road & Sea 68	

GETTING AROUND   **70**

The Airport 70	Car & Motorcycle 71	Walking 74
Bus 71	Taxi 73	Organised Tours 74
Train 71	Bicycle 73	

THINGS TO SEE & DO   **77**

Sightseeing Itineraries 77	Christ Church Cathedral 93	O'Connell St 111
Liffey Quays 79	St Patrick's Cathedral 96	GPO 113
South of the Liffey..............82	National Museum 101	Custom House 114
Trinity College 83	Leinster House 103	Parnell Square 115
Bank of Ireland 87	St Stephen's Green 105	Mountjoy Square 119
Temple Bar 88	Merrion Square 109	James Joyce Cultural Centre 120
Dublin Castle 90	**North of the Liffey.............111**	Old Jameson Distillery 121

King's Inns & Henrietta St ..121
Four Courts 122
Other Sights 122
Guinness Brewery 122

Royal Hospital Kilmainham 123
Kilmainham Gaol 124
Phoenix Park 124
The Royal Canal 126

Casino at Marino 127
The Grand Canal 129
Activities 132
Courses 134

DUBLIN WALKS   135

Walk 1: Mountjoy Square to St
Stephen's Green 135

Walk 2: Custom House to the
Four Courts 138

Walk 3: From the Cathedrals
Through the Liberties 141

PLACES TO STAY   145

Places to Stay – Budget 145
Places to Stay – Mid-Range 149

Places to Stay – Top End 151
Places to Stay – Deluxe 151

Long-Term Rentals 152

PLACES TO EAT   153

Food 153
Drinks 153

Places to Eat – Budget 156
Places to Eat – Mid-Range 160

Places to Eat – Top End 162

ENTERTAINMENT   165

Pubs & Bars 165
Irish Cabaret 165
Discos & Nightclubs 165

Concerts 167
Cinemas 167
Theatre 168

Buskers 168
Spectator Sports 169
Dublin's Pubs & Bars 171

SHOPPING   182

What to Buy 182

Where to Shop 182

SEASIDE SUBURBS   187

Dun Laoghaire 187
Dalkey 192

Bray 192
Howth 193

EXCURSIONS   197

Powerscourt Estate 197
Glendalough 199
Wicklow Way 200
Russborough House 200
Kildare Town 201

Castletown House 201
Malahide ....:..202
Newbridge House 203
Drogheda 204
Boyne Valley 205

Mellifont Abbey 206
Monasterboice 207
Kells 207
Hill of Tara 208
Trim 209

GLOSSARY   210

INDEX   221

Text 221

Boxed Text..........................224

MAP SECTION   225

The Authors

Fionn Davenport
Fionn was born in and spent most of his youth in Dublin, that is when his family wasn't moving him to Buenos Aires or Geneva or New York (all thanks to his Dad, whose job took him far and wide). Infected with the travel disease, he became a nomad in his own right after graduating from Trinity College, moving first to Paris and then to New York, where he spent five years as a travel editor and sometime writer. The call of home was too much to resist however, so armed with his portable computer, his record collection and an empty wallet he returned to Dublin where he decided to continue where he left off in New York. Only it was quieter, wetter and a hell of a lot smaller. When he's not DJing in pubs and clubs throughout the city he's writing and updating travel guides. He has written about many destinations throughout the world. This is his second book for Lonely Planet, having worked already on the *Spain* guide.

Tom Smallman
Tom was born and raised in the UK and now lives in Melbourne, Australia. He had a number of jobs before joining Lonely Planet as an editor and now works full time researching guidebooks. He has worked on Lonely Planet guides to *Canada*, *Ireland*, *New York*, *New Jersey & Pennsylvania*, *New South Wales*, *Sydney*, *Australia*, *Britain*, *Scotland* and *Edinburgh*.

Pat Yale
Pat was born and brought up in London where she spent several happy years selling holidays before deciding she'd rather do the travelling herself. Since then she has interspersed her wanderings in Europe, Africa, Asia and Central America with life as a travel writer, working, among other things, on the Lonely Planet guides to *Turkey*, *Ireland*, *Dublin* and *Britain*. These days her home is in Bristol.

Tony Wheeler
Tony was born in England but spent most of his youth overseas. He returned to England to do a university degree in engineering, worked as an automotive engineer, returned to university to complete an MBA then dropped out on the Asian overland trail with his wife, Maureen. They've been travelling, writing and publishing guidebooks ever since, having set up Lonely Planet Publications in the mid-70s.

FROM THE AUTHOR

Fionn Davenport First, my thanks to everyone at the various attractions, tourist offices, hotels and restaurants (you are too many to name!) who patiently answered all of my questions, sent faxes, posted letters and basically made my task a lot easier. Thanks also to the folks at the Old Jameson Distillery and Dublin Castle who were unfailingly decent about everything. A big thank you to Giuliano, my resident architecture buff and art historian, who gave me an appreciation of Dublin's many architectural and artistic showcases I wouldn't otherwise have; to my mother and father for their advice, encouragement and worthwhile information; to Lucy and Ronan for putting up with my frenetic wanderings from the computer to the kettle and back again; to Brendan for the use of his car; to Paul, Conor, Fergus and Frodo for you-know-what (because I don't!); and to Paolo for going to New York, because if you'd been around I can't even imagine the amount of coffee breaks I would have taken. Lastly, thanks to everyone at Lonely Planet in London, who showed me the way and gave me directions!

This Book

This is the third edition of Lonely Planet's *Dublin* guide. Tony Wheeler wrote the first edition and Tom Smallman and Pat Yale updated the second edition. This edition was updated and expanded by Fionn Davenport.

From the Publisher

This edition of *Dublin* was edited in Lonely Planet's London office by David Rathborne with assistance from John King. Rhonda Carrier and Tim Ryder proofread the book and David and Tim produced the index. Sara Yorke drew the maps and designed the book, colour pages and cover. The illustrations were drawn by Nicky Castle and the photographs were supplied by Lonely Planet Images, Neil Beer and Neil Setchfield. Thanks to Claire Hornshaw for additional research and writing, to Simon Calder, Jen Loy and Leonie Mugavin for checking the travel information, to Quentin Frayne for the language information and to Leonie for help with the health section. Special thanks to Katrina Browning and Michelle Lewis for their invaluable advice and assistance.

Thanks

Many thanks to the travellers who used the second edition of this book and wrote to us with helpful hints, useful advice and interesting anecdotes. Your names follow:

Jadwiga Adamczuk, Wilbur S Bailey, Tracy Bays, John Bourke, Marcella Brown, Sharon Clerkin, Sherla Davies, Kara Davis, Kathy Douglas, Humphrey Evans, Stacy Hague, Tanyia Harrison, Maureen Holland, Steven Holland, Sue Johnson, Patrick James Logue, Tom McCluskey, KS Moore, John Perkins, Lisa Pickard, Mary Rice, Jane Robertson, Sandra Standifer, Matthew Starr, Ursula Thummer-Wolf, Kenneth Wardrop, Teresa Webb, Elad Yom-Tov.

Foreword

ABOUT LONELY PLANET GUIDEBOOKS

The story begins with a classic travel adventure: Tony and Maureen Wheeler's 1972 journey across Europe and Asia to Australia. Useful information about the overland trail did not exist at that time, so Tony and Maureen published the first Lonely Planet guidebook to meet a growing need.

From a kitchen table, then from a tiny office in Melbourne (Australia), Lonely Planet has become the largest independent travel publisher in the world, an international company with offices in Melbourne, Oakland (USA), London (UK) and Paris (France).

Today Lonely Planet guidebooks cover the globe. There is an ever-growing list of books and there's information in a variety of forms and media. Some things haven't changed. The main aim is still to help make it possible for adventurous travellers to get out there – to explore and better understand the world.

At Lonely Planet we believe travellers can make a positive contribution to the countries they visit – if they respect their host communities and spend their money wisely. Since 1986 a percentage of the income from each book has been donated to aid projects and human rights campaigns.

Updates Lonely Planet thoroughly updates each guidebook as often as possible. This usually means there are around two years between editions, although for more unusual or more stable destinations the gap can be longer. Check the imprint page (following the colour map at the beginning of the book) for publication dates.

Between editions up-to-date information is available in two free newsletters – the paper *Planet Talk* and email *Comet* (to subscribe, contact any Lonely Planet office) – and on our Web site at www.lonelyplanet.com. The *Upgrades* section of the Web site covers a number of important and volatile destinations and is regularly updated by Lonely Planet authors. *Scoop* covers news and current affairs relevant to travellers. And, lastly, the *Thorn Tree* bulletin board and *Postcards* section of the site carry unverified, but fascinating, reports from travellers.

Correspondence The process of creating new editions begins with the letters, postcards and emails received from travellers. This correspondence often includes suggestions, criticisms and comments about the current editions. Interesting excerpts are immediately passed on via newsletters and the Web site, and everything goes to our authors to be verified when they're researching on the road. We're keen to get more feedback from organisations or individuals who represent communities visited by travellers.

> Lonely Planet gathers information for everyone who's curious about the planet – and especially for those who explore it first-hand. Through guidebooks, phrasebooks, activity guides, maps, literature, newsletters, image library, TV series and Web site we act as an information exchange for a worldwide community of travellers.

Research Authors aim to gather sufficient practical information to enable travellers to make informed choices and to make the mechanics of a journey run smoothly. They also research historical and cultural background to help enrich the travel experience and allow travellers to understand and respond appropriately to cultural and environmental issues.

Authors don't stay in every hotel because that would mean spending a couple of months in each medium-sized city and, no, they don't eat at every restaurant because that would mean stretching belts beyond capacity. They do visit hotels and restaurants to check standards and prices, but feedback based on readers' direct experiences can be very helpful.

Many of our authors work undercover, others aren't so secretive. None of them accept freebies in exchange for positive write-ups. And none of our guidebooks contain any advertising.

Production Authors submit their raw manuscripts and maps to offices in Australia, USA, UK or France. Editors and cartographers – all experienced travellers themselves – then begin the process of assembling the pieces. When the book finally hits the shops some things are already out of date, we start getting feedback from readers, and the process begins again ...

WARNING & REQUEST

Things change – prices go up, schedules change, good places go bad and bad places go bankrupt – nothing stays the same. So, if you find things better or worse, recently opened or long since closed, please tell us and help make the next edition even more accurate and useful. We genuinely value all the feedback we receive. Julie Young coordinates a well-travelled team that reads and acknowledges every letter, postcard and email and ensures that every morsel of information finds its way to the appropriate authors, editors and cartographers for verification.

Everyone who writes to us will find their name in the next edition of the appropriate guidebook. They will also receive the latest issue of *Planet Talk*, our quarterly printed newsletter, or *Comet*, our monthly email newsletter. Subscriptions to both newsletters are free. The very best contributions will be rewarded with a free guidebook.

Excerpts from your correspondence may appear in new editions of Lonely Planet guidebooks, the Lonely Planet Web site, *Planet Talk* or *Comet*, so please let us know if you *don't* want your letter published or your name acknowledged.

Send all correspondence to the Lonely Planet office closest to you:

Australia: PO Box 617, Hawthorn, Victoria 3122
UK: 10A Spring Place, London NW5 3BH
USA: 150 Linden St, Oakland CA 94607
France: 1 rue du Dahomey, Paris 75011

Or email us at: talk2us@lonelyplanet.com.au

For news, views and updates see our Web site: www.lonelyplanet.com

HOW TO USE A LONELY PLANET GUIDEBOOK

The best way to use a Lonely Planet guidebook is any way you choose. At Lonely Planet we believe the most memorable travel experiences are often those that are unexpected, and the finest discoveries are those you make yourself. Guidebooks are not intended to be used as if they provide a detailed set of infallible instructions!

Contents All Lonely Planet guidebooks follow roughly the same format. The Facts about the Destination chapter or section gives background information ranging from history to weather. Facts for the Visitor gives practical information on issues like visas and health. Getting There & Away gives a brief starting point for researching travel to and from the destination. Getting Around gives an overview of the transport options when you arrive.

The peculiar demands of each destination determine how subsequent chapters are broken up, but some things remain constant. We always start with background, then proceed to sights, places to stay, places to eat, entertainment, getting there and away, and getting around information – in that order.

Heading Hierarchy Lonely Planet headings are used in a strict hierarchical structure that can be visualised as a set of Russian dolls. Each heading (and its following text) is encompassed by any preceding heading that is higher on the hierarchical ladder.

Entry Points We do not assume guidebooks will be read from beginning to end, but that people will dip into them. The traditional entry points are the list of contents and the index. In addition, however, some books have a complete list of maps and an index map illustrating map coverage.

There may also be a colour map that shows highlights. These highlights are dealt with in greater detail in the Facts for the Visitor chapter, along with planning questions and suggested itineraries. Each chapter covering a geographical region usually begins with a locator map and another list of highlights. Once you find something of interest in a list of highlights, turn to the index.

Maps Maps play a crucial role in Lonely Planet guidebooks and include a huge amount of information. A legend is printed on the back page. We seek to have complete consistency between maps and text, and to have every important place in the text captured on a map. Map key numbers usually start in the top left corner.

Although inclusion in a guidebook usually implies a recommendation we cannot list every good place. Exclusion does not necessarily imply criticism. In fact there are a number of reasons why we might exclude a place – sometimes it is simply inappropriate to encourage an influx of travellers.

Introduction

Ireland's capital and its largest and most cosmopolitan city, Dublin defies efforts to pin it down, swinging with bewildering rapidity from rich to poor, and from grandeur to squalor. The elegant and prosperous-looking Georgian squares can quickly give way to streets full of depressing slums, especially as you head from south to north, where the Georgian buildings have fallen into disrepair and there's little modern architecture of any note. But despite its faults, Dublin is curious and colourful, an easy city to like and a fine introduction to Ireland.

Although Dublin celebrated its millennium in 1988, its history dates back much further than 988. Traces of those earliest years are hard to find, but the city offers tantalising hints of the medieval period alongside extensive reminders of its 18th century Georgian heyday when majestic streetscapes and regal squares reflected its wealth and importance as the second city of the British Empire. That period of elegance was followed by one of ongoing problems, which saw, amongst other things, the loss of the limited self-government Ireland had previously enjoyed and the escalation of the struggle for independence from Britain. The horrors of the Potato Famine added to these problems to produce a century of stagnation and even decline.

Since becoming the capital of an independent Ireland in 1922, Dublin has seen two major economic and social upheavals. The first occurred in the 1960s, when a massive programme of construction – brought on by the new wealth of the baby-boom generation – led to the expansion of the city into newly created suburbs, whose rows of new semi-detached houses were filled by young adults looking to escape the dilapidated conditions of the inner city. Consequently, Dublin became a city of commuters, with tens of thousands of people travelling in and out of the city centre every day to go to work, but few people actually living in it. This all changed in the late 80s, when an upturn in Ireland's economic fortunes – largely brought on by massive EU funding and the arrival of

DOUG McKINLAY

The imposing Custom House, which took 10 years to build, seen from the south bank of the Liffey.

multinational companies eager to cash in on favourable tax breaks – resulted in a second construction boom.

Ten years on, Dublin is virtually unrecognisable from the city that clawed its way through the 1980s. The suburbs have continued to grow outward, but the real difference is in the city centre itself (most particularly the south side of the Liffey), which has undergone an extraordinary programme of urban renewal. Old buildings, left to fall into ruin for many decades, were fixed up and converted into modern apartments for a new generation of wage earners tired of living in bland, grey suburbs. The city itself, for so long a 'dirty oul' town' (in the words of a popular song by The Pogues), was cleaned up with a view to restoring its once genteel elegance. After Dublin's tenure as cultural capital of Europe in 1988, huge efforts were made to capitalise on the city's rich heritage, resulting in the opening of new museums and attractions. This is most evident in the Temple Bar area, which was reinvented as Dublin's Left Bank and is now the city's most popular district.

A pillar of Dublin's resurgence, however, is the tourist boom. For many years the city has been a popular destination for foreign students – mostly Spanish and Italian – looking to improve their English, but the economic miracle of the 1990s has begun attracting visitors of all ages and types from all over Europe in their hundreds of thousands. Consequently, dozens of new places to stay – from cheerful backpacker hostels to five-star hotels – have opened up all over the city, and a new, modernised tourist infrastructure was put into place to deal with the increase in visitor numbers. The many new restaurants offer an enticing selection of food, with cuisine from every corner of the world. However, you can still find down-to-earth local specialities such as Irish stew and Dublin coddle.

Despite the changes, Dublin remains a place with soul. The city's literary history bumps against you at every corner and its pub doors are open to all comers; an evening with a succession of pints of Guinness, that noble Irish black brew, is as much a part of the Dublin experience as the Georgian streets and the fine old buildings.

Facts about Dublin

HISTORY

Dublin celebrated its official millennium in 1988, but it's fairly certain that there were settlements long before 988 AD. The first early Celtic habitation was beside the River Liffey and the city's Irish name, *Baile Átha Cliath*, 'the Town of the Hurdle Ford', comes from an ancient river crossing that can still be pinpointed today. St Patrick's Cathedral is said to be built on the site of a well used by Ireland's patron saint for early conversions in the 5th century.

Viking & Norman Invasions

Dublin didn't become a permanent fixture until the Vikings arrived. By the 9th century raids from the north had become a fact of Irish life, but some of the Danes chose to stay rather than rape, pillage and depart. They intermarried with the Irish and established a vigorous trading port where the River Poddle joined the Liffey in a black pool, in Irish a *dubh linn*. Today there's little trace of the Poddle, which has been channelled underground.

At the Battle of Clontarf in 1014, the Irish, led by Brian Ború, defeated the Vikings and broke their military power, but once again many of the Danes remained, marrying with the native Irish, adopting Christianity and building churches. The Normans, having consolidated control in England after the victory of 1066, moved west to Ireland in the 12th century, but, like their Viking predecessors, merged with the Irish rather than ruling over them. Dublin became the centre of Anglo-Norman power. Until Elizabeth I (who ruled from 1558 to 1603), real English control over Ireland was restricted to the narrow eastern coastal strip – the Pale – surrounding Dublin. Beyond the Pale, Ireland remained unbowed, and raids from the fierce Irish warriors encamped in the Wicklow Mountains to the south constantly threatened the Anglo-Norman stronghold in Dublin.

Medieval Dublin

Norman and then early English Dublin remained centred around the black pool that gave the city its name. The black pool to the north and the estuary to the east bounded ancient Dublin, so when the city started to grow it expanded not eastward towards the heart of the modern city but westward.

Dublin's history in the following centuries was a series of misfortunes. The 14th century brought an attempted Scottish invasion in 1316 and the devastation of the Black Death in 1348. It experienced Silken Thomas Fitzgerald's failed revolt against Henry VIII in 1534 and Henry's dissolution of the monasteries in 1537. In 1592, however, Elizabeth I founded Trinity College and gave Dublin an educational tradition that it maintains to the present day.

The Protestant Ascendancy

In 1649, Oliver Cromwell took the city (which had supported Charles I) and seized Ireland's best land to distribute among his soldiers. Ireland backed the losing side at the Battle of the Boyne in 1690, in which William of Orange (1650-1702), king of England since 1688, defeated James II (1633-1701), king of England, Ireland and, as James VII, of Scotland, until deposed by William. When the Catholic James II fled to safety, his supporters found themselves excluded from parliament and from many basic rights by the punitive anti-Catholic Penal Laws.

The period of the Protestant Ascendancy led Dublin into its 18th century boom years when fortunes were made; it became for a time the British Empire's second city, after London, and the fifth-largest city in Europe.

Towards the end of the 17th century many Huguenot weavers settled in Dublin, after fleeing anti-Protestant legislation in France, and established a successful cloth industry that helped fuel the city's growth. As the city expanded, the nouveau riche slowly abandoned the confines of medieval Dublin, located south of the River Liffey around Dublin Castle and the cathedrals of St Patrick's and Christ Church. They moved north across the river to a new Dublin of stately squares surrounded by fine Georgian mansions. The planning of this magnificent Georgian Dublin was assisted by the establishment in 1757 of the Commission for Making Wide & Convenient Streets!

Dublin's teeming, poor, mostly Catholic masses were not so easily abandoned, however, and the city's slums soon spread north in pursuit of the rich, who turned back south to grand new homes around Merrion Square, St Stephen's Green and Fitzwilliam Square.

In 1745, when James Fitzgerald, the earl of Kildare, started construction of Leinster House, his magnificent mansion south of the Liffey, he was mocked for this foolish move away from the centre and into the wilds. 'Where I go society will follow,' he confidently predicted and was soon proved right. Today Leinster House is used as the Irish Parliament and is in the centre of modern Dublin.

Disasters of the 19th Century

The Georgian boom years of the 18th century were followed by more than a century of trouble and unrest. Even before the 18th century ended the problems had started with the abortive French-backed invasion by Wolfe Tone in 1796 and the equally unsuccessful rebellion of Lord Edward Fitzgerald, member of the United Irishmen, in 1798. Five years later in 1803 there was another revolt, but, in what was becoming the Irish fashion, it was badly planned and ill-conceived, though romantic. Robert Emmet, the ringleader, was executed outside St Catherine's Church in the Liberties and joined what would become an increasingly long list of eloquent Irish martyrs in the struggle against Britain.

The Act of Union, which came into effect on 1 January 1801, created the United Kingdom of Great Britain and Ireland and ended the separate Irish Parliament, whose members moved to the British Parliament at Westminster. This was achieved with more than a little bribery and corruption, but the end of Dublin's governmental role led many of the city's leading citizens to head for England. The dramatic growth that had characterised Dublin in the previous century came to an almost immediate halt and the city fell into a steady decline.

In 1823 Daniel O'Connell launched his campaign to recover basic rights for Ireland's Catholic population. For a time he made real progress, including the passing of the Catholic Emancipation Act of 1829, and he gained the nickname of 'The Liberator'. However, he was only willing to agitate within the law, and in the 1840s his efforts and influence faded after he called off one of his 'monster meetings' at Clontarf when it was objected to by the British.

In the late 1840s Ireland was struck by its greatest disaster. The food needs of the burgeoning rural population had become overwhelmingly dependent on the easily grown potato, and when potato blight devastated the crop the human cost was staggering, compounded as it was by the British government's shameful lack of assistance. Although Dublin escaped the worst effects of the Potato Famine between 1845 and 1851, the streets and squares were still packed with refugees trying to escape from the impoverished countryside, living in disease-ridden slums. Dublin's remorseless decline accelerated.

The clamour for Home Rule, effectively calling for a return to the pre-1801 situation when Ireland had its own parliament, grew louder in the 1870s. Charles Stewart Parnell (1846-91), leader of the Home Rule movement, was elected to the British Parliament in Westminster in 1875 and campaigned tirelessly for a Dublin parliament. However, despite support from the British prime minister, William Gladstone, the Home Rule Bill was repeatedly defeated. Parnell, dubbed the 'King of Ireland' at his peak, suffered a dramatic fall from power when his liaison with the married Kitty O'Shea was revealed. The scandal reflected badly on Irish society and the Catholic Church, which found Parnell to be morally unfit as a leader. This was one of the causes of the often bitter mistrust with which the Church, in its conservative mode, is still held by many Irish.

The Struggle for Independence

Resentment against British rule began to show a violent side, and in 1882 the British chief secretary, Lord Cavendish, was assassinated in Phoenix Park by a group known as The Invincibles. The formation of the republican political movement Sinn Féin (We Ourselves) in 1905 was further evidence of increasing anti-British resentment. Socialism gained support, especially among those living in Dublin's appalling tenements, and in 1913 the general strike organised by trade union leaders Jim Larkin and James Connolly threw the city into chaos.

At the same time, agitation against Home Rule was on the increase in the Protestant-dominated northern Irish counties of Ulster, and the authorities turned a blind eye to arms shipments coming into Ireland for irregular Protestant forces. However, this was not the case when the *Asgard* slipped into Howth harbour with a shipment of rifles for the Irish nationalist cause in 1914.

Despite over a century of discontent, punctuated by occasional acts of violence or ill-planned revolts, there was still little widespread support for complete Irish independence and the departure of the British. In 1914 Home Rule was passed into law but its implementation was suspended for the duration of WWI. Thousands of Irish volunteers fought in the war; the nationalists among them believed their efforts would ensure that Britain stood by its promise of Home Rule. In Ireland, opposition to British rule simmered then came to the boil in 1916 in yet another ill-planned, poorly executed revolt – the Easter Rising.

The Easter Rising should have taken place on Easter Sunday, but was delayed at the last moment and rescheduled for Easter Monday. This resulted in a much smaller turnout than planned; however, the stirring words read out by Patrick Pearse (the leader of the rising) and his supporters from the steps of the General Post Office (GPO) on O'Connell St were eventually to lead to Ireland's division and the independence of the south.

Secrecy had been a key element in the planning of the rising since so many previous rebellions had been ruined by betrayals. Unfortunately, the secrecy was so pervasive that many supporters had little idea of what was happening. Nevertheless, the GPO, the headquarters for the rising, was quickly taken by the rebels and other key points in the city were secured. Initially, the British troops in Dublin were taken completely by surprise, but quickly moved into action and the Irish forces were soon both outnumbered and outgunned.

The rebels managed to hold out for a week, by which time large tracts of Dublin were in ruins and the GPO, along with much of O'Connell St, was a smoking shell. Finally, however, the revolt was crushed, the garrisons surrendered and the leaders were marched off to jail. That might have been the end of the matter, as they enjoyed little popular support and were openly jeered as they were taken away. However, the British administration overreacted, with disastrous consequences.

On 3 May, just three days after the Easter Rising ended, Pearse and two other leaders faced the firing squad. Four more were executed on 4 May. Another was executed on 5 May, followed by four more on 8 May. In all, 77 death sentences were passed and, though most of them were not carried out, by the time the 15th and final execution, that of James Connolly on 12 May, had taken place, the leaders of the Easter Rising had been transformed from public nuisances into national heroes. The execution of Connolly was particularly galling to the public: he had been so badly injured in the fighting that he had to be shot while strapped to a chair.

The British government miscalculated again in 1917, when they threatened to impose conscription on Ireland. It was the combination of this threat and the treatment of the leaders of the Easter Rising that turned the tide for the Irish independence movement. The whole country was plunged into turmoil and the general election of 1918 saw republican Sinn Féin candidates win nearly three-quarters of the Irish parliamentary seats. Instead of attending at Westminster, they declared Ireland independent and formed the first *Dáil Éireann* (Irish assembly or lower house). At the same time terrorist strikes against symbols of British control began, led by the Irish Republican Army (IRA), the military wing of Sinn Féin. A prime force in this reversal of Irish opinion was Michael Collins, a visionary political leader of Sinn Féin and a master of undeniably ruthless but effective guerrilla tactics.

The British countered the violence by strengthening the Royal Irish Constabulary and introducing a tough auxiliary force known as the Black and Tans (because of the colour of their uniforms). Their violent tactics simply increased resentment against the British and support for the Irish nationalist cause. The death from a hunger strike of Terence MacSwiney, mayor of Cork, further crystallised Irish opinion, and on 11 November 1920, Ireland's first 'Bloody Sunday' signalled a further escalation in the

Michael Collins was one of the men sent to England to negotiate the Anglo-Irish Treaty.

struggle. Collins' cousin had been inadvertently put in charge of all secret codes at Dublin Castle, leading Collins to exclaim, 'In the name of God how did these people ever get an empire?'. She passed the codes to Collins, allowing him to organise the pre-breakfast killing of 14 undercover British intelligence officers known as the Cairo gang, who had arrived 'in secret' the night before. That afternoon, in reprisal, spectators were fired on with machine guns at a football match. Twelve people, including one of the players, were killed. Later that night, in another act of retribution, two IRA men and a Sinn Féin supporter were murdered in Dublin Castle.

A month later, in another act of reprisal by British forces, the centre of Cork city was burnt and looted. Fire brigades were deliberately prevented from fighting the blaze and the results of a British inquiry into the event were never released. The violence continued. In May, IRA forces burnt down Dublin's Custom House, the centre of British administration in Ireland, but by this time exhaustion was setting in on both sides and a truce was signed on 11 July 1921.

Independence & Civil War

The Anglo-Irish Treaty was signed, after months of argument, on 6 December 1921. Unfortunately for both sides, it was far from being a neat agreement. Instead of setting up the Irish Republic for which the IRA had fought, the Treaty merely created the Irish Free State, which was still subservient to Britain on a number of important issues. Worse, from the Irish perspective, it allowed the six Ulster counties that make up Northern Ireland to opt out of the new state. Thus the seeds were planted for a problem that continues to fester.

The Treaty pitted erstwhile comrades against each other in pro-Treaty and anti-Treaty camps. The latter were led by Eamon de Valera. Although the Dáil narrowly ratified the Treaty and the general public did the same by a larger margin, civil war broke out in June 1922. Anti-Treaty IRA forces had occupied the Four Courts building on the banks of the Liffey in Dublin and when they refused to surrender, pro-Treaty forces led by Collins shelled them from across the river. The building, one of Dublin's Georgian classics, soon went up in flames, just as the equally beautiful Custom House had a year earlier. In a repeat of the 1916 Easter Rising, O'Connell St followed it into the fire and anti-Treaty IRA forces were soon mounting ambushes of Free State forces, just as they had against the Black and Tans a year or two before. On 22 August, Collins was killed in an ambush near Cork.

The Dáil then passed a bill making the death sentence mandatory for any IRA member possessing a gun when captured. On 24 November Robert Erskine Childers, whose yacht, the *Asgard*, had brought arms for the republican cause to Howth in 1914, was executed for possessing a revolver, given to him by Collins. By May 1923, 77 executions had taken place and de Valera, president of Sinn Féin, who had been imprisoned by the Free State authorities for a year, ordered the IRA to drop their arms. The civil war ground to a halt, driving a wedge between Sinn Féin, as a political force, and the IRA, as a terrorist group.

The Irish Republic

Ireland was finally at peace but many questions were left unanswered. The substantial minority of members of parliament who had been elected on the republican and anti-Treaty platform refused to take their seats, particularly as it would involve an oath of allegiance to the British king. Without an armed struggle to pursue, the IRA was becoming a marginalised force in independent Ireland and Sinn Féin was falling apart. In 1926 de Valera created a new party, Fianna Fáil (Warriors of Ireland), and in 1927 almost won power, despite the fact that he and his supporters still refused to sit in parliament. After the election he led his party into the Dáil by the simple expedient of not taking the oath but signing in as if he had.

In 1932 de Valera and Fianna Fáil won the election, repeating this victory, with an increased majority, in 1933. The forces who lost the Civil War in 1922 took power through the ballot box 10 years later. They soon jettisoned the Treaty clauses with which they disagreed. The oath to the British Crown went, the British governor general soon followed and, by the outbreak of WWII, Ireland was a republic in all but name, and even that had been changed from the Irish Free State to Éire.

In 1948 Fianna Fáil lost the general election to Fine Gael (Tribe of the Gaels) – the direct successor party to the first Free State government – in coalition with the new republican Clann an Poblachta led by Sean MacBride, a former IRA officer. The new government declared the Free State to be a republic at last and Ireland left the British Commonwealth in 1949. In 1955 it became a member of the United Nations.

Ireland Today

When Sean Lamass came to power in 1959 as successor to de Valera (whose Fianna Fáil had won the election of 1951) he sought to stem the high rate of emigration by improving the country's economic prospects. By the mid-1960s his policies had been successful enough to reduce emigration to less than half the level of the mid-1950s, and many who had left began to return. Lamass also introduced universal free secondary education.

In 1973 the Republic became a member of the European Economic Community (EEC). At first, membership brought some measure of prosperity, largely through the Common Agricultural Policy (CAP) and Regional Development Funds, but by the early 1980s Ireland was once more in economic difficulties and emigration rose again. In the 1990s, however, Ireland saw a dramatic change in its economic fortunes. Interest rates, which had for many years been prohibitively high, began to tumble, thus encouraging new business; the Irish punt grew stronger and foreign investment, which had been mollycoddled and underpinned by generous tax incentives, began to bring substantial benefits, such as increased employment and injections of finance. The turnaround in Ireland's economic fortunes has led to the country being dubbed the 'Celtic Tiger', and as the European Union proceeds towards economic, social and political integration, tiny Ireland has been paraded as an economic role model for the rest of the EU (see Economy later in this chapter). It wouldn't be Ireland, however, if there wasn't a certain amount of grumbling and begrudging.

Dublin's expansion has continued south to Ballsbridge, Dun Laoghaire and beyond and north to Howth, but the River Liffey remains a rough dividing line between southern haves and northern have-nots. Evidence of EU and private investment adorns the city in the shape of cranes and hoardings, but areas of urban blight and high unemployment linger on. The city is also battling with a rising crime rate linked to rising drug addiction.

In 1997 Belfast-born Mary McAleese was elected president, succeeding Mary Robinson, who – despite having limited power during her term in office – wielded considerable influence on the government's social policies, contributing to a marked shift in attitudes away from the traditionally conservative positions on issues such as divorce, abortion and gay rights. It is perhaps a sign of her impact on the world stage that on leaving office she was appointed UN Commissioner for Human Rights. President McAleese, despite being more conservative than her predecessor, was elected on a promise of following in Robinson's footsteps, and is committed to pursuing a policy of understanding and *rapprochement* with the Unionist community of Northern Ireland.

In 1997 Fianna Fáil, under the leadership of Bertie Ahern, came to power in a coalition with the Progressive Democrats. They are a minority government, however, and rely on the support of three independent TDs (members of the Daíl) to maintain their slim majority.

The one unresolved problem that remains from 1921 is Northern Ireland; however, it seems that the days of violence have finally come to an end. A ceasefire has been in effect since July 1997. The signing of the 1998 Good Friday Agreement and the passing of pro-Agreement referendums in both the Republic and Northern Ireland appear to have consolidated hopes that the resolution to the troubled politics of the six counties lies at the discussion table and not in the use of mortar bombs and sectarian killings. Sadly, it took the explosion of a bomb in the northern town of Omagh in August 1998, killing 29 people (the biggest death toll in a single incident since the beginning of the 'Troubles' in 1969) to convince the overwhelming majority on both sides, north and south of the border, that peace was not simply a political imperative, but a moral one as well. In October 1998, the peace process won major international recognition when nationalist leader John Hume and Unionist leader David Trimble were awarded the Nobel Peace Prize. At the time of writing, the assembly created by the peace agreement was being consolidated, with David Trimble as 'First Minister' and Seamus Mallen, deputy-leader of the nationalist Social, Democratic and Liberal Party (SDLP) as his deputy.

GEOGRAPHY

Dublin lies on the east coast of Ireland, about 53° north of the equator, and is divided by the River Liffey. Greater Dublin sprawls around the arc of Dublin Bay, bounded to the north by the hills at Howth and to the south by the Dalkey headland. Greater Dublin is in the administrative region of County Dublin, which is bordered to the north and north-west by County Meath, to the south-west by County Kildare and to the south by County Wicklow.

Postcodes are divided evenly between north and south of the river; all odd numbers are to the north, all even ones to the south. The postcodes for central Dublin are Dublin 1 immediately north of the river and Dublin 2 immediately south. The up-market Ballsbridge area, which has some of the city's best B&Bs lies to the south-east of the centre in Dublin 4.

CLIMATE

Dublin enjoys a milder climate than its northerly position might indicate. The sea around Ireland is warm for the latitude because of the influence of the North Atlantic Drift, or Gulf Stream. That merely means it's decidedly chilly rather than downright freezing. The water isn't much warmer at the height of summer (about 15°C) than in the depths of winter (10°C).

Dublin's maximum temperature in July and August ranges from 15 to 20°C, so even then it's wise to have a sweater or light coat. During January and February, the coldest months, daily temperatures range from 4 to 8°C. Major snowfalls are rare. May and June are the sunniest months and generally have between five and 6½ hours of sunshine a day. December has an average of only one or two hours a day. There are about 18 hours of daylight in July and August; it's only truly dark after about 11 pm.

It does rain in Ireland; even the drier parts of Ireland – and Dublin is one of the driest – get rain on 150 days in a typical year and it often rains every day for weeks. Dublin receives about 75cm of rainfall annually, so there's much local terminology and humour about the rain – a 'soft day', for instance, is a damp one. Bring an umbrella.

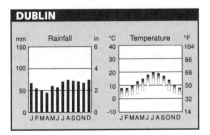

Dun Laoghaire, city centre traffic, especially on the quays, is an ugly, frustrating sight. Ideas on how to resolve the problem have been floated, including the introduction of a scheme whereby cars with even-numbered plates would only be allowed to run on alternate days to those with odd-numbered plates, but the resistance has been strong. Essentially, the vast majority of Dublin's population is suburban and uses cars to get in and out of the city on a daily basis.

Despite the pollution caused by traffic congestion, Dublin does not suffer the same poor air quality as other major European cities such as London and Paris. Nevertheless, it is still pretty bad, despite measures to improve it. Smoke-producing coal is illegal in the city centre, but there is no restriction on motor exhaust. Cigarette smoking, despite restrictions, is still widespread; crowded pubs are certain to prove uncomfortable to the non-smoker, as are some restaurants, which have made few provisions for those looking to enjoy a meal without of smoke invading their dinner.

The Liffey itself is absolutely filthy, largely due to irresponsible dumping further upstream. At low tide, it looks more like a rubbish dump than a river, and to date no effort has been made to clean it up (though that may soon change).

The good news is that Dublin's parks and gardens are havens of ecologically sound tranquillity. Aside from Phoenix Park, which offers seemingly endless acres of pastoral landscape, the Georgian squares are clean and extremely well maintained.

Although recycling is not legally required, the number of recycling bins has increased substantially in recent years. However, there is a certain laziness about the separation of rubbish, even though most people are pretty conscientious.

ECOLOGY & ENVIRONMENT

Dublin's worst environmental problem is traffic congestion, which is a major annoyance in parts of the city centre. Despite the construction of the M50 bypass, which runs from north-west of the city down towards

GOVERNMENT & POLITICS

The Republic of Ireland has a parliamentary system of government. The parliament (*Oireachtas*) has a lower house, or house of representatives, known as the Dáil Éireann, usually shortened to Dáil and pronounced 'doyle'. The prime minister is the *Taoiseach* (pronounced 'teashok'; the plural is *Taosigh*). The Dáil has 166 elected members and sits in Leinster House on Dublin's Kildare St. Members of the Irish Parliament are known as *teachta Dála* (TDs). The upper house (senate) is the *Seanad Éireann*, usually just called the Seanad, and senators are nominated by the taoiseach or elected by university graduates and councillors around the country.

The constitutional head of state is the president (*An tUachtaran*), who is elected by popular vote for a seven year term, but has little real power.

The main political parties are Fianna Fáil, Fine Gael and the Labour Party (which merged with the small Democratic Left party in January 1999). Other parties are the Progressive Democrats, which split from Fianna Fáil in 1986, and the Socialist Workers' Party, which has one sitting member of the Dáil.

The Republic's electoral system is one of proportional representation, where voters mark the candidates in order of preference. As first-preference votes are counted and candidates are elected, the voters' second and third choices are passed on to the various other candidates.

At the local level, Dublin is governed by three elected bodies. Dublin Corporation supervises the city, a county council looks after Dublin County and Dun Laoghaire Corporation administers the port town.

At the time of writing, the major political issues of the day were Northern Ireland and a graft scandal. The Irish government, in accordance with the Good Friday Agreement, has a limited participatory role in the politics of the North, and was, in conjunction with the British government, trying to overcome the major stumbling block to a permanent peace: the decommissioning of IRA weapons.

In the Republic, former taoiseach and leader of Fianna Fáil Charles Haughey is being investigated by the courts over allegations that he received payoffs from the business community. It has emerged that Irish governments throughout the last two decades have been involved in all sorts of political misdeeds.

ECONOMY

Ireland, and especially Dublin, is in the midst of the greatest economic boom since independence. Grandly dubbed the 'Celtic Tiger', the economy is healthy in almost every capacity, from record-low interest rates to a negligible rate of inflation. The success has been attributed to a variety of factors, including the intelligent spending of EU funds (of which Ireland is one of the biggest benefactors); the successful promotion of foreign investment through generous tax incentives, which has seen Ireland lead the field in a number of key industries, such as information technology; the explosion of the tourist industry, which has seen record numbers of visitors in the last decade; and a reversal in the age-old trend of emigration, which since 1995 has seen more people return to Ireland than leave. Lastly, a new entrepreneurial class has emerged since 1990, mostly of young graduates who have taken advantage of the favourable economic atmosphere to start up businesses, which in most cases have been successful, and in some, incredibly so.

Yet doubts persist about the solidity of the economy. A growing consensus suggests that Ireland is in the middle of a boom-and-bust cycle similar to that in Britain in the 1980s. Some economists have argued that Ireland's dependence on multinational corporations, which are attracted by the low corporate tax offered as an incentive to set up here, results in a fragile economy at the tender mercy of world trends. The crash of the Asian markets in 1997 and the resultant threat of world recession cannot be ignored. Furthermore, as Ireland and the other countries of the EU gather pace in their march towards greater union, it seems likely that Europe-wide rules on corporate tax will come into force, eliminating the attractive tax package that has brought so many multinational companies to Ireland's shores.

In Dublin, house prices have rocketed since 1994, making it increasingly difficult for those with even a decent income to afford to buy property, and while many have benefited from the economic boom, it has become evident that the gap between rich and poor has broadened substantially rather than narrowed. Although the slums that were the shame of 19th century Dublin have disappeared, a substantial percentage of the population still lives in sub-standard corporation-run housing estates and flats throughout the city, especially on the north side. A sober reminder of the inequality between rich and poor can be found in the north Dublin working-class estate of Ballymun, which has an infamous set of tower block flats built in the late 60s with the promise that they would offer decent housing in pleasant surroundings for low-income families. Thirty years later, these flats are shameful examples of negligence. Many of the lifts haven't worked in over 15 years, forcing the 7000 residents to walk up as many as 14 floors. Repeated protests on the part of tenants yielded nothing more than vague promises of help until popular outrage finally forced the High Court to declare that Dublin Corporation, the official landlords, must resolve the problem.

POPULATION & PEOPLE

Ireland's population is about 5.2 million – 3.6 million in the South, 1.6 million in the North. This figure is less than it was 150 years ago. Prior to the disastrous Potato Famine between 1845 and 1851, the population was around 8½ million. Deaths and the huge scale of emigration reduced the population to around six million, and emigration continued at a high level for the next 100 years. It wasn't until the 1960s that Ireland's population finally began to increase again. A high proportion of the population is in the younger age groups and over 50% are under the age of 28.

The City of Dublin's population is 500,000 but about 1½ million, or approximately 27% of the whole island, live within commuting distance of the centre.

EDUCATION

With such a young population it's not at all surprising that over 25% of Ireland's population is in full-time education. Attendance at school is compulsory and free for those up to and including the age of 15, when the majority of students take their Junior Certificate exams.

Nearly all primary and secondary schools are run by religious denominations and receive state aid. Secondary schools are for children aged 12 and over and those who successfully complete their education at this level receive their Leaving Certificate. On the basis of points scored in these exams they can then apply through a central applications service for admission to tertiary institutions, which are also heavily subsidised by the state.

Competition for university places is very stiff, and students need to attain relatively high standards to score enough to win a place. University College Dublin (UCD), part of the National University of Ireland, has a large campus in the south of the city, at Belfield, and another at Maynooth, just outside the city in County Kildare. Trinity College, the oldest university in Ireland, has its campus in the city centre. A fourth campus, that of Dublin City University, is in Glasnevin, north of the city centre.

Also at tertiary level, there are a number of technical colleges run by the Dublin Institute of Technology, which provide vocational training. Many courses feature work-placement programmes that ensure practical experience for the young graduates. There are also a number of other private colleges throughout the city, which offer a wide variety of courses.

School-leavers who decide not to opt for tertiary education can enrol with FÁS, a state-sponsored body that works with registered employers to provide training and work experience for young people. With unemployment at only 8%, FÁS has obviously had remarkable success in creating work for young people who might otherwise have been destined for prolonged unemployment.

ARTS

See the special section 'Dublin's Architecture & Architects' on pages 29 to 35.

Literature

Of all the arts it's in literature that Ireland has had the most impact. No other city, Dubliners are proud to boast, can claim three Nobel Prize winners for literature. There's even a Dublin Writers' Museum, which traces Ireland's literary history. Books also take centre stage at Marsh's Library, the Chester Beatty Library and, of course, at the Book of Kells exhibit in the library of Trinity College.

Although writing goes back so far in Ireland – Irish monks were copying Bibles and spreading their learning abroad while England was still in the Dark Ages – it's the Irish mastery of English that is most renowned. One theory to explain this mastery suggests that even though Irish Gaelic is now a minority language, English is in some respects still a foreign tongue to be played and experimented with in a manner that, say, an English writer would never dare. Using turns of phrase and expressions translated directly from Irish, as well as a perspective unique to Ireland, authors have been able to transform written English to great success. Indeed, Dublin has produced so many writers and has been written about so much that you could easily plan a Dublin literary holiday. *A Literary Guide to Dublin* by Vivien Igoe includes detailed route maps, a guide to cemeteries and an eight page section on literary and historical pubs.

See the boxed texts 'James Joyce & *Ulysses*' and 'Dublin Writers' later in this chapter and also the Books section in the Facts for the Visitor chapter for more information on books about Dublin.

Dance

The most important form of dance in Ireland is traditional Irish dancing, performed at *céilidhs* (communal dances), often in an impromptu format and always accompanied by an Irish traditional band. Unfortunately, Dublin is not the best place to engage in, or watch, this form of dancing, its home being in the west and south-west of the country. However, there are a couple of organisations that organise céilidhs – these are usually for the benefit of tourists, but always good fun nevertheless (see the Entertainment chapter).

Up to the 1970s, there were a number of dance halls throughout the city that organised formal dances. However, the popularity of these places has waned in the face of nightclubs and other dance venues. Still, a resurgent interest in ballroom dancing has meant that this particular art is not quite dead yet!

Classical dance does exist in Dublin, but it is hardly one of the more popular pursuits in the city. There are several dance companies, including the Rubato Ballet, The Cois Céim Dance Theatre and the Dance Theatre of Ireland, but it is perhaps indicative of the difficulties they face that none has a permanent home and all are forced to perform in different theatres throughout the city. The Rubato Ballet often gives performances at the National Gallery.

Music

Literature may be the field in which Irish artists have had the greatest influence, but music is the art that you're most likely to come across while visiting Dublin. Just as pubs are an intrinsic part of the Dublin lifestyle, music is an intrinsic part of the pub lifestyle. However, it's not even necessary to go to a pub to find music, as buskers are busy in Dublin's streets at all hours of the day.

Traditional music has survived with greater vigour in Ireland than has comparable music in other European countries, and has influenced Irish musicians working in other musical forms. A wide variety of instruments is used in traditional Irish music, but the most notably Irish include the harp, which is also the country's national emblem; the *bodhrán* (pronounced 'bore-run'), a goatskin drum; and the *uillean* pipes, which are played with a bellows

James Joyce & *Ulysses*

Of course, no commentary on Dublin writers is possible without reference to James Joyce, Ireland's most famous author. The man who claimed Dublin could be rebuilt from scratch using his descriptions as a plan, spent most of his adult life overseas. He was born in Dublin in 1882 and was the eldest of the 10 Joyce children to survive beyond infancy. His father's roller-coaster financial situation led to a rather varied education, which included a two year spell of self-education at home. He completed his school years at Belvedere College (the building stands on Great Denmark St in north Dublin) and went on to University College, Dublin. He was determined to become a writer when he graduated in 1902, but then considered studying medicine and wandered between Dublin and Paris for the next couple of years.

In 1904 three short stories appeared in an Irish farmers' magazine, written under the pen name Stephen Dedalus; these were later to form part of *Dubliners*. In late 1904 Joyce abandoned Ireland and moved to Pula in what was then Austria-Hungary (now in Croatia) with Nora Barnacle, whom he was not to marry until 27 years later. In 1905 they moved on to Trieste, in Italy, where their two children were born and where he reworked *Stephen Hero*, a novel he had started in Dublin, into *A Portrait of the Artist as a Young Man*. He returned to Ireland twice in 1909, but his efforts to find a publisher for *Dubliners* were unsuccessful. It was finally published in 1914, but not until after the first manuscript had been destroyed when the publisher objected to its use of real locations, its language and the stories.

The outbreak of WWI forced the family to move to Zürich, Switzerland, in 1915, where Joyce began work on *Ulysses*. He was always convinced of his own genius but English lessons and grants from literary societies and admirers were his only means of support at the time. His life was further complicated by recurrent eye problems that led to 25 operations for glaucoma, cataracts and other difficulties. *A Portrait of the Artist as a Young Man* was finally published in 1916 and in 1918 the US magazine *Little Review* started to publish extracts from *Ulysses*. Notoriety was already pursuing his epic work and the censors prevented further episodes from being published after 1920.

In 1920 Joyce decided to return to Dublin on a visit. He stopped off in Paris where he was persuaded by Ezra Pound to prolong his stay. Joyce once remarked about his decision, 'I came to Paris for a week and stayed 20 years'. It was a good move for the struggling writer. In 1922, Sylvia Beach of the Paris bookshop Shakespeare & Co finally managed to put *Ulysses* into print. Its earlier censorship difficulties made it an instant success. *Ulysses* follows its characters around Dublin during a single day (16 June 1904, the day Joyce met Nora Barnacle). During this remarkable journey various episodes parallel the voyage of Homer's *Odyssey*, but this literary invention was only a small part of the novel's total achievement. The book ends with Molly Bloom's famous stream of consciousness discourse, a chapter of eight huge and totally unpunctuated paragraphs.

Given the sexually explicit language in parts of the book, it's not surprising that Joyce was labelled a pornographer, and the book, 20th century masterpiece or not, was banned. After long delays, *Ulysses* was finally published in the USA in 1933, but not until 1937 in the UK.

Ulysses has been described as one of the 'great unread works of the English language' and may have bent English into totally new and hitherto unthought-of shapes, but Joyce's final work, *Finnegan's Wake* (published in 1939), was even more complex and went part way to inventing a new language, adding further complications through multilingual wordplays. In 1940 WWII drove the Joyce family back to Zürich where the author died in 1941.

Dublin Writers

Jonathan Swift (1667-1745), the master satirist and author of *Gulliver's Travels*, was the greatest Dublin writer of the early Georgian period but he was followed by many others, such as Oliver Goldsmith (1728-74), author of *The Vicar of Wakefield*, and Thomas Moore (1779-1852), whose poems formed the repertoire of generations of Irish tenor singers.

Oscar Wilde (1854-1900) is renowned for his legendary wit and expertise with the *bon mot*, but he was also a writer of immense talent and striking sensitivity. His best-known works are his plays, including *The Importance of Being Earnest* and his delightful children's tale *The Happy Prince*, but critics agree that his most important and mature work is the *Ballad of Reading Gaol*, which he wrote while serving a prison sentence for his homosexuality. Sadly, Wilde paid a heavy toll for the harsh prison conditions and the ignorance of Victorian society, dying not long after his release.

Oscar Wilde

William Butler Yeats (1865-1939) is perhaps best remembered as a poet though he also wrote plays. He helped found the Abbey Theatre, served as senator in the early years of the Irish Free State and in 1938 received one of Dublin's three Nobel Prizes for literature. George Bernard Shaw (1925) and Samuel Beckett (1969) were the other two prizewinners.

Oliver St John Gogarty (1878-1957) bore a lifelong grudge against James Joyce because of his appearance as Buck Mulligan in Joyce's *Ulysses*, but it didn't prevent Gogarty from presenting his views of Dublin in *As I Was Going Down Sackville Street* (1937) and other volumes of his memoirs. Like Oscar Wilde, he was a renowned wit.

The Informer (1925) by Liam O'Flaherty (1896-1984) is the classic book about the divided sympathies that plagued Ireland during its independence struggle and the ensuing civil war. *The Ginger Man* (1926) by JP Donleavy is a high-energy foray around Dublin from the Trinity College perspective. It received the Catholic Church's 'seal of approval' by being banned in Ireland for many years. From a later era Christy Brown's marvellous *Down all the Days* (1970) summed up Dublin's backstreet energy with equal abandon and was the basis for the acclaimed film *My Left Foot*.

Modern Dublin has continued to produce excellent writers, many of whom have gone on to international recognition. Dublin schoolteacher Roddy Doyle has made a big name for himself with his comic trilogy on north Dublin life – *The Commitments*, *The Snapper* and *The Van* – all of which were made into films. His *Paddy Clarke, Ha Ha Ha*, about a Dublin family, won the 1993 Booker Prize.

Dermot Bolger's *The Journey Home* (1990) depicts the underside of modern Dublin at its darkest. Political corruption, drugs, violence, unemployment and a pervading sense of hopelessness make this a gloomy book, though it still hurtles along at a fast pace. John McGahern is another familiar modern Irish writer, with titles such as *The Barracks*

WB Yeats

(1963) and *Amongst Women* (1990) to his credit. Aidan Carl Mathews' work includes the novel *Muesli at Midnight. A New Book of Dubliners*, edited by Ben Forkner, is a fine collection of Dublin-related short stories written by authors old and new, including James Joyce, Oliver St John Gogarty, Liam O'Flaherty, Samuel Beckett, Flann O'Brien, Sean O'-Faolain, Benedict Kiely and others. Patrick McCabe's *Butcher Boy* (1993) was nominated for the Booker Prize and was also turned into a successful film. *Finbar's Hotel* (1996), edited by Dermot Bolger, is a collection of short stories by the young lions of the Irish literary scene; all the stories are based in a city-centre hotel, which is certainly the U2-owned Clarence Hotel on Wellington Quay.

George Bernard Shaw

Ireland's most important modern writer is John Banville, literary editor of the *Irish Times*. His impressive body of work includes the Booker Prize-winning *Book of Evidence* (1989) and his excellent trilogy *Doctor Copernicus* (1976), *Kepler* (1981) and *The Newton Letter* (1982). His most recent work, *The Untouchable* (1997), is a controversial novel about Cold War spy Anthony Blunt.

Ireland has produced its share of women writers. Edna O'Brien enjoyed the accolade of having her *The Country Girls* (1960) banned. Clare Boylan's books include *Holy Pictures*, *Concerning Virgins* and *Black Baby*. Molly Keane wrote several books in the 1920s and 1930s under the pseudonym MJ Farrell, then had a literary second life in her 70s when *Good Behaviour* and *Time after Time* came out under her real name. Maeve Binchy is *the* writer of blockbusters, which just rise above the sex and shopping genre. Her books have lots of Irish settings and *Circle of Friends*, set in Dublin, was made into a film in 1995.

Dublin is also notable for its literary boozers and hell raisers. Brendan Behan (1923-64), author of *Borstal Boy* and *The Quare Fellow*, fell into both categories and drank himself to death. The poet Patrick Kavanagh (1905-67), a great chronicler of central Dublin, was another writer with a fond attachment to pub life.

Samuel Beckett

Although Dublin and Ireland played a central part in the work of writers like Joyce, others became such international names that their Dublin origins are virtually forgotten. As well as Oscar Wilde, George Bernard Shaw (1856-1950) and Bram Stoker (1847-1912), the creator of Dracula, were both products of the city. In an earlier era it was Dubliner Richard Steele who founded those resolutely English magazines the *Tatler* (1709) and the *Spectator* (1711).

But what about the future? There are plenty of young writers who are ready and willing to fill the shoes of their illustrious predecessors. A quick scan through the lists of newcomers reveals that the quality of Irish writing is still excellent, and that such names as Pat Boran, Philip McCann, Emer Martin and Emma Donoghue will undoubtedly carry the Irish literary torch into the new millennium.

squeezed under the elbow (*uillean* in Irish). The fiddle is less purely Irish, but is a mainstay of traditional music, along with the accordion, the banjo and simple tin whistles or spoons. Unaccompanied music fits into five main categories (jigs, reels, hornpipes, polkas and slow airs) while there are two main styles of song (*sean nós*, old-style tunes often sung in Irish, either unaccompanied or with the backing of a bodhrán, and more familiar ballads).

Of the groups playing traditional Irish music, perhaps the best known is the Chieftains, and adding the words come bands like the Dubliners, the Wolfe Tones and the Fureys. Younger groups like Clannad from Donegal, Altan, Dervish and Nomos espouse a quieter, more mystical style of singing, while the London-Irish band The Pogues help keep things wild.

Christy Moore, whose songs traverse the whole range of 'folk' music themes, is king of the contemporary singer-songwriter tradition and is capable of selling out Dublin's cavernous Point Depot. Moore's younger brother, Luka Bloom, is now carving out a name for himself too. Other male singer-songwriters include Finbar Furey, Mick Hanly, Jimmy MacCarthy, Kieran Goss, Strabane-born Paul Brady, Davy Spillane and Christie Hennessy.

Female singer-songwriters have an equally strong following. The mystical voice of Enya from Donegal has penetrated to a wider audience, as has that of the more controversial Sinéad O'Connor. Among the best-known contemporary female singers are sisters Mary and Frances Black, smoky-voiced Mary Coughlan, Dolores Keane, Eleanor McEvoy and Sinéad Lohan, and wild melodion-player Sharon Shannon.

Ireland also has its rock-music scene, exemplified in the 1970s and 1980s by bands such as Thin Lizzy and the Boomtown Rats and by singers such as Bob Geldof, Elvis Costello and Chris de Burgh. U2 are the biggest of them all, of course, but newer chart-toppers include the Cranberries and, more recently, the spectacularly successful Dublin boy-band Boyzone and the whole-some Corrs, who have achieved worldwide chart success. 1998 saw the meteoric rise of all-girl band B*Witched, who seem intent on reaching the heights of their English counterparts the Spice Girls and All Saints.

In a class of his own, Van Morrison has been performing since the 1960s when he was lead singer with the group, Them, and he now has a hard-core following all over the world.

No account of contemporary Irish music could close without reference to the popularity of country music and to Daniel O'Donnell, the Barry Manilow of the Irish music scene, with millions of album sales (mainly to those over the age of 40). Crooner Joe Dolan, another perennial over-40s favourite, is trying to widen his appeal to younger audiences, and in 1998 released an album covering some of the biggest pop hits of the previous five years.

See the Entertainment chapter for information about music in Dublin and where to find it.

Painting

Although Ireland doesn't have a tradition of painting to match its literary one, the National Gallery does have an extensive Irish School collection, much of it chronicling the personages and pursuits of the Anglo-Irish aristocracy. Just as WB Yeats played a seminal role in the Celtic literary revival, his younger brother Jack Butler Yeats (1871-1957) inspired a surge of creativity in painting. Their father, John Butler Yeats, was also a noted portrait painter. Earlier respected portrait painters were Garrett Murphy (1680-1716) and James Latham (1696-1747). George Barrett, Robert Carver, William Ashford and Thomas Roberts were important 18th and 19th century landscape painters and James Malton captured 18th century Dublin in a series of paintings.

Cinema

Ireland has never had a particularly rich film-making tradition, though hopes were high when James Joyce opened Dublin's first cinema, the Volta, on Mary St in 1909. This absence of a tradition of film-making is largely due to the success of British cinema, which drew the cream of Irish talent across the sea to its own studios, and the general lack of government finance for a domestic film industry. This has changed in recent years, however, and as more money is being spent on the promotion of a home-grown film industry (including a very attractive tax incentive package offered by the government), the number of Irish film-makers making their mark on world cinema is bound to increase.

Furthermore, a number of Irish actors have achieved extraordinary success in the last decade; Liam Neeson, Daniel Day-Lewis and Brenda Fricker have all won Oscars, and Dublin-born Gabriel Byrne has starred in a series of hits including *The Usual Suspects* and *The Man in the Iron Mask*. It is also worth noting that with the exception of Liam Neeson (who is best known for his role as Oskar Schindler in the award winning *Schindler's List*), they have all found fame playing essentially Irish characters: Fricker and Day-Lewis for their roles in *My Left Foot*, Byrne for his role as the Dublin-born gangster in *The Usual Suspects*. Add to this the success of Dublin director Neil Jordan (whose film credits include *Interview with the Vampire*, *The Crying Game* and *Michael Collins*) and Dublin producer Noel Pearson (who produced *My Left Foot* and the recently released *Dancing at Lughnasa*, based on Brian Friel's play) and the list of local talent is looking pretty good. It is no surprise that the current generation of aspiring actors has a new-found confidence in the chances of home-based success.

Dublin itself has been the subject of cinematic interest. The number of domestic and international film crews working in the capital at any given time is higher than ever before, with producers and directors eager to use this 'rare oul' town' as a setting for a film. Dublin's most recent appearance in the movies was in the Noel Pearson production of *The General*, a 1997 film about the life and times of notorious gangster Martin Cahill. Dublin Castle and Newman House can be spotted in the 1997 version of *Moll Flanders* starring Julia Roberts. Previously, Dublin was the spectacular backdrop for Neil Jordan's epic biopic *Michael Collins* (1996), which starred Liam Neeson, Julia Roberts and virtually every other Irish actor working in Ireland and England! Dublin audiences were particularly impressed by the full-scale recreation of the 1916 Easter Rising and the bombing of O'Connell St from the Liffey. The quieter side of the city was seen in *Circle of Friends*, the 1995 film based on Maeve Binchy's novel of college relationships. *A Man of no Importance*, starring Albert Finney as a gay bus conductor, is set in the Dublin of the early 1960s. Kilmainham Gaol provided the set for the 1994 film *In the Name of the Father*, which told the story of the Guildford Four, wrongly convicted of a pub bombing and only released after 14 years in British jails. It starred Daniel Day-Lewis and Emma Thompson. As well as representing itself, Dublin also served as a substitute for Boston in Ron Howard's 1992 film *Far and Away*, a fairly sentimental yarn about Irish emigrants to America starring Tom Cruise and Nicole Kidman.

The Commitments was a wonderful, bright and energetic 1991 hit about a north Dublin soul band. The film accurately records north Dublin's scruffy atmosphere, though some Dublin audiences (well, those in north Dublin at least) were somewhat amused by the geographical jumps around the city that the characters managed to make. *The Snapper* and *The Van*, the other two books in Roddy Doyle's Barrytown trilogy, have also been made into films.

Older films using Dublin include *Educating Rita*, which featured Trinity College as its quintessentially English university. The movie *My Left Foot* was as wonderful as the book it came from, *Down all the Days*. It also managed to make an interesting journey round Dublin, including visits to Mulligan's, the pub where you can find one of the best pints of Guinness in Ireland.

Renowned director John Huston's final film, *The Dead*, released in 1987, was based on a James Joyce story from *Dubliners*.

Theatre

Dublin has a theatrical history as long as its literary one. The city's first theatre was founded in Werburgh St in 1637. Although it was closed by the Puritans only four years later, another theatre named the Smock Alley Playhouse or Theatre Royal opened in 1661 and continued for over a century.

The late 19th century Celtic Revival and the establishment of the Abbey Theatre by WB Yeats and Lady Gregory may be the first images that spring to mind when Irish theatre is mentioned today, but many plays from an earlier era are still staged. Oliver Goldsmith found fame as a playwright, for *She Stoops to Conquer* (1773), as well as a novelist. Richard Brinsley Sheridan (1751-1816) introduced the word 'malapropism' to the language via the tongue-twisted Mrs Malaprop from his play *The Rivals* (1775).

The opening of the Abbey Theatre in 1904 also brought controversy. JM Synge (1871-1909) was already a subject of contention for his earlier plays before *The Playboy of the Western World* caused near riots in 1907 because it upset those with a romantically idealised view of rural Ireland. It was subjected to equally vociferous audience reaction later in the USA. *Juno and the Paycock* by Sean O'Casey (1880-1964) was well received in 1924 but *The Plough and the Stars* in 1926 had a violent reception from its audience as it was seen to be mocking the events of the 1916 Easter Rising. *Waiting for Godot* by Samuel Beckett (1906-89) may not have pleased everybody, but it did contribute to his winning the Nobel Prize for literature in 1969. More recently, Brian Friel's *Dancing at Lughnasa* was a great success, both at the Abbey and on New York's Broadway, where it won several Tony awards.

See the Theatre sections in the Things to See & Do and Entertainment chapters for more details about Dublin's theatres and theatre performances.

SOCIETY & CONDUCT

Ireland's economic success, social changes and cultural changes are dispelling old stereotypes of the country as a predominantly poor, rural, agrarian backwater unable to stop the exodus of its children. It has a booming economy that has embraced high technology, and a young population and flourishing arts.

While this holds true for the majority of Ireland, it is especially so in Dublin. The city has a long tradition of liberal cosmopolitanism, and its citizens pride themselves on living in one of the most easy-going capitals in the world. Social stratification exists, but movement between classes is fairly fluid and all to do with personal wealth rather than birth or background. Dubliners have, for the most part, a keen sense of their own history, and the memories of British rule have made them suspicious of any group or class aspiring to establish any kind of permanent foothold on the social ladder. In Dublin, it is an unwritten social rule that no one is better than anyone else, some just have more money than others.

Yet the growing gap between the 'haves' and the 'have-nots' has widened at an alarming rate. Many Dubliners are enjoying their share of the Celtic Tiger's success, but it hasn't reached areas like the Dublin housing estates where drugs and crime are a major problem. Politicians pay constant lip-service to the need to redress the balance, to ensure that wealth is distributed more evenly, but in actual fact the situation is just getting worse. Property prices in the city have increased by over 150% since 1990 with no signs of levelling off, cutting out a large proportion of the population from the buyers' market. Those living below the poverty line (set at 60% of the average national wage) rose from 31% of the population in 1991 to 38% in 1998. It's paradoxical that there should be a rise in the number of poor at a time of unprecedented national wealth.

The thorny abortion issue, still a bone of contention, has been temporarily resolved in a typically Irish compromise. While abortion is still illegal, it is no longer illegal to provide information on abortion, and women who travel to Britain to terminate their pregnancies can do so without fear of legal sanction. Still, the debate continues, and former president Mary Robinson made a spectacular plea in October 1998 for the legalisation of abortion in Ireland. In 1995 divorce was narrowly accepted in a referendum, making Ireland the last nation in Europe to legalise it.

Dos & Don'ts

Dublin is relaxed and easy-going with few rigid rules and regulations. There is nobody you have to be especially wary of offending, and there are relatively few strict rules of behaviour and dress-code regulations, apart from those dreamed up by ungracious nightclub bouncers. You can jaywalk with impunity and lots of Dublin cyclists even seem to get away with chaining their bikes up to the 'do not park bicycles here' signs in the city.

That said, you should be aware that there is a marked difference in opinion and outlook between the older, more 'traditional' generation, and the younger generations of Dubliners. While the former seem to accept that anything to do with such subjects as sex, contraception, divorce and abortion may be part and parcel of modern Ireland, they are still fundamentally suspicious of this social upheaval and are often less than willing to entertain a conversation on those subjects. Religious belief is still quite strong, and they might take offence at a foreigner who doesn't respect their strongly held opinions on these matters.

Younger Dubliners couldn't be more different. They have embraced social change as long overdue and are often extremely liberal – and sometimes radical – in their views, almost as though they wanted to make up for lost time. It seems that the further they get from the old traditions the better! However, as with anywhere else, Dubliners don't like to be reminded of their faults by anybody but other Dubliners, so the best policy is to be relaxed and to accept the good things the people of Dublin have to offer.

RELIGION

Ireland is strongly Catholic, but has a substantial Protestant minority, as well as smaller numbers of adherents to other faiths. The powerful position of the Roman Catholic Church is a subject of considerable controversy and is frequently cited by the Northern Irish as a major barrier to unification. The constitution introduced by Eamon de Valera in 1937 noted the church's 'special position' in Ireland as the religion of 'the great majority of its citizens'. However, it didn't make Catholicism the country's official religion and in 1970 even the constitutional 'special position' was rescinded. Nevertheless, the church still wields great power, albeit more in rural areas of the country.

The contraceptive pill and condoms are freely available, but in some areas are still taboo subjects not to be discussed. Although abortion is still banned, Ireland is believed to have a greater abortion rate than more liberal countries such as the Netherlands – Irish abortions are simply exported to Britain.

On the other hand, some of the church's influence has been reduced in recent years and church attendance is falling, albeit slowly. More significantly, fewer people, particularly those from the under-30 age group, are entering the religious life. Censorship was once strong, but the enormous list of banned books has been drastically curtailed and in 1995 the film *Priest*, set in Liverpool, England, dealing with sexuality, sin and scandal in the Catholic Church, was shown uncut in Dublin.

LANGUAGE

English is spoken throughout Ireland, but there are parts of western and southern Ireland known as *Gaeltacht* areas where Irish (a Gaelic language) predominates. Officially, the Republic of Ireland is bilingual but in practice few people outside the

Gaeltacht speak Irish fluently. However, the language is experiencing something of a revival and in Dublin there are several Irish-medium primary schools. Irish is one of the official languages of the EU.

See the Glossary chapter for some useful Irish words.

English is spoken with a peculiar Irish character and lilt. Indeed, the Irish accent is one of the most pleasant varieties of English to be heard. Some of the Irish sentence constructions in the English spoken in Ireland are closely related to the Irish language; for instance, the usual word order in Irish sentences is verb, subject, object. The present participle is also used more frequently in sentences such as 'Would you be wanting a room for the night, then?'. Another linguistic peculiarity is the use of 'after' in such constructions as 'I'm just after going to the shop', which has the same meaning as 'I have just been to the shop'.

DUBLIN'S ARCHITECTURE & ARCHITECTS

Dublin's wonderfully unified feel can be credited to a rough-and-tumble history, a century of elegant wealth, a further century of neglect and a final tough century leading up to the present day, perhaps the most fruitful period in urban planning since the Georgian era. Dublin's tangled history from its pre-Viking Celtic beginnings to its Viking, Norman and English periods saw fine buildings thrown up, and equally rapidly torn down. As a result the survivors from Dublin's earliest days are either inconsequential (the Protestant St Audoen's Church), fragmentary (bits and pieces of Dublin Castle) or heavily restored (St Patrick's and Christ Church cathedrals).

Viking & Medieval Architecture

Viking Dublin has been understandably consigned to the architectural dig (wood-and-mud architecture is hardly durable) and there is surprisingly little left to remind us of the city's Norman past. The imposing Dublin Castle has been so heavily reconstructed over the centuries that it bears little resemblance to the fortress erected by the Normans in 1204. Both Christ Church Cathedral (founded in 1038) and St Patrick's Cathedral (finished in 1192) were heavily rebuilt in the 19th century, and while they still have traces of their Norman origins – the crypt in Christ Church is the most obvious example – nothing remains of the private houses built around all sides of the cathedrals. These were torn down in the 18th century to allow for better viewing of the cathedrals. St Audoen's Church (Protestant), whose foundations date from 1190, has three magnificent 15th century bells but little else. St Ann's Guild Chapel, the blocked off south transept of the church, is currently being restored, having been without a roof since 1826. Of the walls that once surrounded the Norman city, only St Andrew's Arch on Cooke St remains.

Georgian Architecture

Dublin's peak was reached during the 18th century when its wealth led to the creation of magnificent streetscapes and fine squares, making it one of the great Georgian cities. The architecture of this era survived because of the century of neglect that followed. The 1801 Act of Union not only destroyed the Irish Parliament but also the basis of Ireland's wealth. The mid-century Potato Famine and the ensuing depopulation of Ireland simply compounded the disaster, one consequence of which was that nothing much was built in the 19th century. Ireland's decline continued into the 20th century, and independence in the 1920s, the Depression in the 1930s and WWII in the 1940s all contributed to the slow pace of change.

Previous Page: One of Edward Smyth's representations of the rivers of Ireland on the Custom House (photograph by Doug McKinlay).

Inset: Georgian door knocker (photograph by Tony Wheeler).

The end result is that despite a spate of destructive modern development since the 1960s, large chunks of modern Dublin are still of a piece – of an 18th century piece. Dublin's splendid Georgian streets and squares, lined with the severe Georgian buildings whose colourful doors have become a symbol of the city, are Dublin's finest architectural elements. Although St Stephen's Green, Merrion Square and Fitzwilliam Square, the city's finest squares, are all south of the Liffey, Dublin's Georgian building spree actually started north of the river and traces of that now-faded glory can still be seen in Mountjoy and Parnell Squares.

The Commission for Making Wide & Convenient Streets, established in 1757, certainly had a hand in providing Dublin's generous supply of such thoroughfares, the most notable of which is O'Connell St in north Dublin. Pedestrianised Grafton St is the most interesting street south of the Liffey and is Dublin's premier shopping street. South of the Liffey, fine Georgian streetscapes can be found along Lower and Upper Fitzwilliam St, which connects Merrion and Fitzwilliam Squares, and also along Ely Place. Upper and Lower Gardiner St in north Dublin would have been equally fine in its prime but is run down today. The first true Georgian street is Henrietta St in north Dublin, which although run-down, is still one of the finest.

Right: Both north and south Dublin have examples of fine Georgian façades.

PAT YALE

The Georgian house style that is so powerfully and consistently displayed in Dublin follows a very standard pattern. Including the basement, Dublin town houses typically have four storeys with symmetrically arranged windows and an imposing, central front door. Granite steps lead up to the door, which, in the best examples, is further embellished with a delicate leaded fanlight. A wide variety of door knockers, door handles and letterboxes decorate the often brightly painted doors, and foot scrapers, once used to scrape mud from the boots of gentlemen visitors, can still be seen beside many doors. The formal exteriors of these houses were often counterpointed internally by exuberant plasterwork and complex staircase railings.

Modern Architecture

The dominant style up to 1916 was a form of classicism based on James Gandon's Custom House but, following the destruction of substantial parts of the city during the Easter Rising and the subsequent creation of the Irish Free State, new styles were introduced. Despite some interesting designs such as those of the Department of Finance building on Kildare St – influenced by the Italian futurist movement and Russian constructivism – and the starkly modernist Dublin airport built at the end of the 1930s, it wasn't until the construction of Busáras after WWII that Dublin began looking like a modern city. This notable International Modernist building, designed by Michael Scott, was to have an influence on architects in Ireland for the next 20 years. Sadly, it was its pioneering use of glass (it used more than any other building in Europe at the time) that was its downfall: huge, unattractive air conditioning systems had to be installed to cool the building during the summer, thus ruining the aesthetic appeal of the design.

Until the late 1970s, the dominant architectural style in Dublin was the Miesian approach (named after the Dadaist Mies Van Der Rohe) advocated by the firm of Scott, Tallon & Walker. Their Bank of Ireland headquarters building and the New Library in Trinity, designed by Paul Koralek, are prime examples. By the 80s, architectural design was in crisis, and Sam Stephenson's two offerings, the Central Bank building on Dame St and the Civic Offices at Wood Quay aroused huge controversy for their ugly, bunker-style design. In fairness to Stephenson, he was not allowed to finish either project: the Central Bank was considered too tall and halfway through the construction of the Civic Offices (which were to be linked by a glass atrium) the remains of Viking Dublin were found, putting an end to Stephenson's projected design. In the mid-90s new buildings were added to the originals, but these haven't improved the site much.

The crisis ended in the 1990s with the development of the Temple Bar area as the city's cultural quarter. The government competition for a plan of how best to develop the area was won by Group 91, whose projects included the Irish Film Centre, the Ark children's centre, the

Top: The unmistakable Corinthian portico, colonnaded drum and copper-covered dome of the Four Courts seen from across the Liffey.

Bottom: The GPO on O'Connell St, with its imposing Ionic portico of Portland stone.

NEIL SETCHFIELD

NEIL SETCHFIELD

DOUG McKINLAY

TONY WHEELER

TONY WHEELER

Left: Throughout Dublin there are constant reminders of the city's Georgian heyday.

Temple Bar Music Centre, the Gallery of Photography, the Designyard Applied Arts Centre and the Arthouse multimedia centre. Two brand new squares and a curved street (Curved St!) were laid out, and the total effect has been remarkably successful. Of particular note is Meeting House Square, the highlight of which is the remarkable titanium stage door designed by Spanish architect Santiago Calatrava, who was also responsible for the design of the extraordinary Lyon-Satolas TGV terminal in France and the Alamillo Bridge in Seville. The Irish Film Centre, housed in the former Friends Meeting House, successfully combines the plain elegance of its Georgian façade with the ultra-modern glass and metal décor of its interior, which you would never guess existed from the outside. Designyard, on East Essex St, is also housed in an 18th century building, but inside is a paragon of modernity, with an elegant use of glass and metal throughout.

One of the more interesting developments in Temple Bar is the Green House on Temple Lane, which is Dublin's only entirely eco-friendly building, using only wind and solar power. The building's best feature is the plant-filled, glass atrium, which has a carefully designed ventilation system that passes air through the building so that it doesn't turn into a solarium.

Outside Temple Bar, other developments are worth mentioning. The Waterways Visitor Centre (known as 'the box on the docks'), designed in 1994 by Irish architects Ciaran O'Connor and Gerard O'Sullivan, has a nautical theme, with a metal frame and panelling on the outside and timber throughout the interior. North of the Liffey, the Harp Regeneration Project is undertaking a huge programme of construction in the Smithfield market area. Its most popular success is the 'new' Old Jameson Distillery, whose ramshackle, abandoned premises were converted into one of Dublin's more interesting museums. And the buildings keep going up: at the time of writing, Dublin was the second-biggest construction site in Europe after Berlin.

Architects

In spite of its many fine Georgian streetscapes and town houses, Dublin would be just another Georgian city if it had only private houses to show from the period. The city's real glory is its wonderful public buildings and for these it has one particular architect to thank – James Gandon (1743-1823).

During its prime, Gandon was the greatest of all Dublin's architects. Among his works are two riverside masterpieces, the Custom House and the later Four Courts, as well as the King's Inns, the O'Connell Bridge (originally the Carlisle Bridge) and the final part of the Houses of Parliament, now the Bank of Ireland. Gandon was English but of Huguenot descent and he looked across the Channel for his inspiration, so his greatest works owe more to Paris' River Seine than to London's Thames.

Francis Johnston (1760-1829) was responsible for numerous buildings, such as the Chapel Royal in Dublin Castle, St George's Church in north Dublin, the Royal Hibernian Military School in Phoenix Park (now St Mary's Hospital) and the GPO in O'Connell St. He was also called upon to design a number of important additions and alterations, including work on King's Inns and the building that is now the Irish president's residence, Áras an Uachtaráin. It was Johnston who redesigned the Irish Parliament building in 1801 when it was taken over by the Bank of Ireland.

The work of Sir William Chambers (1723-96) in Dublin included buildings at Trinity College and Charlemont House on Parnell Square (now the Municipal Gallery of Modern Art), but his Dublin masterpiece is the wonderfully eccentric Casino at Marino. Remarkably, Chambers never visited Dublin. In England he designed Somerset House and the pagoda at Kew Gardens.

Richard Castle (1690-1751) can cause some confusion in Dublin as he is frequently referred to as Richard Cassel. He was born in Hesse-Cassel in Germany and came to Ireland in 1727. Among the buildings he created are those at Nos 80 and 85 St Stephen's Green (now Iveagh House and Newman House respectively), Tyrone House on Marlborough St (near St Mary's Pro-Cathedral), a number of Trinity College buildings (most of which were later replaced, except for the Printing House) and some of Ireland's finest country homes, such as Powerscourt (County Wicklow) and Westport (County Mayo). His crowning achievements were Leinster House (now the Dáil Éireann or Irish Parliament) and the Rotunda Hospital, construction of which started just before he died.

Another of Dublin's prominent architects was Thomas Burgh (1670-1730), who built the original Custom House, Steeven's Hospital near Heuston station and Trinity College Library. Sir William Robinson (1645-1712) was responsible for Marsh's Library and the Royal Hospital Kilmainham, built between 1680 and 1687 and said to be Dublin's finest building in that century.

A number of Dublin's buildings are crowned by fine statuary, and Edward Smyth (1743-1823) created the statues that top the Four Courts and the Custom House.

Dublin's finest Georgian houses, the exteriors of which were so simple and severe, were often decorated inside with superbly crafted plasterwork. Some of the finest is the work of Michael Stapleton (1770-1803), which can be seen in Trinity College, Powerscourt House, Ely House near St Stephen's Green and Belvedere House in north Dublin. Also notable is the work of the LaFranchini brothers, Paolo (1693-1770) and Filippo (1702-79), in Newman House on St Stephen's Green and that of Robert West on the building next door (the home of Richard Chapel Whaley) and in Newbridge House at Donabate. West's own house is still standing at 20 Dominick St, near King's Inns in north Dublin.

In modern times, Michael Scott (of Scott, Tallon & Walker) is one of Dublin's most remarkable architects, as is the controversial Sam Stephenson, who has been nothing short of unlucky with his designs. Plagued throughout much of his career by misunderstanding and confusion at official level, his often brilliant ideas have never been completely realised, and he has left a legacy of unfinished buildings that have earned him more criticism than he has deserved.

Of course, architects are nothing without developers to employ them, and the greatest of all the Georgian Dublin property speculators was Luke Gardiner (1745-98), later Viscount Mountjoy. Dublin in its Georgian prime started north of the river, then spread south. Gardiner's Mall was one of the viscount's greatest achievements, and when a bridge linked it (as Sackville St) with south Dublin it became the new central axis of the city. It remains so to this day, though it is now known as O'Connell St. Mountjoy Square, which began as Gardiner's Square, was another Gardiner creation. The very first of Dublin's great Georgian streets was Henrietta St, leading to King's Inns in north Dublin, and Gardiner lived there at No 10.

William Dargan (1799-1867) also played a major part in the development of Dublin. He opened the Dublin-Dun Laoghaire train line in 1834 and mounted the Dublin Industrial Exhibition on the lawn in front of Leinster House in 1853. The proceeds from that exhibition were then used to found the National Gallery in 1864.

Right: The north side of the quadrangle at the Royal Hospital Kilmainham is dominated by the clock tower and spire.

TONY WHEELER

Facts for the Visitor

WHEN TO GO

The weather is warmest in July and August and the daylight hours are long, but the crowds will be greatest, the costs the highest and accommodation harder to come by. In the quieter winter months, however, you may get miserable weather, the days are short and many tourist facilities will be shut. Visiting Dublin in June or September has a number of attractions: the weather can be better than at any other time of the year, it's less crowded and everything is open. A visit to Dublin during the weekend nearest St Patrick's Day (March 17) is also recommended. On this day the holiday is celebrated throughout the city centre with a parade, fireworks, street dancing and other special events.

What to Bring

The Irish climate is changeable and even at the height of summer you should be prepared for cold weather and sudden rainfall. A raincoat or an umbrella is a necessity. Otherwise, Dublin presents few surprises; dress is usually casual and you are unlikely to be required to wear a jacket and tie except in the most exclusive restaurants.

You should also bring a couple of traveller's necessity items, such as a portable medical kit, a universal electric plug adapter and a universal sink plug. You might not need any of these, but emergencies do arise, and besides, they won't take up much room in your luggage.

ORIENTATION

The central area of Dublin is neatly divided by the River Liffey into southern and northern halves. The Viking and medieval city of Dublin developed first to the south of the river. The city's Georgian heyday began in the north then moved south again as the northern part prospered then declined.

Nowadays, the River Liffey marks a sharp divide in Dublin's fortunes, made even more marked by the success of the Temple Bar development. The further north you go, the poorer and more run down Dublin tends to become. Conversely, the further south you go, the more prosperous the streets become.

North of the river the important streets for visitors are O'Connell St, the major shopping thoroughfare that leads north to Parnell Square, and Gardiner St, with lots of B&Bs. Many of the hostels are in this area. Busáras, the main bus station, and Connolly station, one of the two most important train stations, are near the southern end of Gardiner St, which becomes rather dilapidated as it continues north. Immediately south of the river is the revitalised Temple Bar area and the expanse of Trinity College. Nassau St, along the southern edge of the college's campus, and the pedestrianised Grafton St are the main shopping streets south of the river.

Finding Addresses

There are several problems inherent in finding addresses in Dublin and the same problems exist in other Irish towns. One is the tendency for street names to change every few blocks. Another is that streets are subdivided into upper and lower (and even middle) or north and south. On maps, the 'upper' or 'lower' always appears at the end of the street name, and that convention has been followed on the maps in this book. However, in conversation the 'upper', 'lower', 'north' or 'south' is placed at the beginning of the street name, and this is how such names appear in the text of this book. So, on a map you will see Great George's St Lower, but in the text the same street will be referred to as Lower Great George's St. Street numbering often runs up one side of a street and down the other, rather than having odd numbers on one side and even on the other. Added to this, some streets don't have signs to tell you which street you're on.

MAPS

For most purposes free maps of Dublin are quite adequate. Dublin Tourism has detailed maps of the city covering hotels, restaurants and sights to see. If you need an indexed street directory, the *Dublin Street Guide* published by the Ordnance Survey is the best. The Ordnance Survey also publishes a *Map of Greater Dublin* (scale 1:20,000), which includes a street index and details of bus routes.

TOURIST OFFICES
Local Tourist Offices

The privately run Dublin Tourism provides all tourist information concerning the city, whereas the state-run Bord Fáilte (Irish Tourist Board) has offices throughout the rest of the country. If you arrive by air or sea, you'll find tourist offices at the airport and on the waterfront at Dun Laoghaire. In the city the Dublin Tourism office (Map 7, ☎ 605 7700/7799, reservations ☎ 605 7777) is in St Andrew's Church, 2 Suffolk St, Dublin 2 but it can get crowded, with long queues for accommodation bookings and information. From July to September it's open from 8.30 am to 6 pm Monday to Saturday, 11 am to 5.30 pm on Sunday. For the rest of the year it's open from 9 am to 6 pm Monday to Saturday. It's also worthwhile having a look at their Web site at www.visit ireland.com.

The tourist offices can reserve accommodation for you: the charge for a Dublin booking will be IR£1, for anywhere else IR£2, and you also pay a 10% deposit to the tourist office that is deducted from your bill at the end of your stay.

The head office of Bord Fáilte (Map 6, ☎ 676 5871, 602 4000) is at Baggot St Bridge (entrance on Wilton Terrace) and has an information desk. Although it's less conveniently located – to the south of the city centre, beyond St Stephen's Green – it's much less crowded. It's open from 9 am to 5.15 pm Monday to Friday and also has a Web site (www.ireland.travel.ie). There is also a suburban tourist office in The Square shopping centre, Tallaght, Dublin 24, which

is open from 9.30 am to 5 pm daily between March and December. It has no telephone.

Gulliver

This is a computerised tourist information and reservation service available at tourist offices. It provides up-to-date information on events, attractions and transport, and can also book accommodation. Eventually, anyone intending to visit Ireland will be able to go to a travel agency and access this information and make reservations from anywhere in the world. In Ireland call ☎ 1 800 600 800.

Tourist Offices Abroad

Offices of Bord Fáilte can be found in the following countries:

Australia
   (☎ 02-9299 6177) 5th floor, 36 Carrington St, Sydney, NSW 2000
Canada
   (☎ 416-929 2777) 160 Bloor St East, Suite 934, Toronto, Ontario M4W 1B9
France
   (☎ 01 47 42 03 36) 33 rue de Miromesnil, 75008 Paris
Germany
   (☎ 069-23 6492) Untermainanlage 7, 60329 Frankfurt Main 1
Netherlands
   (☎ 020-622 3101) Leidsestraat 32, 1017 PB Amsterdam
New Zealand
   (☎ 09-379 3708) Dingwall Building, 87 Queen St, Auckland 1 (PO Box 279)
Northern Ireland
   (☎ 01232-327 888) 53 Castle St, Belfast BT1 1GH
UK
   (☎ 020-7493 3201) Ireland House, 150 New Bond St, London W1Y 0AQ
USA
   (☎ 212-418 0800) 345 Park Ave, New York, NY 10154

DOCUMENTS
Visas

Citizens of most western countries don't need a visa to visit Ireland. UK nationals born in Great Britain or Northern Ireland don't require a passport, though may be asked for some form of identification. Visas are required from Indians, Pakistanis, non-UK passport Hong Kong citizens and citizens of some African states. See Embassies & Consulates later in this chapter for addresses of where to apply for visa extensions if necessary.

Travel Insurance

A travel insurance policy to cover theft, loss and medical problems is a wise idea. Citizens of EU countries are eligible for free medical care (with an E111 certificate, which they must obtain from their local health authority before travelling), but other visitors should have medical insurance or be prepared to pay. There is a wide variety of policies and your travel agency will have recommendations. Make sure the policy includes health care and medication in the countries you plan to visit en route to Ireland, covers 'dangerous' activities, such as diving or rock climbing, if they're on your agenda, and includes a flight home for you, and anyone you're travelling with, should your condition warrant it.

Driving Licence & Permits

If you take your own vehicle, you should always carry a Vehicle Registration Document as proof that it's yours. Your normal driving licence is legal for one year from the date you last entered Ireland, unless you have an EU licence, which is treated the same as an Irish licence. If you have a driving licence from outside the EU, it's generally a good idea to obtain an International Driving Permit (IDP). These can be obtained from your automobile association for a small fee.

Hostel Cards

The An Óige (Irish Youth Hostel Association) card, costing IR£10, can be bought at the An Óige offices (Map 4, ☎ 830 4555, 61 Mountjoy St, Dublin 1) or over the phone with a credit card. The An Óige card entitles the holder to discounts at hostels and also gives access to the international youth hostel booking network.

Seniors' Cards

Senior citizens usually need only show proof of age to benefit from the many discounts available to them. These include discounts at museums and galleries and free public transport.

Other Documents

Many parks, monuments and gardens in the Republic are operated by Dúchas (formerly the Office of Public Works). From any of these sites, you can get a Heritage Card for IR£15 (seniors IR£10, students and children IR£4), giving you unlimited access to all of these sites for one year.

Photocopies

All important documents (for instance your passport data page and visa page, credit cards, travel insurance policy, travel tickets and driving licence) should be photocopied before you leave home. Leave one copy with someone at home and keep another with you in a safe place, separate from the originals, of course.

EMBASSIES & CONSULATES
Irish Embassies & Consulates

Irish diplomatic offices overseas include:

Australia
   (☎ 02-6273 3022) 20 Arkana St, Yarralumla, Canberra, ACT 2600
Canada
   (☎ 613-233 6281) 130 Albert St, Ottawa, Ontario K1P 5G4
France
   (☎ 01 44 17 67 60) 12 ave Foch, 75116 Paris
Germany
   (☎ 0228-95 9290) Godesberger Allee 119, 53175 Bonn
Netherlands
   (☎ 070-363 0993) Dr Kuyperstraat 9, 2514 BA The Hague
UK
   (☎ 020-7235 2171) 17 Grosvenor Place, London SW1X 7HR
USA
   (☎ 202-462 3939) 2234 Massachusetts Ave NW, Washington, DC 20008
   In addition there are consulates in Boston, Chicago, New York and San Francisco.

Embassies in Dublin

For citizens of New Zealand, the closest embassy is in London. You'll find embassies of the following countries in Dublin:

Australia
   (☎ 676 1517) 2nd floor, Fitzwilton House, Wilton Terrace, Dublin 2
Canada
   (Map 6, ☎ 478 1988) 4th floor, 65-68 St Stephen's Green, Dublin 2
France
   (☎ 260 1666) 36 Ailesbury Rd, Dublin 4
Germany
   (☎ 269 3011/3123)
   31 Trimleston Ave, Booterstown, County Dublin
Netherlands
   (☎ 269 3444) 160 Merrion Rd, Dublin 4
New Zealand (in London)
   (☎ 020-7930 8422) New Zealand House, Haymarket, London SW1 4QT
UK
   (☎ 205 3700) 31-33 Merrion Rd, Dublin 4
USA
   (☎ 668 8777) 42 Elgin Rd, Dublin 4

CUSTOMS

There is a two-tier system for imported goods: the first tier is for goods bought duty free, the second for goods bought in an EU country where taxes and duties have been paid. The second is relevant because a number of products (including alcohol and tobacco) are cheaper on the Continent. Under the EU rules, as long as taxes have been paid somewhere in the EU there are no additional taxes if the goods are exported within the EU – provided they're for personal consumption. The amounts that officially constitute personal use are 800 cigarettes (400 cigarillos, 200 cigars or 1kg of tobacco) and either 10L of spirits, 20L of fortified wine, 60L of sparkling wine, 90L of still wine or 110L of beer.

Goods purchased duty free in the EU remain subject to the normal restrictions. You're allowed to import 200 cigarettes, 1L of spirits, 2L of wine, 60cc of perfume, 250cc of toilet water and other dutiable goods to the value of IR£34. It's well worth checking the regulations before you leave home because duty-free shopping within the EU is under review.

Apart from the usual bans on firearms, explosives and illegal drugs, it is illegal to bring into Ireland such things as oral smokeless tobacco, indecent or obscene books and pictures, all meat and meat products, and all plants and plant products (including seeds). Dogs and cats from anywhere outside the United Kingdom are subject to strict quarantine laws (which at the time of writing were under review to bring them into line with proposed changes in the UK).

MONEY
Currency

The Irish pound or punt (IR£) is divided into 100 pence (p). There are coins of one, two, five, 10, 20 and 50 pence and IR£1. Notes come in denominations of IR£5, IR£10, IR£20, IR£50 and IR£100.

Don't confuse Northern Irish pounds (issued by the Bank of Ireland, First Trust, and the Northern and Ulster banks) with Republic of Ireland pounds (issued by the Central Bank of Ireland). 'Sterling' or 'Belfast' are giveaway words found on the Northern Irish notes, which are worth the same as British notes. The Irish punt is worth about 10 pence less than the pound sterling. Ireland is participating in the euro, the European single currency. See the boxed text 'Introducing the euro' on the next page for an account of this process and what it means for the visitor.

Exchange Rates

country	unit		punt
Australia	A$1	=	IR£0.44
Canada	C$1	=	IR£0.46
euro	€1	=	IR£0.79
France	1FF	=	IR£0.12
Germany	DM1	=	IR£0.40
Japan	¥100	=	IR£0.60
New Zealand	NZ$1	=	IR£0.37
UK	UK£1	=	IR£1.14
USA	US$1	=	IR£0.69

euro currency converter IR£1 = €1.27

Introducing the euro

On 1 January 1999 a new currency, the euro, was introduced in Europe. It's all part of the harmonisation of the European Union (EU) countries. Along with national border controls, the currencies of various EU members are being phased out. Not all EU members have agreed to adopt the euro, however: Denmark, Greece, Sweden and the UK rejected or postponed participation. The 11 countries which have participated from the beginning of the process are Austria, Belgium, Finland, France, Germany, Ireland, Italy, Luxembourg, the Netherlands, Portugal and Spain.

The timetable for the introduction of the euro runs as follows:

- On 1 January 1999 the exchange rates of the participating countries were irrevocably fixed to the euro. The euro came into force for 'paper' accounting and prices could be displayed in local currency and in euros.
- On 1 January 2002 euro banknotes and coins will be introduced. This ushers in a period of dual use of euros and existing local notes and coins (which will, in effect, simply be temporary denominations of the euro).
- By July 2002 local currencies in the 11 countries will be withdrawn. Only euro notes and coins will remain in circulation and prices will be displayed in euros only.

The new currency will be standardised in the participating countries; the €5 note in France is the same €5 note you will use in Italy and Portugal. There will be seven euro notes. In different colours and sizes they come in denominations of 500, 200, 100, 50, 20, 10 and five euros. There are eight euro coins, in denominations of two and one euros, then 50, 20, 10, five, two and one cents. On the reverse side of the coins each participating state will be able to decorate the coins with their own designs, but all euro coins can be used anywhere that accepts euros.

So, what does all this mean for the traveller? It is somewhat uncertain exactly what practices will be adopted between 1999 and 2002, and travellers will probably find differences in 'euro-readiness' between different countries, between different towns in the same country, or between different establishments in the same town. It is certain, however, that euro cheque accounts and travellers cheques will be available. Credit card companies can bill in euros, and shops, hotels and restaurants might list prices in both local currency and euros. Travellers

Exchanging Money

Most major currencies are readily accepted in Ireland. The best exchange rates are obtained at banks, which are usually open from 10 am to 4 pm Monday to Friday and stay open until 5 pm on Thursday. Bureaux de change and other exchange facilities usually stay open longer but the rate or commission will be worse. Building societies often handle foreign exchange and are open longer hours than the banks. Many post offices have a currency-exchange facility and have the advantage of being open on Saturday morning.

The foreign-exchange counter at Dublin airport is in the baggage-collection area and opens from approximately 7 am to 9.30 pm in summer (April to September) and from 7.30 am to 8.30 pm in winter (October to March). There is also an office on the departures level upstairs.

There's a cluster of banks in College Green (Map 7) opposite Trinity College and most have exchange facilities and automated teller machines (ATMs). The Bank of Ireland bureau de change, in Westmoreland St (Map 7) beside the bank, is open from 9 am to 9 pm Monday to Saturday (including should check bills carefully to make sure that any conversion from local currency to euros has been calculated correctly. The most confusing period will probably be between January 2002 and July 2002 when there will be two sets of notes and coins.

Luckily for travellers, the euro should make everything easier. One of the main benefits will be that prices in the 11 countries will be immediately comparable, avoiding all those tedious calculations.

Also, once euro notes and coins are issued in 2002, you won't need to change money at all when travelling to other single-currency members. Banks may still charge a handling fee (yet to be decided) for travellers cheques but they won't be able to profit by buying the currency from you at one rate and selling it back to you at another, as they do at the moment. However, even EU countries not participating may price goods in euros and accept euros over shop counters.

There are many Web sites dealing with the introduction of the euro but most are devoted to the legal implications and the processes by which businesses may adapt to the single currency and are not particularly interesting or informative for the traveller. The Lonely Planet Web site at www.lonelyplanet.com has a link to a currency converter and up-to-date news on the integration process.

country	unit		euro
Australia	A$1	=	€0.55
Canada	C$1	=	€0.58
France	1FF	=	€0.15
Germany	DM1	=	€0.51
Ireland	IR£1	=	€1.27
Japan	¥100	=	€0.75
New Zealand	NZ$1	=	€0.47
Spain	100 pta	=	€0.60
United Kingdom	UK£1	=	€1.45
United States	US$1	=	€0.88

FACTS FOR THE VISITOR

bank holidays) and from 10 am to 7 pm on Sunday. American Express and Thomas Cook are across the road from the Bank of Ireland and the Trinity College entrance (Map 7). American Express is open from 9 am to 5 pm Monday to Friday; on Saturday the travel agency closes at noon, but the foreign-exchange counter stays open until 5 pm. From June to September you can also change money here on Sunday between 11 am and 4 pm. Thomas Cook is open from 9 am to 5.30 pm from Monday to Saturday.

The main offices of major Irish banks in Dublin are:

Allied Irish Bank
  (☎ 660 0311) Bankcentre, Ballsbridge, Dublin 4
Bank of Ireland
  (Map 6, ☎ 661 5933) Lower Baggot St, Dublin 2
National Irish Bank
  (Map 7, ☎ 678 5066) 7-8 Wilton Terrace, Dublin 2
Ulster Bank
  (☎ 677 7623) 33 College Green, Dublin 2

Travellers Cheques & Eurocheques
Most major brands of travellers cheques are readily accepted in Ireland, but carrying

them in pounds sterling has the advantage that in Northern Ireland or Britain you can change them on your return without losing out over exchange rates. American Express and Thomas Cook travellers cheques are widely recognised and branches don't charge commission for cashing their own cheques. Travellers cheques are rarely accepted for everyday transactions so you'll need to cash them beforehand.

Eurocheques can be cashed in Dublin but special arrangements must be made before you travel if you are thinking of using personal cheques.

ATMs Plastic cards make the perfect travelling companions – they're ideal for major purchases and let you withdraw cash from selected banks and ATMs. ATMs are usually linked up internationally, so you can get instant cash from your account back home by punching in a personal identification number (PIN). The Allied Irish Bank (AIB) and Bank of Ireland have many conveniently central ATMs.

Needless to say, ATMs aren't infallible, and they have been known to accidentally swallow cards, which can be an awful inconvenience. If you can, withdraw money from a teller, who will simply run your card through a magnetic slide and access your account that way.

Credit Cards Major credit cards – particularly American Express, MasterCard and Visa – as well as other credit and charge cards are widely accepted, though some B&Bs will only take cash. You can also use credit cards to withdraw cash, but be sure to obtain a PIN from your bank *before* you leave. You should also ask which ATMs in Ireland accept your credit card. This service usually carries an extra charge, so if you're withdrawing money, take out enough so that you don't have to keep going back.

Security
Dublin isn't a particularly dangerous city but, like any urban centre, it has its fair share of problems with crime. Pickpocket-

ing, though not a widespread problem, does occur; more frequent are incidents of bags and other items stolen from pubs and cafés while sitting at the feet of their owners. Muggings also occur, though mostly in run-down parts of the city and late at night.

Your best bet is to split your money into different stashes, preferably keeping the bulk of it in a pouch that you can wear around your neck inside your clothing or in a money belt, which you can wrap firmly around your waist and under your shirt or sweater. It is highly inadvisable to carry a wallet in your back pocket; not only is it easy prey for pickpockets, but it can fall out without you noticing.

Costs
Costs in Dublin are not as high as in London or other major European cities, but they are certainly not low. Many places to stay, particularly hostels, have different high and low-season prices. Some places may have not just a high-season but a *peak* high-season price. In this book the highest price levels are quoted. Entry prices to such places as museums and galleries are usually lower for children, students and senior citizens than the standard adult fee. These child, student and senior prices may sometimes differ.

At the bottom of the scale a hostel dormitory bed will cost from IR£6 to IR£11 a night. A cheap B&B will cost about IR£15 to IR£20 per person, and a more luxurious B&B or guesthouse with attached bathroom costs about IR£20 to IR£45. Dinner with a glass of wine or a beer in a reasonable restaurant costs from IR£10 to IR£18.

Sightseeing Discounts
If you're planning a serious onslaught on Ireland's many castles, monasteries and other sites, it can be worthwhile purchasing a Heritage Card (see Documents earlier in this chapter).

Dúchas sites in Dublin that charge an entry fee are the Casino at Marino (IR£2), St Mary's Abbey (IR£1) and Kilmainham Jail (IR£2). Dúchas sites within day-trip

What's Free

Dublin has only recently joined the list of major European tourist destinations and many of the more important places of interest charge fairly high entrance fees. However, all art galleries, including the National Gallery and the Irish Museum of Modern Art, are free, as are all the public gardens and parks, including the Botanic Gardens in Glasnevin. There are also a number of museums that have resisted cashing in on the tourist boom. They are:

Chester Beatty Library
Dublin Civic Museum
Garda Museum (police museum in Phoenix Park)
Heraldic Museum & Genealogical Office
Natural History Museum
National Museum
Pearse Museum
Royal Irish Academy

Of Dublin's churches, only Christ Church Cathedral and St Patrick's Cathedral charge an admission fee; all the others are free to visitors, as are all cemeteries, including the notable ones at Glasnevin and Arbour Hill.

There is no charge to enter government buildings. Leinster House, the seat of the Irish legislature, does not charge admission should you wish to sit in on a debate when it is in session; and although arranging tours of the building can be difficult, they too are free.

You can have great fun just ambling through the streets of Dublin, especially round the two main markets, the South George's St covered market, south of the Liffey, and Mother Redcap's Market on the north side of the city (see the Shopping chapter for details).

distance of Dublin are Mellifont Abbey (IR£1.50), Knowth (IR£2) and Newgrange (IR£2) in the Boyne Valley to the north; Glendalough to the south charges an entry fee to the visitor centre (IR£2) but not to the site itself.

The Dublin Cultural Connection costs IR£2.50 and gives you 10% discount on some of the city's main heritage sites including Dublinia, the Dublin Writers' Museum, the Guinness Hop Store, the National Museum, Trinity College and Malahide Castle. It's available from the tourist offices or at the sites.

A SuperSaver card is available from Dublin Tourism, covering entry to eight attractions: Malahide Castle, Newbridge House, the James Joyce Museum and Tower, the Dublin Writers' Museum, Dublin's Viking Adventure, the Fry Model Railway and the George Bernard Shaw House. The SuperSaver card costs IR£16.50 (students IR£12.50).

Tipping

Although tipping is less prevalent in Ireland than elsewhere in Europe, things are changing fast. Fancy hotels and restaurants usually add a 15% service charge and no additional tip is required, but good service is usually rewarded with a gratuity. Simpler places usually do not add service, and if you decide to tip, it's acceptable to round up the bill or add 15% at most. You don't have to tip taxi drivers, but if you do 10% is fine. For hotel porters 50p per bag is acceptable.

Taxes & Refunds

Value-added tax (VAT) is a sales tax that applies to most goods and services in

Ireland, excluding books and children's footwear. Residents of the EU cannot claim a VAT refund. Visitors from non-EU countries can claim back the VAT on large purchases that are subsequently exported from the EU through the Cashback scheme. If you're a resident of a country outside the EU and buy something from a store displaying a Cashback sticker, you'll be given a Cashback voucher with your purchase. This voucher can be refunded in US, Canadian or Australian dollars, British pounds sterling or Irish punts at Dublin or Shannon airport. Alternatively, you can have the voucher stamped at the ferry port and mail it back for a refund.

If you reclaim more than IR£200 on any of your vouchers you'll need to get the voucher stamped at the customs booth in the arrivals hall at Dublin or Shannon airport before you can get your refund from the Cashback desk.

If you leave the EU from terminal three or terminal four of London's Heathrow airport you must get British customs to stamp your vouchers and then leave them at the Tax Free Shopping Desk. In some circumstances refunds can be posted to you or credited to your credit card.

POST & COMMUNICATIONS
Post
Post offices are open from 8.30 am to 5.30 or 6 pm Monday to Friday and from 9 am to noon on Saturday; smaller offices close for lunch. Dublin's historically significant GPO (Map 6), on O'Connell St north of the river, has longer opening hours: 8 am to 8 pm Monday to Saturday, 10 am to 6.30 pm Sunday and holidays. The post office (Map 7) on South Anne St, just off Grafton St, is handy for the centre. Many newsagencies also operate as sub-post offices.

Mail can be addressed to poste restante at post offices, but is officially held for two weeks only. If you write 'hold for collection' on the envelope it may be kept for a longer period.

Postal rates by air for letters up to 20g and other items are:

item	destination	cost
aerograms	all destinations	45p
postcards	Ireland/other EU countries	28p
	other countries	38p
letters	Ireland/other EU countries	32p
	non-EU Europe	44p
	other countries	52p

All mail to Britain and Europe goes by air so there is no need to use air-mail envelopes or stickers.

Telephone
The Telecom Éireann Telecentre (Map 4, ☎ 661 1111), Findlater House on Upper O'Connell St, has public phones that use cash or phonecards. The staff there will also help you with any queries or problems you may have regarding the phone system.

You can dial international calls directly from pay phones. Phone calls between the Republic and Northern Ireland are classified as international calls. The number of the operator for inquiries or making reverse-charge calls within Ireland is 10.

Overseas Calls To call a UK number (except for Northern Ireland) from the Republic dial 0044 plus the area code (minus the 0) then the number. Thus an 020 number in London would start 0044-20. To call elsewhere overseas dial 00 then the international code for that country (1 for the USA or Canada, 61 for Australia, 64 for New Zealand) then the area code (dropping any leading 0) and then the number. The one variation is that to call Northern Ireland from Ireland you dial 08 and then the Northern Irish area code *without* dropping the leading 0. The number of the international operator for inquiries or for making reverse-charge calls is 114, or 10 for help with calls to Britain.

The cost of a direct-dialled international call from Ireland varies according to the time of day. Reduced rates apply after 6 pm and before 8 am. They also apply between midnight and 8 am and between 2 and 8 pm on calls to Australia and New Zealand. Standard charges for one minute are:

Australia	88p
France	39p
Germany	39p
North America	36p
New Zealand	88p
UK	24p

Home Direct Calls Rather than placing reverse-charge calls through the operator in Ireland, you can dial direct to your home country operator and then reverse the charges or charge the call to a local phone credit card. To use the home-direct service dial the following codes then the area code and, in most cases, the number you want. Your home country operator will come on the line before the call goes through:

Australia	☎ 1800 5500 61 + number
France	☎ 1800 5500 33 + number
Italy	☎ 1800 5500 39 + number
New Zealand	☎ 1800 5500 64 + number
Spain	☎ 1800 5500 34 + number
UK – BT	☎ 1800 5500 44 + number
UK – Mercury	☎ 1800 5500 04 + number
USA – AT&T	☎ 1800 5500 00 + number
USA – MCI	☎ 1800 5510 01 + number
USA – Sprint	☎ 1800 5520 01 + number

Payphones & Phonecards Phonecards are available in 10 (IR£2), 20 (IR£3.50), 50 (IR£8) and 100-unit (IR£16) versions. Each unit is equivalent to one local phone call. Phonecards are useful for making international calls. Note that you cannot make international calls via the operator from a card-operated phone.

Fax & Telegrams You can send faxes from post offices or other specialist offices. It can be quite expensive, however: about IR£1 per page locally, between IR£2 and IR£3 to Europe and approximately IR£4 per page to such overseas destinations as Australia or the USA. Phone the operator on ☎ 196 to send international telegrams (known as telemessages).

Area Codes The area code for calls to Dublin from outside the city is 01. Other

area codes in the Republic of Ireland and Northern Ireland include:

Athlone	☎ 0902
Bantry	☎ 027
Belfast	☎ 028 90
Cork	☎ 021
Derry	☎ 028 71
Dingle	☎ 066
Donegal	☎ 073
Drogheda	☎ 041
Galway	☎ 091
Glendalough	☎ 0404
Kilkenny	☎ 056
Killarney	☎ 064
Kilronan	☎ 099
Limerick	☎ 061
Shannon	☎ 061
Tipperary	☎ 062
Waterford	☎ 051
Wexford	☎ 053

Email & Internet Access

Travelling with a portable computer is a great way to stay in touch, but unless you know what you're doing it's fraught with problems. If you plan to carry your notebook or palmtop computer with you, remember that the power supply voltage in Ireland is 220V, so if your machine isn't compatible you risk damage to your equipment. The best investment is a universal AC adapter for your appliance, which will enable you to plug it in anywhere without frying the innards. You'll also need a three pin plug adapter, which you can pick up at any electrical appliance store.

Also, your PC-card modem may not work once you leave your home country – you won't know for sure until you try. The safest option is to buy a reputable 'global' modem before you leave home, or buy a local PC-card modem if you're spending a long time in a country. Keep in mind that the telephone socket in each country you visit will probably be different from that at home, so ensure that you have at least a US RJ-11 telephone adapter for your modem. You can almost always find an adapter that will convert from RJ-11 to the local variety. The Web sites at www.teleadapt.com or www.warrior.com have information on travelling with a portable computer.

Major Internet service providers (ISPs) such as AOL (www.aol.com), CompuServe (www.compuserve.com) and IBM Net (www.ibm.net) have dial-in nodes throughout Europe; it's best to download a list of the dial-in numbers before you leave home. If you access your Internet email account at home through a smaller ISP or your office or school network, your best option is either to open an account with a global ISP, such as those mentioned above, or to use cybercafés and other public access points.

If you intend to rely on cybercafés, you'll need to know three things to access your email account: your incoming (POP or IMAP) mail server name, your account name and your password. Your ISP or network supervisor will give you these. With this information, you should be able to access your Internet email account from any net-connected machine in the world, provided it runs some kind of email software (remember that Netscape and Internet Explorer both have mail modules). It pays to become familiar with the process for doing this before you leave home. A final option for collecting mail through cybercafés is to open a free Web-based email account such as those provided by Hotmail (www.hotmail.com) or Yahoo! (mail.yahoo.com). You can then access your mail from anywhere in the world from any net-connected machine running a standard Web browser.

Dublin is pretty Internet-friendly, and there are several cybercafés in the city centre where you can check and send email or simply surf the Internet. These include:

Betacafé Arthouse
    (Map 6, ☎ 671 5717) Curved St, Temple Bar, Dublin 2
Cyberia
    (Map 6, ☎ 679 7607) The Granary, Temple Lane South, Dublin 2
Planet Cyber Café
    (Map 6, ☎ 679 0583) 23 South Great George's St, Dublin 2

INTERNET RESOURCES

The World Wide Web is a rich resource for travellers. You can research your trip, hunt down bargain air fares, book hotels, check on weather conditions or chat with locals and other travellers about the best places to visit (or avoid!).

There's no better place to start your Web explorations than the Lonely Planet Web site (www.lonelyplanet.com). On this site you'll find succinct summaries on travelling to most destinations on earth, postcards from other travellers and the Thorn Tree bulletin board, where you can ask questions before you go or dispense helpful advice when you get back. You can also find travel news and updates to many of our most popular guidebooks, and the subWWWay section has links taking you to the most useful travel resources to be found elsewhere on the Web.

Other interesting and informative links relating specifically to Dublin include the following:

Blarney Woollen Mills
    www.blarney.ie
    (the famous Irish clothing store's site lists accommodation options, places to eat and activities throughout the country)
Bord Fáilte
    www.ireland.travel.ie
    (the Irish Tourist Board's official site)
Dublin Tourism's official site
    www.visitdublin.com
    (gives access to most of the services it offers in its city centre office)
The Hedonist's Guide to Dublin
    www.shaw.iol.ie/~smytho/dublin
    (aimed at young people – this is a fun look at pubs, clubs, cafés, shopping and what's on in the capital)
Indigo
    www.indigo.ie
    (the biggest Irish server, with comprehensive services including a full tourist menu, with everything from where to eat to what to do with young children)
Ostlan
    www.ostlan.ie
    (has a list of over 270 restaurants in the Dublin area and a comprehensive list of pubs)

BOOKS

A glance in most Dublin bookshops will reveal huge Irish interest sections, whether it's fiction, history and current events, or numerous local and regional guidebooks. See the Literature section in the Facts about Dublin chapter for information on fiction by Irish writers.

Most books are published in different editions by different publishers in different countries. As a result, a book might be a hardcover rarity in one country while it's readily available in paperback in another. Fortunately, bookshops and libraries search by title or author, so they are best placed to advise you on the availability of the following recommendations.

Lonely Planet

Lonely Planet publishes *Ireland* and *Walking in Ireland*, which provide detailed information for people planning to travel around the country, and *Travel with Children*, a guide specifically for those travelling with young children.

History & Politics

Dublin – One Thousand Years by Stephen Conlin is a fascinating book about the development of Dublin, with a series of illustrations showing how the city looked at various times in its history. The paintings of the area around the black pool (*dubh linn*) in 988 and the same scene again in 1275, with the addition of Dublin Castle, are particularly interesting. *Dublin* by VS Pritchett is a little old but gives an evocative and engaging account of an often eccentric city.

The two best books on Ireland's more recent history are JJ Lee's *Ireland 1912-1985* and the classic FSL Lyons tome, *Ireland since the Famine*. Lee's book caused something of a stir when it first came out, as it contends that Ireland's problems were not entirely due to 'perfidious Albion'. Lyons' book is the standard history for all students of modern Ireland; its author was professor of history at Trinity College.

A Concise History of Ireland by Máire and Conor Cruise O'Brien is a readable and comprehensively illustrated short history of Ireland. Readers may be familiar with the highly controversial Conor Cruise O'Brien; a staunch supporter of the underdog, he was a member of the pro-Union UK Unionist Party until November 1998, when he resigned from the party, arguing that Northern Irish Unionists had been betrayed by the British Government and that their future lay in a united Ireland. *Ireland – a History* by Robert Kee covers similar ground in a similar format in a book developed from a BBC/RTE TV series.

For all sorts of minutiae about Dublin buildings and streets check the *Encyclopaedia of Dublin* by Douglas Bennett.

The Irish bookshop chain Eason's publishes a series of slim booklets on specific fields of Irish interest, including several on personages and buildings of Dublin. Interesting titles in this series include *The American Ambassador's Residence, Christ Church Cathedral, The City Hall, Georgian Dublin, Guinness, James Joyce's Dublin, Malahide Castle, Masterpieces of the National Gallery of Ireland, The National Library, The Royal College of Surgeons, The Shelbourne Hotel, St Mary's Pro-Cathedral, St Patrick's Cathedral, Swift's Ireland, Trinity College* and *The World of George Berkeley*.

Literary Dublin – a History by Herbert A Kenny traces the history of Dublin's rich and diverse literary culture. *A Literary Guide to Dublin* by Vivien Igoe includes detailed route maps, a guide to cemeteries and an eight page section on literary and historical pubs.

NEWSPAPERS & MAGAZINES

The main Irish dailies are the *Irish Times* and the *Irish Independent*. The *Irish Times* is Ireland's oldest newspaper and famous for its good journalism, while the *Irish Independent*'s content is lighter. Irish versions of the English tabloid papers (including the *Sun* and the *Mirror*) are also available. The *Evening Herald* is an evening tabloid. Sunday papers include the *Sunday Tribune*, which has an excellent reputation for good

FACTS FOR THE VISITOR

investigative journalism, and the *Sunday Business Post*, the best financial newspaper in the country. For political content, the best magazines are the weekly *Magill* and the satirical fortnightly *Phoenix*. British papers and magazines are available on the day of issue and are cheaper than their Irish equivalents. Eason's on O'Connell St has a wide selection of foreign and regional Irish newspapers, which are also available in larger newsagents.

RADIO & TV

Radio na Telefís Éireann (RTE) is Ireland's government-sponsored national broadcasting body. There are three state-controlled radio stations. Two of them – RTE Radio 1 and RTE's 2FM – are broadcast in English, and Radio na Gaeltachta is in Irish. There are also various independent radio stations. In Dublin, 98FM, 104FM and Today FM (100 to 102 on the dial) play classic rock music and are popular; Today FM is especially good on weekdays from 5 pm to midnight, when it has an interesting blend of informative talk radio and good alternative music. For a complete list of Dublin's radio stations and their frequencies – including some excellent pirate stations – look in the *Event Guide*.

Ireland has two state-controlled TV channels, RTE 1 and Network 2, as well as an independent station, TV3, which began broadcasting in October 1998. British BBC, ITV and Channel 4 programmes can also be picked up. An advantage Ireland has over Britain is that the two main Sky satellite channels, Sky One and Sky News, are available without recourse to a satellite dish.

VIDEO SYSTEMS

Ireland uses the PAL I (VHF) system for video recorders, which is unique to Ireland.

PHOTOGRAPHY & VIDEO

Dublin is a photogenic but often gloomy city, so photographers should bring high-speed film. The best times of day for taking pictures are early morning and late evening, when the sunlight – if there is any – is low and warm. Remember the rain and bring a plastic bag to keep your camera dry.

Fast-developing services are readily available. Developing and printing a 24 exposure print film typically costs around IR£8.50 for a one hour service or from IR£4 to IR£5 for a slower turnaround. Slide processing costs about IR£6 a roll and takes a few days, though the Film Bank (Map 6, ☎ 662 4420), 102 Lower Baggot St, has a two hour service. However, they mainly cater for professionals and have prices to match their high quality.

TIME

Dublin is on Greenwich Mean Time (GMT) or Universal Time Co-ordinated (UTC), as is London. Without taking daylight-saving time changes into account, when it's noon in Dublin or London, it is 8 pm in Singapore, 10 pm in Sydney or Melbourne, 3 am in Los Angeles or Vancouver and 7 am in New York.

Also, as in Britain, clocks are advanced by one hour in mid-March and put back one hour at the end of October.

ELECTRICITY

Electricity is 220V, 50Hz AC. Plugs are of the flat three pin type, as in Britain.

WEIGHTS & MEASURES

Like Britain, progress towards metrication in Ireland is slow and piecemeal. Green roadsigns give distances in kilometres, older white ones measure them in miles and newer white ones give them in kilometres. Speed limits are usually given in miles, food in shops is priced and weighed in metric, beer in pubs is served in pints and half pints.

LAUNDRY

Most of the hostels offer laundry facilities at lower than commercial rates. Irish self-service laundrettes almost all offer a service-wash facility, where for IR£3.75 to IR£5 they'll wash, dry and neatly fold your washing. Many guesthouses and hotels will

James Joyce in nonchalant pose, North Earl St.

NEIL SETCHFIELD

No 1 Merrion Square, the Wilde family home.

NEIL SETCHFIELD

If it's Bloomsday (June 16) it must be Burgundy and Gorgonzola at Davy Byrne's.

PAT YALE

The National Gallery, opened in 1864.

Leinster House, site of the Irish parliament.

Here comes the summer! Escape the hustle and bustle of the city in St Stephen's Green.

offer a similar service in conjunction with a local laundry, simply tacking on an extra IR£2 or so delivery charge.

Otherwise, there are several convenient laundries, such as the Laundry Shop (Map 4, ☎ 872 3541) at 191 Parnell St, Dublin 1, off Parnell Square in north Dublin. Also in north Dublin is the Launderette at 110 Lower Dorset St (Map 4) near the An Óige Hostel. South of the centre at 40 Great George's St is the lively All American Laundrette Company (Map 7, ☎ 677 2779), which has a handy notice board. Just north of the Grand Canal is Powders Launderette (☎ 478 2655), 42A South Richmond St, Dublin 2. If you're staying north-east of the centre at Clontarf there's the Clothes Line (☎ 833 8480), 53 Clontarf Rd. In Dun Laoghaire there's the Star Laundrette (☎ 280 5074), 47 Upper George's St.

TOILETS

The old public toilets once found in the city centre are now gone, leaving Dublin with virtually no public facilities. If you need to go, your best bet is to walk into a bar and use the facilities there; if the bar is empty, it might be a good idea to ask the bartender for permission to use the toilet. Restaurants can be very fussy and often put up signs indicating that toilets are for patrons' use only. The law states that all places open to the public should have facilities for the disabled. Quite a few of the newer bars and restaurants do have these facilities, but many others are slow in upgrading their facilities to comply with the law.

LEFT LUGGAGE

For details of locations and prices of left luggage facilities, see the Airport, Bus and Train sections in the Getting Around chapter.

HEALTH

Travel health depends on your predeparture preparations, your daily health care while travelling and how you handle any medical problem that does develop. While the potential dangers can seem quite frightening,

in reality few travellers experience anything more than upset stomachs.

There are no serious health problems in Dublin apart from the effects of traffic pollution and the dangers posed by the Irish high-cholesterol breakfast; you might even see mobile cholesterol-testing units around town. Although Ireland is still a largely rural country, there is no risk of rabies infection due to stringent laws that ban the import of any animals or animal products.

Make sure you're healthy before you start travelling. If you wear glasses take a spare pair and your prescription. If you require a particular medication take an adequate supply, as it may not be available locally. Take part of the packaging showing the generic name, rather than the brand, which will make getting replacements easier. It's a good idea to have a legible prescription or letter from your doctor to show that you legally use the medication, to avoid any problems.

Health Insurance

Make sure that you have adequate health insurance. See under Travel Insurance in the Documents section earlier in this chapter for details.

Medical Kit

It's always a good idea to travel with a basic medical kit, even when your destination is a country like Ireland, where first-aid supplies are readily available; don't forget any medication you may already be taking. See the medical kit check list on the next page.

Medical Services

The Eastern Health Board (Dublin Area) (☎ 679 0700, freephone 1800 520 520), 138 Thomas St, Dublin 8 (Map 5), has a Choice of Doctor Scheme, which can advise you on a suitable doctor from 9 am to 5 pm, Monday to Friday. Your hotel or embassy can also suggest a doctor. The Eastern Health Board also provides services for those with physical and mental disabilities.

If you experience an immediate health problem, contact the casualty section of the

Medical Kit Check List

Following is a list of items you should consider including in your medical kit – consult
your phamacist for brands available in
your country.

☐ **Aspirin** or **paracetamol** (acetamino-
phen in the US) – for pain or fever.

☐ **Antihistamine** – for allergies, eg hay
fever; to ease the itch from insect bites
or stings; and to prevent motion sick-
ness.

☐ **Antibiotics** – consider including these;
see your doctor, as they must be prescribed, and carry the prescription
with you.

☐ **Loperamide** or **diphenoxylate** –
'blockers' for diarrhoea; **prochlorper-
azine** or **metaclopramide** for nausea
and vomiting.

☐ **Calamine lotion, sting relief spray** or
aloe vera – to ease irritation from
sunburn and insect bites or stings.

☐ **Antiseptic** (such as povidone-iodine)
– for cuts and grazes.

☐ **Bandages, Band-Aids (plasters)** and
other wound dressings.

☐ **Scissors, tweezers** and a **thermometer**
(note that mercury thermometers are
prohibited by airlines).

☐ **Cold** and **flu tablets, throat lozenges**
and **nasal decongestant**.

☐ **Multivitamins** – consider for long
trips, when dietary vitamin intake may
be inadequate.

nearest public hospital; in an emergency,
call an ambulance ☎ 999. North of the river
is Mater Misericordiae Hospital (Map 4,
☎ 830 1122), Eccles St off Lower Dorset St;
south of the river are St James's Hospital (Map 5, ☎ 453 7941) on James's St
and Baggot St Hospital (Map 6, ☎ 668
1577), at 18 Upper Baggot St.

The following chemists stay open until
10 pm: O'Connell's Late Night Pharmacy,
O'Connell St (Map 4) and Dame St Pharmacy, Dame St (Map 7).

Condoms are now widely available in
Dublin, in both pharmacies and in many
bars and clubs. They're also available at the
Dublin Well Woman Centre (☎ 872 8095),
35 Lower Liffey St (Map 6), which can also
prescribe the morning-after pill for emergencies. The centre is open from 9 am to 8
pm on weekdays, and from 10 am to 5 pm
on Saturday. There's another branch (☎ 661
0083) at 73 Lower Leeson St (Map 6),
which opens on Sunday morning from 10
am to 12.30 pm, and other branches in Bray
and Dun Laoghaire. These centres can
advise on various women's-health problems
and charge consultation fees on a sliding
scale.

The contraceptive pill is available only
on prescription, so a visit to a doctor will be
necessary.

HIV & AIDS

HIV, the Human Immunodeficiency Virus,
develops into AIDS, Acquired Immune De-
ficiency Syndrome, which is a fatal disease.
HIV is a major problem in many countries.
Any exposure to blood, blood products or
body fluids may put the individual at risk.
The disease is often transmitted through
sexual contact or dirty needles – vaccin-
ations, acupuncture, tattooing and body
piercing can be potentially as dangerous as
intravenous drug use. HIV/AIDS can also
be transmitted through infected blood transfusions; some developing countries cannot
afford to screen blood used for transfusions.

If you do need an injection, ask to see the
syringe unwrapped in front of you, or take
a needle and syringe pack with you.

Fear of HIV infection should never
prevent you from having treatment for
serious medical conditions.

WOMEN TRAVELLERS

In many ways Ireland is one of the safest
and least harassing countries for women.
However, outside Dublin, old attitudes
often prevail, with women treated more or
less as second-class citizens. In Dublin
women are treated in the same way as they
are in any other westernised, cosmopolitan

city. Dublin can even offer some advantages – for example, as pornography has an unusually low profile, women aren't subjected to the daily parade of breasts and bottoms common in British newsagencies. They are also not subjected as frequently to the silly comment on the street as they would be in London or Paris, but this has less to do with Dublin males' respect for women and more with the traditional Irish manner of keeping all emotions under wraps! Still, women can find themselves in awkward situations, especially in a pub full of drunken men. Polite but firm refusals of unwanted advances is normally sufficient.

Lone women should exercise care when walking in dodgy parts of town (mainly north of the Liffey). See Dangers & Annoyances later in this chapter for more information.

GAY & LESBIAN TRAVELLERS

Gay or lesbian life is simply not acknowledged in most parts of Ireland, but in Dublin there is an openly gay and lesbian community. For more information contact the National Lesbian & Gay Federation (☎ 671 0939), Hirschfield Centre, 10 Fownes St, Dublin 2 (Map 7). The Gay Switchboard (☎ 872 1055) is in Carmichael House, North Brunswick St, Dublin 7 (Map 3); call between 8 and 10 pm, Sunday to Friday or between 3.30 and 6 pm on Saturday. The Lesbian Line (☎ 661 3771) is open from 7 to 9 pm on Thursday.

The magazine *In Dublin* has a section on gay and lesbian services, organisations and entertainment. The monthly publication *Gay Community News* is available through the Temple Bar Information Centre (Map 7, ☎ 671 5717), 18 Eustace St, Temple Bar.

DISABLED TRAVELLERS

If you have a physical disability, get in touch with your national support organisation (preferably the travel officer if there is one). They often have complete libraries devoted to travel, and can put you in touch with travel agencies who specialise in tours for the disabled.

Guesthouses, hotels and sights in Ireland are increasingly being adapted for people with disabilities though there is still a long way to go. Bord Fáilte's annual accommodation guide, *Be Our Guest*, indicates which places are accessible by wheelchair. Travel agencies may have access to the most recent details about facilities available for disabled people. Alternatively, you can obtain information from the National Rehabilitation Board (☎ 874 7503), 44 North Great George's St, Dublin 1 (Map 7).

SENIOR TRAVELLERS

Senior citizens are entitled to many discounts in Europe on such things as public transport and museum admission fees, provided they show proof of their age. The minimum qualifying age varies between 60 and 65 for men, and 55 to 65 for women.

In your home country, a lower age may already entitle you to all sorts of interesting travel packages and discounts through organisations and travel agencies catering for senior travellers. Start hunting at your local senior citizens' advice bureau.

DUBLIN FOR CHILDREN

Successful travel with young children requires effort, but it can be done. Try not to overdo things and consider using some sort of self-catering accommodation as a base. This frees you from the limited opening hours of restaurants and hotels and gives more flexibility. Having said that, Dublin is one of the more child-friendly cities in Europe, with provisions made for children in hotels and restaurants.

Include children in the planning process; if they've helped to work out where you're going, they'll be more interested when they get there. Include a range of activities – for example, balance a visit to Trinity College with one to the National Wax Museum. Like most big cities, Dublin has plenty to keep children just as entertained as their parents. Some of the sites (World of Wax, Dublin Writers' Museum, the dinosaur section of the National Museum, The Ark in Temple Bar and Christ Church) are right in

FACTS FOR THE VISITOR

the centre, within easy walking distance of O'Connell St. Others (Dublin Zoo and Phoenix Park Visitor Centre) are a short bus ride away. A few (Fry Model Railway and Newbridge Demesne) are further out. Family bus passes are available, allowing up to two adults and four children under 16 years of age to use all Dublin Bus services for the day for IR£5.50; for another 50p you can get a pass covering DART and suburban rail services too. Buy passes in advance from the Dublin Bus office in O'Connell St (Map 4) or from ticket agencies around town. For further information about most of the sights mentioned here, see the Things to See & Do chapter. For further general information see Lonely Planet's *Travel with Children* by Maureen Wheeler.

The Ark (Map 7)

The Ark (☎ 670 7788), or Children's Cultural Centre, Eustace St, Temple Bar, Dublin 2, is aimed at youngsters between the ages of four and 14. Its activities are aimed at promoting an interest in science and the environment as well as the arts. It also offers a good opportunity for visiting youngsters to meet their Dublin counterparts. The centre also has an open-air stage for summer events. It's open from 9.30 am to 4 pm Tuesday to Friday and from 10 am to 4 pm on Saturday. Admission is free.

Christ Church Cathedral (Map 6)

If your children usually find anything to do with churches boring, take heart. Christ Church Cathedral on Christchurch Place addresses the problem with a free *Young Person's Guide to Christ Church Cathedral*, providing a series of numbered questions. You hunt for the matching numbers as you walk round and should then be able to answer the questions. The biggest one likely to remain is why so many numbers seem to be missed out! Kids are likely to be fascinated by the gruesome mummified cat and mouse in the crypt, but bear in mind that it's pretty spooky, not to mention dusty, down there. The cathedral is open from 10 am to 5 pm daily and entry is IR£3.95/1.

The Dublin Writers' Museum (Map 4)

The first two floors of the Writers' Museum (☎ 872 2077), 18 Parnell Square North, Dublin 1, have little to enthrall children, but upstairs things get better with a whole room devoted to modern children's authors such as Michael Mullen, Carolyn Swift, Vincent Banville and Margrit Cruickshank. As well as having pictures and biographies of the authors, the exhibiton features models taken from their books, the best of them being the giant Magus the Lollipop Man, the eponymous hero of Michael Mullen's book, who greets you as you come in. Perhaps best of all, you can sit your brood down and have other (recorded) voices read bedtime stories to them.

In the next room stands Tara's Palace, an outsize doll's house. The original 'Titania's Palace' was built by Major Sir Neville Williamson for his daughter Gwendoline in 1907. In 1967 it was sold to the owners of Wookey Hole in England, and in 1978 to Lego. Tara's Palace is a replica, with 14 of its 23 rooms finished and furnished with fittings from all round the world. The façades are based on Leinster House, Carlton House and Castleton House. The museum is open from 10 am to 5 pm, Monday to Saturday and from 11.30 am to 6 pm on Sunday. In July and August it opens until 7 pm on Friday. Admission costs IR£2.95/2.50.

Dublin Zoo (Map 3)

Like so many zoos, Dublin Zoo (☎ 677 1425) in Phoenix Park is past its prime, although the government has agreed to plough more money in to revive it. Unfortunately the saddest part is the Pet's Corner where you wonder about the nature of sponsorship when a sponsor's name plaque continues to adorn a filthy, abandoned cage. To be fair, some bits of the zoo are much better. Summer feeding times are as follows: 11.30 am polar bears, noon hippos, 12.15 pm tamarins, 2.15 pm rhinos and tapirs, 3 pm sealions, 3.45 pm elephants, 4.15 pm penguins and 4.45 pm ring-tailed lemurs. The zoo is open from 9.30 am to 6 pm, Monday to Saturday and from 10.30 am to 6 pm on Sunday (closing at sunset in winter). A family ticket for two adults and two children costs IR£15.50, for two adults and up to four children it's IR£18.

Fort Lucan

This is essentially an assault course for children, complete with slides, trampolines, mazes and suspension bridges. It is just off the Strawberry Beds Rd in Westmanstown, Lucan, in north-west County Dublin; you'll need a car to get here. It's opening times depend on the weather, so be sure to call ☎ 628 0166 before setting off. In good weather it is open from 1.30 to 6 pm daily. Admission is IR£3 (IR£3.50 on Sunday); adults and tots get in free.

Fry Model Railway Exhibition

The Fry Model Railway Exhibition (☎ 845 2758) is the world's largest display of model narrow-gauge trains, trams, boats and vehicles and covers 240 sq metres of ground in a purpose-built house in the grounds of Malahide Castle (Map 8). Children can also while away the time in the excellent playground in the grounds of the estate. From April to September the exhibition is open from 10 am to 5 pm, Monday to Thursday, 11 am to 6 pm on Saturday and from 2 to 6 pm on Sunday and public holidays. From October to March it only opens from 2 to 5 pm on Saturday and Sunday. Family tickets for two adults and two children cost IR£6.75, or IR£10 if you want to visit Malahide Castle too.

Museum of Childhood

The Museum of Childhood (☎ 497 3223), 10 Palmerston Park, Rathmines, Dublin 6, sounds more promising than it actually is. Although it contains a collection of dolls and toys dating back to 1730, they're all jumbled in together, in dire need of cleaning and redisplaying. There's another huge doll's house here, Tanya's Crystal Palace, which has 21 rooms and more than 7500 fittings. The museum only opens on Sunday

from 2 to 5.30 pm; admission is IR£1.50, IR£1 for children under 12 years old.

National Museum (Map 6)

Dinosaur-fixated youngsters may want to visit the National Museum's geological offshoot at 7-9 Merrion Row, Dublin 2, where they can sit on squashy seats in the shape of dinosaur paws and watch a video narrated by Richard Attenborough. Admission is free but this is a visit only worth making if you have time on your hands. It's open from 10 am to 5 pm, Tuesday to Saturday and from 2 to 5 pm on Sunday.

Newbridge Demesne Traditional Farm

The courtyard and grounds of Newbridge Demesne Traditional Farm (☎ 843 6064), Donabate, have been converted to accommodate an imitation self-sufficient 18th century farm. Alongside more familiar domestic animals and birds there are also rare breeds like the Kerry cow, Connemara pony and Jacob sheep; children will like the exotic chickens with punk hairdos too. In restoring the courtyard buildings and deciding what to grow and rear, Dublin County Council Parks Department has been able to draw on the records of the Cobbe family who used to own the house and still live there occasionally.

Between April and October the farm is open from 10 am to 5 pm Tuesday to Friday, from 11 am to 6 pm on Saturday and from 2 to 6 pm on Sunday. From November to March it opens from 2 to 5 pm on weekends only. A family ticket for the farm for two adults and four children costs IR£2; for the house as well, family tickets cost IR£7.95.

Phoenix Park Visitor Centre

Children keen on all things furry should enjoy the Great Slumber Party exhibition upstairs in the Phoenix Park Visitor Centre (☎ 677 0095), Dublin 8 (see the Phoenix Park map in the Things to See & Do chapter). A walk-through tunnel looks at animals' sleeping habits, letting youngsters peep in on a mock-up badger's den, fox's earth, and so on. The visitor centre is open from 9.30 am to 5 pm daily, staying open until 6.30 pm from June to September and closing at 4.30 pm from December to February. Admission costs IR£2/1.

Premier Indoor Karting

Children as young as three are strapped into karts and let loose on the 400-yard course of Premier Indoor Karting (☎ 626 1444), Unit 1A, Kylemore Industrial Estate, Killeen Road, Dublin 10. This place is great, offering thrills (but thankfully no spills) for children and adults alike. There's all kinds of racing here, including a Grand Prix championship race (for the bigger kids), which comes complete with a voice-over from TV commentator Murray Walker. The downside is the price; it's very expensive. A 10 minute practice session costs IR£15, a full race costs up to IR£25 per person. If you win a race, you get a trophy. To get here, take the No 19 or 79 bus from D'Olier St in the city centre.

World of Wax (Map 4)

The National Wax Museum (☎ 872 6340), Granby Row, Parnell Square, Dublin 1, has something to amuse children of all ages. The youngest might enjoy the Children's World of Fairytale & Fantasy section with models of pantomime favourites such as Jack and the Beanstalk and Aladdin, alongside more modern interlopers like the Flintstones and ET. There's also the inevitable Hall of (distorting) Mirrors and a roomful of laser-generated monsters that can be frightening for nervous youngsters. Older children will get more out of the Chamber of Horrors, which has tunnels to creep along and all sorts of gruesome sights ... again, not for the squeamish. There's also a Hall of Megastars, although picky teenagers are unlikely to get too worked up about static models of Michael Jackson, Freddie Mercury and U2. The wax museum has an educational side too. The Main Hall contains figures from many aspects of Irish history with buttons to press to have their significance explained. It's open from 10

am to 6 pm, Monday to Saturday and from noon to 6 pm on Sunday (last admissions 5.15 pm daily). A family ticket for two adults and two children costs IR£10.

USEFUL ORGANISATIONS

An Óige (Map 4, ☎ 830 4555, fax 830 5808), the Irish Youth Hostel Association, has its office at 61 Mountjoy St, near the hostel; it's open from 9.30 am to 5.30 pm Monday to Friday and from 10 am to 12.30 pm on Saturday from April to September.

The Backpackers Centre (☎ 836 4700), 21A Store St immediately opposite Busáras (Map 4), provides information on hostels run by Independent Holiday Hostels (IHH; a tourist board-approved co-operative group), tours and public transport. It's open Monday to Friday from 10 am to 8 pm and at weekends from noon to 8 pm.

The Automobile Association or AA (Map 7, ☎ 677 9481) is at 23 Suffolk St, Dublin 2.

LIBRARIES

In keeping with Dublin's tradition as a literary capital, the city has plenty of libraries, both private and public. For information on public libraries, contact Dublin Corporation (☎ 661 9000), Cumberland House, Fenian St, Dublin 2 (Map 6). The public library in the ILAC Centre (Map 4, ☎ 873 4333), Henry St, Dublin 1, is well stocked with books and videos on virtually every subject. The Irish Architectural Association archive (Map 6, ☎ 676 3430), 73 Merrion Square, Dublin 2, has books on Dublin's rich architectural heritage as well as specialised books on, and plans of, significant buildings throughout the city.

CULTURAL CENTRES

Dublin has an international selection of cultural centres that includes:

Alliance Française
    (Map 6, ☎ 676 1732) 1 Kildare St, Dublin 2
British Council
    (☎ 676 4088/6943) Newmount House, 22-24 Lower Mount St, Dublin 2

Goethe Institut
(Map 6, ☎ 661 1155) 37 Merrion Square, Dublin 2
Italian Cultural Institute
(Map 6, ☎ 676 6662, 662 3268) 11 Fitzwilliam Square, Dublin 2
Spanish Cultural Institute
(☎ 668 2024) 58 Northumberland Rd, Dublin 4

DANGERS & ANNOYANCES

Ireland is probably safer than most European countries, but in recent years Dublin's good reputation as a safe city has been dented by a spate of muggings in the city centre. Some are linked to an upsurge in drug addiction since the late 1980s and the frighteningly high rates of unemployment in Dublin's sprawling housing estates. Tourists are not at particular risk but it's a sad hint at what may be to come.

Dublin has its fair share of pickpockets and sneak thieves (many of them young children) waiting to relieve the unwary of unwatched bags. The city is also notorious for car break-ins, and foreign-registered cars and rental cars are a particular target. If you have a car, don't leave valuables inside it when it's parked, and bear in mind that insurance policies often don't cover losses from cars. See the Car & Motorcycle section of the Getting Around chapter for more details.

Cyclists should always lock their bikes securely and be cautious about leaving bags on their bicycles.

Certain parts of Dublin are unsafe after dark and visitors should avoid run-down, deserted-looking and poorly lit areas. Phoenix Park is not safe at night and you should not camp there. Unfortunately, some

Dealing with Drugs

While working as crime correspondent for the *Sunday Independent*, Veronica Guerin was shot dead in her car as she waited in traffic. A well known anti-drugs campaigner, she has been widely credited with exposing and putting out of business some of the biggest names on the Dublin drug dealing scene.

In November 1998, 2½ years after her murder, Paul 'Hippo' Ward was convicted of the crime and now faces life imprisonment. The verdict came at the end of a trial slowed by appeals and dogged with complaints about police procedures. Vital evidence against Ward, a known cannabis dealer, was given by gang member, Charles Bowden, the state's first 'supergrass'. Bowden was granted immunity from prosecution and given police protection in exchange for taking the stand. A marksman with military training, he admitted to cleaning and loading the murder weapon. Bowden will now give evidence at the trials of two more men charged in relation to Guerin's murder.

Regarded as a passionate, if sometimes reckless, journalist, Guerin grew up in inner city Dublin. She was seen as fighting the good fight and her cause was one close to the hearts of local people. Several high-profile sweeps drove dealers out of O'Connell St and local communities contributed by ostracising known drug dealers. After the initial shock of Guerin's death, the high profile trial continued to stir public opinion. Blame was laid at the door not just of those involved in the trial but also of the newspapers that had, allegedly, put Guerin at risk by pushing her for a good story.

Controversial in life and death, Guerin's story has already been made the subject of several 'warts and all' documentaries and books. Preparations are being made for a Hollywood biopic with filming scheduled for June 1999.

Claire Hornshaw

of the hostels are also in the rougher parts of north Dublin.

Beggars are a common sight on Dublin streets, and some of them are school-age children, which makes it all the more depressing. If you don't want to give them money, but would like to help in some way, consider buying a copy of the magazine the *Big Issue* (IR£1) from a street vendor. It can be a good read, with lots of local insight, and some of the proceeds go to help the homeless. At the time of writing the magazine was facing financial pressures and might have ceased publication by the time you read this.

Smoking has yet to die the social death it seems to have in other western countries. While cinemas are smoke-free, even some quite pricey restaurants still let people light up freely. When you add in the pollution from Dublin's increasingly heavy traffic, you might feel your lungs are due for a bit of fresh air after a few days in the city.

EMERGENCIES

For emergency assistance phone ☎ 999. This call is free from any phone and the operator will connect you with the type of assistance you specify: fire, police (*gardaí*), ambulance, boat or coastal rescue. There are gardaí stations at Fitzgibbon St (Map 4, ☎ 836 3113), Harcourt Terrace (☎ 676 3481), Pearse St (Map 6, ☎ 677 8141) and Store St (Map 4, ☎ 874 2761).

Some other emergency services include:

Alcoholics Anonymous
  (☎ 453 8998, 679 5967 after hours) 109 South Circular Road, Dublin 8
Drugs Advisory & Treatment Centre
  (Map 6, ☎ 677 1122) Trinity Court, 30-31 Pearse St, Dublin 2
Poisons Information Centre
  (☎ 837 9964/6) Beaumont Hospital, Beaumont Rd, Dublin 9
Rape Crisis Centre
  (Map 6, ☎ 661 4911, toll free 1800 778 888) 70 Lower Leeson St, Dublin 2
The Samaritans
  (☎ 1850 60 90 90, 872 7700) 112 Marlborough St, Dublin 1 (Map 4) – for people feeling lonely, depressed or suicidal

LEGAL MATTERS

If you need legal assistance contact the Legal Aid Board (☎ 661 5811), Stephen's Green House, Dublin 2 (Map 6).

Drugs

The importation of prohibited drugs is illegal and automatically leads to arrest and possible imprisonment. The possession of small quantities of marijuana or hashish attracts a fine and a warning, but most other drugs are treated more seriously. So-called 'party' drugs such as cocaine and ecstasy are considered class 'A' drugs, as is heroin, and possession can result in a prison term.

Public Drunkenness

Although illegal, enormous leeway is granted by the police to displays of public drunkenness. If matters get out of hand, a word in your ear from a police officer is usually enough to send you on your way. Fighting is treated a little more harshly; if you're involved in a fight you may have to spend a night in a cell, to 'cool off'.

Drinking & Driving

The legal drinking age is 18 (although some pubs and clubs won't serve people under 21 years old) and you may need photographic identification to prove your age. The legal blood-alcohol limit for driving is 80mg of alcohol per 100mL of blood, and although this is the highest in Europe, a crackdown on drunk drivers in the last decade has gone a long way towards eradicating the tolerance shown by the authorities to those caught driving while under the influence. Stiff fines – and sometimes a jail term – can be incurred. Spot checks by the gardaí are increasingly common, especially around holidays such as Christmas.

Traffic offences (such as illegal parking or speeding) usually incur a fine, for which you're normally allowed 30 days to pay.

BUSINESS HOURS

Offices are open from 9 am to 5 pm Monday to Friday, but shops stay open a little later. Thursday is a late shopping day, usually until 8 pm. All shops open on Saturday and some on Sunday. In winter, tourist attractions are often open shorter hours, and some may be open fewer days per week or may be shut completely.

Pubs are open from 10.30 am to 11.30 pm, Monday to Saturday, between June and September. For the rest of the year closing time is 11 pm. However, they close for a 'holy hour', which may actually be one or more hours, in the afternoon. On Sunday the opening hours are 12.30 to 2 pm and 4 to 11 pm. The only days when pubs will definitely be closed are Christmas Day and Good Friday.

PUBLIC HOLIDAYS & SPECIAL EVENTS
Public Holidays
Ireland has the following public holidays:

New Year's Day	1 January
St Patrick's Day	17 March
Good Friday	March/April
Easter Monday	March/April
May Day Holiday	1 May
June Holiday	first Monday in June
August Holiday	first Monday in August
October Holiday	last Monday in October
Christmas Day	25 December
St Stephen's Day/ Boxing Day	26 December

St Patrick's Day, St Stephen's Day and May Day holidays are taken on the following Monday should they fall on a weekend.

Special Events
St Patrick's Day The most important holiday of the year in Dublin is undoubtedly Christmas, but St Patrick's Day runs it a close second. The main Dublin parade, where up to 500,000 spectators watch over 100 marching bands from all over the world, is preceded by a weekend-long street party featuring street theatre, music, a fireworks display and lots of drinking. On St Stephen's Green a large *céilidh* attracts thousands of revellers who dance the afternoon away.

Other cultural, musical and sporting highlights of the Dublin year include the following events:

February to April
England vs Ireland rugby match
Played at Lansdowne Rd stadium every second year. Next staged there in 2001.
March
Dublin Film Festival
Features a usually excellent selection of big and small-budget films, both domestic and international, at a selected number of cinemas. Call ☎ 679 2939 for details.
World Irish Dancing Championship
At the Royal Dublin Society in Ballsbridge.
Easter Monday
Howth Jazz Festival
Takes place in the seaside suburb of Dublin, north of the city. Most gigs are free.
June
Irish Open golf championship
Annual competition. Call ☎ 676 6650 for information on dates.
July
Temple Bar Blues Festival
At venues throughout the city centre, culminating in a live show in front of the Bank Of Ireland at College Green.
August
Dublin Horse Show
At the Royal Dublin Society Showground, features an international showjumping competition. Ireland's answer to Wimbledon and Ascot when it comes to showing off one's social status.
September
All Ireland Hurling Final and **All Ireland (Gaelic) Football Final**
Take place in September at Croke Park, to the north-east of the city centre (Map 4).
October
Dublin Theatre Festival
Europe's biggest theatre festival, takes place over two weeks.
Dublin marathon
Held on the last Monday of the month. Contact ☎ 677 8439.
November
French Film Festival
Organised by the French embassy's cultural department. Contact ☎ 676 2197 for details.
Junior Film Festival
Focuses on the work of film-makers under 18 years old. It takes place at the Irish Film Centre in Eustace St, Dublin 2 (Map 7).

Bloomsday

On 16 June (Bloomsday) Leopold Bloom's journey around Dublin in *Ulysses* is re-enacted; various readings and dramatisations take place around the city. Many of the places visited on that well documented 1904 journey around Dublin can still be found. Some of the interesting reminders of Joyce's Dublin and the chapters of *Ulysses* in which they appear are described here. The names in parentheses refer to the episodes in Homer's *Odyssey* to which Joyce's chapters correspond.

The Martello Tower, Sandycove near Dun Laoghaire, Chapter 1 (Telemachus). After the open-air shave with which the book begins, Buck Mulligan goes for a swim in the nearby Forty Foot Pool. The tower houses the James Joyce Museum, and it's still traditional to swim unclothed in the pool before 9 am.

St Andrew's Church & Sweny's Chemist Shop, south Dublin, Chapter 5 (Lotus Eaters). On his way into the centre, Leopold Bloom stops to observe part of the mass at All Hallows Church. This is now St Andrew's Church on Westland Row, just east of Trinity College and right beside Pearse station. From there Bloom goes to Sweny's Chemist Shop on Lincoln Place, which is still a chemist shop, still has the name Sweny prominently displayed and still sells lemon soap, though a bar will now cost you IR£2 or IR£3, rather than the fourpence Bloom paid in 1904.

The Oval & Mooney's, north Dublin, Chapter 7 (Aeolus). Leopold Bloom and Stephen Dedalus both visit the office of the *Freeman's Journal* and the *Evening Telegraph* on Prince's St North. A branch of BHS now occupies the site. Visits are then made to two pubs. The Oval on Abbey St Middle is still the Oval, but Mooney's on the other side of O'Connell St on Lower Abbey St has changed markedly since Joyce's day and is now the Abbey Mooney. In 1988 a series of 14 pavement plaques were placed in the city to trace Bloom's peregrinations from Middle Abbey St in this chapter to the National Library in Chapter 9.

Thomas Moore statue, north Dublin, Chapter 8 (Lestrygonians). Leopold Bloom crosses the River Liffey by the O'Connell St Bridge and walks down Westmoreland St by the Bank of Ireland, ruminating on the amusing position of the statue of poet Thomas Moore on the traffic island where College St meets Westmoreland St. To this day it's a local joke that the author of the poem *The Meeting of the Waters* should have his commemorative statue plonked in front of a public urinal.

Davy Byrne's, Duke St, south Dublin, Chapter 8 (Lestrygonians). Having 'crossed under Tommy Moore's roguish finger' Bloom continues by Trinity College, noting the provost's house, where the college provost still resides, and various shops along Grafton St, particularly Brown Thomas. This is still one of Dublin's best-known shops although it has now moved across the road and its former location is occupied by Marks & Spencer. Finally he turns into Duke St and having glanced into Burton's (no longer there) decides he doesn't like the look of the patrons and turns back to Davy Byrne's. Bloom would hardly recognise Joyce's 'moral pub' today as it was extensively remodelled in the 1940s and then yuppified in the 1980s. If Joyce turned up today he would probably be turned away by the bouncers.

National Library, Kildare St, south Dublin, Chapter 9 (Scylla and Charybdis). From Davy Byrne's, Bloom continues down Molesworth St to the National Museum and National Library, both on Kildare St. Stephen Dedalus is also in the library, discussing Shakespeare with a group of famous Dubliners, including Æ (George Russell).

Ormond Hotel, Ormond Quay, north Dublin, Chapter 11 (Sirens). Although it has been changed considerably over the course of this century, the Ormond Hotel still overlooks the Liffey from Upper Ormond Quay and a plaque outside commemorates its role in *Ulysses*. On the way there from the National Library, Bloom walks along Wellington Quay on the Temple Bar side of the Liffey and contemplates a stop at the Clarence Hotel before crossing the Liffey to the Ormond.

Bella Cohen's & Olhausen's, north Dublin, Chapter 15 (Circe). Once near St Mary's Pro-Cathedral, the red-light district of north Dublin (dubbed Nighttown in *Ulysses* and known as Monto to Dubliners in 1904) is no more. The prostitutes left the area when the British army departed in 1922 after Ireland's independence. Bella Cohen was indeed a brothel madam in 1904, though her premises were at 82, not 81, Railway St (then known as Lower Tyrone St). There are still some colourful pubs in the vicinity but this area contains nothing of interest today: it has been totally redeveloped, contains soul-destroying public housing and is definitely not a place to linger at night. In this chapter Bloom also drops into Olhausen's, the pork butcher, at 72 Talbot St to pick up a pig's trotter and a sheep's hoof as a snack. Olhausen's is still in business.

Amiens St, north Dublin, Chapter 16 (Eumaeus). Leopold Bloom and Stephen Dedalus, whose paths have crossed several times during the day, finally meet in Nighttown and wander down Amiens St, the main road into the city from Clontarf, which passes Connolly Station and ends by the Busáras. On the way they pass Dan Bergin's Pub (now Lloyd's), Mullett's (still there), the Signal House (now J&M Cleary), the North Star Hotel (still there) and the 1842 Dock Tavern (which, after a spell as the Master Mariner Bar, is now Kenny's Lounge). They then turn into Store St (beside today's Busáras) past the Dublin City Morgue (still there) and the City Bakery (now the Kylemore Bakery).

Gardiner St to Eccles St, north Dublin, Chapters 17 and 18 (Ithaca; Penelope). Bloom and Dedalus make the long walk up Gardiner St, now known to travellers as a favourite strip for central B&Bs. At Mountjoy Square they turn left then right to pass by St George's Church and end up at Bloom's home at 7 Eccles St. A private hospital now occupies the site where Molly Bloom's soliloquy ends *Ulysses*, but Georgian houses similar to the original No 7 still stand on the opposite side of the street.

For Joyce fans there are several books that follow the wanderings of *Ulysses'* characters in minute detail. *Joyce's Dublin – a Walking Guide to Ulysses* by Jack McCarthy traces the events chapter by chapter with clear maps. *The Ulysses Guide – Tours Through Joyce's Dublin* by Robert Nicholson has easy-to-follow maps. It concentrates on certain areas and follows the events of the various related chapters.

DOING BUSINESS

A key element of Ireland's economic success over the last decade has been the successful encouragement of foreign business interests to set up in Ireland. Since the early 1980s, successive Irish governments have pursued a policy of using favourable tax incentives to attract foreign investment; in short, if you have a foreign company and are willing to set up in Ireland, you will be exempt from virtually all corporate tax for your first 10 years in Ireland. Furthermore, Ireland is renowned for its highly skilled labour force, which has consistently and expertly adapted itself to the constantly changing requirements of modern industry.

The Industrial Development Authority (IDA) is the state-run organisation responsible for attracting new business to Ireland and encouraging those already here to expand their interests. Traditionally, the IDA has sought to target a fairly diverse range of companies, but has especially concentrated on those industries deemed to be internationally mobile, such as electronics, pharmaceuticals, engineering and financial services providers.

The success of the IDA's campaign is seen in the number of foreign businesses now present in Ireland; for example, in electronics alone there are approximately 200 foreign-owned companies using Ireland as a base, employing over 33,000 people on a permanent basis and an additional 5500 people on a temporary or contract basis. In 1997, foreign-owned electronics businesses accounted for IR£8 billion worth of exports from Ireland, 36% of the country's total exports.

At a smaller level, the IDA's sister authority, Forbáirt, is responsible for the distribution of start-up grants to local businesses. In order to receive a grant, you must apply to the local enterprise board for your area (there is at least one board for each county; the larger, more populated counties, such as Dublin and Cork, have four) who will then consider your application on the basis of viability and potential for growth. Furthermore, it will investigate similar businesses operating within the area, and if none are deemed to be in direct competition with your venture, you have more than a good chance of receiving a grant. Grants are available to anyone whose business address falls within the jurisdiction of the enterprise board, including all citizens of the EU (as long as they are based in Ireland) and legal residents from outside the EU.

For further information about both the IDA and Forbáirt, check out their Web sites at www.idaireland.com and www.forbairt .com respectively.

WORK

The success of the Celtic Tiger has resulted in unemployment dropping to an all-time low of about 8%. Consequently, opportunities for work have increased, especially in the tourist industry, usually in restaurants and pubs. However, without skills, it is difficult to find a job that pays sufficiently well to enable you to save money. You're almost certainly better off saving in your country of origin. As Ireland is a member of the EU, citizens of any other EU country can work legally in Ireland.

Getting There & Away

AIR

Dublin is Ireland's major international airport and Aer Lingus is the Irish national airline with connections to other countries in Europe and to the USA. Ryanair is the next largest Irish airline, also with routes to Britain and mainland Europe.

Departure Tax

There is an airport departure tax but it is built into the price of the ticket.

Buying Tickets

World aviation has never been so competitive, making air travel better value than ever. But you have to research the options carefully to make sure you get the best deal. The Internet is a useful resource for checking air fares: many travel agencies and airlines have a Web site.

Discounted tickets are released by airlines through selected travel agencies, and these are often the cheapest deals going. Some airlines now sell discounted tickets direct to the customer, and it's worth contacting airlines anyway for information on routes and timetables. Sometimes, there is nothing to be gained by going direct to the airline – specialist discount agencies often offer fares that are lower and/or carry fewer conditions than the airline's published prices. You can expect to be offered a wider range of options than a single airline would provide, and, at worst, you will just end up paying the official airline fare.

The exception to this rule is the new breed of 'no-frills' carriers, which mostly sell direct. Of these carriers, only Ryanair and Cityjet had flights to Dublin at the time of writing, but the city is sure to be on the wish list of easyJet and Go of the UK.

Unlike the 'full-service' airlines, the no-frills carriers often make one-way tickets available at half the return fare – meaning that it is easy to stitch together an open-jaw itinerary, where you fly in to one city and

out of another. Regular airlines may offer open-jaws, particularly if you are flying in from outside Europe.

Fares quoted in this chapter are approximate high-season return fares, based on advertised rates at the time of writing. None of them constitutes a recommendation for any airline.

Travellers with Special Needs

Airlines can often make special arrangements for travellers if they're warned early enough, such as wheelchair assistance at airports or vegetarian meals on the flight; note, however, that Ryanair makes a charge for wheelchair users. Children under two years travel for 10% of the standard fare (or free on some airlines) as long as they don't occupy a seat. They don't get a baggage allowance. 'Skycots', baby food and nappies should be provided by the airline if requested in advance. Children aged between two and 12 years can usually occupy a seat for half to two-thirds of the full fare, and do get a baggage allowance.

Other Parts of Ireland

There are flights between Dublin and Cork, Donegal, Galway, Kerry, Shannon and Sligo. Most journeys within Ireland take between 30 and 40 minutes. The two main companies operating within the country, as well as handling international flights, are Aer Lingus and Ryanair. Aer Lingus has offices in Dublin (see Airline Offices later in this chapter), Belfast, Cork, Limerick and Shannon. Ryanair's head office is in Dublin (see Airline Offices) with ticket offices at Dublin, Cork, Galway, Knock, Kerry, Shannon and Waterford airports.

For student travel information in Ireland, contact the Union of Students in Ireland Travel (USIT). The USIT Travel Office (Map 7, ☎ 679 8833, 677 8117), Aston Quay, beside O'Connell Bridge on the south side of the Liffey, is open from 9 am

Air Travel Glossary

Baggage Allowance This will be written on your ticket and usually includes one 20kg item to go in the hold, plus one item of hand luggage.

Bucket Shops These are unbonded travel agencies specialising in discounted airline tickets.

Bumped Just because you have a confirmed seat doesn't mean you're going to get on the plane (see Overbooking).

Cancellation Penalties If you have to cancel or change a discounted ticket, there are often heavy penalties involved; insurance can sometimes be taken out against these penalties. Some airlines impose penalties on regular tickets as well, particularly against 'no-show' passengers.

Check-In Airlines ask you to check in a certain time ahead of the flight departure (usually one to two hours on international flights). If you fail to check in on time and the flight is overbooked, the airline can cancel your booking and give your seat to somebody else.

Confirmation Having a ticket written out with the flight and date you want doesn't mean you have a seat until the agent has checked with the airline that your status is 'OK' or confirmed. Meanwhile you could just be 'on request'.

Courier Fares Businesses often need to send urgent documents or freight securely and quickly. Courier companies hire people to accompany the package through customs and, in return, offer a discount ticket which is sometimes a phenomenal bargain. In effect, what the companies do is ship their freight as your luggage on regular commercial flights. This is a legitimate operation, but there are two shortcomings – the short turnaround time of the ticket (usually not longer than a month) and the limitation on your luggage allowance. You may have to surrender all your allowance and take only carry-on luggage.

Full Fares Airlines traditionally offer 1st class (coded F), business class (coded J) and economy class (coded Y) tickets. These days there are so many promotional and discounted fares available that few passengers pay full economy fare.

ITX An ITX, or 'independent inclusive tour excursion', is often available on tickets to popular holiday destinations. Officially it's a package deal combined with hotel accommodation, but many agents will sell you one of these for the flight only and give you phoney hotel vouchers in the unlikely event that you're challenged at the airport.

Lost Tickets If you lose your airline ticket an airline will usually treat it like a travellers cheque and, after inquiries, issue you with another one. Legally, however, an airline is entitled to treat it like cash and if you lose it then it's gone forever. Take good care of your tickets.

MCO An MCO, or 'miscellaneous charge order', is a voucher that looks like an airline ticket but carries no destination or date. It can be exchanged through any International Association of Travel Agents (IATA) airline for a ticket on a specific flight. It's a useful alternative to an onward ticket in those countries that demand one, and is more flexible than an ordinary ticket if you're unsure of your route.

No-Shows No-shows are passengers who fail to show up for their flight. Full-fare passengers who fail to turn up are sometimes entitled to travel on a later flight. The rest are penalised (see Cancellation Penalties).

On Request This is an unconfirmed booking for a flight.

Air Travel Glossary

Onward Tickets An entry requirement for many countries is that you have a ticket out of the country. If you're unsure of your next move, the easiest solution is to buy the cheapest onward ticket to a neighbouring country or a ticket from a reliable airline which can later be refunded if you do not use it.

Open Jaw Tickets These are return tickets where you fly out to one place but return from another. If available, this can save you back-tracking to your arrival point.

Overbooking Airlines hate to fly empty seats and since every flight has some passengers who fail to show up, airlines often book more passengers than they have seats. Usually excess passengers make up for the no-shows, but occasionally somebody gets bumped. Guess who it is most likely to be? The passengers who check in late.

Point-to-Point Tickets These are discount tickets that can be bought on some routes in return for passengers waiving their rights to a stopover.

Promotional Fares These are officially discounted fares, available from travel agencies or direct from the airline.

Reconfirmation At least 72 hours prior to departure time of an onward or return flight, you must contact the airline and 'reconfirm' that you intend to be on the flight. If you don't do this the airline can delete your name from the passenger list and you could lose your seat.

Restrictions Discounted tickets often have various restrictions on them – such as needing to be paid for in advance and incurring a penalty to be altered. Others are restrictions on the minimum and maximum period you must be away, such as a minimum of 14 days or a maximum of one year.

Round-the-World Tickets RTW tickets give you a limited period (usually a year) in which to circumnavigate the globe. You can go anywhere the carrying airlines go, as long as you don't backtrack. The number of stopovers or total number of separate flights is decided before you set off and they usually cost a bit more than a basic return flight.

Stand-by This is a discounted ticket where you only fly if there is a seat free at the last moment. Stand-by fares are usually available only on domestic routes.

Transferred Tickets Airline tickets cannot be transferred from one person to another. Travellers sometimes try to sell the return half of their ticket, but officials can ask you to prove that you are the person named on the ticket. This is less likely to happen on domestic flights, but on an international flight tickets are compared with passports.

Travel Agencies Travel agencies vary widely and you should choose one that suits your needs. Some simply handle tours, while full-services agencies handle everything from tours and tickets to car rental and hotel bookings. If all you want is a ticket at the lowest possible price, then go to an agency specialising in discounted tickets.

Travel Periods Ticket prices vary with the time of year. There is a low (off-peak) season and a high (peak) season, and often a low-shoulder season and a high-shoulder season as well. Usually the fare depends on your outward flight – if you depart in the high season and return in the low season, you pay the high-season fare.

euro currency converter IR£1 = €1.27

to 6 pm Monday to Friday (8 pm on Thursday) and 10 am to 5.30 pm on Saturday. It has a good notice board for travellers. As well as providing travel information USIT also issues International Student Identity Cards (ISICs).

Other Countries

The UK London to Dublin has just taken over from London-New York and London-Paris as the busiest international air route in the world. There are dozens of services on numerous airlines to the Irish capital. Aer Lingus and British Midland fly from Heathrow; Aer Lingus also flies from Stansted; Cityflyer/British Airways Express flies from Gatwick; Ryanair flies from Gatwick, Luton and Stansted; and KLM uk/Cityjet fly from London City airport.

The regular one-way economy fare from London to Dublin is approximately UK£95, but cheap advance-purchase fares are available offering round-trip tickets for as low as UK£50 to UK£75 and many limited-offer deals become available from time to time. These should be booked well in advance as seats are often limited.

UK phone numbers and Web site addresses (where applicable) are:

Aer Lingus
☎ 0645 737747
www.aerlingus.ie
British Airways
☎ 0345 222111
www.british-airways.com
British Midland
☎ 020-8745 7321
www.iflybritishmidland.com
Cityjet
☎ 0345 445588
Jersey European
☎ 0990 676676
www.jea.co.uk
KLM uk
☎ 0990 074074
www.airuk.co.uk
Ryanair
☎ 0541 569569
www.ryanair.ie

From Dublin the Aer Lingus or British Midland fare to Heathrow or Gatwick is about IR£140 for a standard one-way ticket, or IR£99 for a budget or off-peak one-way ticket. Many return fares require a variety of advance-purchase arrangements, minimum stays and so on. They range from as low as IR£59 to as high as IR£185 or IR£230. Fares vary depending on which city you fly to and from.

Special budget fares are often available and if you're between 12 and 25 years old you can fly from Dublin to London for IR£49 one way.

USIT's London office is at USIT Campus Travel (☎ 020-7730 3402), 52 Grosvenor Gardens, London SW1W 0AG.

Other places in the UK connected with Dublin and the relevant airlines are:

Birmingham:	Aer Lingus, Ryanair
Blackpool:	Executive Express
Bournemouth:	Ryanair
Bristol:	Aer Lingus, Ryanair
Cardiff:	Ryanair
East Midlands:	British Midland, Cityjet
Edinburgh:	Aer Lingus
Exeter:	Jersey European
Glasgow:	Aer Lingus, Ryanair
Guernsey:	Jersey European
Isle of Man:	Manx Airlines
Jersey:	Jersey European
Leeds/Bradford:	Aer Lingus, Ryanair
Liverpool:	Ryanair
Luton:	Ryanair, Britannia Airways
Manchester:	Aer Lingus, Ryanair
Newcastle:	Aer Lingus
Southampton:	British Airways Express
Teesside:	Ryanair.

Europe Dublin is connected with major centres in Europe. Standard return fares are: Amsterdam f349, Milan L510,000, Paris 1440F, and Stockholm 2255 kr. Relevant airlines are:

Amsterdam:	Aer Lingus, British Airways, British Midlands
Barcelona:	Iberia
Berne:	Air Engiadina
Brussels:	Aer Lingus, Ryanair, Sabena
Copenhagen:	Aer Lingus, Scandinavian Airlines (SAS)
Düsseldorf:	Aer Lingus
Frankfurt:	Aer Lingus, Lufthansa

Geneva: Air Engiadina
Helsinki: Aer Lingus, Finnair
Madrid: Iberia
Malaga: Cityjet, Viva Air
Milan: Aer Lingus, Alitalia
Moscow: Aeroflot
Paris: Aer Lingus, Air France, Ryanair
Rome: Aer Lingus, Alitalia
Stockholm: Aer Lingus, Finnair
Vienna: Tyrolean Airways
Zürich: Aer Lingus, Crossair

USA & Canada Direct flights from North America put down in Dublin as well as Shannon, but because competition on flights to London is so fierce it's generally cheaper to fly to London first then pick up a London to Dublin flight.

Aer Lingus connects Dublin (and Shannon) with Boston, Chicago, New York and Newark. Its New York office (☎ 1-800 474 7424) is at 538 Broadhollow Rd, Melville. Continental Airlines links Dublin (and Shannon) with Newark. The other US operator with direct connections to Ireland is Delta Airlines (☎ 1-800 241 4141), which operates Atlanta-Shannon-Dublin, linking into its huge US network.

During the summer high season the round trip between New York and Dublin with Aer Lingus costs US$780 midweek or US$800 at weekends. Usually there are advance-purchase fares offered early in the year that allow you to fly from New York to Dublin for just under US$700 return. In the low season, discount return fares from New York to London are in the US$350 to US$500 range; in the high season they're from US$600 to US$700. From the west coast, fares to London cost from around US$150 more.

Currently there are no direct flights from Canada to Ireland – visitors have to fly to London and get a connection there. In Canada, Aer Lingus can be contacted by calling ☎ 1-800 223 6537, although it doesn't actually fly to Canada.

Check the travel sections of the Sunday editions of such papers as the *New York Times*, *Los Angeles Times*, *San Francisco*

Chronicle-Examiner or *Chicago Tribune* for the latest fares.

The USIT office in the USA is at the New York Student Center (☎ 212-663 5435), 895 Amsterdam Ave (103rd St), New York, NY 10025. Offices of Council Travel or STA Travel in the USA or Travel CUTS in Canada are good sources of reliable discounted tickets.

Australia & New Zealand Excursion or Apex fares from Australia or New Zealand to most major European destinations can have a return flight to Dublin tagged on at no extra cost. Return fares from Australia vary from around A$1600 (low season) to A$2900 (high season) but there are often short-term special deals available. STA Travel and Flight Centres International are good sources of reliable discounted tickets in Australia or New Zealand.

The cheapest fares from New Zealand are available on services travelling via Asia, but the connections on these flights are generally not as good as those on flights via the USA. Fares from New Zealand to major European cities range from NZ$2099 in the low season to NZ$2499 in high season.

Aer Lingus has an office (☎ 02-9244 2123) in Sydney at 64 York St.

Airline Offices

You'll find the following airline offices in Dublin:

Aer Lingus
　(☎ 844 7777, 705 3333 for UK inquiries, 844 7747 for elsewhere)
　40-41 Upper O'Connell St, Dublin 1
　13 St Stephen's Green, Dublin 2
　Jury's Hotel, Ballsbridge, Dublin 4
　12 Upper George's St, Dun Laoghaire
Aeroflot
　(☎ 679 1453) Dublin airport
Air Canada
　(☎ 1800 70 99 00) Dublin airport
Air France
　(☎ 844 4129) Dublin airport
Alitalia
　(☎ 677 5171) 4 Dawson St, Dublin 2
British Airways
　(☎ 1800 62 67 47) Dublin airport

British Midland
(☎ 283 8833) Dublin airport
Delta Air Lines
(☎ 676 8080) 3 Dawson St, Dublin 2
Iberia
(☎ 677 9486) 54 Dawson St, Dublin 2
Lufthansa Airlines
(☎ 844 5000) Dublin airport
Manx Airlines
(☎ 1800 62 66 27) Dublin airport
Qantas Airways
(☎ 874 7747) Dublin airport
Ryanair
(☎ 844 4411, 677 4422) 3 Dawson St, Dublin 2
Sabena
(☎ 679 1729) 7 Dawson St, Dublin 2
Scandinavian Airlines (SAS)
(☎ 844 5440) Dublin airport

BUS

Busáras (Map 4), on Store St, Dublin 1, just north of the Custom House and the River Liffey, is Dublin's central bus station.

Other Parts of Ireland

Bus Éireann (☎ 836 6111), at Busáras, is the Republic's national bus line, with services all over the Republic and to the North. There's also a Bus Éireann desk in the Dublin Bus office (Map 4) on O'Connell St. Standard one-way fares to/from Dublin include Cork IR£12, Limerick IR£10 or Wexford IR£7. These fares are cheaper than the regular train fares, return fares are usually only a little more expensive than one-way fares and special deals are often available (see Bus & Train Discount Deals later in this chapter).

There are several private bus companies that run services to various towns and cities throughout Ireland. Although not nearly as regular as Bus Éireann's, their services are usually much cheaper. Nestor Coaches (☎ 832 0094) has a daily service to Galway, leaving Dublin at 2, 6 and 10 pm. The fare is IR£8 return. All coaches leave from Tara St DART station, George's Quay (Map 6). George Kavanagh Rapid Express (☎ 679 1549) offers a service to Waterford, leaving Dublin nine times daily Monday to Saturday and eight times on Sunday. The fare is

IR£6 one-way. It also runs a service to Limerick, departing Dublin five times on Monday, four times a day from Tuesday to Saturday and three times on Sunday. The fare is IR£5 single (there is no student discount). All George Kavanagh buses leave from Custom House Quay (Map 4).

Buses to Belfast in Northern Ireland leave from Busáras four times a day Monday to Saturday and three times on Sunday. Services from the Europa bus station in Belfast operate at the same frequency. The trip takes about three hours and costs IR£9.50 one way or IR£12 for a return within one month.

TRAIN
Other Parts of Ireland

Iarnród Éireann (Irish Rail; Map 4, ☎ 836 6222), 35 Lower Abbey St, Dublin 1, operates the Republic's trains on routes that fan out from Dublin. Connolly station (Map 4, ☎ 836 3333), just north of the Liffey and the city centre, has trains going to Belfast, Derry, Sligo, Wexford and other points to the north. Heuston station (Map 5, ☎ 836 5421), just south of the Liffey and west of the centre, is the station for services to Cork, Galway, Killarney, Limerick, Waterford and other points to the west, south and south-west.

Distances are short in Ireland and the longest trip you can make by train from Dublin is 4½ hours to Tralee. However, fares are relatively high. Examples of regular fares from Dublin are: Belfast IR£14 (six daily, 2¼ hours), Cork IR£32 (up to eight daily, 3¼ hours), Galway IR£15 (up to 10 daily, three hours) and Limerick IR£27 (up to 13 daily, 2¼ hours). As with buses, special fares are often available. A same-day return to Belfast can cost as little as IR£13, a pound less than a one-way ticket! First-class tickets cost about IR£4 to IR£8 over the standard fare for a single journey. If you're aged under 26 you can get a FairCard for IR£8.50, which gives you a 50% discount on regular fares. See the next section for information on tickets giving unlimited travel.

BUS & TRAIN DISCOUNT DEALS

Irish Rambler tickets are available from Bus Éireann for unlimited bus travel within the Republic of Ireland. They cost IR£28 (three days), IR£68 (eight days) or IR£98 (15 days). Bus Éireann's Boomerang service allows you to buy a return ticket, valid for one month, for the cost of a one-way ticket but you can only travel on Tuesday, Wednesday and Thursday.

The Emerald Card gives you unlimited travel throughout Ireland on all scheduled services of Iarnród Éireann, Northern Ireland Railways, Bus Éireann, Dublin Bus, Ulsterbus and Citybus. The card costs IR£105 (or the equivalent in pounds sterling) for eight days or IR£180 for 15 days.

Children under 16 years of age pay half fare for all these passes.

Eurail passes are available to residents of non-European countries and are valid for unlimited travel on national railways and some private lines in Austria, Belgium, Denmark, Finland, France (including Monaco), Germany, Greece, Hungary, Ireland, Italy, Luxembourg, the Netherlands, Norway, Portugal, Spain, Sweden and Switzerland. Great Britain and Northern Ireland are not covered. The pass also gives you a discount on Bus Éireann's three day Irish Rambler ticket.

There are several different types of Eurail pass. The standard Eurailpass costs from US$538 for 15 days up to US$1512 for three months. The Flexipass costs US$634 for 10 days travel or US$836 for 15 days travel, to be taken on any chosen days within a two month period. These passes are available in 1st class only. Two people travelling together can save around 15% each by buying 'saver' versions (child fares are also available).

The Youthpass, for travellers aged 26 or under, is valid for unlimited 2nd class travel within a given time period, ranging from 15 days for US$376 up to three months for US$1059. The Youth Flexipass, also for 2nd class, is valid for freely chosen days within a two month period: 10 days for US$444 or 15 days for US$585.

Inter-Rail passes are available in Europe to people who have been resident there for at least six months. The standard Inter-Rail pass is for travellers aged under 26, though an Inter-Rail 26+ version is available. The pass divides Europe into eight zones (A to H); Ireland is in zone A, along with the UK. The standard/26+ fare for any one zone is UK£159/229, valid for 22 days. A one month pass covering two/three/all zones costs UK£209/229/259, or UK£279/309/349 for the 26+ version. The pass also gives discounts on Irish Ferries and Stena Line connecting ferries.

For IR£8.50 full-time students can have a Travelsave Stamp affixed to their ISIC card. This gives a 50% discount on Iarnród Éireann trains, and 15% on Bus Éireann services for fares over IR£1. Inquire at a USIT office for details (see under Other Parts of Ireland in the Air section earlier in this chapter for contact details).

The Rail Travel Centre (Map 4, ☎ 836 6222) at 35 Lower Abbey St, Dublin 1, sells tickets giving unlimited rail travel. A weekly ticket costs IR£10.50 and a month's travel is IR£40.

FERRY

Ferry services from Britain and France operate to a variety of ports in Ireland.

The ferry terminal at Dun Laoghaire, the port on the southern side of Dublin Bay, is well equipped and easily accessible by either the DART or bus. The Dublin ferry terminal is a 3km walk from the city centre and public transport is linked to departure and arrival times. See the Getting Around chapter for details of public transport to and from the terminals.

Departure Tax

There's no departure tax if you leave Dublin by ferry.

Other Countries

The UK There are two direct routes to Dublin – one from Holyhead, on the northwestern tip of Wales, to Dublin itself, and the other from Holyhead to Dun Laoghaire, the port on the southern side of Dublin Bay. The range of prices given below reflects seasonal differences and special offers, which may or may not be available.

Stena Line (☎ 0990 707070), operates a passenger and car service between Holyhead and Dun Laoghaire. The high-speed catamaran (High-Speed Service or HSS) takes a little over 1½ hours and costs from UK£22 to UK£26 for a foot passenger and from UK£159 to UK£189 for a car (prices are for cars with up to four passengers). Stena Line also runs a conventional ferry service from Holyhead to Dublin, but this service does not take foot passengers. The crossing takes 3½ hours and tickets cost from UK£129 to UK£279 for a five day return and UK£198 to UK£378 for a standard return.

Irish Ferries (☎ 0990 171717) operates ferries between Holyhead and Dublin. Foot passenger fares range from UK£20 to UK£35 (UK£16 to UK£28 for those under 26 years old) and car fares range from UK£99 to UK£184.

In Dublin, Stena Line (Map 7, ☎ 204 7777) is at 15 Westmoreland St, Dublin 2, and at Adelaide House, Haddington Terrace, Dun Laoghaire. The Irish Ferries office (Map 6, ☎ 661 0511) is at 2-4 Merrion Row, Dublin 2.

Other ferry services to Ireland from Britain include Swansea to Cork (Swansea Cork Ferries), Fishguard to Rosslare (Stena Line), Pembroke to Rosslare (Irish Ferries) and a variety of services to Northern Ireland (Norse Irish Ferries, P&O, Seacat).

France From France there are services from Roscoff to Cork, Cherbourg to Cork and Rosslare, and Le Havre to Cork and Rosslare. You can also travel to Ireland from France via Britain. These services are operated by Irish Ferries, and can be used by Eurail pass holders.

ROAD & SEA
Bus Éireann and National Express operate Eurolines services direct from London and other UK centres to Dublin and other cities.

Contact Eurolines (☎ 020-7730 8235) or National Express (☎ 0990 808080) for details. Slattery's (☎ 020-7730 3666, 7482 1604) of London is an Irish bus company with routes from Bristol, Leeds, London, Liverpool, Manchester and northern Wales to Dublin and other Irish cities.

London to Dublin takes about 12 hours and in 1999 fares fell to about UK£10 one way or UK£20 return. Be warned that the buses are cramped and usually full, and delays are not uncommon.

ORGANISED TOURS
Most organised tours to Ireland devote at least some time to Dublin.

In the UK, All Ireland Leisure Holidays (☎ 01704-531999) organises customised trips. You give details of places to be visited, the number of people, when you want to go and what grade of accommodation you require and the company plans a route for you. Celtic Links (☎ 01292-511133) will also put together an itinerary for any budget, and only sell directly, rather than through travel agencies, thus keeping costs down. CIE Tours International (☎ 020-8667 0011) organises five different tours ranging from seven to 10 days, each with one or two days in Dublin. Their season runs from mid-May to October.

Europe Express (☎ 0800 426 3615) in Washington, USA, can organise customised packages to Ireland and the ETM Travel Group (☎ 0800 992 7700) of Connecticut runs three-night 'weekend gem' packages to Dublin with accommodation, breakfast and a city tour included.

In Australia, Adventure World (☎ 02-9956 7766) of Sydney provides a full range of escorted tours to Ireland, some of which take in Dublin.

WARNING
The information in this chapter is particularly vulnerable to change: prices for international travel are volatile, routes are introduced and cancelled, schedules change, special deals come and go, and rules and visa requirements are amended.

Airlines and governments seem to make price structures and regulations as complicated as possible. Check directly with the airline or a travel agency to make sure you understand how a fare (and any ticket you may buy) works. In addition, the travel industry is highly competitive and there are many lurks and perks.

The upshot of this is that you should get information, opinions, quotes and advice from as many airlines and travel agencies as possible before you go ahead and part with your hard-earned cash. The details given in this chapter should be regarded as pointers and are not a substitute for your own careful, up-to-date research.

Getting Around

THE AIRPORT

Dublin airport (☎ 704 4222) has a *bureau de change* in the baggage arrivals area, a branch of the Bank of Ireland on the second level, which keeps regular banking hours and also offers currency exchange, a post office (open Monday to Friday from 9 am to 5 pm), an Aer Rianta (Irish airport authority) desk with information about the airport's facilities, a Dublin Tourism office that books accommodation, a CIE desk with information on trains and buses, plus shops, restaurants, bars, a hairdresser, a nursery, a church and car-hire counters. In the car park atrium there's a left-luggage office (☎ 704 4633), open daily from 6 am to 10 pm.

TO/FROM THE AIRPORT

Dublin airport is 10km north of the centre and public-transport options between the airport and city consist of two bus services or taxis.

Airport Bus Services

The Airlink Express Coach, operated by the Dublin Bus company (☎ 872 0000, 873 4222), runs to/from Busáras (the central bus station just north of the River Liffey in central Dublin, Map 4) and less frequently to/from Heuston station (Map 5) for IR£3 (children IR£1.50). It takes about half an hour. Timetables are available at the airport or in the city. Monday to Saturday, city-to-airport services go about every 20 to 30 minutes from 7.30 am to 10.40 pm. On Sunday they operate less frequently from 7.35 am to 10 minutes past midnight. Monday to Saturday airport-to-city services operate from 6.40 am to 11 pm. On Sunday they run from 7.30 am to 10.55 pm. The demand for seats sometimes exceeds the capacity of the bus, in which case it's worth getting a group together and sharing a taxi.

Alternatively, there are the slower bus Nos 41 and 41A, which make a number of useful stops on the way, terminate on Eden Quay near O'Connell St and cost IR£1.10. The trip can take up to one hour, but they operate longer hours and run more frequently than the express bus.

Airport Taxi Services

Taxis are subject to all sorts of additional charges for baggage, extra passengers and 'unsocial hours'. However, a taxi between the airport and the centre usually costs IR£12, so between four people it's unlikely to be more expensive than the express bus. There's a supplementary charge of 80p from the airport to the city, but this charge does not apply from the city to the airport. Make sure the meter is switched on, as some Dublin airport taxi drivers can be as unscrupulous as some of their counterparts elsewhere in the world.

TO/FROM THE FERRY TERMINALS

Buses go to Busáras from the Dublin Ferryport terminal (☎ 855 2222), Alexandra Rd, after all ferry arrivals from Holyhead. Buses also run from Busáras to meet ferry departures. For the 9.45 am ferry departure from Dublin, buses leave Busáras at 8.45 am. For the 9.45 pm departure, buses depart from Busáras at 8.15 and 9 pm and from Heuston station at 8.15 pm.

To travel between Dun Laoghaire's Carlisle terminal (☎ 280 1905) and Dublin, take bus No 46A to St Stephen's Green, or bus Nos 7, 7A or 8 to Burgh Quay, or take the DART (see Train later in this chapter) to Pearse station (for south Dublin) or Connolly station (for north Dublin).

TO/FROM CONNOLLY & HEUSTON STATIONS

The 90 Rail Link Bus runs between the two stations up to six times an hour at peak periods and costs 60p. Connolly station is a short walk north of Busáras; Heuston is by the Liffey, on the eastern side of town.

BUS

Dublin Bus has an information office (Map 4, ☎ 873 4222) at 59 Upper O'Connell St. It's open from 9 am to 5.30 pm Tuesday to Friday and from 8.30 am on Monday. On Saturday it closes at 2 pm. Free single-route timetables are available.

The city centre is divided into a 13 stage Citizone, within which the cheapest fare is 55p and the maximum IR£1.10. Ten-ride tickets offer discounts of between 50p and IR£1.50. One-day passes cost IR£3.30 for the bus, or IR£4.50 for bus and rail. Other passes include a weekly bus pass for IR£11 (students IR£9), or a bus and rail pass for IR£15.50 (plus IR£2 for an ID photo). See the Train section for information on the Dublin Explorer pass. Bus passes must be bought in advance, at 59 O'Connell St or at any of the bus agencies listed there.

Late-night buses run from the triangle formed by College St, Westmoreland St and D'Olier St (Map 6) until 3 am on Friday and Saturday night and go as far as Howth, Dun Laoghaire and Swords.

Busáras (Map 4), the central bus station, is just north of the river and the Custom House; it has a left-luggage facility costing IR£1.50 per item.

TRAIN

The Dublin Area Rapid Transport (DART, Map 2) provides quick rail access to the coast as far north as Howth and as far south as Bray. Pearse station is convenient for central Dublin south of the Liffey and Connolly station for north of the Liffey. From Monday to Saturday there are services every 10 to 20 minutes, sometimes more frequently, from around 6.30 am to midnight. Services are less frequent on Sunday. It takes about 30 minutes from Dublin to Bray at the southern extreme or Howth at the northern extreme. Dublin to Dun Laoghaire only takes about 15 to 20 minutes. There are also Suburban Rail services north as far as Dundalk, inland to Mullingar and south past Bray to Arklow.

A one way DART ticket from Dublin to Dun Laoghaire or Howth costs IR£1.10; to Bray it's IR£1.30. Within the DART region, a one day, unlimited travel ticket costs IR£3.50 for an adult, IR£1.75 for a child or IR£5 for a family. A one day ticket combining DART and Dublin Bus services costs IR£4 for an adult, IR£2 for a child or IR£6 for a family, but this ticket cannot be used from Monday to Friday during peak hours (7 to 9.45 am, 4.30 to 6.30 pm). A weekly rail and bus ticket costs IR£15.50 but requires an ID photo (IR£2). Dublin Explorer passes allow you four days DART and bus travel for IR£11.50 but can't be used until after 9.45 am from Monday to Friday.

Bicycles can't be taken on DART services, but can be taken on the less-frequent Suburban Rail services, either in the guard's van or in a special carriage at the opposite end of the train from the engine. There is an IR£2 charge for transporting a bicycle.

Heuston station has left-luggage lockers of three sizes, costing IR£1.50/2.50/4 for 24 hours. At Connolly station the facility costs IR£1 (backpacks IR£2).

CAR & MOTORCYCLE

As in most big cities, a car in Dublin is as much a millstone as a convenience, though it can be useful for day trips. If you're going farther afield, a car is a wonderful means of getting around Ireland since there are always interesting diversions down back roads where public transport doesn't venture. The two big disadvantages in central Dublin are traffic, which is a major problem, and parking, which is difficult to find outside official car parks. The clamping of illegally parked vehicles is becoming increasingly common.

Central Dublin has parking meters and a selection of open and sheltered car parks. You don't have to go far from the centre to find free roadside parking, especially in north Dublin. However, the police warn visitors that it's safer to park in a supervised car park, since cars are often broken into even in broad daylight close to major tourist attractions. Rental cars and cars with foreign number plates, which may contain valuable personal effects, are a prime target.

Dublin Driving

Apart from the problems of traffic jams and pollution from car exhausts, visitors to Dublin may be surprised (not to mention physically injured) by the ferocity of some drivers in what is generally seen as a relaxed city.

There are many accidents at traffic lights, where a car at the front of the queue stops for a red light only to be shunted into by the driver behind, who has 'naturally' assumed that the first few cars to reach the light will just drive right through.

The extent to which traffic signals are treated with contempt is witnessed in a piece of typical Irish wordplay, with the existence of red lights simply not being acknowledged, and the lights being referred to as 'deep amber'!

When booking accommodation you may want to check on parking facilities. Some B&Bs that claim to offer private parking, especially in the centre, may have a sharing arrangement with a nearby hotel to use its car park – provided it hasn't been filled by the hotel patrons' cars.

As in Britain, driving is on the left and you should only overtake on the outside (to the right) of the vehicle in front of you. Safety belts must be worn by the driver and front-seat passengers. Children under 12 years of age are not allowed to sit in the front seats. Motorcyclists and their passengers must wear helmets. Despite frequent apologies from Irish people about the roads there's really little to complain about, although minor roads may sometimes be potholed and are often narrow.

Speed limits are 70mph (112km/h) on motorways, 60mph (96km/h) on other roads and 30mph (48km/h) or as signposted in towns, but are often treated in a somewhat cavalier fashion. Leaded petrol costs about 70p a litre, unleaded costs three or four pence less.

The Automobile Association of Ireland, or AA (Map 7, ☎ 677 9481), is at 23 Suffolk St, Dublin 2 and the AA breakdown number in the Republic is ☎ 1800 667 788.

Rental

Car rental in Ireland is expensive because of high rates and a 12½% tax, so you're often better off making arrangements in your home country with some sort of package deal. In high season it's wise to book ahead. There are often special deals, the longer you hire the car the lower the daily rent, and off season some companies discount all rates by about 25%. Most companies make an extra daily charge if you cross the border into Northern Ireland. Most cars are manual; automatics are available but they are more expensive to hire.

Avis, Budget, Hertz, Thrifty and the major local operators, Argus, Dan Dooley and Murrays Europcar are the big rental companies. Murrays Europcar, Budget, Avis and Hertz have desks at the airport, but numerous other operators are based close to the airport and deliver cars for airport collection. Typical high-season rental rates per week with insurance, collision-damage waiver (CDW), VAT and unlimited kilometres are around IR£250 for a small car (Ford Fiesta), IR£300 for a medium-sized car (Toyota Corolla 1.3) and IR£350 for a larger car (Ford Mondeo). There are many smaller local operators with lower prices, but they don't offer the same kind of insurance coverage or unlimited mileage deals as the bigger operators.

People aged under 21 years of age are not allowed to hire a car; for the majority of rental companies you have to be at least 23 years old and to have had a valid driving licence for a minimum of 12 months. Some companies will not rent to you if you're over 70 or 75 years old. Your driving licence is usually enough to hire a car for stays of up to three months.

Motorbikes and mopeds are not available for rent in the Republic of Ireland.

The main car rental companies are:

Avis Rent-a-Car
   (☎ 677 5204) 1 East Hanover St (Map 6),
   Dublin 2
   (☎ 844 5204) Dublin airport
Budget Rent-a-Car
   (☎ 837 9802) 151 Lower Drumcondra Rd,
   Dublin 7
   (☎ 844 5919) Dublin airport, Dublin 9
Dan Dooley Car & Van Rentals
   (☎ 677 2723) 42-43 Westland Row (Map 6),
   Dublin 2
   (☎ 844 5156) Dublin airport
Hertz Rent-a-Car
   (☎ 660 2255) 149 Upper Leeson St (Map 6),
   Dublin 2
   (☎ 844 5466) Dublin airport
Murrays Europcar
   (☎ 668 1777) Baggot St Bridge (Map 6),
   Dublin 4
   (☎ 844 4179) Dublin airport
Payless Car Rental
   (☎ 844 4092) Dublin airport
Sixt Rent-a-Car
   (☎ 862 2715) Old Airport Rd, Santry,
   Dublin 9
   (☎ 844 4199) Dublin airport
Windsor Motors
   (☎ 454 0800) Rialto, South Circular Rd (Map
   5), Dublin 8
   (☎ 840 0800) Dublin airport

TAXI

Taxis in Dublin are expensive with an IR£1.80 flagfall and 80p per half-mile thereafter. In addition there are a number of extra charges – 40p for each extra passenger, 40p for each piece of luggage, IR£1.20 for telephone bookings and 40p for unsocial hours (8 pm to 8 am and all day Sunday). Public holidays are even more unsocial and require a higher supplement.

Taxis can be hailed on the street and are found at taxi ranks around the city, including on O'Connell St in north Dublin, College Green in front of Trinity College and St Stephen's Green at the end of Grafton St. There aren't nearly enough taxis around, however, and it can be extremely frustratingly trying to get one, especially at weekends and in rainy weather. Queues at taxi ranks can lead to waits of up to an hour

at night. Many companies dispatch taxis by radio, but they too can run out of cars at peak times; be sure to book as early as you can. Try City Cabs (☎ 872 7272) or National Radio Cabs (☎ 677 2222).

Phone the Garda Carriage Office (☎ 873 2222, ext 395/406) with any complaints about taxis.

BICYCLE

Despite the shortage of cycle lanes and the traffic, Dublin isn't a bad place to get around by bicycle, as it is small enough and flat enough to make bike travel easy. Many visitors explore farther afield by bicycle, a popular activity in Ireland despite the often less-than-encouraging weather.

The hostels seem to offer secure bicycle parking areas, but if you're going to have a bike stolen anywhere in Ireland, Dublin is where it'll happen. Lock your bike up well. Surprisingly, considering how popular bicycles are in Dublin, there's a scarcity of suitable bike-parking facilities. Grafton St and Temple Bar are virtually devoid of places to lock a bike. Elsewhere, there are signs on many likely stretches of railing announcing that bikes must not be parked there. Nevertheless, there are places where you can park your bike, such as the Grafton St corner of St Stephen's Green.

Square Wheel Cycleworks (☎ 679 0838), Temple Lane, Temple Bar, Dublin 2 (Map 7), is a good, central bike repair shop where you can also get up-to-date information on forthcoming cycling events.

Rental

You can either bring your bike with you or rent in Dublin, where typical costs are IR£7 to IR£10 a day or IR£32 to IR£38 a week.

Rent-a-Bike has eight outlets around the country and offers one-way rentals between its outlets for an extra IR£5. The head office of Rent-a-Bike is at Bike Store (☎ 872 5399/5931), 58 Lower Gardiner St, Dublin 1 (Map 4). They don't do daily rentals, but you can extend a weekly rental by the day.

Raleigh Rent-a-Bike agencies can be found all over Ireland, north and south of the border. Contact them at Raleigh Ireland (☎ 626 1333), Raleigh House, Kylemore Rd, Dublin 10. Raleigh agencies in Dublin include the following:

Joe Daly
  (☎ 298 1485) Lower Main St, Dundrum, Dublin 14
C Harding for Bikes
  (☎ 873 2455) 30 Bachelor's Walk (Map 6), Dublin 1
Hollingsworth Bikes
  (☎ 296 0255) 1 Drummartin Rd, Stillorgan, Dublin 14
Hollingsworth Cycles
  (☎ 490 5094, 492 0026) 54 Templeogue Rd, Templeogue, Dublin 6
Little Sport
  (☎ 833 0044) 3 Marville Ave, Fairview, Dublin 3
McDonald's Cycles
  (☎ 475 2586) 38 Wexford St (Map 6), Dublin 2
  (☎ 497 9636) 1 Orwell Rd, Rathgar, Dublin 6
Shankill Cycle Shack
  (☎ 282 7577) Barbeque Centre, Old Bray Rd, County Dublin

WALKING
Walking is the best way to explore Dublin. It is a small, compact city, with most sights and areas of interest within easy walking distance of each other. For example, it should take you no more than an hour to walk from the northern tip of O'Connell St down past the Liffey, through the city centre and back out again through the Liberties down to Kilmainham in the west of the city. The suburbs of Ballsbridge and Donnybrook are no more than a 20 minute walk from Grafton St and you could easily reach Phoenix Park in under half an hour.

But Dublin is not really about getting from one place to another in the shortest possible time. It is about taking your time, deviating from your intended route to have a look in a shop window or check out the doorway of a building; it is about stopping to watch a silver-painted mime artist entertain the crowd or listen to a busking duo sing the latest pop hit; it is about having a lie down in St Stephen's Green or Merrion Square because the warm sun is too precious to ignore; it is about having an impromptu drink in a pub. An old Dublin brain-teaser lays down the challenge of walking through the city without passing a pub: considering that there are over 700 in the city centre alone, it seems an impossible task. But it can be done, Dubliners will tell you: just go into every one you see!

For walks through the city, see the Dublin Walks chapter and for more information on walks in the Dublin area, see Lonely Planet's *Walking in Ireland*.

ORGANISED TOURS
Many Dublin tours operate only during summer, but at that time you can take bus tours, walking tours and bicycle tours. You can book these directly with the operators, through your hotel, at the various city tourist offices or with a travel agent.

Bus Tours
Bus Éireann You can book Bus Éireann tours directly at Busáras (Map 4, ☎ 836 6111), or through the Bus Éireann desks at the Dublin Bus office (Map 4), 59 Upper O'Connell St, or at the Dublin Tourism office (Map 7), St Andrews' Church, Suffolk St. During the summer months they operate a Monday to Saturday city tour that takes 3¾ hours and costs IR£9/4.50, including entry to the Book of Kells display.

Bus Éireann has several day tours outside Dublin. From January to March, tours to Glendalough run between 10.30 am and 4.30 pm on Wednesday, Saturday and Sunday (IR£14/7); from April to October they run from 10.30 am to 5.45 pm daily (IR£17/9). Tours to Newgrange and Boyne Valley run to the following timetable: 10 am until 4.15 pm, Thursday and Saturday, in February, March and November (IR£14/7); 10 am until 5.45 pm, Thursday and Saturday, in April and October (IR£17/9); and 10 am until 5.45 pm, daily except Friday, between May and September (IR£17/9). In the summer, there are also day tours farther afield to places such as Kilkenny, the River Shannon, Waterford, the Mourne Mountains, Armagh and Navan, and Lough Erne.

Dublin Bus Dublin Bus (☎ 872 0000, 873 4222) tours can be booked at their office at 59 Upper O'Connell St or at the Bus Éireann counter in the Dublin Tourism office (Map 7) in St Andrew's Church, Suffolk St. The three hour tour uses an open-top double-decker bus, weather permitting, and operates twice daily year-round, leaving from the Dublin Bus office at 10.15 am and 2.15 pm. You can leave or join the tour at any of 12 designated stops on the route. The tour costs IR£7/4.

Dublin Bus also operates a hop-on hop-off Heritage Trail bus, which does a city tour, with commentary, 11 times daily from mid-April to late September. From June to August there are eight additional circuits daily. The IR£5/2.50 ticket lets you travel all day, getting on or off at any of the eight stops around the city.

There are also two tours out of the city that operate daily during the summer months, take 2¾ hours and cost IR£8/4. The North Coast Tour does a loop via Howth, Malahide, the Casino at Marino and the Botanic Gardens. The South Coast Tour goes via Dun Laoghaire, Bray and Greystones and then returns through the mountains via Enniskerry.

For a taste of Dublin at its weirdest, Dublin Bus runs a Ghost Bus tour, a trip through Dublin's macabre legends. A storyteller is on hand to relate tales of haunted houses, body snatchings and mummies. At journey's end, everyone is invited to a pub, where an Irish wake is recreated. The tour departs from the Dublin Bus office at 7.30 pm on Tuesday and from Thursday to Sunday. It costs IR£12.

Gray Line Gray Line (☎ 670 8822) runs tours around Dublin and farther afield but only in the summer. Reservations can be made through Dublin Tourism (☎ 605 7777) and all tours depart from the Dublin Tourism office on Suffolk St. Are tours to Glendalough (IR£15.50) lasting from 2.45 pm until 6 pm on Tuesday and from 10 am to 2 pm on Thursday. Tours to Glendalough, Powerscourt and Russbor-

ough House (IR£27) last from 10 am to 5.30 pm on Friday and from 10.30 am to 5.30 pm on Sunday. Tours to Boyne Valley and Newgrange (IR£15.50) last from 10 am to 2 pm on Monday and Tuesday and from 2.30 to 6 pm on Thursday and Saturday.

Gray Line also has nightlife tours to Jury's Irish Cabaret (IR£18.90 with two drinks; IR£31.50 with dinner) and Doyle's Irish Cabaret (IR£18.90 with two drinks; IR£29.90 with dinner). See Irish Cabaret in the Entertainment chapter for details.

Other Tour Operators Mary Gibbons Tours (☎ 283 9973) does 2½ hour Dublin city tours daily at 9.45 am (IR£12); Boyne Valley tours on Monday, Wednesday and Friday (1.20 to 6 pm, IR£15); and Wicklow tours on Tuesday, Thursday, Saturday and Sunday (12.45 to 6.45 pm, IR£16). All depart from the Dublin Tourism office.

Old Dublin Tours (☎ 458 0054) does city sightseeing tours in a double-decker bus that leaves from outside the old tourist office at 14 Upper O'Connell St. From April to October, they run daily every seven minutes from 9.30 am until 5.30 pm. From November to March they run every 15 to 20 minutes between 9.30 am to 4 pm. The cost is IR£7 (IR£6 for concessions) and IR£3 for children.

Aran Tours (☎ 280 1899) runs an exciting and informative tour of Wicklow on Friday, Saturday and Sunday from April to September. The price is IR£22, including admission to Glendalough. It picks up at four points in the city (the Dublin Tourism office, the Shelbourne, the Gresham and Jury's, Ballsbridge), beginning at 8.50 am and returning at about 4 or 4.30 pm.

Walking Tours

During summer there are various walking tours, which are a great way to explore this city. A Trinity College walking tour departs frequently from Front Square just inside the college and costs IR£5.50/5, including entry to the Book of Kells exhibition. See the Trinity College section in the Things to See & Do chapter.

GETTING AROUND

Dublin Footsteps Walking Tours (☎ 496 0641) operates 1½ to two-hour walks for IR£5. The tours start from Bewley's Café (Map 7) on Grafton St and explore either medieval or 18th century Dublin together with literary Dublin. Ninety-minute walking tours of north Dublin, focusing on sites associated with James Joyce, depart from the James Joyce Centre (Map 4) at 35 North Great George's St at 2.30 pm Monday to Saturday; outside the summer months phone ☎ 873 1984 to check departure times. The cost of a tour of the centre and the walk is IR£5/3.50.

Historical Walking Tours (☎ 845 0241) are conducted by Trinity College history graduates, take two hours and depart from the front gates of Trinity College. The walks take place several times daily from mid-May to September and cost IR£5/4.

The Dublin Literary Pub Crawl (☎ 454 0228) operates daily, starting at 7.30 pm from Davy Byrne's (Map 7) on Duke St, just off Grafton St. From May to September there are also tours at 3 pm (and at noon on Sunday). The walk is great fun and costs IR£6.50/5, though Guinness consumption can quickly add a few pounds to that figure. The two actors who lead the tour put on a theatrical performance appropriate to the various places and pubs along the way; the pubs chosen vary from night to night. The quality of this tour has made it very popular and advance booking is recommended.

The Dublin Musical Pub Crawl (☎ 478 0191) leaves from upstairs in St John Gogarty's pub in Temple Bar (Map 7) at 7.30 pm Saturday to Thursday. A couple of musicians take you to McDaid's and The Clarendon, put on sample traditional music

sessions and explain the development of the Irish musical tradition. The tour ends in O'Donohue's with a final session at about 10 pm. Once again, this is great fun. Tours cost IR£7.

You can also buy various heritage trail leaflets in the tourist office and guide yourself around the city sites. Walks include a Georgian Heritage Trail and a Rock & Stroll Tour of sites associated with Irish music. Around town you'll also spot boards outlining a Malton Trail of sites portrayed by 18th century artist James Malton in his *A Picturesque & Descriptive View of the City of Dublin*.

The Zozimus Experience (☎ 661 8646) leaves from the gates of Dublin Castle daily at 6.45 pm on a tour of Dublin's superstitious and seedy medieval past. The costumed guide recounts stories of murders, great escapes and mythical events. The tour finishes with a macabre surprise. Tours must be booked and cost IR£5.

Carriage Tours

At the junction of Grafton St and St Stephen's Green you can pick up a horse and carriage with a driver/commentator. Half-hour tours cost up to IR£25 and the carriages can take four or five people. Tours of different lengths can be negotiated with the drivers.

Tour Guides

Bord Fáilte-approved guides can be contacted via the tourist board. The recommended fees for a full-day approved guide in Dublin are from IR£35 to IR£50 for an English-speaking guide or IR£45 to IR£65 for a guide speaking another language.

Things to See & Do

Central Dublin is relatively compact and reasonably uncrowded so getting around the city on foot is generally both efficient and pleasurable. Most of the attractions in this chapter are within easy reach of the centre and the walks in the Dublin Walks chapter take you past many of the most important and interesting sites. To travel further out there are taxis, buses and sightseeing tours and, for the energetic, bicycles are easy to hire. See the Facts for the Visitor chapter for information about Heritage Card entry to sites administered by Dúchas (formerly the Office of Public Works) and the Dublin Cultural Connection pass to other sites.

SIGHTSEEING ITINERARIES

Below are three itineraries that can be used as a guide to making your visit to Dublin as complete, informative and fun as possible. See also the Dublin Walks chapter for specific routes through the city. More detailed information on the sites mentioned in the itineraries can be found either later in this chapter or in the Excursions chapter.

Weekend

If you arrive on a Friday afternoon, your best introduction to Dublin is a meal and a drink in one of the city's hundreds of pubs. To work up an appetite, take a walk from

Highlights

Like any great city, Dublin has a number of sights that every visitor feels obliged to see. It's easy to spend several days seeing the central highlights and several more exploring the rest of the city and going on excursions in the surrounding countryside. Trinity College, with the Book of Kells, and the displays of the National Museum are two of Dublin's 'must see' attractions. Also close to the centre the medieval cathedrals of Christ Church and St Patrick's make a compact triangle with Dublin Castle and should feature on any sightseeing list. Between the college and the cathedrals is the intriguing, rejuvenated Temple Bar, one of the brightest, most energetic areas of the city.

Dublin is great for aimless wandering and an amble from the regal Georgian squares of south Dublin to their decaying counterparts in north Dublin makes a good introduction to the city. A stroll along the banks of the River Liffey takes you by the Custom House and the Four Courts, two Georgian-era masterpieces. St Stephen's Green is a fine place to sit and watch the world go by, or you might prefer the wide expanses of Phoenix Park with its gardens, sports pitches and castle.

Farther away are the Royal Hospital Kilmainham and Kilmainham Gaol to the west of the centre or the Casino at Marino to the north-east. Dun Laoghaire, with the nearby James Joyce Museum, and Howth are two ports that make good short excursions from the centre. If you have time, the prehistoric burial site at Newgrange north of Dublin and the ruined monastery at Glendalough to the south are well worth a visit.

Night-time in Dublin is the time to explore the city's plentiful supply of pubs, and a literary or musical pub crawl on a summer evening makes a fine introduction. Finally, having sampled Guinness in the pubs, a pilgrimage to the Guinness Hop Store should complete a visit to Dublin's highlights. Should whiskey be your tipple, you could pop into the Old Jameson Distillery as well.

Trinity College to St Stephen's Green along Grafton St to give yourself an impression of the city centre. Devote Saturday morning to visiting Trinity College and the Book of Kells before moving on to the National Gallery and/or the National Museum on Kildare St. Take a walk up O'Connell St, past the GPO and on up to Parnell Square, where you'll find the Hugh Lane Municipal Gallery of Modern Art and the Dublin Writers' Museum. You might want to go shopping on the streets around O'Connell St or back towards Grafton St, as most shops are closed on Sunday except in the month leading up to Christmas. Alternatively, you could make the relatively short journey to the Guinness Hop Store and check out the museum devoted to the dark stout, and sample a glass (or two) of the best Guinness to be found anywhere in the world. On your way, you can pop your head into Christ Church Cathedral. In the evening, take in a play at the Abbey or Gate Theatres, after which you can get a drink in a pub before going on to a club in or near Temple Bar. Sunday offers less in terms of museum visits, so you might want to take a stroll around the city's landscaped squares, including St Stephen's Green and Merrion Square. If the weather is particularly pleasant, you can either walk the length of the quays (or take a bus) to Phoenix Park and check out Dubliners at play, either picnicking or engaging in sports.

One Week

A week affords you plenty of time to see the best of what Dublin has to offer. Devote the first day or two to visiting the sights of major importance, such as Trinity College, the National Gallery, the National Museum, Dublin Castle and, on Parnell Square, the Hugh Lane Gallery and the Writers' Museum. In the evenings, be sure to sample some of Dublin's excellent nightlife, including a visit to a few of the different pubs around the centre, both traditional and modern. Pay a visit to both Christ Church Cathedral and the nearby St Patrick's Cathedral, both a short walk away from

Trinity College. The cathedrals are near the area that once formed Viking Dublin and you can check out Dublin's Viking history at Dublinia, next door to Christ Church. A short walk away is the Liberties, the city's oldest standing neighbourhood, dating back to the Middle Ages. Over the next couple of days, extend your area of discovery beyond the immediate city centre, taking in such sights as the Casino at Marino, a splendid example of Palladian architecture, the Irish Museum of Modern Art and the gaol at Kilmainham, a short bus ride away from the Guinness Hop Store. Fans of Irish whiskey will enjoy a visit to the Old Jameson Distillery, on the north side of the Liffey in the Victorian neighbourhood of Smithfield, just a short walk from Father Mathew Bridge. Devote one evening to a play at one of Dublin's famous theatres.

You should still have a couple of days to spare, which you may want to devote to exploring the southern suburbs of Dublin, especially the small seaport towns of Dun Laoghaire, Sandycove and Dalkey, all within easy reach of the centre by DART. In Sandycove you can visit the 18th century James Joyce Martello Tower, where the writer lived for a short time. If the weather is even mildly pleasant, you might fancy an invigorating stroll along Sandymount Strand, a little closer to the city. Otherwise, you can leave Dublin and devote a day to the monastic ruins of Glendalough in County Wicklow, an hour south of the city and set in a wonderfully picturesque valley of woodland and rushing streams. Nearby is the magnificent Powerscourt House and its equally splendid landscaped gardens.

10 Days

If you have the benefit of a prolonged stay, you can visit virtually all of the city-centre sights covered in this chapter and still have time to make excursions out of the city. Malahide Castle, 17km north of the city, makes for an excellent day trip, as you can also walk around the scenic town and down towards the seashore. The wonderful fishing village of Howth, at the northern end of the DART line, also affords some scenic walks, along the beaten path around Howth Head. If you have time, you should make an effort to get to the Neolithic passage graves at Newgrange, 60km north of Dublin in County Meath. The tombs are among the most spectacular tourist attractions in all of Europe. Fifty kilometres south-west of Dublin is the town of Kildare, a pleasant town that is home to the National Stud – which horse enthusiasts will enjoy – and the adjacent Japanese Gardens, considered to be the best example in Europe of the ancient Japanese art of landscaping.

The River Liffey

The River Liffey divides Dublin psychologically and socially, as well as physically, into northern and southern halves. The Liffey is spanned by an interesting collection of bridges, bounded by an equally historic array of quays, and overlooked by two of Dublin's finest Georgian buildings, the Custom House and the Four Courts.

The river flows down to Dublin from the Wicklow Hills, passing Phoenix Park and flowing under 14 city bridges before reaching Dublin Harbour and Dublin Bay. In a straight line it's only about 20km from the Liffey's source to the sea, but it meanders for over 100km and changes remarkably in that distance. Well into the city, around Phoenix Park, the Liffey is still rural-looking, although a far cry from the prehistoric *An Ruiteach* (as it was known in Irish), when it was four times wider than at present and fed by numerous smaller rivers.

The Liffey isn't a particularly notable river except for the fact that it's absolutely filthy – the water is never blue or green but various shades of grey. Although Liffey water was once a vital constituent of Guinness, you may be relieved to hear that this is no longer the case. However, James Joyce immortalised the river's spirit as Anna Livia, the woman you see lying in sculpted form in the middle of O'Connell St (and irreverently known as 'the floozy in the Jacuzzi' by the locals).

The best Liffey views are from O'Connell Bridge or, just upstream, from Dublin's most famous bridge, the pedestrian-only Ha'penny Bridge, which leads into the colourful Temple Bar area and has virtually become a symbol for the city.

LIFFEY QUAYS & DUBLIN HARBOUR
The Liffey's riverside quays have had a history almost as replete with name changes as its bridges.

Wolfe Tone & Victoria Quays (Map 5)
The furthest quay from the sea is immediately downstream from Heuston station and was originally named Albert Quay after Queen Victoria's husband. It was later renamed after the Protestant Irish patriot Wolfe Tone. Queen Victoria's own quay has somehow retained its name since her 1861 visit to Dublin.

Ellis, Arran, Inns & Ormond Quays (Maps 5 & 6)
On the north side of the Liffey, Ellis Quay was built on land leased to Sir William Ellis in 1682 and has kept his name. Still on the north side, Arran Quay dates from 1683. Lord Arran was the son of the Duke of Ormonde, whose name (minus the final 'e') graces the next north-side quay downstream after Inns Quay.

Upper and Lower Ormond Quay stretch east and west from Grattan Bridge and date from 1676 to 1678. The original plan was to build houses down to the riverside, but Sir Humphrey Lewis was persuaded to construct the quay instead and this set a pattern for later quays.

Usher's Island & Usher's Quay (Map 5)
On the south side of the Liffey, Victoria Quay gives way to Usher's Island and Usher's Quay. John Ussher leased the land here in 1597, but the quay wasn't built until the 18th century when it adopted his name, dropping an 's' on the way.

Liffey Bridges

Although there have been bridges over the Liffey for nearly 800 years, the oldest remaining bridge dates from 1768. The Liffey bridges have been through a series of names: under the British many were named after the Lords Lieutenant of the time, but since independence many have been renamed after notable republicans. Travelling downstream (west to east) you will come across the following city bridges (see Maps 5 and 6).

Island Bridge

The first city bridge over the Liffey is north of Kilmainham Gaol and its foundation stone was laid by Sarah Fare, wife of the earl of Westmoreland, John Fare, Lord Lieutenant of Ireland from 1790 to 1795. The official name, Sarah Bridge, never caught on and it was generally known as either Kilmainham Bridge or Island Bridge, after the island formed at this point by the weir. It was officially renamed Island Bridge in 1922.

Heuston & Frank Sherwin Bridges

The bridge beside Heuston station started as King's Bridge in 1821 to commemorate the visit to Ireland by King George IV, though the bridge wasn't actually completed until 1828. In 1922 it was renamed Sarsfield Bridge and in 1941 Heuston Bridge, after Sean Heuston, one of the leaders of the 1916 Easter Rising executed at nearby Kilmainham Gaol.

Frank Sherwin Bridge, just downstream from Heuston Bridge, was opened in 1982 and named after a city councillor.

O'More Bridge

The current bridge north of the St James's Gate Guinness Brewery dates from 1860, but a wooden bridge was first built here in 1674. It was known as Bloody Bridge after a riot that took place nearby in 1671. The present bridge started life as the Victoria Bridge, but was generally referred to as the Barrack Bridge after the nearby Royal Barracks (now Collins Barracks). In 1922 it was renamed after Rory O'More, ringleader of an uprising in 1641.

Liam Mellowes Bridge

Opened in 1768 as Queen's Bridge, this is the oldest surviving bridge on the Liffey. It's had several other names and is still popularly known as Queen St Bridge, for the simple reason that Queen St runs down to it. It was renamed in 1942 after Liam Mellowes, executed in 1922 during the Civil War.

Father Mathew Bridge

The first recorded bridge over the Liffey was built in 1210 at the present site of Father Mathew Bridge. The earlier ford of hurdles at this site, upstream from the Four Courts, gave Dublin its Irish name, *Baile Átha Cliath*, the Town of the Hurdle Ford. Two ancient Irish roads met and crossed the river together at this point: one, Sligh Chualann, ran from Tara to County Wicklow; the other, Sligh Midhluachara, ran from Derry to Waterford. There are records of a bridge collapsing here in 1385 and being rebuilt in 1428, but until the bridge at the site of the present O'More Bridge was built in 1674 no other structure spanned the Liffey.

The present bridge, built in 1818, was first named the Charles Whitworth Bridge after the Lord Lieutenant from 1813 to 1817. It was renamed Dublin Bridge in 1922 then renamed again in 1938 after Ireland's 'apostle of temperance'.

Liffey Bridges

O'Donovan Rossa Bridge
The bridge was built in 1813 and was originally named the Richmond Bridge after the duke of Richmond, Lord Lieutenant from 1807 to 1813. It was later renamed after Republican hero and publisher of the paper *United Ireland*, Jeremiah O'Donovan Rossa, who died in 1915. It's slightly upstream from the former Arran Bridge, which was opened in 1683 but destroyed by a storm in 1806 and never rebuilt.

Grattan Bridge
Better known as Capel St Bridge, Grattan Bridge crosses the river from Capel St and leads into Temple Bar and the road to Dublin Castle. It was originally built in 1676 and named Essex Bridge after the then Lord Lieutenant, Arthur Capel (earl of Essex). The new name came with the replacement bridge built between 1874 and 1875. The River Poddle joined the Liffey at this point, at the black pool or *dubh linn* that gave the city its name. Today the Poddle runs its final 5km in an underground channel and trickles into the Liffey through a grating on the south side of the river downstream from the bridge.

Ha'penny Bridge
This cast-iron bridge was built in 1816 as Wellington Bridge, but is officially known as the Liffey Bridge, being renamed as such in 1922. Earlier this century there was a toll of half a penny to cross it and that's how Dublin's best-loved and most photogenic bridge received its unofficial name.

O'Connell Bridge
James Gandon, Dublin's most important architect, was responsible for its most important bridge. Its construction from 1794 to 1798 made O'Connell St the premier avenue in Dublin and shifted the city's axis eastward from Capel St. Originally named Carlisle Bridge after the Lord Lieutenant from 1780 to 1782, it received its current name in 1882, at the same time that the statue of Daniel O'Connell, 'The Liberator', was unveiled at the river end of O'Connell St. Two years earlier, in 1880, the bridge had been widened so it's now actually wider than it is long.

Butt & Loop Line Bridges
The Butt Bridge (1878) was named after Isaac Butt, leader of the Home Rule movement. It was rebuilt in 1932 and officially renamed the Congress Bridge but that name never caught on. The railway Loop Line Bridge, which also crosses the river here, is the ugliest, worst-placed bridge on the river, obscuring what would otherwise be fine views of the Custom House.

Talbot Memorial & East Link Toll Bridges
The Talbot Memorial Bridge (1978) was named after Matt Talbot, a gentleman whose principal claim to fame was that, like Father Mathew, he disapproved of alcohol. The final Liffey bridge, the East Link Toll Bridge, was opened in 1985, beyond the point where the Grand Canal enters the Liffey.

THINGS TO SEE & DO

Merchant's & Wood Quays (Maps 5 & 6)

These are the oldest quays in the city. Wood Quay was built of wood back in the 13th century, but rebuilt in stone in 1676. Many Viking-era archaeological finds were made when the land behind Wood Quay was excavated in the 1970s to construct the controversial Dublin Corporation offices. Merchant's Quay came a century after Wood Quay and merchant ships unloaded here until the construction of the original Custom House slightly downstream in 1621, when the area became residential rather than commercial.

Essex & Wellington Quays (Map 7)

Essex Quay, ending at Grattan Bridge, was named after Arthur Capel, earl of Essex and Lord Lieutenant of Ireland from 1672 to 1677, and his name also survives on Capel St on the north side of the bridge. On the other side, the Clarence Hotel on Wellington Quay in Temple Bar was built on the site of the original Custom House (1621-1791), after which the quay was named. The name changed from Custom House Quay to Wellington Quay in 1817, two years after Lord Wellington's defeat of Napoleon at Waterloo.

Bachelor's Walk & Aston Quay (Map 6)

Bachelor's Walk, between Ha'penny and O'Connell bridges on the north side, is infamous for a clash between civilians and British troops in 1914. Following the landing of arms for the republican cause by the ship *Asgard* at Howth, a crowd gathered here and jeered the soldiers. They in turn opened fire, killing three civilians and injuring 38. On the south side, Aston Quay was named after a mayor of Dublin who acquired the land in 1672.

Other Quays

East of O'Connell Bridge on the north side are Eden and Custom House quays and finally North Wall Quay, built by the Dublin Corporation in 1729. On the south side is Burgh Quay, built in 1808 and possibly named after the architect Thomas Burgh. It's followed by George's Quay, named after King George I, then by City Quay. Finally, Sir John Rogerson's Quay was named after the member of parliament and mayor of Dublin who acquired the marshy land here in 1713.

Dublin Harbour

In medieval times the River Liffey spread out into a broad estuary as it flowed east into the bay. Today the low-lying estuary land has long been reclaimed (Trinity College has stood on it for over 400 years) and the Liffey runs right to the sea.

Dublin Harbour came into existence in 1714, when the Liffey embankments were constructed. North Wall Quay was then built and, later, a 5km breakwater known as the South Wall was added – the engineer in charge of the construction of the South Wall was the notorious Captain William Bligh of *Mutiny on the Bounty* fame. This was followed by the North and South Bull Walls. The South Wall starts at Ringsend and runs past the Pigeon House Fort, which was built in 1748 and now used as a power station. From there the South Wall continues a further 2km out to the Poolbeg Lighthouse (1762) at the end of the breakwater. It's a pleasant, if somewhat lengthy, stroll out to the lighthouse.

Ferry services to Holyhead in Britain run from the Dublin Harbour ferry terminal as well as from the Dun Laoghaire Harbour, at the southern end of the bay (see Ferry in the Getting There & Away chapter).

South of the Liffey

South Dublin is the affluent, touristed Dublin where you'll find the fanciest shops, most restaurants of note and the majority of the hotels. You'll also find most reminders of Dublin's early history and the finest Georgian squares and houses. South Dublin is certainly not all there is to Dublin, but it's a good place to start.

THINGS TO SEE & DO

TRINITY COLLEGE & THE BOOK OF KELLS (Map 6)

Ireland's premier university was founded by Elizabeth I in 1592 on land confiscated from a monastery. By providing an alternative to education on the Continent, the queen hoped that the college's students would avoid being 'infected with popery'. The college is in the centre of Dublin, though when it was founded it lay outside the city walls. Archbishop Ussher, whose scientific feats included the precise dating of the act of creation to 4004 BC, was one of the college's founders.

Officially, the university's name is the University of Dublin, but Trinity College is the sole college. Until 1793 Trinity College remained completely Protestant apart from one short break. Even when the university relented and began to admit Catholics, the Catholic Church authorities forbade it, a restriction not completely lifted until 1970. Today, Trinity College is still something of a centre of British and Protestant influence although the majority of its 9500 students are Catholic. Women were first admitted to the college in 1903, earlier than at most British universities.

The college grounds cover 16 hectares. For visitors the college has no admission charge or restrictions on entry apart from a ban on dogs, a request not to ride bicycles in the Library Square area and another request not to sunbathe in any part of the grounds except College Park.

In summer, walking tours depart regularly from the main gate on College Green (the street in front of the college) from 9.30 am to 4.30 pm, Monday to Saturday, and from noon to 4 pm on Sunday. The IR£5.50/5 cost is good value since it includes the fee to see the Book of Kells.

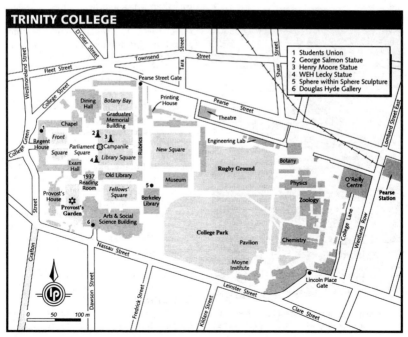

TRINITY COLLEGE

1 Students Union
2 George Salmon Statue
3 Henry Moore Statue
4 WEH Lecky Statue
5 Sphere within Sphere Sculpture
6 Douglas Hyde Gallery

Main Entrance

Much of the college today dates from Dublin's 18th century heyday. The Front Gate or Regent House entrance on College Green was built between 1752 and 1759 and is guarded by statues of the poet Oliver Goldsmith (1730-74) and the orator Edmund Burke (1729-97).

Around the Campanile

The open area reached from Regent House is divided into Front Square, Parliament Square and Library Square. The area is dominated by the 30m-high Campanile, designed by Edward Lanyon and erected from 1852 to 1853 on what was believed to be the centre of the monastery that preceded the college. Earlier there had been a bell tower, designed by the architect Richard Castle, on the same spot. To the north of the Campanile is a statue of George Salmon, the college provost from 1886 to 1904, who fought bitterly to keep women out of the college. He carried out his threat to permit them in 'over his dead body' by dropping dead when the worst happened. To the south of the Campanile is a statue of historian WEH Lecky (1838-1903). On the grassy expanse of Library Square are a 1969 sculpture by British sculptor Henry Moore (1898-1986) and two large Oregon maples.

Chapel & Dining Hall

Clockwise around the Front Square from the entrance gate, the first building is the Chapel, completed in 1799 to plans made in 1777 by architect Sir William Chambers (1723-96). It has been open to all denominations since 1972. The Chapel has fine plasterwork by Michael Stapleton, Ionic columns and painted, rather than stained, glass windows. The main window is dedicated to Archbishop Ussher.

Next to the Chapel is the Dining Hall, originally designed and built in 1743 by Richard Castle but dismantled 15 years later because of problems caused by inadequate foundations. The replacement was completed in 1761 and may retain elements of the original design. It was extensively restored after a fire in 1984. The popular Buttery Café & Bar is in the basement.

Graduates' Memorial Building & the Rubrics

The Graduates' Memorial Building (1892) forms the north side of Library Square. Behind it are tennis courts in the area known as **Botany Bay**. Legend has it that unruly students housed around the square were considered suitable candidates for the British penal colony at Botany Bay in Australia. On the east side of Library Square, the red-brick Rubrics building dates from around 1690, making it the oldest building in the college. It was extensively altered in an 1894 restoration then underwent serious structural modifications in the 1970s.

Old Library

To the south of the square is the Old Library, built in a rather severe style by

It is rumoured that if students pass beneath the Campanile they will fail their final exams.

TONY WHEELER

Thomas Burgh between 1712 and 1732. The Old Library's 65m-long Long Room contains numerous unique, ancient texts and the Book of Kells is displayed in the library Colonnades. Despite Ireland's independence, the 1801 Library Act entitles Trinity College Library to a free copy of every book published in the UK. Housing this bounty requires nearly 1km of extra shelving every year and the collection amounts to around five million books. These can't all be kept at the college library, so there are library storage facilities dotted around Dublin.

The magnificent Long Room (see later in this section) is mainly used for the library's oldest volumes. Until 1892 the ground floor Colonnades formed an open arcade, but this was enclosed at that time to increase the storage area. Earlier, in 1853, the Long Room's storage capacity had been increased by raising its ceiling.

Book of Kells

Trinity College's prime attraction is the magnificent Book of Kells, an illuminated manuscript from around 800 AD – one of the oldest books in the world. Although the book was brought to the college for safe-keeping from the monastery at Kells in County Meath in 1654, it undoubtedly predates the monastery. It was probably produced by monks at St Columba's Monastery on the remote island of Iona, off the coast of Scotland. After repeated Viking raids the monks moved to the temporarily greater safety of Ireland in 806 AD, bringing their masterpiece with them to Kells. In 1007 the book was stolen then rediscovered three months later, buried in the ground. Some time before the dissolution of the monastery, the metal shrine or *cumdach* was lost, possibly taken by looting Vikings who wouldn't have valued the text itself. About 30 of the beginning and ending folios (double-page spreads) are also missing.

The manuscript contains the four New Testament gospels, written in Latin, as well as prefaces, summaries and other text. If it contained merely words, it would simply

be an old book – it's made so wonderful by the superbly decorated opening letters of each chapter and the extensive, complex, smaller illustrations between the lines.

The 680 page (340 folio) book was rebound in four calfskin volumes in 1953. Two volumes are usually on display, one showing an illuminated page, the other showing text. The pages are turned regularly, but if you can't spare the time for the numerous daily visits required to view the entire book, you can purchase a reproduction available via the Trinity College Library for a mere US$18,000. If that's too much, an information brochure and 'documentation kit' are available for US$98. If that's still too steep, the library bookshop has various cheaper books, including *The Book of Kells*, which has some attractive colour plates and text, for IR£12.95.

The Book of Kells is displayed in the East Pavilion of the library Colonnades, underneath the actual library, alongside the 807 AD **Book of Armagh** and the 675 AD **Book of Durrow**, all of which are part of a new exhibition called 'The Book of Kells: Turning Darkness into Light' (the exhibition will run until at least the year 2001). Ironically, efforts have been made to improve the poor lighting that protects the fragile manuscripts, but another problem remains. Around 500,000 people a year come to see it, leading to queues of at least 30 minutes in June, July and August. If you can, try and visit at some other time of year or arrive early.

The Book of Kells exhibition and the Long Room are open from 9.30 am to 5.30 pm Monday to Friday, and from noon to 5 pm on Sunday. Entry is IR£4.50/4 (children under 12 free). The entry price includes admission to the Long Room and to temporary exhibitions in the East Pavilion. The Colonnades also houses a busy book and souvenir shop and temporary exhibitions.

Library Long Room

The Long Room is lined with shelves containing 200,000 of the library's oldest books and manuscripts, but a continual process of restoring and protecting them means that some, at any given time, may not be viewable. Also on display is the so-called Brian Ború's harp, which wasn't in use when he defeated the Danes at the Battle of Clontarf in 1014 AD, as it actually dates from around 1400, making it one of the oldest harps in the country.

Other exhibits in the Long Room include a rare copy of the Proclamation of the Irish Republic, read by Patrick Pearse at the beginning of the 1916 Easter Rising. The collection of 18th and 19th century marble busts around the walls features Jonathan Swift, Edmund Burke and Wolfe Tone, former members of Trinity College.

Reading Room, Exam Hall & Provost's House

Continuing clockwise around the Campanile there's the Reading Room and the Exam Hall or Public Theatre, which dates from 1779 to 1791. Like the Chapel that it faces and closely resembles, it was the work of William Chambers and also has plasterwork by Michael Stapleton. It contains an oak chandelier rescued from the Irish Parliament (now the Bank of Ireland) and an organ said to have been salvaged from a Spanish ship in 1702, though evidence indicates otherwise. Portraits of Swift, Ussher, Berkeley, Elizabeth I and others connected with the college's history are hung in the Exam Hall.

Behind the Exam Hall is the Provost's House (1760), a fine Georgian building where the provost or college head still resides. The house and its garden are not open to the public.

Berkeley Library

To the south-east of the old library is the solid, square, brutalist-style 1967 Berkeley Library designed by Paul Koralek. It has been hailed as the best example of modern architecture in Ireland. It's fronted by Arnaldo Pomodoro's sculpture *Sphere Within Sphere* (1982-83).

George Berkeley, born in Kilkenny in 1685, studied at Trinity when he was only 15 years old and had a distinguished career in many fields, particularly in philosophy. His influence spread to the new English colonies in North America where he helped to found the University of Pennsylvania. Berkeley in California, and its namesake university, are named after him.

Arts & Social Science Building & Douglas Hyde Gallery

South of the old library, the Arts & Social Science Building (1978) backs on to Nassau St and forms the alternative main entrance to the college. Designed by Paul Koralek it houses the Douglas Hyde Gallery of Modern Art (☎ 608 1116), which features some extremely good contemporary pieces. The gallery is open from 11 am to 6 pm Monday to Friday (Thursday until 7 pm) and 11 am to 4.45 pm on Saturday; admission is free. Fellows' Square is bordered on three sides by the two library buildings and the Arts & Social Science Building.

The Dublin Experience

The college's other big tourist attraction is the Dublin Experience (☎ 608 1688), a 45 minute audiovisual introduction to the city, shown at the back of the Arts & Social Sciences Building every hour from 10 am to 5 pm daily from May to early October. It's well signposted and entry is IR£2.75/2.25. Combined tickets for the Book of Kells and the Dublin Experience are IR£5/4.

Around New Square

Behind the Rubrics building, at the eastern end of Library Square, is New Square. In the highly ornate **Museum Building** (1853-57) exhibits include skeletons of two enormous giant Irish deer just inside the entrance and geological artefacts in the Geological Museum upstairs. It's open by prior arrangement only (☎ 608 1477). The **Printing House** (1734), designed by Richard Castle to resemble a Doric temple and housing the microelectronics and electrical engineering departments, is at the north-west corner of New Square. One of Dublin's best early architects, Castle was responsible for a number of buildings at Trinity College but, apart from this building, little of his work here has survived.

Towards the eastern end of the college grounds are the **Rugby Ground** and **College Park**, where cricket games are played. There are several science buildings at the eastern end of the grounds. **Lincoln Place Gate** at this end is usually open and provides a good short cut through the college from Leinster St and Westland Row.

BANK OF IRELAND (Map 7)

The imposing Bank of Ireland (☎ 671 1488), on College Green directly opposite Trinity College, was originally begun in 1729 to house the Irish Parliament. When the parliament voted itself out of existence through the 1801 Act of Union, the building was sold with instructions to alter the interior to prevent it being used as a debating chamber in the future. Subsequently, the central House of Commons was remodelled, but the smaller House of Lords chamber survived. After independence the Irish government installed the new parliament in Leinster House, ignoring the possibility of restoring this fine building to its original use.

Over time a number of architects worked on the building, yet it avoids looking like a hotchpotch of styles. Edward Lovett Pearce designed the original circular part of the building, which was constructed between 1729 and 1739. The curving windowless Ionic portico has statues of Hibernia (the Roman name for Ireland), Fidelity and Commerce, and the east front, designed by James Gandon in 1785, has Corinthian columns and statues of Wisdom (or Fortitude), Justice and Liberty. Architects Robert Park and Francis Johnston converted it from a parliament building to a bank after it was sold in 1803.

Now the Bank of Ireland, this was the first-ever purpose-built parliament building.

euro currency converter IR£1 = €1.27

Inside, the banking mall occupies what was once the House of Commons, but offers little hint of its former role. The House of Lords is more interesting with its Irish oak woodwork, mahogany longcase parliament clock and late 18th century Dublin crystal chandelier. The tapestries date from the 1730s and depict the Siege of Derry (1689) and the Battle of the Boyne (1690), the two Protestant victories over Catholic Ireland. In the niches are busts of George III, George IV, Lord Nelson and the Duke of Wellington. The 10kg, silver-gilt mace on display was made for the House of Commons and retained by the Speaker of the House when the parliament was dissolved. It was later sold by his descendants and bought back from Christies in London by the Bank of Ireland in 1937.

The building is open from 10 am to 4 pm, Monday to Friday (to 5 pm on Thursday). Free talks – as much about Ireland, and life in general, as the bank – take place on Tuesday at 10.30 and 11.30 am and 1.45 pm. The building's alternative role as a tourist attraction isn't pushed hard and you'll probably have to ask somebody the way to the House of Lords.

AROUND THE BANK OF IRELAND (Map 7)

Close to the bank are several places of interest. In Foster Place, to the west, is the Bank of Ireland Arts Centre, refitted and reopened in 1995. The area between the bank and Trinity College, today a constant tangle of traffic and pedestrians, was once a green swathe and is still known as College Green. In front of the bank on College Green is a statue of Henry Grattan (1746-1820), a distinguished parliamentary orator. Further up Dame St is a modern memorial to the patriot Thomas Davis (1814-45).

On the traffic island, where College Green, Westmoreland St and College St meet, are public toilets (no longer in use) and a statue of the poet and composer Thomas Moore (1779-1852), subject of James Joyce's comment in *Ulysses* that standing atop a public urinal wasn't a bad place for the man who penned the poem *The Meeting of the Waters*. At the other end of College St, where it meets Pearse St (Map 6), another traffic island is topped by a 1986 sculpture known as *Steyne*. It's a copy of the *steyne* (the Viking word for stone) erected on the riverbank in the 9th century to stop ships from grounding and removed in 1720.

TEMPLE BAR (Map 7)

West of College Green and the Bank of Ireland the maze of streets making up Temple Bar is sandwiched between Dame St and the river. It's one of the oldest areas of the city but since its revitalisation has become a Dublin delight, with numerous restaurants and pubs and a growing collection of trendy shops.

Dame St forms part of the southern boundary of Temple Bar and links new Dublin (centred around Trinity College and Grafton St) and old (stretching from Dublin Castle to encompass Christ Church and St Patrick's cathedrals). Along its route Dame St changes name to Cork Hill, Lord Edward St and Christchurch Place.

Information

The Temple Bar Information Centre (☎ 671 5717), 18 Eustace St, has specific details on the area and publishes a *Temple Bar Guide*. The notice board in the Resource Centre/ Well Fed Café on Crow St offers a useful round-up of local goings-on.

Temple Bar has two hostels and several hotels (see the Places to Stay chapter). Bloom's Hotel stands on the site of the original Jury's Hotel, which started life here in 1839 and moved to its present suburban location in 1973. The number of restaurants in Temple Bar has increased dramatically in the past few years and is still growing (see the Places to Eat chapter). Pubs are also well represented and in summer an international outdoor drinking party takes place every evening along East Essex St between the Norseman and the Temple Bar pubs.

Two of Dublin's most popular late-night music venues – the Eamonn Doran Imbibing Emporium for rock music and Bad Bob's Backstage Bar for country music – are in Temple Bar along with the Olympia Theatre from 1982 (see the Entertainment chapter). Finally, Temple Bar is packed with all manner of colourful one-off shops, some of which are described in the Shopping chapter.

History

This stretch of riverside land was owned by Augustinian friars from 1282 until Henry VIII's dissolution of the monasteries in 1537, after which Sir William Temple (1554-1628) acquired the land that bears his name. The term 'bar' referred to a riverside walkway. Until 1537 Temple Lane was known as Hogges Lane and gave access to the friars' house. During its monastic era the Temple Bar area was marshy land that had only recently been reclaimed from the river. Much of it was outside the city walls and the River Poddle flowed through it, connecting the black pool (*dubh linn* in Gaelic, hence the city's name) with the Liffey. In Eustace St is St Winifred's Well, built in 1680 on the site of a medieval well.

The narrow lanes and alleys of Temple Bar date from the early 18th century when this was a disreputable area of pubs and prostitution. Through the 19th century it developed a commercial character with small craft and trade businesses, but in the first half of the 20th century went into a steady decline, along with most of central Dublin.

In the 1960s it was decided to flatten the area to build a major bus depot but these plans took a long time to develop and, meanwhile, the properties acquired for the purpose were rented out on short-term leases at low rents, mostly to artists and artisans. Temple Bar thus gradually became a thriving countercultural centre, and in the 1980s the bus depot plan was dropped in favour of developing the area as a centre for restaurants, shops and entertainment.

The official decision to recognise that local energy was already rehabilitating the area accelerated the development of Temple Bar. It has changed dramatically since 1991 when Dublin was nominated Europe's City of Culture and the revitalisation of Temple Bar was given a further push. The area now boasts two public squares, apartments, a student housing centre, a Viking museum, a children's cultural centre, an independent cinema and many art galleries. The renovation work in Temple Bar is all but finished but the conversion of old buildings into flats and the construction of new apartments continues. Meanwhile, rents have soared, leading to accusations of gentrification.

Exploring Temple Bar

The western boundary of Temple Bar is formed by Fishamble St, the oldest street in Dublin, dating back to Viking times – not that you'd know that to see it now. Christ Church Cathedral, beside Fishamble St, dates from 1170, but there was an earlier Viking church on this site. Brass symbols in the pavement direct you towards a mosaic laid out to show the ground plan of the sort of Viking dwelling excavated here from 1980 to 1981. The parliamentarian Henry Grattan (whose statue stands outside Trinity College on College Green) and the poet James Clarence Mangan (whose bust can be seen in St Stephen's Green) were both born on Fishamble St.

In 1742 Handel conducted the first performance of his *Messiah* in the Dublin Music Hall, behind Kinlay House (on Lord Edward St), now part of a hotel that bears the composer's name. The chorus was made up of the choirs from the two cathedrals. The Music Hall, opened in 1741, was designed by Richard Castle, but the only reminder of it today is the entrance and the original door, which stand to the left of Kennan's engineering works.

Parliament St, which runs south from the river to the City Hall and Dublin Castle, has Read's Cutlers at No 4, the oldest shop in Dublin, having operated under the same name since 1760. At the other end of the street, beside the river, the filthy Sunlight Chambers has a beautiful frieze around the façade. Sunlight was a brand of soap manufactured by Lever Brothers, who were responsible for the late 19th century building. The frieze shows the Lever Brothers' view of the world and soap: men make clothes dirty, women wash them!

Eustace St is an interesting road, with the popular Norseman pub near the river end. Buildings on the street include the Presbyterian Meeting House (1715). The Dublin branch of the Society of United Irishmen, who sought parliamentary reform and equality for Catholics, was first convened in 1791 in the Eagle Tavern, now the Friends Meeting House. This should not be confused with the other Eagle Tavern, which is on Cork St.

Cecilia St, named after St Cecilia the patron saint of music, once had a popular music hall and Ha'penny Bridge was built partly to give easy access to the hall from north Dublin. Fownes St, named after the mayor of Dublin in 1697, a notorious wheeler-dealer, has the Boy Scout Shop, and the headquarters of both the Irish green and gay movements.

Merchant's Arch leads to Ha'penny Bridge. If you cross the bridge to the north side, you'll see the statue of two Dublin matrons sitting on a park bench with their shopping bags, dubbed, in typically irreverent Dublin fashion, 'the hags with the bags'.

Back on the south side of the river, the Stock Exchange is on Anglesea St, in a building dating from 1878. The Bank of Ireland occupies the south-eastern corner of Temple Bar.

DUBLIN CASTLE (Map 7)

The centre of British power in Ireland and originally built on the orders of King John in the early 13th century, Dublin Castle is more correctly described as a palace. Although the castle's construction, on Viking foundations, dates back to the 13th century the older parts have been built over through the centuries since then. Only the Record Tower remains intact from the original Norman castle.

Under the more recent additions, parts of the castle's earliest foundations remain, and a visit to the subterranean excavations,

which clearly reveal the development of the castle from its original construction, is the most interesting part of the castle tour. The castle moats, now covered by more modern developments, were filled by the River Poddle on its way to joining the Liffey at Dublin's black pool.

The castle has enjoyed a relatively quiet history despite a siege by Silken Thomas Fitzgerald in 1534, a fire that destroyed much of the castle in 1684 and the events of the 1916 Easter Rising. The building served as the official residence of the British viceroys of Ireland until the Viceregal Lodge was built in Phoenix Park. Earlier it had been used as a prison, though not always with great success, as Red Hugh O'Donnell managed to escape from the Record Tower in 1591 and again in 1592.

The castle tops Cork Hill, behind the City Hall on Dame St, and tours, costing IR£3/2, are held from 10 am to 5 pm Monday to Friday, afternoons only on weekends. The castle is still used for government business and tours are often tailored around meetings and conferences or sometimes cancelled altogether, so it's wise to phone ☎ 677 7129 beforehand.

Castle Tour

The main **Upper Yard** of the castle with a pedestrian entrance beneath the **Throne Room** can also be reached directly from Cork Hill or via the **Lower Yard**. From the main (Lower Yard) entrance, the castle tour takes you round the state chambers, developed during Dublin's British heyday, but still used for state occasions. The sequence of rooms visited on the tour may vary. From the entrance you ascend the stairs to the **Battle-Axe Landing**, where the viceroy's guards once stood, armed with battle-axes.

Turning left you pass through a series of drawing rooms, formerly used as bedrooms by visitors to the castle. One contains a Van Dyck painting of Elizabeth, second Viscountess of Southampton, at the age of 17, another a book painted on vellum between 1989 and 1991 as a sort of latterday Book of Kells. The castle gardens, visible from

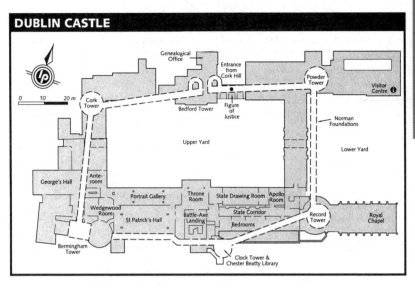

DUBLIN CASTLE

Genealogical Office

Entrance from Cork Hill

Powder Tower

Visitor Centre

Cork Tower

Bedford Tower

Figure of Justice

Norman Foundations

Upper Yard

Lower Yard

George's Hall

Ante-room

Portrait Gallery

Throne Room

State Drawing Room

Apollo Room

Wedgewood Room

St Patrick's Hall

Battle-Axe Landing

State Corridor

Record Tower

Royal Chapel

Bedrooms

Bermingham Tower

Clock Tower & Chester Beatty Library

0 10 20 m

the windows, end in a high wall said to have been built for Queen Victoria's visit to block out the distressing sight of the Stephen St slums. The wounded James Connolly was detained in the first of these rooms after the GPO siege of 1916 before being taken to Kilmainham Gaol to face a firing squad. The ceilings are notable for their beautiful plasterwork, some of which was rescued from Georgian buildings facing demolition elsewhere in the city.

At the end of this series of rooms you cross the **State Corridor** to enter the **Apollo Room** or Music Room, which has a lovely delicate ceiling dating from 1746 and originally installed in a house on Merrion Row but installed here in the 1960s. You then pass through the long State Corridor and enter the **State Drawing Room**, which suffered serious fire damage in 1941. It has been restored with period furniture and paintings dating from 1740. From there you enter the ornate **Throne Room**, built in 1740. It contains a large throne, said to have been presented to the castle by William of Orange (King William III) after he defeat-

ed King James II at the Battle of the Boyne, and a brass 'Act of Union' chandelier that weighs over a tonne and is decorated with roses, thistles and shamrocks.

The long **Portrait Gallery** has portraits of 19th century British viceroys and ends at an anteroom from where you enter George's Hall, added to the castle in 1911 for George V's visit to Ireland. From these rooms you return through the anteroom to the blue **Wedgewood Room** (yes, the whole room does look like Wedgewood china), which in turn leads to the **Bermingham Tower**, originally dating from 1411 but rebuilt between 1775 and 1777 after the original was damaged by an explosion. The tower was used as a prison on a number of occasions, especially during the independence struggle from 1918 to 1920.

Leaving the tower you pass through the 25m-long **St Patrick's Hall**. The knights of the Order of St Patrick, an order created in 1783, were invested here and their standards are displayed around the walls. Now, Irish presidents are inaugurated here and it is used for receptions. The painting on the ceiling shows St Patrick lighting the fire on Slane Hill, the Irish chieftains ceding power to the Anglo-Normans and the coronation of George III, who created the Order of St Patrick.

St Patrick's Hall ends at the Battle-Axe Landing, but the tour takes you down to the **Undercroft**. Remnants of the earlier Viking fort, the 13th century Powder Tower and the city wall can be seen in this excavation of the original moat, now below street level.

Bedford Tower & Genealogical Office

Other points of interest include the Bedford Tower and the Genealogical Office (established in 1552, though the present building dates from the 18th century), across the Upper Yard from the main entrance. In 1907 the collection known as the Irish

Crown Jewels was stolen from this tower and never recovered.

The entrance to the Upper Yard beside the Bedford Tower is topped by a figure of justice that has been a subject of both controversy and mirth. The fact that she faces the castle and has her back to the city was taken as an indicator of how much justice Irish citizens could expect from the British. Also, the scales of justice had a tendency to fill with rain and tilt in one direction or the other rather than balancing evenly. Eventually a hole was drilled in the bottom of each pan so the rainwater could drain out.

Royal Chapel

In the Lower Yard is the Church of the Holy Trinity, previously known as the Royal Chapel, which was built in Gothic style by Francis Johnston between 1807 and 1814. Decorating the cold, grey exterior are over 90 heads of various Irish personages and saints carved out of Tullamore limestone. The interior is wildly exuberant, with fan vaulting alongside quadripartite vaulting, wooden galleries, stained glass and lots of lively-looking sculpted angels.

Record Tower

Rising over the chapel is the Record Tower, used as a storage facility for official records from 1579 until their transfer to the Record Office in the Four Courts in the early 19th century. Although the tower was rebuilt in 1813 it retains much of its original appearance, including the massive 5m-thick walls. It now houses the Garda Museum, with exhibits dedicated to the history of the Irish police force.

Architect Francis Johnston refaced and added Gothic elements to the Record Tower in 1813.

Chester Beatty Library

Reached by a separate entrance on Ship St and housed in the Clock Tower is the castle's newest attraction, the world-famous Chester Beatty Library (☎ 269 2386), home of the collection of the mining engineer Sir Alfred Chester Beatty (1875-1968). It includes over 20,000 manuscripts, rare books, miniature paintings, clay tablets, costumes and other objects, predominantly from the

Middle East and Asia. There are various ancient bibles and the Arabic collection includes over 270 copies of the Koran. You'll also find texts and books from Tibet, Myanmar (Burma), Thailand and Mongolia and a large collection of Japanese prints. The European collection has fine examples of early books and numerous maps and prints, including a set of Turner's mezzotints. For many years housed in the fashionable suburb of Ballsbridge, the library completed its move to the castle in the spring of 1999 and was scheduled to open to the public in June that year. Opening hours are 10 am to 5 pm Tuesday to Friday and 2 to 5 pm on Saturday. Tours of the library are available on Wednesday and Saturday at 2.30 pm. Entry is free.

CITY HALL & MUNICIPAL BUILDINGS (Map 7)

Fronting Dublin Castle on Lord Edward St, the City Hall was built by Thomas Cooley from 1769 to 1779 as the Royal Exchange and later became the offices of the Dublin Corporation. The building has a Corinthian portico with six columns, statues of notable Irish citizens and a fine dome. It was built on the site of the Lucas Coffee House and the Eagle Tavern (Cork Hill rather than Eustace St version). Patrons of the tavern set up Dublin's infamous Hell Fire Club in 1735 (see the boxed text 'Dublin Clubs' under Newman House later in this chapter). Parliament St (1762), which leads up from the river to the front of City Hall, was the first of Dublin's wide boulevards to be laid out by the Commission for Making Wide & Convenient Streets.

The Municipal Buildings (1781), immediately west of the City Hall, were built by Thomas Ivory (1720-86), who was also responsible for the Genealogical Office in Dublin Castle.

ST WERBURGH'S CHURCH (Map 7)

In Werburgh St, south of Christ Church Cathedral and beside Dublin Castle, St Werburgh's stands on ancient foundations. Its early history, however, is unknown. It was rebuilt in 1662, 1715 and again in 1759 (with some elegance) after a fire in 1754. It is linked with the Fitzgerald family; Lord Edward Fitzgerald, who turned against Britain, joined the United Irishmen and was a leader of the 1798 Rising, is interred in the vault. In what was a frequent theme of Irish uprisings, compatriots gave him away and his death resulted from the wounds he received when captured. Major Henry Sirr, his captor, is buried in the graveyard.

Despite its long history, fine design and interesting interior, the church is rarely used today. Visiting hours are 10 am to 4 pm Monday to Friday. If you want to see inside, walk round the corner to 8 Castle St, where you'll find the caretaker who will open the church. Otherwise phone ☎ 478 3710.

Werburgh St was the location of Dublin's first theatre (see South Dublin Theatres later in this chapter), and Jonathan Swift was born off the street in Hoey's Court.

CHRIST CHURCH CATHEDRAL (Map 6)

Christ Church Cathedral (Church of the Holy Trinity; ☎ 677 8099) is on Christchurch Place, just south of the river, at the southernmost edge of Dublin's original Viking settlement. This was also the centre of medieval Dublin, with Dublin Castle nearby and the Tholsel or town hall (demolished in 1809) and the original Four Courts (demolished in 1796) both beside the cathedral. Nearby on Back Lane is the only remaining guild hall in Dublin, the Tailor's Hall (1706), now the office of An Taisce (National Trust for Ireland).

Originally built in wood by the Danes in 1038, the cathedral was rebuilt in stone from 1172, by Richard de Clare, earl of Pembroke, better known as the legendary Strongbow, the Anglo-Norman noble who invaded Ireland in 1170. The archbishop of Dublin at that time was Laurence (Lorcan in Irish) O'Toole, later to become St Laurence, patron saint of Dublin. Neither lived to see the building of the church completed, as Strongbow died in 1176 and O'Toole at Eu in Normandy in 1180. Nor was their cathedral destined to have a long life: the foundations were essentially a peat bog and the south wall collapsed in 1562, though it was soon rebuilt. Most of what you see from the outside dates from a major restoration (1871-78) by architect George Edmund Street. Above ground the north wall, the transepts and the western part of the choir are almost all that remain from the original.

Through much of its history Christ Church vied for supremacy with nearby St Patrick's Cathedral but, like its neighbour, it fell on hard times in the 18th and 19th centuries and it was virtually derelict by the time restoration took place. Earlier, the nave had been used as a market and the crypt had housed taverns. Today, both Church of Ireland cathedrals are somewhat neglected by the largely Catholic population of Dublin and making ends meet in an overwhelmingly Catholic country is not easy.

From the south-eastern entrance to the churchyard you walk past the ruins of the old Chapterhouse (1 on map), dating from 1230. The entrance to the cathedral (2) is at the south-western corner and you face the north wall as you enter. This wall survived the collapse of its southern counterpart, but has also suffered from subsidence, and from its eastern end it leans visibly – at the top it's about 0.5m out of perpendicular.

The southern side aisle has a monument to Strongbow (3). The armoured figure on the tomb is unlikely to be Strongbow (it's more probably the earl of Drogheda), but his internal organs may have been buried here. A popular legend relates that the half-figure beside the tomb is of Strongbow's son, who was cut in two by his father when his bravery in battle was suspect.

The South Transept (4) is one of the most original parts of the cathedral and contains the superb Baroque tomb of the 19th earl of Kildare (5), who died in 1734. His grandson, Lord Edward Fitzgerald, was a member of the United Irishmen and died in the abortive 1798 Rising. The entrance to the Chapel of St Laurence (6) is off the South Transept and contains two effigies, one of them reputed to be of either Strongbow's wife or sister. On a more macabre

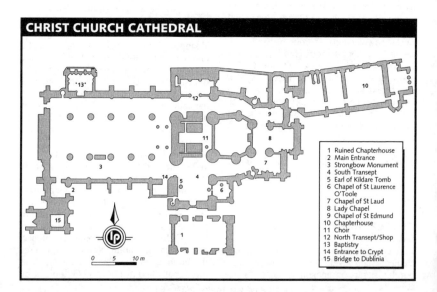

CHRIST CHURCH CATHEDRAL

1 Ruined Chapterhouse
2 Main Entrance
3 Strongbow Monument
4 South Transept
5 Earl of Kildare Tomb
6 Chapel of St Laurence O'Toole
7 Chapel of St Laud
8 Lady Chapel
9 Chapel of St Edmund
10 Chapterhouse
11 Choir
12 North Transept/Shop
13 Baptistry
14 Entrance to Crypt
15 Bridge to Dublinia

0   5   10 m

note, Laurence O'Toole's embalmed heart is in the Chapel of St Laud (7).

At the eastern end of the cathedral is the Lady Chapel (8) or Chapel of the Blessed Virgin Mary. Also at the east end is the Chapel of St Edmund (9) and the Chapterhouse (10), the latter closed to visitors. Parts of the Choir (11), in the centre of the church, and the North Transept (12) are original, but the Baptistry (13) was added during the 1871-78 restoration. There's a gift shop in the North Transept.

An entrance (14) by the South Transept descends to the unusually large arched crypt, which dates back to the original Viking church. Curiosities in the crypt include a glass display-case housing a mummified cat in the act of chasing a mummified mouse, frozen in pursuit inside an organ pipe in the 1860s. From the main entrance a bridge (15), part of the 1871-78 restoration, leads to Dublinia (see the following section).

Christ Church Cathedral is open from 10 am to 5.30 pm daily and a donation of IR£2/1 is requested.

DUBLINIA

Inside what was once the Synod Hall, which was added to Christ Church Cathedral in the restoration of 1871 to 1878, the Medieval Trust has created Dublinia (☎ 679 4611), an attempt to bring medieval Dublin to life. The ground floor has models of 10 episodes in Dublin's history, which are explained through headsets as you walk around. On the 1st floor, objects from medieval excavations on Wood Quay are displayed alongside a large model of the city. There are also models of the medieval quayside and of a cobbler's shop. On the top floor is the 'Medieval Fayre', a replica of a medieval fair outside the city gates. Displays include merchants' wares, a medicine stall, an armourer's pavilion, a medieval confessional booth and a bank. You can climb neighbouring St Michael's Tower for panoramic views over the city to the Dublin Hills. There is also a pleasant café and the inevitable souvenir shop.

Dublinia is open from 10 am to 5 pm daily between April and September and from 11 am to 4 pm Monday to Saturday and 10 am to 4.30 pm on Sunday in all other months. Admission costs IR£3.95/2.90 and includes entry into Christ Church Cathedral (accessible via the link bridge).

ST AUDOEN'S CHURCHES (Map 5)

St Audoen has two churches to his name, both just west of Christ Church Cathedral. The Church of Ireland version is the older and smaller building, and is the only surviving medieval parish church in the city. Its tower and door date from the 12th century, the aisle from the 15th century and various other parts from early times, but the church today is mainly a product of its 19th century restoration. The tower's bells include the three oldest in Ireland, dating from 1423. Further bells were added in 1790, 1864 and 1880; the newer ones were recast in 1983, and the original bells were retuned at the same time. The church is entered from the north through an arch beside Cook St. Part of the old city wall, this arch was built in 1240 and is the only surviving reminder of the city gates. At the time of writing the church was undergoing restoration by Dúchas (formerly the Office of Public Works).

Joined onto the Protestant church is the newer Catholic St Audoen's, a large church whose chief claim to local fame is Father Flash Kavanagh, who apparently used to read Mass at high speed so that his large congregation could head off to more absorbing Sunday pursuits, such as football matches. This St Audoen's was completed in 1846 after almost 30 years under construction; the dome was replaced in 1884 after it collapsed and the front, with its imposing Corinthian columns, was added in 1899. Inside, the church's high altar is flanked by reliefs of St Laurence O'Toole (see Christ Church Cathedral earlier in this chapter) and St Audoen.

Unfortunately, you're unlikely to find either church open.

ST PATRICK'S CATHEDRAL (Map 6)

St Patrick's Cathedral (☎ 475 4817) stands on one of Dublin's earliest Christian sites and the saint is said to have baptised converts at a well within the cathedral grounds. Like Christ Church Cathedral it was built on unstable ground, with the subterranean River Poddle flowing beneath its foundations. Because of the high water table, St Patrick's doesn't have a crypt but, again like its rival, it has had frequent restorations, alterations and additions.

The cathedral's current configuration dates mainly from some rather overenthusiastic restoration in 1864, which included the addition of the flying buttresses. More recently, the dismal slums that stood between the two cathedrals have been redeveloped. St Patrick's Park, the expanse of green beside the cathedral, was a crowded slum until it was cleared and its residents relocated in the early years of this century.

Although a church stood on the Patrick St site from as early as the 5th century, the present building dates from 1190 or 1225 – opinions differ. The stone Norman construction was rebuilt in the early 13th century in a style similar to its present form. At that time a struggle for religious supremacy was being waged between St Patrick's, outside the Dublin city walls, and Christ Church, within the walls. That Dublin ended up with two Protestant cathedrals indicates clearly that neither won a complete victory. St Patrick's still bears traces of the fortifications necessitated by its unprotected position.

Like Christ Church, the building has suffered a rather dramatic history. A storm brought down the spire in 1316, and soon afterwards the building was badly damaged in a fire. Another more disastrous fire fol-

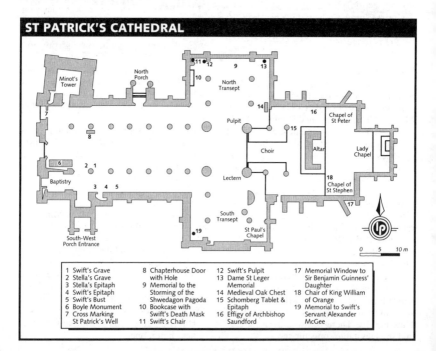

ST PATRICK'S CATHEDRAL

1 Swift's Grave	8 Chapterhouse Door	12 Swift's Pulpit	17 Memorial Window to
2 Stella's Grave	with Hole	13 Dame St Leger	Sir Benjamin Guinness'
3 Stella's Epitaph	9 Memorial to the	Memorial	Daughter
4 Swift's Epitaph	Storming of the	14 Medieval Oak Chest	18 Chair of King William
5 Swift's Bust	Shwedagon Pagoda	15 Schomberg Tablet &	of Orange
6 Boyle Monument	10 Bookcase with	Epitaph	19 Memorial to Swift's
7 Cross Marking	Swift's Death Mask	16 Effigy of Archbishop	Servant Alexander
St Patrick's Well	11 Swift's Chair	Saundford	McGee

The decorative cast-iron arch of Dublin's Ha'penny Bridge has virtually become a symbol for the city.

At Trinity College the main buildings are arranged around interconnecting open spaces.

lowed in 1362. In 1370 Archbishop Minot added the west tower that bears his name. For some reason it was built at a slight angle to the rest of the cathedral. In 1560 one of the first clocks in Dublin was added to the tower, and the 43m-high tower was subsequently topped by a 31m spire in 1749. During his visit to Ireland in 1649, Cromwell converted St Patrick's to a stable for his army's horses, an indignity to which he subjected other Irish churches. Jonathan Swift was the dean of the cathedral from 1713 until 1745 (see the boxed text on the following page), but prior to its mid-19th century restoration it was badly neglected.

Entering the cathedral from the south-west porch you come almost immediately to the graves of Swift (1) and Esther Johnson (2) or Stella, Swift's long-term companion. On the wall are the Latin epitaphs of Stella (3) and Swift (4), both written by the latter, and a bust of Swift (5). Also at this end of the cathedral is the huge Boyle Monument (6). Erected in 1632 by Richard Boyle, earl of Cork, it was decorated with numerous painted figures of members of his family. It briefly stood beside the altar until, in 1633, Dublin's viceroy, Thomas Wentworth, earl of Strafford, had it shifted from its prominent position. Wentworth won this round in his bitter conflict with Boyle, but the latter had the final say when he contrived to have Wentworth impeached and executed. The figure in the centre of the bottom level of the monument is the earl's five-year-old son, Robert Boyle (1627-91), who became a noted scientist. His contributions to physics include Boyle's Law, which sets out the relationship between the pressure and the volume of a gas.

In the north-western corner of the church is a cross on a stone slab (7), which once marked the position of St Patrick's original well. The South Transept was formerly a separate chapterhouse, and an old door (8), now simply leaning against a column at the west end of the cathedral, was once the entry to this.

During the cathedral's years of neglect and decay in the 18th and 19th centuries the

He's 'Armless

In 1492 a furious argument occurred in St Patrick's Cathedral between the earl of Kildare and the earl of Ormonde. Each was supported by his armed retainers, but when strong words were about to lead to blows the earl of Ormonde retreated to the chapterhouse. Fortunately, a peaceful settlement was reached and a hole was chopped through the door so the earls could shake hands on the agreement. In extending his arm through the door, thus making it vulnerable to attack from his opponent, the earl of Kildare added the phrase 'chancing one's arm' to the English language. The hole is still in the door.

North Transept was virtually a separate church. It now contains various military memorials to the Royal Irish Regiments. The first shots in the American War of Independence were fired at one of these Irish military banners. The military monuments also include a depiction of the British forces storming the great Shwedagon Pagoda in Yangon (Rangoon), Myanmar (9).

The Swift corner in the North Transept features a book-filled glass cabinet (10) containing his death mask, his chair (11) and Swift's pulpit (12). At the other side of the transept is a difficult-to-read memorial (13) to a certain Dame St Leger (1566-1603), who outlived two husbands before dying while giving birth to a child by her third, and a 14th century oak chest (14).

The northern choir aisle has a tablet (15) indicating the grave of the duke of Schomberg, who died during the Battle of the Boyne. Swift provided the duke's epitaph, caustically noting on it that the duke's own relatives couldn't be bothered to provide a suitable memorial. The aisle also has a marble effigy (16) of Archbishop Saundford, who built the Lady Chapel at the eastern end of the building in 1251 and died in 1271.

Jonathan Swift

St Patrick's Cathedral is inextricably linked with its famous dean, Jonathan Swift (1667-1745), the noted satirist, author of *Gulliver's Travels* among other writings, and tireless campaigner for fair treatment for the Irish. Swift was born at Hoey's Court, now a derelict little alley beside St Werburgh's Church and a stone's throw from either of Dublin's cathedrals. By the age of three he was said to be a fluent reader and, remarkably, he entered Trinity College when he was just 15 years old.

In 1689 Dublin was in turmoil, following the seizure of the British throne by William of Orange, and Swift moved to England, where he worked as secretary to the wealthy diplomat Sir William Temple. Swift's intelligence and scholarship were much appreciated by Sir William and, despite various trips to Ireland, Swift remained in his employ until the diplomat's death in 1699. Swift had been ordained as a priest in 1695 and he returned to Ireland to take up a variety of positions in the Irish church, first near Belfast, then near Dublin.

The publication of *The Battle of the Books* and *A Tale of a Tub* in 1704, together with a series of political pamphlets, began to cement Swift's reputation not only as a noted satirist and wit but also as an eccentric. He still commuted between Ireland and England, spending three years in England from 1710 to 1713, and yearned for a higher ecclesiastical position (a 'fat deanery or a lean bishopric') in the English church. His writings, however, had made him enemies and when the Whigs took over from the Tories in 1714 Swift found himself on the wrong side of the political divide. He retreated to Dublin, where he had become dean of St Patrick's Cathedral a year earlier.

Over the next 20 years Swift developed a keen social conscience and a deep concern for Irish impoverishment. He also made the transition from minor to major eccentric. His pen worked overtime righting wrongs, taking tyrants to task and attacking injustice wherever he saw it. His writing often took the form of anonymous tracts, such as his *Proposal for the Universal Use of Irish Manufactures* (1720), which suggested that the Irish take their revenge on England by burning anything from that country except its coal. Swift's *Drapier's Letters* (1724-25), ostensibly written by a humble trader, tore into a corrupt German duchess and her Irish business partner who were planning a crooked financial coup using a permit from the English king to mint coins. Their plan was to gain money by minting coins of copper instead of the standard gold or silver.

In 1729 *A Modest Proposal* modestly suggested that the children of poor Irish parents be eaten by the rich in order to reduce their parents' financial burden. First choice of the children, suggested Swift, should go to landlords who 'have already devoured their parents'. Despite this satirical defence of Irish children, it was said that Swift had absolutely no time

The Guinness family were big contributors to the cathedral's restoration and a monument (17) to Sir Benjamin Guinness' daughter stands beneath a window bearing the words 'I was thirsty and ye gave me drink'! The chapel also has a chair (18) used by William of Orange at a service in the cathedral after his victory at the Boyne.

The South Transept, where the clash between the earls of Ormonde and Kildare came to its conclusion, has various memorials, including one from Swift for his servant Alexander McGee (19).

The cathedral is open from 9 am to 6 pm Monday to Friday, 9 am to 5 pm on Saturday (to 4 pm November to February), and

Jonathan Swift

for them, so it is a curious twist that he is remembered today primarily for what is often seen as a children's tale, *Gulliver's Travels*, published in 1726.

Jonathan Swift

Swift's private life is full of intriguing mysteries, particularly those relating to Esther Johnson (1681-1728), better known as Stella, who was, depending on the tale, his innocent companion, his lover, his wife from a secretly conducted marriage, his niece or even his sister. He met her in England when she was just eight years old (and he was 22). She was the daughter of Sir William Temple's widowed housekeeper and it has been speculated that both Swift and Stella may have been the illegitimate offspring of Sir William. In 1701 he brought Stella to Ireland, with her chaperone, and lived with or near her until her death. At that time Swift lived in the deanery in the garden beside the cathedral (the present house is a replacement, built in 1781 after its predecessor burnt down). On the night when Stella's body lay in the church before her burial, Swift slept in a different bedroom so that he would not see the light in his cathedral. He completed *Journal to Stella* in the darkened cathedral on the nights following her death.

Swift's name is also associated with another Esther, Esther Vanhomrigh or Vanessa. Swift wrote to her with the suggestion that she should come to Dublin, because: 'you will get more for your money in Dublin than in London, and St Stephen's Green has the finest walking gravel in Europe'. Vanessa duly turned up in 1714, but the Irish attraction was more probably the dean than Dublin. The two soon fell out and Vanessa retreated to her town house on Foster Place (at that time known as Turnstile Alley) off College Green where she died, so it is said, of a broken heart. Her grave is said to be somewhere nearby, but now submerged under centuries of urban development.

Jonathan Swift's cantankerous final years were unhappy ones. Hearing loss, terrible headaches and dizzy spells combined to convince him that he was heading towards insanity. It was a possibility his enemies had, no doubt, been suggesting for years. He is remembered not only for his writing and his colourful but secretive personal life, but also for the steps he made towards identifying and promoting a uniquely Irish conscience and spirit.

10 to 11 am (from 9.30 am in summer) and 12.45 to 3 pm on Sunday (and 4.15 to 5 pm in summer). Entry is IR£2/1.50. The cathedral is accessible on bus No 50, 50A or 56A from Aston Quay or No 54 or 54A from Burgh Quay. The cathedral's choir school dates back to 1432 and the choir took part in the very first performance of

Handel's *Messiah* in 1742. You can hear the choir perform at 5.35 pm from Monday to Thursday (times may vary at Christmas).

MARSH'S LIBRARY (Map 6)

In St Patrick's Close beside St Patrick's Cathedral is Marsh's Library (☎ 454 3511), founded in 1701 by Archbishop Narcissus

Marsh (1638-1713) and opened in 1707. It was designed by Sir William Robinson, who was also responsible for the Royal Hospital Kilmainham. The oldest public library in the country, it contains 25,000 books dating from the 16th to the early 18th centuries, as well as maps, manuscripts (including one in Latin dating back to 1400) and a collection of incunabula, the technical term for a book printed before 1500. One of the oldest and finest of these is a volume of Cicero's *Letters to his Friends* printed in Milan in 1472.

The heart of the collection was the library of Edward Stillingfleet, bishop of Worcester. This hoard of almost 10,000 books was bought by Marsh in 1705 for UK£2500. Marsh's own extensive collection is also in the library, though he left his collection of Asian manuscripts to the Bodleian Library at Oxford University in England.

The collection also includes various items of Swifts, including his copy of *History of the Great Rebellion*. His margin notes include a number of comments vilifying Scots, of whom he seemed to have a low opinion. Swift also held a low opinion of Archbishop Marsh, whom he blamed for his not achieving the position in the church he, Swift, felt he deserved. Marsh died in 1713 and was buried in St Patrick's Cathedral. Ironically, when Swift died in 1745, he was buried near his former enemy.

Like the rest of the library, the three alcoves, in which scholars were once locked to peruse rare volumes, have remained virtually unchanged for three centuries. The skull in the furthest one doesn't, however, belong to some poor forgotten scholar – it's a cast of Swift's Stella's head. A bindery to repair and restore rare old books operates from the library, which makes an appearance in Joyce's *Ulysses*.

The library is open from 10 am to 12.45 pm and 2 to 5 pm on Monday and from Wednesday to Friday and from 10.30 am to 12.45 pm on Saturday. A donation of IR£2 is requested. You can reach the library by taking bus No 50, 50A or 56A from Aston Quay or No 54 or 54A from Burgh Quay.

DUBLIN CIVIC MUSEUM (Map 7)

In the 18th century Assembly House beside the Powerscourt Townhouse shopping centre, the Dublin Civic Museum (☎ 679 4260), 58 South William St, is close to Grafton St. Its displays are related to the city's history. In particular look out for the stone head of Lord Nelson toppled from its column in O'Connell St by the IRA in 1966. A showcase houses the small wax artists' models upon which the stone heads representing Ireland's rivers on the Custom House were based. Changing exhibits might include postcards, Dublin coal-hole covers or items relating to local shipwrecks.

The museum is open from 10 am to 5.45 pm, Tuesday to Saturday, and 11 am to 2 pm on Sunday; entry is free. It's worth dropping in just to see the architecture.

POWERSCOURT TOWNHOUSE SHOPPING CENTRE (Map 7)

Back from Grafton St on South William St is the elegantly converted Powerscourt Townhouse shopping centre, originally designed by Richard Castle. Built between 1771 and 1774 this grand house has a balconied courtyard and, following its conversion in 1981, shelters three levels of modern shops and restaurants. The Powerscourt family's main residence was Powerscourt House in County Wicklow and this city mansion was soon sold for commercial use. Currently it forms a convenient link from Grafton St to the South City Market on South Great George's St. The building features plasterwork by Michael Stapleton, who also worked on Belvedere House in north Dublin.

GRAFTON ST (Map 7)

Grafton St is the premier street south of the Liffey. It was the major traffic artery of south Dublin before it became a pedestrian precinct in 1982. It's now Dublin's fanciest, most colourful shopping centre with plenty of street life and the city's most entertaining buskers, including poets. The street is equally alive after dark as some of Dublin's most interesting pubs are clustered around it (see the Entertainment chapter).

As well as fine shops, such as the Brown Thomas department store (opened in 1848), Grafton St features the main branch of Bewley's Oriental Café, a Dublin institution for anything from a quick cup of coffee or tea to a filling meal. Upstairs in this branch the Joshua Museum relates the history of Bewley's. At the College Green end of the street is the statue of Molly Malone, rendered in such extreme deshabille that she's nicknamed 'the tart with the cart'.

MANSION HOUSE (Map 7)
The Mansion House, on Dawson St, was built in 1710 by Joshua Dawson, after whom the street is named. Five years later the house was bought as a residence for the lord mayor of Dublin. The building's original brick Queen Anne style has all but disappeared behind a stucco façade added in the Victorian era. The building was the site for the 1919 Declaration of Independence, but isn't open to the public.

ROYAL IRISH ACADEMY (Map 7)
Next door to the Mansion House is the seat of Ireland's pre-eminent society of letters, the Royal Irish Academy (☎ 676 2570). Its 18th century library houses many important documents, including an extensive collection of ancient manuscripts such as the Book of Dun Cow. Also held there is the entire library of 18th century poet Sir Thomas Moore. Opening hours are 10.30 am to 5 pm Monday to Friday; entry is free.

NATIONAL MUSEUM (Map 6)
The National Museum (☎ 677 7444), on Kildare St, was designed by Sir Thomas Newenham Deane and completed in 1890. The star attraction is the Treasury, with its two superb collections (one of Bronze and Iron Age gold objects, the other from the medieval period) and a related audio-visual display.

Other exhibits focus on the 1916 Easter Rising and the independence struggle from 1900 to 1921. Numerous displays relate to this important period of modern Irish history, although sadly the moving prison letters written by leaders of the Easter Rising have been put into storage. Viking Age Dublin upstairs displays exhibits from the excavations at Wood Quay – the area between Christ Church Cathedral and the river, where Dublin Corporation has its headquarters. Recent additions to the Viking display include a full-scale longboat in the square at the front of the museum.

An appendage of the National Museum in Merrion Row (Map 6) houses its geological collections. The museum's collections of Irish decorative arts, ceramics and musical instruments, and of Japanese decorative arts, have been moved to Collins Barracks (Map 3) in Benburb St off Ellis Quay.

The museum is open from 10 am to 5 pm, Tuesday to Saturday and from 2 to 5 pm on Sunday. Entry is free but donations are welcome; guided tours cost IR£1. There's a good café on the ground floor.

Bronze & Iron Age Gold Objects
Ireland's early Celtic artisans produced beautiful gold objects and many of those on display are stunning. The Royal Irish Academy started the collection in the late 18th century and archaeological finds continue to be made. Little is known about the source of Ireland's gold, but wherever it came from gold, bronze and copper were all being worked in Ireland by 2000 BC.

In the 500 years from around 2200 BC, gold was often beaten into thin sheets to produce sun discs or crescent-shaped ornaments known as *lunalae*. The sheet gold was decorated with patterns either from the front or by making a raised pattern from behind by the technique known as repoussé.

Around 1200 to 1000 BC, larger quantities of gold were used to make earrings, bracelets, necklaces or even waistbands. During this period gold in sheet form was also beaten into armbands. Later still, a wider range of highly decorated gold objects were produced using gold wire or gold foil or by techniques such as casting.

Among the items produced were neck rings, dress-fasteners and bracelets.

The many gold objects found in Ireland have only rarely been found during archaeological excavations. It was common for gold objects to be hidden in remote hoards, and in recent times these have been discovered in the course of ploughing land for farms, cutting peat for fuel, quarrying for building materials or preparing railway tracks. One of the earliest recorded discoveries of a gold hoard was in 1670. Many hoards have been found in bogs, which suggests that these areas had some important significance to Irish people in the Bronze Age. During a 70 year period in the 18th century numerous hoards were found in County Tipperary's Bog of Cullen, but almost all of the gold was melted down.

The following are some of the museum's finest displays.

Broighter Hoard Discovered in County Derry in 1896, this collection of fine gold objects from the 1st century BC includes a large gold collar of a standard of artisanship unsurpassed anywhere in Europe. Other finds include twisted-gold neck ornaments and a model of a galley complete with oars.

Gleninsheen Gorget This magnificent gold collar dating from around 800 to 700 BC was found in County Clare in 1932.

Mooghaun Hoard The Mooghaun Hoard from County Clare was discovered by railway workers in 1854, and in that year the Royal Irish Academy displayed 146 objects weighing a total of 5kg, including sheet gold collars, gold neck rings and gold bracelets. Unfortunately, only 29 objects have survived; the rest of the find was probably melted down. Replicas are displayed at the museum.

Other Displays The Ballinesker Hoard is a collection of cloak-fasteners, boxes and discs discovered in 1990 in County Wexford. The Dowris Hoard of the 8th to 6th centuries BC was a huge find made in 1820.

The wonderful Loughnasade bronze war trumpet dates from the 1st century BC. There are other superb gold collars from the same era as the Gleninsheen Gorget.

Medieval Objects

During the Dark Ages in Europe, Ireland's monasteries were beacons of knowledge and scholarship. Some of the beautiful religious objects in the gallery amply reflect the strengths of that period.

Ardagh Chalice This 8th century chalice from County Limerick was found in 1868 and is thought to have been hidden around the 10th century AD. The elaborately constructed and decorated chalice was used to dispense wine during religious ceremonies. The bowl and base of the chalice are of silver but the find also included silver-gilded brooches and a bronze chalice.

Cross of Cong The 12th century Cross of Cong was made of wood, bronze and silver to enshrine a fragment of wood said to come from the True Cross. This holy relic was presented by Pope Calixtus II to the King of Connaught in 1123 but has since disappeared. The cross remained in Cong, County Mayo, until 1839, when it was bought by the National Museum.

St Patrick's Bell & Shrine Dating from sometime between the 5th and the 8th centuries, St Patrick's Bell is said to have belonged to Ireland's patron saint. Around 1100 AD a shrine of gold wire on a silver backplate was made to house the bell. Originally from Armagh in County Armagh, the bell and shrine were once carried off by a Norman baron and subsequently handed down through generations of the Mulholland family until the late 18th century.

Tara Brooch The elaborately decorated, 8th century Tara Brooch, found in County Meath, is made of gold wire and gold strips embellished with amber and enamel. It consists of three parts – a ring, a pin and a long chain. It has no connection with the ancient kingdom of Tara, but is one of the finest examples of craftwork from that time. The Tara Brooch is classified as a pseudo-penannular brooch. Penannular brooches were used between the late Iron Age and the early medieval period to fasten cloaks.

NATIONAL GALLERY (Map 6)

Opened in 1864, the National Gallery (☎ 661 5133) looks out on Merrion Square. Its excellent collection is strong in Irish art, but there are also high-quality collections of every major school of European painting. On the lawn in front of the gallery is a statue of the Irish railways magnate William Dargan, who organised the 1853 Dublin Industrial Exhibition at this spot; the profits from the exhibition were used to found the gallery. The building itself was designed by Francis Fowke, whose architectural credits also include London's Victoria & Albert Museum. Nearby is a statue of George Bernard Shaw, who was a major benefactor of the gallery. The gallery has three wings: the original Dargan Wing, the Milltown Rooms, which were added between 1899 and 1903, and the Modern Wing added from 1964 to 1968.

The Dargan Wing's ground floor has the imposing Shaw Room, lined with full-length portraits and illuminated by a series of spectacular Waterford-crystal chandeliers. Upstairs, the rooms are dedicated to the Italian Early and High Renaissance, 16th century north Italian art and 17th and 18th century Italian art. The highlight here is undoubtedly Caravaggio's *The Taking of Christ*, which lay undiscovered for over 60 years in a Jesuit house in Leeson St, and was found accidentally by the chief curator of the gallery, Sergio Benedetti, in the early 1990s. Fra Angelico, Titian and Tintoretto are among the other artists represented.

The central Milltown Rooms were built to hold Russborough House's art collection, which was presented to the gallery in 1902. The ground floor displays the gallery's fine Irish collection plus a smaller British collection, with works by Reynolds, Hogarth, Gainsborough, Landseer and Turner. One

highlight is the room at the back of the gallery displaying works by Jack B Yeats (1871-1957), younger brother of WB Yeats. Other rooms relate to specific periods and styles of Irish art. Upstairs, the Milltown Rooms contain works from Germany, the Netherlands and Spain. There are rooms of works by Rembrandt and his circle and by Spanish artists of Seville. The Spanish collection features works by El Greco, Goya and Picasso.

The Modern Wing houses modern works and also has French works by Degas, Delacroix, Millet, Monet and Pissarro.

The gallery also has an art reference library, a lecture theatre, a good bookshop and an excellent and deservedly popular restaurant. The gallery hours are from 10 am to 5.30 pm Monday to Saturday (to 8.30 pm Thursday), and 2 to 5 pm on Sunday. Entry is free and there are guided tours at 3 pm on Saturday and at 2.30, 3.15 and 4 pm on Sunday.

LEINSTER HOUSE – IRISH PARLIAMENT (Map 6)

Ireland's parliament, the *Oireachtas na hÉireann*, meets in Leinster House on Kildare St. Both the lower house (*Dáil*) and the upper house or senate (*Seanad*) meet here. The entrance to Leinster House from Kildare St is flanked by the National Library and the National Museum. The house was originally built as Kildare House from 1745 to 1748 for the earl of Kildare, but its name was changed when he also became the duke of Leinster in 1766.

Leinster House was designed by Richard Castle in the Palladian style (Castle was a big fan of the Italian architect Palladio) and is considered the forerunner of the Georgian style that became the norm for the city's finer residences. The Kildare St frontage was designed to look like a town house (which inspired Irish architect James Hoban's designs for the American White House), whereas the Merrion Square frontage was made to resemble a country house. Interestingly, the Duke of Leinster was the first of Dublin's genteel class to settle on the south side of the Liffey, away from the then posh north side, thus beginning a trend that continues today.

At the other end of the lawn from the statue of Dargan is a statue of Prince Albert, Queen Victoria's consort. Queen Victoria herself was commemorated in massive form on the Kildare St side from 1908 until the statue was removed in 1948. The obelisk in front of the building is dedicated to Arthur Griffith, Michael Collins and Kevin O'Higgins, architects of independent Ireland.

The Dublin Society, later renamed the Royal Dublin Society, bought the building in 1814 but moved out in stages between 1922 and 1925, when the first government of the Irish Free State decided to establish its parliament there.

The Seanad meets in the north-wing saloon, while the 166 member Dáil meets in a less-interesting room that was originally a lecture theatre added to the original building in 1897. When parliament is sitting visitors are admitted to an observation gallery. You get an entry ticket from the Kildare St entrance on production of some identification. Parliament sits for 90 days a year, usually between November and May, on Tuesday (from 2.30 to 8.30 pm), Wednesday (from 10.30 am to 8.30 pm) and Thursday (from 10.30 am to 5.30 pm). When the Daíl is not in session, guided tours of the parliament building are available from Monday to Friday. Call ☎ 618 3000 for details.

GOVERNMENT BUILDINGS (Map 6)

On Upper Merrion St, on the south side of the Natural History Museum, the domed Government Buildings, designed in a rather heavy-handed Edwardian interpretation of the Georgian style, were opened in 1911. On Saturdays free 40-minute tours are conducted from 10.30 am to 12.30 pm and 1.30 to 4.50 pm. Tickets are available from the National Gallery ticket office. Each tour takes about 16 people, so you may have to wait a while for a group to assemble. Tours can't be booked in advance, but on Saturday

morning you can put your name down for one later in the day. You get to see the Taoiseach's office, the cabinet room, the ceremonial staircase with a stunning stained-glass window designed for the 1939 New York Trade Fair, and innumerable fine examples of modern Irish arts and crafts.

NATIONAL LIBRARY (Map 6)

To the north of the Kildare St entrance to Leinster House is the National Library, built from 1884 to 1890 at the same time as the National Museum and to a similar design by Sir Thomas Newenham Deane and his son Sir Thomas Manly Deane. Leinster House, the library and museum belonged to the Royal Dublin Society (formed in 1731), which aimed to improve conditions for poor people and to promote the arts and sciences. The library's extensive collection has many valuable early manuscripts, first editions, maps and other items of interest. Temporary displays are often held in the entrance area, and the library's reading room features in *Ulysses*. There's also an hour-long audiovisual presentation on the mezzanine floor. The library is open between 10 am and 9 pm on Monday, from 2 to 5 pm on Tuesday and Wednesday, from 10 am to 5 pm Thursday and Friday and 10 am to 1 pm on Saturday.

HERALDIC MUSEUM & GENEALOGICAL OFFICE (Map 6)

On the corner of Kildare St and Leinster St, the former home of the Kildare St Club (an important right-wing institution during Dublin's Anglo-Irish heyday) is shared by the Heraldic Museum, the Genealogical Office and the Alliance Française. The Genealogical Office is a popular destination for visitors attempting to trace their Irish roots. A session with a genealogical expert costs IR£25 per hour, so you're better off attempting the trace yourself. Note the whimsical though rather worn stone carvings of animals that decorate the building's windows, especially the monkeys playing billiards to the right of the door.

The Heraldic Museum's displays follow the story of heraldry in Ireland and Europe. It's open from 10 am to 8.30 pm, Monday to Wednesday, from 10 am to 4.30 pm, Thursday and Friday, and from 10 am to 12.30 pm on Saturday; admission is free.

NATURAL HISTORY MUSEUM (Map 6)

Just as the National Library and the National Museum flank the entrance to Leinster House on the Kildare St side, the National Gallery and Natural History Museum do the same on the Upper Merrion St/Merrion Square side.

The Natural History Museum (☎ 677 7444) is a rather musty place, scarcely changed since 1857 when Scottish explorer Dr David Livingstone delivered the opening lecture. It's hardly surprising that it's known as 'the dead zoo'. Despite this, the museum is worth a visit, as its collection is huge and well kept. That moth-eaten look often afflicting neglected stuffed-animal collections has been kept at bay and children are likely to find it fascinating. The collection includes three skeletons of the giant deer, the Irish elk, which became extinct about 10,000 years ago; a Tasmanian tiger (mislabelled as a Tasmanian wolf), the probably extinct but still much-searched-for Australian marsupial; a giant panda from China; several African and Asian rhinoceroses and plenty more.

The museum hours are from 10 am to 5 pm Tuesday to Saturday, and 2 to 5 pm on Sunday. Entry is free.

ST STEPHEN'S GREEN (Map 6)

On warm summer days the nine hectares of St Stephen's Green provide a popular lunch-time escape for city workers. The green was originally an expanse of open common land where public whippings, burnings and hangings took place. The green was enclosed by a fence in 1664

Tracing Your Ancestors

Tracing your ancestors is a popular activity for visitors to Ireland, and many tourists, mainly from Canada, the USA and Australia, come to Ireland purely to track down their Irish roots. Success in this activity is more likely if you've conducted some basic research in your home country – in particular, if you've been able to obtain the date and point of arrival of your ancestor(s) – before you come to Ireland.

In Dublin the Genealogical Office (Map 6, ☎ 661 8811), which includes the Heraldic Museum, is at 2 Kildare St, Dublin 2, on the corner with Leinster St. For a small fee they offer a consultation service on how to trace your ancestry, which is a good way to begin your research if you have no other experience. For information on commercial agencies that will do the research for you contact the Association of Professional Genealogists in Ireland (APGI), c/o the Genealogical Office. The Birth, Deaths & Marriages Register (☎ 671 1863) of Dublin City, the files of the National Library (☎ 661 8811) and the National Archives (☎ 478 3711) at the Four Courts are all potential sources of genealogical information. The National Archive Records in Dublin Castle are of particular interest to Australians whose ancestors may have arrived in Australia as convicts.

A huge number of books is available on the subject. *The Irish Roots Guide* by Tony McCarthy serves as a useful introduction. Other publications include *Tracing Your Irish Roots* by Christine Kineally and *Tracing Your Irish Ancestors: A Comprehensive Guide* by John Grenham. All these publications, and other items of genealogical concern, may be obtained from the Genealogy Bookshop, 3 Nassau St, Dublin 2 (Map 7).

when the Dublin Corporation sold off the surrounding land for buildings. A stone wall replaced the fence in 1669 and trees and gravel paths soon followed within. By the end of the 17th century restrictions were already in force prohibiting buildings of less than two storeys or those constructed of mud and wattle. At the same time Grafton St, the main route to the green from what was then central Dublin, was upgraded from a 'foule and out of repaire' laneway to a crown causeway.

The fine Georgian buildings around the square date mainly from Dublin's mid to late 18th century Georgian prime. At that time the northern side was known as the Beaux Walk and it is still a centre for some of Dublin society's most esteemed meeting places. Further improvements were made, with seats being put in place in 1753, but in 1814 railings and locked gates were added and an annual fee of one guinea was charged to use the green. This private use continued until 1877 when Sir Arthur Edward Guinness, later Lord Ardilaun, pushed an act through parliament once again opening the green to the public. He also financed the central park's gardens and ponds, which date from 1880.

A variety of statues and memorials dot the green and, since it was Guinness money that created the park you see today, it's only right that there should be an 1892 statue of Sir Arthur, on the western side of the park. Just north of the Guinness statue, but outside the railing, is a statue of Irish patriot Robert Emmet (1778-1803), born across the road at No 124-25, though his actual birthplace has been demolished. The statue was placed here in 1966 and is a replica of an Emmet statue in Washington DC.

Across the road from the western side of the green are the **Unitarian Church** (1863) and the **Royal College of Surgeons**, which has one of the finest façades on St Stephen's Green. It was built in 1806 and extended from 1825 to 1827 to the design of William Murray. Forty years later Murray's son, William G Murray, designed the Royal College of Physicians building on Kildare

St. In the 1916 Easter Rising, the Royal College of Surgeons was occupied by the colourful Countess Markievicz (1868-1927), an Irish nationalist married to a Polish count. The columns still bear bullet marks from the fighting.

The main entrance to the green was once on this side, but is now reached through the **Fusiliers' Arch** at the north-western corner of the green, which leads from Grafton St. Modelled to look like a smaller version of the Arch of Titus in Rome, the arch commemorates the 212 soldiers of the Royal Dublin Fusiliers who were killed while fighting for the British in the Boer War (1899-1902).

A path from the arch passes by the murky duck pond where you can see bar-headed geese, Canada geese, greylag geese, white-fronted geese, wigeons, tufted ducks, mandarin ducks, moorhens, coots and mallards. Around the fountain in the centre of the green are several statues, including a bust of Countess Markievicz. Nearby are a bust of the poet James Clarence Mangan (1803-49) and a curious sculpture (1967) of WB Yeats by Henry Moore. The centre of the park also has a garden for the blind, complete with signs in Braille and plants that can be handled.

On the eastern side of the green is a children's play park and to the south there's a fine old bandstand, erected to celebrate Queen Victoria's jubilee in 1887. Musical performances often take place here in the summer. Near the bandstand is a bust of James Joyce, facing Newman House of University College Dublin, where he was once a student.

Just inside the green at the south-eastern corner, near Leeson St, is a statue of the Three Fates, presented to Dublin in 1956 by West Germany in gratitude for Irish aid after WWII. The north-western corner, opposite the Shelbourne Hotel and Merrion Row, is marked by the Wolfe Tone Monument to the leader of the abortive 1796 invasion. The vertical slabs serving as a backdrop to Wolfe Tone's statue have been dubbed 'Tonehenge'. Just inside the park at this entrance is a memorial to the victims of the mid-19th century Potato Famine.

Unfortunately, some of Dublin's biggest architectural mistakes have been made around St Stephen's Green. Some notable buildings still remain, however, such as the imposing Shelbourne Hotel (1867) on the northern side of the green, with statues of Nubian princesses and their ankle-fettered slave girls decorating the front. Just to the east of the Shelbourne is a small Huguenot cemetery dating from 1693, when many French Huguenots fled here from persecution under Louis XIV.

Some of Dublin's most interesting streets radiate from the green. Grafton St, the main shopping avenue of Dublin, runs from the north-western corner, while Merrion Row, with its popular pubs, runs from the north-eastern. At the south-east is Leeson St, replete with fine Georgian residences. The Hotel Conrad, Dublin's Hilton Hotel, is just off the square from this corner on Earlsfort Terrace, as is the National Concert Hall.

Harcourt St, from the south-western corner, was laid out in 1775. Well known names associated with the street include Edward Carson, born at No 4 in 1854; as the architect of Northern Irish 'Unionism' he is an easy scapegoat for many of the problems caused by Ireland's division. Bram Stoker, author of *Dracula*, lived at No 16 and George Bernard Shaw at No 61. From 1859 to 1958 the Dublin-Bray railway line finished at Harcourt St station, then at the bottom of this road.

Iveagh House

At No 80-81 on the southern side of the green is Iveagh House, the former home of the Guinness family. Today the building houses the Department of Foreign Affairs. Designed by Richard Castle in 1730, this was his first project in Dublin.

Newman House

At No 85-86 on the southern side of the green is Newman House, which has had an interesting history and is now part of University College Dublin. The main campus is out at Belfield in Donnybrook, between Dublin and Dun Laoghaire.

These buildings have some of the finest plasterwork in the city. No 85 was built between 1736 and 1738 by Richard Castle for the parliamentarian Hugh Montgomery. The plasterwork was by the Italian stuccodores Paulo and Filipo LaFranchini and can be best appreciated in the wonderfully detailed Apollo Room on the ground floor. In 1865 the building was acquired by the Catholic University of Ireland, predecessor of University College Dublin, and was then passed to the Jesuits. Some of the plasterwork was a little too detailed for Jesuit tastes, however, so covers were prescribed for parts of the work. On the ceiling of the upstairs Saloon, previously naked female figures were covered with what can best be described as furry swimsuits. One such modesty vest has survived restoration.

Richard Chapel Whaley MP had taken possession of No 85 in 1765 but decided to display his wealth by constructing a grander home next door at No 86. This was still the southern edge of the city at the time and open fields spread to the south. Whaley commissioned Robert West to do the plasterwork, but despite the larger scale the work is not up to the standards set by No 85. Like Hugh Montgomery, the original owner of No 85, Whaley was a member of the Irish Parliament and his son, Buck Whaley, contrived to become a member of parliament while still a teenager. Buck Whaley also became one of the more notorious members of Dublin's Hell Fire Club (see the boxed text 'Dublin Clubs' on the next page). He was also a noted gambler, once walking all the way to Jerusalem for a bet.

After the buildings were acquired by the Catholic University, the names of James Joyce, Gerard Manley Hopkins and Flann O'Brien were all connected with the university, and Newman House was named after its first rector, John Henry Newman. Gerard Manley Hopkins, professor of classics at the college from 1884 until his death in 1889 aged just 44, lived upstairs at No 86. His rather gloomy writing only gained

Dublin Clubs

In its Georgian heyday Dublin had a number of colourful gentlemen's clubs where distinctly ungentlemanly conduct was frequently tolerated. Daly's Club, 2-3 Dame St, opposite the Bank of Ireland near the Trinity College entrance, was founded around 1750 in Patrick Daly's coffee house. It is said that members of the club used to use the statue of St Andrew in St Andrew's Church on Suffolk St for target practice. Forty years later the club had become so popular among Dublin's socialites that a new clubhouse had to be built. By the early 1820s, however, it had retreated into exclusiveness and folded up.

By this time the Kildare St Club was the prestige Dublin club, having moved to its site on the corner of Kildare and Leinster Sts, beside Trinity College, in 1782. The Venetian-style building they erected on this site in 1861 has been described as one of the most distinguished Dublin constructions of the period. The comical stone animals that decorate the windows are one of the building's more appealing touches. It's now occupied by the Alliance Française, and the Kildare St Club has amalgamated with the University Club and can be found beside St Stephen's Green.

The most colourful of the Dublin clubs was undoubtedly the Hell Fire Club, which was founded in 1735 and used to meet in the Eagle Tavern on Cork Hill, in front of Dublin Castle. The members liked to play up to their colourful image and it is said they once burnt the building down in an attempt to create a more infernal ambience. On at least one occasion the devil is said to have made a personal appearance at a club function, but there's no evidence that debauchery, black magic or other such lurid activities really took place.

The club's founder, Richard Parsons, earl of Rosse, is said to have been 'fond of all the vices which the beau monde call pleasures, and by those means first impaired his fortune as much as he possibly could do; and finally, his health beyond repair'. Buck Whaley (see the section on Newman House, St Stephen's Green) was another notorious Hell Fire Club member. The club's out-of-town premises on top of Montpelier Hill in the Dublin Mountains still stands. To get there, go to Rathfarnham, about 6km south-west of central Dublin, and then follow the road through Ballyboden and Woodtown to the summit.

wide appreciation some time after his death. Hopkins' bedroom is preserved as it would have been during his residence. Joyce was a Bachelor of Arts student of the college between 1899 and 1902; Patrick Pearse, leader of the 1916 Easter Rising, and Eamon de Valera, leader of Sinn Féin and Fianna Fáil and, later, president of Ireland were also students here.

The house is open from June to August and can only be visited as part of an organised tour. Tours run at 12, 2, 3 and 4 pm, Tuesday to Friday, on the hour from 11 am to 1 pm on Saturday and on the hour from 2 to 4 pm on Sunday. Entry costs IR£2/1 and each tour lasts about 40 minutes. Tours can be organised at other times of the year; call ☎ 475 7255 for details.

Newman University Church

Next to Newman House is the Catholic Newman University Church, built between 1854 and 1856 with an incongruous neo-Byzantine interior that attracted a lot of criticism at the time. It features much coloured marble, lots of gold leaf, and all in all, the effect is pleasant. Around the walls are plaques illustrating the Stations of the Cross and there's a bust of Cardinal Newman on the right-hand side. Today this is one of the most fashionable churches in Dublin for weddings.

Iveagh Gardens

Just behind Newman House and visible from Hopkins' room in Newman House are the landscaped Iveagh Gardens, accessible from Earlsfort Terrace or Harcourt St. The gardens are one of the city's secret jewels, scarcely visited as the imposing walls that surround them give the impression that they are private. It is one of the best places to relax on a summer's day or before a show in the National Concert Hall. They are open all year from dawn to dusk.

RHA Gallagher Gallery

Just off St Stephen's Green at Ely Place is the Royal Hibernian Academy Gallagher Gallery (☎ 661 2558), a large, well lit gallery that concentrates exclusively on the work of modern Irish and international artists. It is commonly accepted that if your work is shown here, you must either be very good and dead or extremely good and alive. The gallery is open from 11 am to 5 pm Monday to Wednesday, Friday and Saturday, 11 am to 9 pm Thursday and 2 to 5 pm on Sunday.

MERRION SQUARE (Map 6)

Merrion Square, with its well kept central park, dates back to 1762 and has the National Gallery on its western side, while the other three sides are lined with elegant Georgian buildings. Around this square are the hallmarks of the best Georgian Dublin entrances – elegant doors and peacock fanlights, ornate door knockers and more than a few foot-scrapers where gentlemen removed mud from their shoes before venturing indoors. Merrion Square residents have included, at 1 North Merrion Square, the surgeon Sir William Wilde and the poet Lady 'Speranza' Wilde, parents of the even more famous Oscar Wilde, who was born in 1854 at the now near-derelict 21 Westland Row, just north of the square. Wilde enthusiasts will enjoy the new statue of the playwright at the north-western corner of the square. It is surrounded by inscriptions of some of the witty one-liners, for which he was famous.

Other Merrion Square personalities were WB Yeats (1865-1939), who lived first at 52 East Merrion Square and later, from 1922 to 1928, at 82 South Merrion Square. Others along South Merrion Square included George (Æ) Russell (1867-1935), the 'poet, mystic, painter and co-operator', who worked at No 84. Daniel O'Connell (1775-1847) was a resident of No 58 in his later years. The Austrian Erwin Schrödinger (1887-1961), co-winner of the 1933 Nobel Prize for physics, lived at No 65 between 1940 and 1956. Dublin seemed to attract authors of horror stories and Joseph Sheridan Le Fanu (1814-73), who penned the vampire classic *Carmilla*, was a resident of No 70. The UK embassy occupied 39 East Merrion Square until it was burnt out in 1972 in protest against events in Derry, Northern Ireland, when 13 civilians were killed by the British army.

Damage to fine Dublin buildings hasn't always been the prerogative of vandals, terrorists or protesters. East Merrion Square once continued into Lower Fitzwilliam St in the longest unbroken series of Georgian houses in Europe. Despite this, in 1961 the Electricity Supply Board knocked down 26 of them to build an office block. The Architectural Association, however, is based in a genuine Georgian house, at 8 North Merrion Square, a few doors along from the Wilde residence.

The Leinster Lawn at the western end of the square has the fine Rutland Fountain (1791) and an 18m-high obelisk honouring the founders of independent Ireland. On the south side is a statue of Michael Collins (1890-1922), one of the architects of Ireland's independence, who was assassinated during the ensuing Civil War. Merrion Square hasn't always been merely graceful and affluent, however. During the Potato Famine (1845-51), soup kitchens were set up in the gardens, which were crowded with starving rural refugees.

Number 29

At the south-eastern corner of Merrion Square the Electricity Supply Board, having demolished most of Lower Fitzwilliam St for its new office block, had the decency to preserve one of the fine old Georgian houses. Originally built in 1794, it has been restored by the National Museum to give a good impression of genteel home life in Dublin between 1790 and 1820. Everything is genuine, from the furniture to the paint on the walls. The first occupants were Mrs Olivia Beatty, the widow of a wealthy wine merchant, and her children. Property speculation was obviously a consideration even at that time as she paid UK£320 for it in 1794 but sold it 12 years later for UK£700.

The house (☎ 702 6165) is open from 10 am to 5 pm Tuesday to Saturday and 2 to 5 pm on Sunday, closing for two weeks before Christmas. Visitors are shown a short film on the house's history then join a 30 minute tour in groups of nine or less. Entry is IR£2.50/1.

UPPER MERRION ST & ELY PLACE (Map 6)

Upper Merrion St runs south from Merrion Square towards St Stephen's Green. Mornington House, 24 Upper Merrion St, is thought to be the birthplace of the Duke of Wellington, who downplayed his Irish origins, although it's possible that his actual birthplace was Trim in County Meath. The building is now part of the Merrion Hotel (see the Places to Stay chapter), Dublin's newest and most upmarket hotel.

On the other side of Baggot St, Upper Merrion St becomes Ely (pronounced 'e-lie') Place. Built around 1770 this classic Georgian street features some well preserved houses and has many interesting historical associations.

John Philpot Curran (1750-1817), a great advocate of Irish liberty, once lived at No 4, as did the novelist George Moore (1852-1933). No 6 was the residence of the earl of Clare. Better known as Black Jack Fitzgibbon (1749-1802), he was a bitter opponent of Irish political aspirations and in 1794 a mob attempted to storm the house. **Ely House**, at No 8, is one of the best examples of a Georgian mansion in Dublin. The plas-

terwork is by Michael Stapleton and the staircase, which illustrates the Labours of Hercules, is one of the finest in the city. At one time the surgeon Sir Thornley Stoker (brother of Bram Stoker the creator of Dracula) lived here. Oliver St John Gogarty (1878-1957) lived for a time at No 25, but it's now occupied by the art gallery of the Royal Hibernian Academy.

FITZWILLIAM SQUARE (Map 6)

South of Merrion Square and east of St Stephen's Green is Fitzwilliam Square. Built between 1791 and 1825, it was the smallest and the last of Dublin's great Georgian squares. It's also the only one where the central garden is still the private domain of the square's residents. William Dargan (1799-1867), the railway pioneer and founder of the National Gallery, lived at No 2, and the artist Jack B Yeats (1871-1957) lived at No 18. Look out for the attractive 18th and 19th century metal coal-hole covers. Today the square is a centre for the Dublin medical profession.

OTHER SOUTH DUBLIN CHURCHES
St Andrew's Church (Map 7)

This Protestant Gothic-style former church, on the corner of Suffolk St and St Andrew's St near Trinity College and Grafton St, was designed by Charles Lanyon and built between 1860 and 1873 on the site of an ancient nunnery. It is now the headquarters of the Dublin Tourism organisation. There is also a Catholic St Andrew's Church (Map 6) behind Trinity College on Westland Row, beside Pearse station.

Whitefriars Carmelite Church (Map 6)

On Aungier St, the Carmelite Church stands on the former site of the Whitefriars Carmelite monastery founded in 1278. The monastery was suppressed by Henry VIII in 1537 and its lands and wealth seized by the crown. Eventually the Carmelites returned to their former church and re-established it, dedicating the new building in 1827.

In the north-eastern corner is a 16th century Flemish oak statue of the Virgin and Child, believed to be the only wooden statue to escape destruction during the Reformation. The church's altar contains the remains of St Valentine, of St Valentine's Day fame, donated to the church by the pope in 1836.

St Stephen's Church (Map 6)

Built in 1825 in Greek Revival style, St Stephen's, complete with cupola, is at the far end of Upper Mount St from Merrion Square and has been converted into business units. Because of its appearance, it has earned the nickname the 'Peppercanister Church'. You can see the interior between 12.30 and 2.30 pm, Monday to Friday.

SOUTH DUBLIN THEATRES

The city's first theatre opened in 1637 on Werburgh St, near Dublin Castle. Although that venue is long gone, there are still theatres south of the Liffey, including the **Gaiety Theatre** (Map 7) on South King St, just off Grafton St. Built in 1871 this is Dublin's oldest theatre and hosts a variety of performances.

The **Olympia Theatre** (Map 7), built in 1892 on Dame St in Temple Bar, is the city's largest and second-oldest theatre and is a venue for popular performances. It was previously known as the Palace Theatre and Dan Lowry's Music Hall. Also south of the Liffey is the **Tivoli Theatre** (Map 5) on Francis St in the Liberties.

North of the Liffey

Though south Dublin is noticeably more affluent than north Dublin and has the lion's share of the city's tourist attractions, there are many reasons to head across the Liffey, starting with Dublin's grandest avenue.

O'CONNELL ST (MAP 4)

O'Connell St is the major thoroughfare in north Dublin and qualifies as the most important, imposing street in the whole city,

though its glory has faded somewhat. It started life in the early 18th century as Drogheda St, named after Viscount Henry Moore, earl of Drogheda. There are still a Henry St, a Moore St and an Earl St nearby. The earl even managed to squeeze in an Of Lane! At that time Capel St, further to the west, was the city's main artery and Drogheda St, which then had no bridge to connect it to the south side of the Liffey, was of little importance.

In the 1740s Luke Gardiner, later Viscount Mountjoy, widened the street to 45m, turning it into an elongated promenade bearing his name. Then the completion of the Carlisle Bridge across the Liffey in 1794 quickly made it Dublin's most important street. In 1880 the Carlisle Bridge was replaced by the much wider O'Connell Bridge that stands today.

Gardiner's Mall became Sackville St but was renamed again in 1924 after Daniel O'Connell, the Irish nationalist leader whose statue stands at the river end. The 1854 bronze statue features four winged figures that are not, despite their appearance, angels. In fact they're the four Victories and are supposed to illustrate O'Connell's courage, eloquence, fidelity and patriotism. If you inspect them closely you'll notice that two of them are bullet marked, a legacy of the 1916 Easter Rising and the Civil War in 1922.

The central pedestrian area, continuing north from the river, is home to a variety of other statuary, one of which is a monument to William Smith O'Brien (1803-64), leader of the Young Ireland Party. The inscription on his monument notes that he was sentenced to death for high treason in 1848, so it either took a long time to carry out the sentence or it was done with remarkable inefficiency. There is also a statue of Sir John Gray (1815-75), a newspaper publisher and a pioneer in the provision of mains water in Dublin. Outside the GPO, Jim Larkin (1876-1947), a trade union leader and organiser of the general strike of 1913, is represented in a dramatic pose, throwing his arms in the air.

The Name's the Game

It seems that Dubliners just aren't happy with the names given to the various statues, monuments and other assorted sights throughout the city, and in an effort to convey the deeper significance of what these sights represent, they are compelled to make up humorous rhyming names for them. Silly or not, they are often quite funny, perhaps a sign of how iconoclastic Dubliners really are.

Just next to the north side of the Ha'penny Bridge is a bronze sculpture of two women sitting on a bench with shopping bags at their feet that is commonly known as 'the hags with the bags'.

At the end of Grafton St is a statue of a woman with a wheelbarrow loaded with cockles and mussels; she is Molly Malone, street vendor extraordinaire and the subject of Dublin's most famous song. But how do

'Cockles and mussels alive, alive o' – Molly Malone

Dubliners treat such a venerable figure? By referring to her as 'the tart with the cart'.

Not content with giving names to statues, Dubliners express their disapproval of buildings they consider ugly with rhyming names. Consequently, an unappealing apartment complex above The Oak bar on Dame St is 'the yoke on The Oak', and the rather box-like Waterways Visitor Centre in the docklands area is – you guessed it – 'the box on the docks'.

One of the funnier names was given to a well intentioned but ill-advised plan to place a luminous millennium clock in the Liffey underneath the Ha'penny Bridge. It would count down to the end of the century and people would see it from down the river; quite effective, you might think. But the problem was that you couldn't see the luminous numbers due to the dirt in the Liffey, and so 'the time in the slime' was removed.

Dublin's newest monument, a 130m-high spire to replace Nelson's Pillar, hasn't even been built yet – it's expected to be up in time for the millennium – but Dublin's wags have already taken to calling it 'the skewer by the sewer', 'the stiletto in the ghetto' and, in a macabre reference to the area's drug problem, 'the biggest needle in O'Connell St'.

The best names of all are reserved for the Anna Livia statue on O'Connell St. Joyce enthusiasts will know that the author gave the Liffey a woman's personality and name, Anna Livia, and the statue of a woman lying in water was designed and built in tribute. The problem is that it's an ugly statue and the locals don't really like it, so 'the floozy in the Jacuzzi' and 'the 'hooer in the sewer' were coined. And it doesn't end there. Modern medicine has provided the latest name, which describes the small waterfall at the back of Anna Livia's head that drips water over her suggestively prone body: 'Viagra Falls'.

The Bedford Tower, Dublin Castle, built in 1760

Much-criticised figure of justice, Dublin Castle

'The hags with the bags', by Ha'penny Bridge

'The floozy in the Jacuzzi', O'Connell St

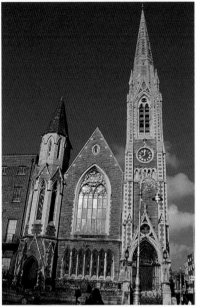
Abbey Presbyterian Church, Parnell Square

Boyle family monument, St Patrick's Cathedral

The nave of St Patrick's, Ireland's largest church

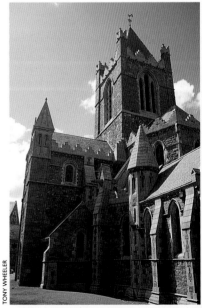
Dublin's other medieval cathedral, Christ Church

O'Connell St's most famous monument was a victim of the tendency to 'redevelop' the street in an explosive fashion. In 1815 the street was graced with a Doric pillar topped by a statue of Nelson, the British naval captain who defeated the French navy at Trafalgar in 1805. It predated the famous Nelson's Column in London's Trafalgar Square by 32 years. In 1966, as an unofficial celebration of the 50th anniversary of the 1916 Easter Rising, this symbol of British imperialism was badly damaged by an explosion and subsequently demolished. An aspect of the demolition that never ceases to amuse Dubliners is that while the explosion that originally ruined the statue caused no damage to anything other than poor Nelson, the charges set by the Irish army to demolish the remaining pedestal blew out virtually every window in O'Connell St! Nelson's stone head survives in the Dublin Civic Museum but the statue's demise put an end to the quip that the main street of the capital city of this most piously Catholic of countries had statues honouring three noted adulterers: O'Connell at the bottom of the street, Parnell at the top and Nelson in the middle.

The site of Nelson's demolished pillar is halfway up the street, between Henry and Earl Sts, near the GPO. Close by, a figure of James Joyce stands nonchalantly at the corner of pedestrianised North Earl St. In a fountain just beyond the site of the former column is a sculpted figure of Joyce's spirit of the Liffey, Anna Livia – a 1988 addition to the streetscape.

Continuing north, the tourist office is to the right, as is the Gresham Hotel, one of Dublin's most genteel. Further on is the figure of Father Theobald Mathew (1790-1856), the 'apostle of temperance' – an utterly hopeless role in Ireland. However, this quixotic task resulted in a Liffey bridge bearing his name. The top of the street is completed by the statue of Charles Stewart Parnell (1846-91), who was an advocate of Home Rule and became a political victim of Irish intolerance. Despite this it's Parnell who gets the most imposing monument.

O'Connell St has had its share of dramatic events; its rapid redevelopment began during the 1916 Easter Rising when the GPO building became the starting point for, and centre of, the abortive revolt. The fighting badly damaged the GPO and destroyed most of that side of the street. Six years later in 1922 the unfortunate avenue suffered more destruction when a Civil War clash here burnt down most of the eastern side of the street. O'Connell St was further damaged in the 1960s and 70s when Dublin went through a period of rampant development under extremely lax government controls. The fast-food and cheap office block atmosphere of O'Connell St today is a reminder of that era. A succession of governments have made promises to restore the street to its former glory, but so far nothing concrete has emerged.

Among the attractions close to O'Connell St is an energetic and colourful open-air market to the west on Moore St. The Abbey Theatre and the Catholic St Mary's Pro-Cathedral are to the east, as is the imposing Custom House. At the top of O'Connell St in Parnell Square are the notable Rotunda Hospital and the Gate Theatre. The Hugh Lane Municipal Gallery of Modern Art and the Dublin Writers' Museum are on the north side of the square.

GPO (GENERAL POST OFFICE, Map 4)

The GPO, on O'Connell St, is an important landmark and its seminal role in the history of independent Ireland has made it a prime site for everything from official parades to personal protests. The huge building, designed by Francis Johnston and opened in 1818, was the focus of the 1916 Easter Rising when Patrick Pearse, James Connolly and other leaders read their proclamation of a republic from its steps. In the subsequent siege the building was completely burnt out. The façade with its Ionic portico is still pockmarked from the 1916 clash and from further damage wrought at the start of the Civil War in 1922. The GPO was not re-opened until 1929.

By an inside window the *Death of Cuchulainn* statue commemorates Cuchulainn, the greatest of the Knights of the Red Branch, who were loyal to the king of the Ulaids (Ulster). He defended Ulster against the forces of Maeve, queen of Connaught, but is said to have been slain at the age of 27 after being tricked into an unfair fight.

ABBEY THEATRE (Map 4)

Opened in 1904 the Abbey Theatre (☎ 878 7222) is just north of the Liffey on the corner of Marlborough St and Lower Abbey St. The Irish National Theatre Society soon made a name not only for playwrights such as JM Synge and Sean O'Casey but also for Irish acting ability and theatrical presentation. The theatre became renowned as much for the uproars it provoked as for artistic appreciation. The use of the word 'shift' (petticoat) at the 1907 premiere of Synge's *The Playboy of the Western World* brought a storm of protest from theatregoers and O'Casey's *The Plough and the Stars* prompted a similar reaction in 1926. On the latter occasion WB Yeats himself came on stage after the performance to remonstrate with the audience!

The original theatre burnt down in 1951 and it was 15 years before the replacement was completed. Unfortunately, that interval wasn't long enough to engender any artistic inspiration and the dull building is in no way equal to its famous name or continuing reputation. The smaller Peacock Theatre at the same location presents new and experimental works.

CUSTOM HOUSE (Map 4)

James Gandon was 18th century Dublin's pre-eminent architect. The Custom House, his first great building, was built between 1781 and 1791 just past Eden Quay, despite opposition from city merchants and dock workers at the original Custom House upriver in Temple Bar. Nor were local residents very happy about this commercial intrusion, and Gandon sometimes appeared on site wielding a sword! He was supported by the era's foremost property developer,

Luke Gardiner, who saw the new Custom House as a major part of his scheme to shift the axis of the city eastward from medieval Capel St to what was then Gardiner's Mall (now O'Connell St).

In 1921, during the independence struggle, the Custom House was set alight and completely gutted in a five day fire, but was later totally rebuilt. The interior, however, was extensively redesigned and another major renovation occurred between 1986 and 1988.

The building stretches for 114m along the Liffey; the best complete view is from across the river, though a close-up inspection of its many fine details is also worthwhile. Arcades, each with seven arches, join the centre to the end pavilions and the columns along the front have harps carved in their capitals. Motifs allude to transportation and trade, including the four rooftop statues of Neptune, Mercury, Plenty and Industry, destroyed in the 1921 fire and replaced in 1991. Below the frieze are heads representing the gods of Ireland's 13 principal rivers. The sole female head above the main door represents the River Liffey. The cattle heads honour Dublin's beef trade and the statues behind the building represent Africa, America, Asia and Europe. The building is topped by a copper dome with four clocks and, above that, a 5m-high statue of Hope.

ST MARY'S PRO-CATHEDRAL (Map 4)

On the corner of Marlborough and Cathedral Sts, just east of O'Connell St, is Dublin's most important Catholic church, built between 1816 and 1825. The Pro-Cathedral was originally intended for O'Connell St, but fears that such a prominent position would provoke anti-Catholic British attitudes led to its comparatively inconspicuous location. Unfortunately, the cramped Marlborough St location makes it almost impossible to stand back far enough to admire the front with its six Doric columns, modelled on the Temple of Theseus in Athens.

Some intriguing questions are connected with the Pro-Cathedral's design and even its name. The competition held in 1814 to find the best design for the church was won by John Sweetman, a former owner of Sweetman's Brewery. But who organised the competition? Why, it was none other than William Sweetman, John Sweetman's brother. And did John Sweetman design the building himself? Possibly not, since he was living in Paris at the time and may have bought the plans from the French architect who designed the similar Notre Dame de Lorette in northern France. The only clue as to the church's architect is in the ledger, which lists the builder as 'Mr. P.' And what does 'pro' mean? It's not clear, but Pro-Cathedral seems to imply something like 'unofficial cathedral'. It is open daily from 8 am to 6 pm.

PARNELL SQUARE (Map 4)

The main squares of north Dublin are poor relations of their great counterparts south of the Liffey, and are generally far less well tended. However, they do have their points of interest.

The northern side of Parnell Square was built on lands acquired in the mid-18th century by Dr Bartholomew Mosse, the founder of the Rotunda Hospital, and was originally named Palace Row. The terrace was laid out in 1755 and Lord Charlemont bought the land for his home at No 22 in 1762. Charlemont's home was designed by Sir William Chambers, who also designed Lord Charlemont's extraordinary Casino at Marino (see later in this chapter). Today the building houses the Hugh Lane Municipal Gallery of Modern Art. The street was completed in 1769 and the gardens were

The Children of Lir

The children of Lir were the daughter and four sons of the ancient King Lir. As in most fairy-tales involving ill-treated children, a wicked stepmother (who in this case was also the sister of the children's dead mother) played a key part in the legend. The king's new wife, Aoife, developed an insane jealousy of the children but, lacking the resolve to drown them, she merely enticed them into a lake, Lough Derravaragh (in modern-day Westmeath), to bathe and then cast a spell on them, turning them into swans.

They were forced to spend 900 years on the waters of Ireland – 300 years each on Lough Derravaragh, the Sea of Moyle and the Bay of Erris. Feeling remorseful about what she had done, Aoife allowed them to keep their human voices and to make beautiful music. It wasn't long before the king discovered a group of talking swans and proclaimed that no swan should ever be killed in Ireland. King Dearg,

The Children of Lir Monument

Aoife's father, punished his dastardly daughter by turning her into a demon, but the unfortunate children still had to live out their 900 years as swans.

Christianity had just arrived in Ireland when the time span was up, so the children of Lir, by then old and careworn, were baptised by St Patrick when they once again took on human form, but they died soon after. Swans remain a protected species in Ireland.

renamed Rutland Square in 1786, before acquiring their current name in 1921.

Next to the gallery is the Dublin Writers' Museum, and overlooking the square from the northern corner is the Abbey Presbyterian Church. In 1966 a section at the north of the square was turned into a **Garden of Remembrance** for the 50th anniversary of the 1916 Easter Rising. Its centrepiece is a sculpture by Oisin Kelly depicting the myth of the Children of Lir.

There are some fine, though rather run-down, Georgian houses on the eastern side of the square. Oliver St John Gogarty, who was immortalised as Buck Mulligan in Joyce's *Ulysses*, was born at **No 5** in 1878, Dr Bartholomew Mosse was once a resident of **No 9** and the earls of Ormonde used **No 11** as a town house. On the other side of the square is the Sinn Féin Bookshop, at 44 West Parnell Square. The square also contains the Gate Theatre, Ambassador Cinema and Rotunda Hospital.

ROTUNDA HOSPITAL (Map 4)

Dr Bartholomew Mosse set up the Rotunda Hospital in 1757. This was the first maternity hospital in Ireland or Britain and was built at a time when Dublin's burgeoning urban population was leading to horrific infant-mortality figures. The hospital shares its basic design with Leinster House: Richard Castle was the architect of both and re-used the Leinster House floor plan as an economy measure.

To his Leinster House design Castle added a three storey tower. To raise funds for the hospital's operation, Mosse intended to charge visitors to climb the tower, which provided a fine view over the city. The Rotunda Assembly Hall, now occupied by the Ambassador Cinema, was built as an adjunct to the hospital also to raise operating funds. Over the main entrance of the hospital is the Rotunda Chapel, built in 1758 with superb coloured plasterwork by Bartholomew Cramillion.

The Rotunda Hospital still functions as a maternity hospital today. The Patrick Conway pub opposite dates from 1745 and

has been hosting expectant fathers since the day the hospital opened.

GATE THEATRE (Map 4)

At the top of O'Connell St, in the eastern corner of Parnell Square, the Gate Theatre was opened in 1929 by Micheál MacLiammóir and Hilton Edwards. The former continued to act at his theatre until 1975, when he retired at the age of 76 after making his 1384th performance of the one-man show *The Importance of Being Oscar* (Oscar being Oscar Wilde, of course). The Gate Theatre was also the stage for Orson Welles' first professional appearance and also featured James Mason early in his career. The building dates from 1784 to 1786 when it was built as part of the Rotunda Hospital complex. Today, the theatre stages some of the best plays to be seen in Dublin, with a repertory of American and European plays as well as the work of Irish dramatists.

HUGH LANE MUNICIPAL GALLERY OF MODERN ART (Map 4)

The Hugh Lane Gallery (☎ 874 1903), 22 North Parnell Square, has a fine collection of work by the French Impressionists and 20th century Irish artists. The exhibits include sculptures by Rodin and Degas, works by Corot, Courbet, Manet and Monet from the Lane Bequest and numerous works by Irish artists, including Jack B Yeats.

The gallery was founded in 1908 and moved to its present location in the splendid 18th century Charlemont House, formerly the earl of Charlemont's town house, in 1933. The gallery was established by Lady Gregory's (WB Yeats' patron) wealthy nephew, Sir Hugh Lane, who died in 1915, a passenger on the *Lusitania*, torpedoed off the southern coast of Ireland by a German U-boat. The Lane Bequest pictures, which formed the nucleus of the gallery, were the subject of a dispute over Lane's will between the gallery and the National Gallery in London. A settlement wasn't reached until 1959 and modified in

Hugh Lane

If wealthy Sir Hugh Lane (1875-1915) became more than a little miffed by the Irish and decided to give his paintings to some other nation, it was scarcely surprising, as he was treated with less respect than he felt he deserved in his own land. Born in County Cork he began to work in London art galleries from 1893 and five years later set up his own gallery in Dublin. He had a true art dealer's nose for the directions in which art would be heading and built up a superb collection, particularly of the Impressionists.

Unfortunately for Ireland, neither his talents nor his collection were much appreciated and in exasperation he turned his attention to opportunities in London and South Africa. Irish rejection led him to rewrite his will and bequeath some of the finest works in his collection to the National Gallery in London. Later he relented and added

Hugh Lane Municipal Gallery of Modern Art, Parnell Square

a rider to his will leaving the collection to Dublin but failed to have it witnessed, thus causing a long legal squabble over which gallery had rightful ownership.

Lane was only 40 years old when he went down with the ill-fated *Lusitania* in 1915 after it was torpedoed off the southern coast of Ireland by a German U-boat.

1993 allowing for 35 of the 39 paintings to be viewed in Dublin over a period of 12 years. Twenty-seven are here for the full duration of the term; the remaining eight alternate in two groups of four between London and Dublin, changing after six years. From November 1999 the gallery is displaying Manet's *Eva Gonzales*, Pissarro's *Printemps*, Morisot's *Jour d'Été*, and the most important painting of the whole collection, Renoir's *Les Parapluies*.

The gallery includes a shop and the Gallery restaurant. Operating hours are from 9.30 am to 6 pm, Tuesday to Thursday, from 9.30 am to 5 pm, Friday and Saturday, and from 11 am to 5 pm on Sunday. From April to August, it is open until 8 pm on Thurday. Entry is free.

DUBLIN WRITERS' MUSEUM (Map 4)

The Dublin Writers' Museum (☎ 872 2077), 18 North Parnell Square, is next to

the Municipal Gallery of Modern Art. The building was probably first owned by Lord Farnham, who died in 1800, and bequeathed it to his son. After his death George Jameson, of the whiskey distilling Jameson family, bought the house.

The museum celebrates the city's long and continuing history as a literary centre. Downstairs there's a collection of letters, photographs, first editions and other memorabilia of Ireland's best-known writers. Upstairs, in a wonderful room with plastered ceilings and painted doors, the Gallery of Writers has portraits and busts of some of Ireland's most famous writers, mainly copies of originals on display in the National Gallery. There is, however, a dearth of material about more recent writers, other than the children's authors highlighted in a top-floor room. The museum even has a rooftop Zen Garden.

Entry is IR£2.95/2.50. It's open from 10 am to 5 pm Monday to Saturday, and 11 am

James Malton & 18th Century Dublin

James Malton was an 18th century English artist who spent perhaps 10 years in Dublin. While there he drew a series of watercolours of the city in its heyday and used these to produce a set of 25 prints, being, as he wrote in his prospectus, 'desirous to make a display of (Dublin) to the world'. The prints remain one of the finest early records of any European capital city.

Despite the importance of the prints, little is known about the man responsible for them. He was certainly the son of Thomas Malton, who wrote textbooks on geometry and architectural design and who seems to have spent the last 15 years of his life in Dublin, but even the date of James' birth is uncertain. A Malton is known to have worked for the architect James Gandon from 1781 to 1784, during the period when the Custom House was being built. Assuming that a reference to 'a youth of seventeen' in the office refers to James Malton, he would have been born about 1764 and would have produced his great works while still in his late 20s or early 30s. Malton probably died of a fever in 1803, although there are also suggestions that he killed himself in London's Marylebone Fields.

Malton seems to have made the sketches and notes for his prints in 1791 when some of the buildings depicted were still incomplete. The discrepancies between the drawings and the completed buildings lend weight to the suggestion that Malton quarrelled with Gandon (he may even have been sacked by him) and that the two were on such bad terms that the artist was unable to ask the architect to check his sketches before they were finalised.

Malton's original prints were probably uncoloured, although some were inked more lightly, presumably to facilitate colouring. The colour was probably added sometime after 1820.

The 25 prints depict some of Dublin's most famous buildings (the Four Courts, Trinity College, the Custom House and Parliament House) as well as some that are less well known or lost (the Tholsel, the Royal Infirmary, the Barracks and the Blue Coat Hospital). Malton was as good at portraying street life as he was at drawing buildings, a fact which partly explains the popularity of his prints. However, he is thought to have made changes to the sketches

---

to 5 pm on Sunday; from June to August it stays open until 6 pm Monday to Friday. The admission fee includes taped guides with readings from relevant texts; these are available in English and other languages. There's also a bookshop and the Chapter One café, which is open for the same hours as the museum.

While the museum concerns itself primarily with authors of the deceased variety, next door at No 19 the **Irish Writers' Centre** provides a meeting and working place for their living successors.

WORLD OF WAX (Map 4)

Every city worth its tourist traps has a wax museum. Dublin's National Wax Museum (☎ 872 6340) is on Granby Row, north of Parnell Square. It has the usual fantasy and fairy-tale offerings, the inevitable chamber of horrors and a rock music 'megastars' area. There are also figures of Irish heroes and politicians such as Wolfe Tone, Robert Emmet, Charles Parnell, the leaders of the 1916 Easter Rising, the *Taosigh* (prime ministers, plural of *Taoiseach*), the presidents, a number of popes and prominent figures from the northern Troubles – John Hume and Ian Paisley, soon to be joined by Gerry Adams and David Trimble. Recorded commentaries explain their roles in Irish history.

There are also models of Irish cultural figures and numerous Irish TV and sporting personalities. The museum is open from 10 am to 5.30 pm, Monday to Saturday, noon

James Malton & 18th Century Dublin

(for example, to make a group of lone women look less like prostitutes) and his images present Dublin as being much cleaner than was probably the case.

The prints were published in six parts as *A Picturesque and Descriptive View of the City of Dublin*, with a commentary believed to have been written by Malton himself. Whatever the state of his relationship with Gandon, his comments on the architect's buildings suggest he remained a fan of Gandon's work. The book's frontispiece showed a print of the arms of the city of Dublin, also designed by Malton.

In 1993 Baileys sponsored 11 signboards outlining a 'Malton Trail' round central Dublin.

The boards show the Malton prints opposite the buildings that inspired them and reproduce relevant sections from his commentary. The longer version of the trail takes 2¾ hours to complete, the shorter version 1¼ hours.

A complete set of Malton prints is on display in the Malton Room teashop inside Dublinia, and Dublin airport is festooned with enlargements of Malton scenes. Almost unbelievably, none of the specialist books about Malton is currently in print, although the National Gallery booklet *Fifty Views of Ireland* includes reproductions of five of his drawings. The Neptune Gallery at 41 South William St sometimes has original prints for sale. The most expensive of these show the most acclaimed scenes. Cheaper 'wedding-present Maltons' depict the more offbeat buildings.

Dublin's coat of arms, designed by
James Malton

---

to 5.30 pm on Sunday. Entry is IR£3.50/2.50 (family IR£10).

ABBEY PRESBYTERIAN CHURCH (Map 4)

The slim, soaring spire of the Abbey Presbyterian Church at the corner of Frederick St and North Parnell Square, overlooking Parnell Square, is a convenient landmark. Dating from 1864 the church was financed by the Scottish grocery and brewery magnate Alex Findlater and is often referred to as Findlater's Church.

GREAT DENMARK ST (Map 4)

From the corner of Parnell Square, Great Denmark St runs north-east to Mountjoy Square, passing Belvedere House at No 6.

The construction of this house began in 1775 and it has been used as the Jesuit **Belvedere College** since 1841. James Joyce was a student here between 1893 and 1898 and describes it in *A Portrait of the Artist as a Young Man*. The building is renowned for its magnificent plasterwork by the master stuccodore Michael Stapleton and for its fireplaces by the Venetian artisan Bossi.

MOUNTJOY SQUARE (Map 4)

Built between 1792 and 1818, Mountjoy Square was a fashionable and affluent centre at the height of the Anglo-Irish ascendancy, but today is a run-down example of north Dublin urban decay. Money and some sensitivity, however, could work wonders on what are still fine buildings.

Viscount Mountjoy, after whom the square was named, was the developer Luke Gardiner, who briefly gave his name to Gardiner's Mall before it became Sackville St and then O'Connell St. The square has been named after him twice, as it started life as Gardiner Square.

Legend relates that this was the site where Brian Ború pitched his tent at the Battle of Clontarf in 1014. Residents of the square included Sean O'Casey, who set his play *The Shadow of a Gunman* here, though he referred to it as Hilljoy Square. As a child, James Joyce lived just off the square at 14 Fitzgibbon St.

ST GEORGE'S CHURCH (Map 4)

St George's Church, on Hardwicke Place off Temple St, was built by Francis Johnston from 1802 in Greek Ionic style and has a 60m-high steeple, which was modelled on that of St Martin-in-the-Fields in London. The church's bells were added in 1836. Although this was one of Johnston's finest works and the Duke of Wellington was married here, the church is no longer in use.

ST MARY'S CHURCH (Map 4)

On Mary St, between Wolfe Tone and Jervis Sts, St Mary's was designed in 1697 by Sir William Robinson, also responsible for the Royal Hospital Kilmainham. It was completed in 1702 and is the most important church to survive from that period. The church was a popular one among 18th century Dublin's social elite: many famous Dubliners were baptised there and Arthur Guinness was married there in 1793. In 1747 John Wesley, the founder of Methodism, preached for the first time in Ireland in St Mary's. Today, however, like so many other fine old Dublin churches, it's no longer in use.

ST MARY'S ABBEY (Map 4)

All that remains of this Cistercian abbey, in Meeting House Lane, near the junction of Capel St and Mary's Abbey, is the chapterhouse, which hardly does justice to what was once the most powerful and wealthy monastery in Ireland. Built in 1180 the abbey played a dominant role in Irish church politics until Henry VIII ordered the dissolution of the monasteries in 1537. Only three years earlier Silken Thomas Fitzgerald, the most important of Leinster's Anglo-Norman lords, had renounced his allegiance to Henry in the chapterhouse, which had been a popular meeting place for rebels conspiring against the English monarch. The chapterhouse can be visited between 10 am and 5 pm on Wednesday from mid-June to mid-September. Admission costs IR£1/40p.

JAMES JOYCE CULTURAL CENTRE (Map 4)

North Great George's St was a fashionable address in 18th century Dublin but, like so much of the north side of the city, fell on hard times when the Act of Union turned the city into a backwater. James Joyce's family lived in north Dublin for a time and he would have been familiar with the street. The dancing instructor, Denis Maginni, who taught in the front room of No 35, appears several times in *Ulysses*. In the 20th century many of the houses became run-down tenements. In 1982 Senator David Norris, a charismatic Joycean scholar and gay-rights activist, moved into the street and took over No 35. This has now been restored and has been converted into a centre for the study of James Joyce and his books.

Visitors see the room where Maginni taught and a collection of pictures of the 17 different Dublin homes occupied by Joyce's family and of the real individuals fictionalised in his books. Some of the building's fine plaster ceilings are restored originals, others careful reproductions of Michael Stapleton's designs.

Admission is IR£2.75/2. The house (☎ 878 8547) is open from 9.30 am to 5 pm, Monday to Friday, and from 12.30 to 5 pm on Saturday and Sunday. Tours of north Dublin costing IR£3 and lasting just over an hour depart from here at 2.30 pm, Monday to Saturday.

Incidentally, North Great George's St as

a whole has benefited from a much-needed facelift and boasts some fine Georgian doorways and fanlights.

ST MICHAN'S CHURCH (Map 3)
Named after a Danish saint, St Michan's Church on Lower Church St was founded by Danes in 1095, though there's little trace of the original. The battlement tower dates from the 15th century, but the church was rebuilt in the late 17th century, considerably restored in the early 19th century and again in this century after the Civil War, during which it had been damaged.

The church contains an organ from 1724, which Handel may have played for the first-ever performance of his *Messiah*. The organ case is distinguished by the fine oak carving of 17 entwined musical instruments on its front. A skull on the floor on one side of the altar is said to represent Oliver Cromwell. On the opposite side is the Stool of Repentance, where 'open and notoriously naughty livers' did public penance. The church's main attraction lies underground in the crypts, where bodies have been preserved to varying degrees not by mummification, but by the constant dry atmosphere. They make a gruesome sight.

Tours lasting about 15 minutes run between 10 am and 12.45 pm and 2 and 4.45 pm, Monday to Friday, and on Saturday morning (12.30 to 3.30 pm, Monday to Friday, and 10 am to 4.45 pm on Saturday, from the end of September until April). They cost IR£2/50p.

OLD JAMESON DISTILLERY (Map 3)
Where does Irish whiskey get its particular colour and smooth bouquet from? While most people have heard the term 'single malt', how many actually know what this means? These are just some of the secrets you can learn at the Old Jameson Distillery (☎ 807 2355) on Bow St, a museum devoted to Irish whiskey. It opened in 1997 after a IR£7 million renovation of the old Jameson distillery, where Ireland's best-loved whiskey was produced from 1791

until its closure in 1966, when Jameson, along with the other main Irish producers, united to form Irish Distillers, with an ultra-modern distillery in Middleton, County Cork. The museum can only be visited by guided tour, but it's well worth it. A short film kicks off the tour, after which visitors are led through a recreation of the old factory, where the guide explains the entire process of whiskey distilling from grain to bottle. Visitors are then invited into the Jameson Bar where they are offered a complimentary glass of the 'hard stuff' (as it is referred to in Dublin vernacular). The tour finishes with a surprise competition, but you'll have to visit to find out what it is! There is also a restaurant on the premises. The museum is open daily 10 am to 5 pm; tours depart every 30 minutes. Admission costs IR£3.50.

ARBOUR HILL CEMETERY (Map 3)
West of the Jameson distillery at Arbour Hill is a small cemetery that is the final resting place of all 14 of the executed leaders of the 1916 Easter Rising, including Patrick Pearse and James Connolly. The burial ground is plain, with the 14 names inscribed in stone. Beside the graves is a cenotaph bearing the Easter Proclamation. Government leaders come every Easter Monday to pay their respects to the fallen heroes of Ireland, and it is also a popular gathering place for Irish republicans of all shades. The cemetery is open from 9 am to 4.30 pm Monday to Saturday, 9.30 am to noon on Sunday. Admission is free.

KING'S INNS & HENRIETTA ST (Map 4)
Accessible from Constitution Hill and Henrietta St, King's Inns is home to the Dublin legal profession. This classical building by James Gandon suffered many delays between its design in 1795, the start of construction in 1802 and its completion in 1817. Along the way several other architects were recruited, including Francis Johnston, who added the cupola late in the

day. The building is normally open only to members of the Inns and their guests.

The city's original law courts stood just to the west of Christ Church Cathedral, south of the Liffey. Collett's Inn, the first gathering place for lawyers, was later established in Exchequer St and was in turn followed by Preston Inn, which stood on Cork Hill where the City Hall stands today. In 1541, when Henry VIII staked his claim to be King of Ireland as well as England, the lawyers' society took the title of King's Inns. The society moved to a new site on land which had been confiscated from the Dominican Convent of St Saviour, but when that site by the Liffey was taken over to become the Four Courts the King's Inns moved to their present home.

Henrietta St, running south-east from the building, was Dublin's first Georgian street and has buildings dating from 1720. Sadly, this is another of north Dublin's run-down areas and the street is now in a state of disrepair. These early Georgian mansions were both larger and more varied in style than their later counterparts. For a time Henrietta St rejoiced in the name 'Primate's Hill', as the archbishop of Armagh and other high church officials lived there. Luke Gardiner, responsible for so much of the early development of Georgian north Dublin, lived at No 10. Plaques at Nos 5 and 7 identify a certain Alderman Meade as the villain who split what was originally one building into two in 1908 and ripped out many of the original features in the course of turning them into tenements.

FOUR COURTS (Map 5)

On Inns Quay, the Four Courts, with its 130m-long façade, was designed by James Gandon and built between 1786 and 1802 engulfing and incorporating the Public Records Office built a short time earlier. The more recent building includes a Corinthian-columned central block connected to flanking wings with enclosed quadrangles. The ensemble is topped by diverse statuary.

There are fine views over the city from the upper rotunda of the central building. The original four courts – Exchequer, Common Pleas, King's Bench and Chancery – branched off this circular central building. The Dominican Convent of St Saviour (1224) formerly stood here, but was replaced first by an early version of the King's Inns and then by the present building. The last parliament of James II was held on the site in 1689.

The Four Courts played a brief role in the 1916 Easter Rising without suffering any damage, but in 1922 anti-Treaty republicans seized the building and couldn't be persuaded to leave. Michael Collins shelled the building from across the river. As the republican forces retreated, the building was set on fire and many irreplaceable early records were destroyed. This event sparked off the Civil War and the building wasn't restored until 1932.

Other Sights

After working your way along the River Liffey then exploring south and north Dublin, you'll have seen a fair amount of the city's attractions, but there's still much more. To the west are the St James's Gate Guinness Brewery in the colourful Liberties area, Kilmainham Gaol and Phoenix Park. To the north and north-east are the Royal Canal, Prospect Cemetery, the Botanic Gardens, the Casino at Marino and Clontarf. To the south and south-east are the Grand Canal, Ballsbridge and the Royal Dublin Showground. There are also more galleries and museums apart from those already covered.

ST JAMES'S GATE GUINNESS BREWERY & GUINNESS HOP STORE (Map 5)

Heading westward from central south Dublin, past St Audoen's churches, Thomas St metamorphoses into James's St in the area of Dublin known as the Liberties. Along James's St stretches the historic St James's Gate Guinness Brewery. From its foundation by Arthur Guinness in 1759, on the site of the earlier Rainsford Brewery, the Guinness operation has expanded down to the Liffey and across both sides of the street. In all, it covers 26 hectares and for a time was the largest brewery in the world. The oldest parts of the site are south of James's St; at one time there was a gate spanning the entire street.

While the brewery itself is off limits to the public, the Guinness Hop Store (☎ 453 3645) on Crane St is the historic brewery's old storehouse for hops (an essential ingredient in beer-making) where visitors can watch a Guinness audiovisual display and inspect an extensive Guinness museum. Upstairs, the 'Guinness Zone' is an interactive exhibition highlighting the history of Guinness advertising: post-WWII posters bearing the legend 'Guinness is Good For You' have become *objets d'art* in their own right. It may not be a tour of the actual brewery, but it makes for an interesting visit and your entry fee includes a glass of the black stuff. Children pay less and don't get a drink! It's frequently claimed that Guinness tastes exactly as it should only at its source, and you can't get any closer to the source than here. Guinness aficionados claim the Guinness 'pulled' in the hop store is better than at even the most traditional of Dublin's pubs.

In its early years Guinness was only one of dozens of Dublin breweries but it outgrew and outlasted them all. At one time a Grand Canal tributary was cut into the brewery to enable special Guinness barges to carry consignments out onto the Irish canal system or to the Dublin port. When the brewery extensions reached the Liffey in 1872, the fleet of Guinness barges became a familiar sight. There was also a Guinness railway on the brewery site, complete with a corkscrew tunnel. Guinness still operates its own ships to convey the vital fluid to the British market. Over 50% of all the beer consumed in Ireland is brewed here, four million pints of it a day.

It's open from 9.30 am to 5 pm, Monday to Saturday (4.30 pm from October to March) and from 10.30 am to 4.30 pm on Sunday (from noon from October to March). Entry is IR£4/3. To get there take bus No 21A, 78 or 78A from Fleet St. The upper floors of the building house temporary art exhibits.

Around the corner at 1 Thomas St a plaque marks the house where Arthur Guinness lived, and in a yard across the road is **St Patrick's Tower**, Europe's tallest smock windmill (one with a revolving top), dating from about 1757.

IRISH MUSEUM OF MODERN ART & ROYAL HOSPITAL KILMAINHAM (Map 5)

The Irish Museum of Modern Art or IMMA (☎ 612 9900) at the old Royal Hospital Kilmainham is close to Kilmainham Gaol. The gallery opened in 1991 with a particular focus on the work of contemporary Irish artists such as Louis Le Brocquy, Sean Scully, Richard Deacon, Richard Gorman and Dorothy Cross. Regular temporary exhibitions top up the permanent collection, which also includes such heavy hitters as Picasso and Miró.

The Royal Hospital Kilmainham was built from 1680 to 1687 not, as its name suggests, as a hospital but as a home for retired soldiers, a role it fulfilled until after Irish independence. It preceded the well known Chelsea Royal Hospital in London, which had a similar role. Royal Hospital inmates were often referred to as 'Chelsea Pensioners' although there was no connection. At the time of its construction it was one of the finest buildings in Ireland. It was designed by William Robinson, whose other work included Marsh's Library.

There's a good café and bookshop at the IMMA, which is open from 10 am to 5.30 pm Tuesday to Saturday and noon to 5.30 pm on Sunday. Entry is free, as are the guided tours of the museum, which are held on Wednesday and Friday at 2.30 pm and on Sunday at 12.15 pm. Tours for groups are held from Tuesday to Friday but bookings must be made two weeks in advance. Heritage tours, which discuss the historical significance of the building, run at 2.30 and

3.30 pm on Sunday (IR£1). To get there, take bus No 24, 79 or 90 from Aston Quay.

KILMAINHAM GAOL

Built between 1792 and 1795, Kilmainham Gaol (☎ 453 5984), on Inchicore Rd, to the west of IMMA, is a solid, grey, threatening, old building. During each act of Ireland's long, painful path to independence from Britain at least one part of the performance took place at the prison.

The uprisings of 1799, 1803, 1848, 1867 and 1916 all ended with the leaders' confinement in Kilmainham. Robert Emmet, Thomas Francis Meagher, Charles Stewart Parnell and the 1916 Easter Rising leaders were all visitors, but it was the executions in 1916 that most deeply etched the jail's name into the Irish consciousness. Of the 15 executions that took place between 3 and 12 May after the Easter Rising, 14 were conducted here. As a finale, prisoners from the Civil War struggles were held here from 1922, but that chapter is played down when you visit the jail. Even the passing comment that the final prisoner released from Kilmainham was Ireland's future president, Eamon de Valera, doesn't reveal that he had been imprisoned by his fellow Irish citizens. The building was finally closed for good as a jail in 1924.

Kilmainham Gaol was used as the setting for the film *In the Name of the Father*, which told the story of the Guildford Four, Irishmen imprisoned for 14 years for bombings in Britain during the 1970s. It was eventually conceded that they weren't responsible for carrying out the bombings.

An excellent audiovisual introduction to the old building is followed by a lively, thought-provoking guided tour. Incongruously sitting outside in the yard is the *Asgard*, the ship that successfully broke the British blockade and delivered arms to nationalist forces in 1914. The tour finishes in the gloomy yard where the 1916 executions took place.

It's open from 9.30 am to 6 pm daily between May and September, and from 9.30 am to 5 pm Monday to Friday and 10 am to 6 pm on Sunday between October and April. Last admissions are 45 minutes before closing. Entry is IR£3/1.25 and you can get there by bus No 23, 51, 51A, 78 or 79 from the city centre.

Kilmainham Gate was designed by Francis Johnston in 1812 and originally stood, as the Richmond Tower, at Watling St Bridge near the Guinness Brewery. It was moved to its current position opposite the prison in 1846 as it obstructed the increasingly heavy traffic to the new Kingsbridge station (now Heuston station). The railway company paid for the gate's dismantling and reassembly.

PHOENIX PARK

Comprising more than 700 hectares, Phoenix Park is one of the world's largest city parks, dwarfing Central Park (337 hectares) in New York or any of the major London parks: Hyde Park is 138 hectares, Regent's Park is 190 hectares and Hampstead Heath is 324 hectares. The park has gardens and lakes, a host of sporting facilities (including a motor-racing track), the second-oldest public zoo in Europe, a visitor centre and castle, various government offices, the Garda Síochána (police) Headquarters, the residences of the US ambassador and the Irish president, and even a herd of 300 deer.

Lord Ormonde turned this land into a park in 1671 but it wasn't opened to the public until 1747 by Lord Chesterfield. The land had been confiscated from the Kilmainham priory of St John to create a royal deer park, but was then given as a grant by Charles II. The name Phoenix is probably a corruption of the Irish phrase for clear water, *fionn uisce*. The park played a crucial role in Irish history, as Lord Cavendish, the British chief secretary for Ireland, and his assistant were murdered here in 1882 by members of an Irish nationalist group called The Invincibles. Lord Cavendish's home is now called Deerfield, and is used as the US ambassador's residence. His murder occurred outside what is now the Irish president's residence.

Near the Parkgate St entrance to the park is the 63m-high **Wellington Monument** obelisk. This took from 1817 to 1861 to build, mainly because the Duke of Wellington fell from public favour during its construction. At this south-eastern corner of the park are the **People's Garden**, dating from 1864, and the bandstand in the **Hollow**. Just north of the Hollow is **Dublin Zoo**. Chesterfield Ave separates the Hollow and the zoo from the Phoenix Park Cricket Club of 1830 and from **Citadel Pond**, usually referred to as the Dog Pond. Behind the zoo, on the edge of the park, the **Garda Síochána Headquarters** has a small police museum, usually open during weekday business hours.

Going north-west along Chesterfield Ave, which runs right through the park, you pass the **Áras an Uachtaráin**, the Irish president's residence on the right. On the left the **Papal Cross** marks the site where Pope John Paul II preached to 1¼ million people in 1979. In the centre of the park the **Phoenix Monument**, erected by Lord Chesterfield in 1747, looks so unphoenix-like that it's often referred to as the Eagle Monument. To the north-west of the monument stand the **Phoenix Park Visitors' Centre** and **Ashtown Castle**. The southern part of the park has many football and hurling pitches; although they occupy about 80 hectares (200 acres), the area is known as the Fifteen Acres.

At the north-western end of the park near the White's Gate entrance are the offices of the **Ordnance Survey**, the government mapping department. This building was originally built in 1728 by Luke Gardiner, who was responsible for the architecture in O'Connell St and Mountjoy Square in north Dublin. South of this building is the attractive rural-looking **Furry Glen** and **Glen Pond** corner of the park.

Back towards the Parkgate St entrance is

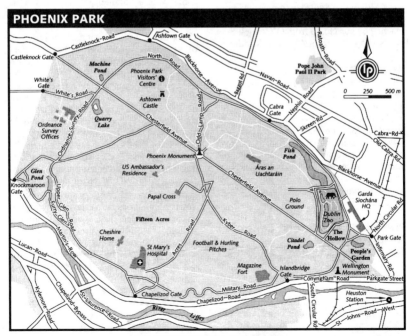

PHOENIX PARK

Magazine Fort on Thomas's Hill. Like the nearby Wellington Monument, the fort was no quick construction, the process taking from 1734 to 1801. It was also a target in the 1916 Easter Rising.

Dublin Zoo

Designed by Decimus Burton in 1830, the 12 hectare Dublin Zoo (☎ 677 1425), in the south-eastern corner of Phoenix Park, is starting to show its age. However, the Irish government has agreed to an IR£15 million grant for a five year programme of expansion and modernisation. The zoo is well known for its lion-breeding programme, which dates back to 1857 and includes among its offspring the lion that roars at the start of MGM films. One of the most up-to-date exhibit halls is the one housing African reptiles and one of the zoo's more pleasing sights is the polar bear that ploughs up and down a swimming pool on its back. Entry is IR£5.90/4.20 and it's open from 9.30 am to 6 pm Monday to Saturday (4 pm in winter), and from 10.30 am on Sunday. It can be reached by bus No 10 from O'Connell St or bus No 25 or 26 from Abbey St Middle.

Áras an Uachtaráin

The residence of the Irish president was built in 1751 and enlarged in 1782, and then again in 1816, on the latter occasion by the noted Irish architect Francis Johnston, who added the Ionic portico. From 1782 to 1922 it was the residence of the British viceroys or Lords Lieutenant. After independence it became the home of Ireland's governor general until Ireland cut its ties with the British crown and set up the office of president in 1937.

Phoenix Park Visitors' Centre & Ashtown Castle

The Phoenix Park Visitors' Centre (☎ 821 3021) is in what were the stables of the papal nunciate. A 20 minute video outlines the history of the park, and two floors of exhibits include a reconstruction of the Knockmaree Cist, a tomb containing two skeletons dating back to about 3500 BC dis-

covered in Fifteen Acres in 1838. Visitors are taken on a tour of the adjacent four storey Ashtown Castle, a 17th century tower-house that had been concealed inside the later building of the papal nunciate until the latter was demolished in 1986; box hedges surrounding the tower trace the ground-plan of the lost building. The visitor centre is open from 9.30 am to 5 pm daily in March and from October to November (until 6 pm from April to September), and from 9.30 am to 4.30 pm on Saturday and Sunday only from November to March. Last admission is 45 minutes prior to closing, and entry costs IR£2/1.50.

THE ROYAL CANAL

Two canals encircle central Dublin: the older Grand Canal to the south, and the newer Royal Canal to the north. Constructed from 1790, by which time the Grand Canal was already past its prime, the Royal Canal was a commercial failure, but its story is a colourful one. It was founded by Long John Binns, a director of the Grand Canal Company who quit the board because of a supposed insult over his being a shoemaker. He established the Royal Canal for revenge but since it duplicated the purpose of the earlier canal it never made money. The duke of Leinster became a major backer for the canal on condition that it was routed past his mansion near Maynooth. In 1840 it was sold to a railway company that considered the canal's route convenient for a railway line. Tracks still run alongside much of the disused canal through the city.

The Royal Canal towpath provides a relaxing walk to the north of the city centre. You can join it beside Newcomen Bridge at North Strand Rd, just north of Connolly station, and follow it to the suburb of Clonsilla over 10km away, and beyond. The walk is particularly pleasant past Binns Bridge in Drumcondra. At the top of Blessington St, near the Dublin International Youth Hostel, is a large pond that was used as a filter bed when the canal also supplied drinking water to the city. It now attracts swans and other water birds.

NATIONAL BOTANIC GARDENS

Founded in 1795 the National Botanic Gardens, directly north of the centre on Botanic Rd in Glasnevin, function both as a scientific resource and as a popular public park. The area was used as a garden long before 1795 but only Yew Walk, also known as Addison's Walk, has trees dating back to the first half of the 18th century.

The 19 hectare gardens are flanked to the north by the River Tolka, and in the gardens is a series of curvilinear glasshouses dating from 1843 to 1869. The creator of the glasshouses, Dubliner Richard Turner, was also responsible for the glasshouse at the Belfast Botanic Gardens and the Palm House at London's Kew Gardens. Within these Victorian masterpieces you will find the latest in botanical technology, including a series of computer-controlled climates reproducing environments in different parts of the world. The gardens also have a palm house, built in 1884. Among the pioneering botanical work conducted here was the first attempt to raise orchids from seed, back in 1844. Pampas grass and the giant lily were first grown in Europe in these gardens.

The gardens are open from 9 am to 6 pm, Monday to Saturday, and 11 am to 6 pm on Sunday from April to October, and from 10 am to 4.30 pm, Monday to Saturday, and 11 am to 4.30 pm on Sunday from November to March. Entry is free. You can reach the gardens on bus No 13, 13A or 19 from O'Connell St or bus No 34 or 34A from Middle Abbey St.

GLASNEVIN CEMETERY

Beside the National Botanic Gardens (though not accessible from them) is Glasnevin or Prospect Cemetery, the largest in Ireland. It was established in 1832 for Roman Catholics, who faced opposition when they conducted burials in the city's Protestant cemeteries. Many of the monuments and memorials have overtly patriotic overtones with numerous high crosses, harps, shamrocks, and other Irish symbols. The most imposing memorial is the enormous monument to Cardinal McCabe (1837-1921), archbishop of Dublin and primate of Ireland.

A modern replica of a round tower is a handy landmark for locating the tomb of Daniel O'Connell, who died in 1847 but was reinterred here in 1869, when the tower was completed. Charles Stewart Parnell's tomb (1891) is topped with a huge granite rock. Other notable people buried here include Sir Roger Casement, executed for treason by the British in 1916 and whose remains were not returned until 1964; Michael Collins (1890-1922), a leading figure in Ireland's final struggle for independence; Jim Larkin, a prime force in the 1913 general strike and Gerard Manley Hopkins (1844-89), the poet. There's also a poignant memorial to the men who have starved themselves to death for the cause of Irish freedom over the century.

The most interesting parts of the cemetery are at the south-eastern end, near Prospect Square. The cemetery wall still has watchtowers, from which lookouts watched for body snatchers. Part of *Ulysses* is set in the cemetery and there are several clues for Joyce enthusiasts to follow among the tombstones.

Bus No 40 from Parnell St stops outside the cemetery gates.

CASINO AT MARINO

The casino (☎ 833 1618) is just off Malahide Rd, north of the junction with Howth Rd in Marino, north-east of central Dublin. In Italian, the word *casino* is used to mean a house of pleasure (as in gambling) or a summer home, and this 18th century folly is one of Ireland's finest examples of the latter meaning. It is a Palladian summer house, built for the somewhat eccentric James Caulfield (1728-99), later earl of Charlemont, who had returned from a grand European tour with a huge art collection and a burning passion for Italian architectural style.

On his return, he appointed the architect Sir William Chambers to build the casino, a process that started in the late 1750s, continued through the 1760s and much of the 1770s. The project never really came to a conclusion, in part because the earl's extravagances had frittered away his fortune.

Externally, the building's 12 Tuscan columns, forming a temple-like façade, and huge entrance doorway suggest that it encloses a simple single open space. Only when you go inside do you realise what a wonderful extravagance it is. The interior is a convoluted maze planned as a bachelor's retreat but eventually put to a quite different use. Flights of fancy include carved draperies, ornate fireplaces, chimneys for central heating disguised as roof urns, downpipes hidden in columns, beautiful parquet floors built of rare woods and a spacious wine cellar. All sorts of statuary adorn the outside, the amusing fakes being the most enjoyable. The towering front door is a sham, and a much smaller panel opens to reveal the interior. The windows have blacked-out panels to disguise the fact that the interior is a complex of rooms rather than a single chamber.

When the earl married, the casino became a garden retreat rather than a bachelor's quarters. The casino was designed to accompany another building where he intended to house the art and antiquities he had acquired during his European tour, so it's perhaps fitting that his town house on Parnell Square, also designed by Sir William Chambers, is now the Municipal Gallery of Modern Art.

Despite his wealth, Charlemont was a comparatively liberal and free-thinking aristocrat. He never fenced-in his demesne and allowed the public to use it as an open park. Nor was he the only eccentric in the area at that time. In 1792 a painter named Folliot took a dislike to the earl and built Marino Crescent at the bottom of Malahide Rd purely to block his view of the sea. Bram Stoker (1847-1912), author of *Dracula*, was born at 15 Marino Crescent.

After Charlemont's death his estate, crippled by his debts, quickly collapsed. The art collection was dispersed and in 1870 the town house was sold to the government. The Marino estate followed in 1881 and the casino in 1930, though it was in a decrepit condition when the government acquired it. Not until the mid-1970s did serious restoration begin, and it's still continuing. Although the current casino grounds are a tiny fragment of the original park-like Marino estate, trees around the building help to hide the fact that it's now surrounded by a housing estate.

Marino Casino is open from 10 am to 5 pm daily, May and October; 9.30 am to 6 pm daily, June to September; noon to 4 pm Sunday and Wednesday, November, February and March. At other times of the year call ☎ 833 1618 for details of opening hours. You can visit the building only on a guided tour; entry is IR£2/1. Bus Nos 20A, 20B, 27, 27A, 27B, 32A, 42, 42B, 42C and 43 run there from the centre.

CLONTARF & NORTH BULL ISLAND

Clontarf, a bayside suburb about 5km north-east of the centre, takes its name from *cluain tarbh*, the bull's meadow. On Good Friday in 1014, Brian Ború defeated the Danes at the Battle of Clontarf, though in the struggle the Irish hero was killed, along with his son and grandson. The Normans

The casino is the result of the finest 18th century Irish research into Roman architecture.

DOUG McKINLAY

DOUG McKINLAY

DOUG McKINLAY

DOUG McKINLAY

DOUG McKINLAY

Wherever you go, there's always something happening or someone to watch in the streets of Dublin.

NEIL SETCHFIELD

DOUG McKINLAY

NEIL BEER

DOUG McKINLAY

DOUG McKINLAY

DOUG McKINLAY

DOUG McKINLAY

From markets to corner shops and streetside stalls to shopping centres, whether you're after fish or flowers, crafts or cucumbers, Dublin will have it somewhere.

later erected a castle here that was handed on to the Knights Templar in 1179, rebuilt in 1835 and later converted into a hotel.

The North Bull Wall, extending from Clontarf about 1km into Dublin Bay, was built in 1820 at the suggestion of Captain William Bligh of HMS *Bounty* fame, in order to stop Dublin Harbour from silting up. The marshes and dunes of North Bull Island, which formed behind the wall, are a popular nature reserve. Many birds migrate here from the Arctic in winter, and at times the bird population can reach 40,000; watch for shelducks, curlews, and oystercatchers on the mud flats and listen for larks in the dunes. You reach the interpretive centre on the island by walking across the 1.5km-long northern causeway. Bus Nos 30 and 32X run to the start of the causeway on James Larkin Rd. The Royal Dublin and St Anne's golf courses are also on the island.

THE GRAND CANAL

Built to connect Dublin with the River Shannon in the centre of Ireland, the Grand Canal makes a 6km loop around south Dublin. At its eastern end the canal forms a harbour connected with the Liffey at Ringsend. The Royal Canal performs a similar loop through north Dublin. True Dubliners, it is said, are born within the confines of the canals. The canal hasn't been used commercially since 1960 but some stretches are attractive and enjoyable to stroll along. It's about 2km from Mount St Bridge west to Richmond St along a particularly beautiful part of the canal, with a cluster of pubs providing refreshment at the Richmond St end. The canalside path also makes a fine bicycle ride.

History

An Act of Parliament to build the canal was first proposed in 1715 but things moved slowly due to lack of funds. Work didn't begin until 1756 and only 20km had been built by 1763. At this time the Dublin Corporation took over the project from private interests – the canal was partly designed to bring water to the city and the corporation was concerned about the slow rate of progress. They handed it back in 1772 and eventually, in 1779, the first cargo barges started to operate between Dublin and Sallins, about 35km west of Dublin.

Passenger services started a year later but at that time the terminus of the canal was the St James's St Harbour, near the St James's Gate Guinness Brewery. By 1784 the canal had been extended a farther 10km to Robertstown, and the construction of the Circular Line, completed in 1791, extended the canal around the south of Dublin to meet the River Liffey at Ringsend. The locks between the Grand Canal Docks and the Liffey were opened in 1796, making the completed canal the longest in Ireland or Britain. In all, the Grand Canal system extended for 550km, of which about 250km were along the Rivers Shannon and Barrow.

The Grand Canal Company operated five hotels along the route from Dublin to Shannon (on Ireland's west coast). The Portobello Hotel, opened in 1807, was the Dublin terminus and was soon busy with passengers arriving and departing. Though never speedy, canal travel became a popular alternative to the hardships of road journeys. Horses towed the barges along the canals at a steady 5 or 6km/h. Passenger boats, divided into 1st and 2nd class, carried 80 passengers. In 1834 lightweight flyboats pulled by four horses were introduced and could reach up to 15km/h.

Railways spread across Ireland from the mid-19th century and the canal quickly declined. Passenger services ended in 1852 and the canal was used only for cargo services. During this era Guinness deliveries were often made by barge departing from the harbour at the brewery, but by the end of the century steam power began to supplant horses. The barges were pulled by horse from Dublin to Robertstown from where a steam tug towed up to six barges the 40km to Ballycommon; from there horses again took over for the final stretch to the River Shannon. In 1911 diesel engines started to replace both horses and steam, and by 1924 all the Grand Canal

Company barges were diesel powered, although horse-drawn barges continued to be operated by other traders. The decline continued, however, and though the canal was used more frequently during WWII, the private canal company folded in 1950; the last barge-carried cargo of Guinness left Dublin in 1960.

The canal fell into disrepair and in the early 1970s the St James's St Harbour and the stretch of canal from there to the Circular Line were filled in. Today the canal enjoys a modest revival as a tourist attraction and, despite the limited number of boats now plying the canal, all the locks are kept in working order.

Along the Circular Line to Ringsend

The Grand Canal enters the Liffey at Ringsend, through locks opened in 1796. The large Grand Canal Docks, flanked by Hanover and Charlotte quays, are now used by windsurfers (see the Activities section later in this chapter).

At the north-western corner of the dock is Misery Hill, once the site of public executions. Even more macabre was the practice of bringing the corpses of those already hanged at Gallows Hill, near Upper Baggot St, to be strung up here for public display for between six and 12 months.

Waterways Visitors' Centre

Upstream from the Grand Canal Docks is the visitors' centre, built by Dúchas as an exhibition and interpretive centre covering the construction and operation of Irish canals and waterways. The centre stands in striking contrast to the dereliction surrounding it. A 10 minute video outlines the role of the canals in general, while display boards and an interactive video give more detailed information. Particularly impressive is a model of a barge slowly working its way through a pair of locks. The visitors' centre is open daily from 9.30 am to 6.30 pm between June and September, and from 2.30 to 5 pm in October and May. Admission costs IR£2/1.

Mount St to Leeson St

On Mount St Bridge is a memorial to the Easter Rising of 1916. A little further along, Baggot St crosses the canal on the Macartney Bridge, built in 1791. The head office of Bord Fáilte (the Irish Tourist Board) is on the northern side of the canal and Bridge House (an old pub) and Parson's shop are on the southern side.

This lovely stretch of the canal with its grassy, tree-lined banks was a favourite haunt of the poet Patrick Kavanagh. One of his poems requested that he be commemorated by 'a canal bank seat for passers-by' and his friends obliged with a seat beside the lock. A little farther along on the north side you can sit beside Kavanagh himself, or at least a bronze replica of him, comfortably lounging on a bench watching his beloved canal.

Canalside Pubs

The next stretch of the canal has some fine pubs, such as the Barge and the Portobello, both right by the water. The Portobello is an old-fashioned place with music on weekend evenings and Sunday lunchtimes. The Lower Deck on Richmond St is also near the canal. You could pause for a meal at the Locks Restaurant on Windsor Terrace. The Institute of Education Business College by the Portobello was built in 1807 as Portobello House; then as the Portobello Hotel it was the Dublin terminal for passenger traffic on the canal. The artist Jack B Yeats lived here for the last seven years of his life until his death in 1957.

Further west the Circular Line isn't quite as interesting and is better appreciated on a bicycle rather than on foot. The spur running off the Circular Line alongside Grand Canal Bank to the old St James's St Harbour has been filled in and is now a park and bicycle path.

BALLSBRIDGE

South-east of central Dublin, the suburb of Ballsbridge was mainly laid out between 1830 and 1860 and many of the streets have British names with a distinctly military bearing. Many embassies, including the flashy circular US embassy, are in Ballsbridge. It also has some mid-range B&Bs and several top-end hotels. The main attractions in Ballsbridge are the Royal Dublin Society Showground and the Lansdowne Rd rugby and football (soccer) stadium (see the Football & Rugby section in the Entertainment chapter).

Royal Dublin Society Showground

Founded in 1731, the Royal Dublin Society was involved in the establishment of the National Museum, Library, Gallery and Botanic Gardens. The showground, on Merrion Rd in Ballsbridge, is used for exhibitions throughout the year, but the main event, the Dublin Horse Show, reflects the society's agricultural background. The show takes place in the first week of August and includes an international showjumping contest amoong other events.

Tickets for the horse show (IR£5 for general entry, from IR£6 to IR£10 for seating) can be booked in advance by contacting the Ticket Office (☎ 668 0866), Royal Dublin Society, PO Box 121, Ballsbridge, Dublin 4. Ask at the tourist office or consult a listings magazine for details of other events held at the showground.

PEARSE MUSEUM

Patrick (or Padráig in the Irish he worked hard to promote) Pearse was a leader of the 1916 Easter Rising and one of the first to be executed at Kilmainham Jail. St Enda's, the school he established with his brother Willie to further his ideas of Irish language and culture, is now a museum (☎ 493 4208) and memorial to the brothers. It's in St Enda's Park (sometimes known as Pearse Brothers Park) at the junction of Grange Rd and Taylor's Lane in Rathfarnham, southwest of the city centre.

The museum is open from 10 am to 5.30 pm daily between May and August, to 5 pm from February to April and in September and October and to 4 pm from November to January. It is closed daily between 1 and 2

pm. There is no admission charge; you can get there on bus No 16 or 47A from the city centre.

OTHER MUSEUMS

As well as the institutions described earlier in this chapter, Dublin has a number of smaller museums or museums of specialist interest such as the following:

George Bernard Shaw House
  (Map 6, ☎ 872 2077) 33 Synge St, Dublin 2; open from 10 am to 5 pm Monday to Saturday, 2 to 6 pm Sunday and holidays, May to October; entry is IR£2/1.10 (students IR£1.60).
Irish Jewish Museum
  (☎ 453 1797) 3-4 Walworth Rd, off Victoria St, Portobello, Dublin 8; housed in a former synagogue, this museum relates the history of Ireland's Jewish community; open Sunday, Tuesday and Thursday from 11 am to 3.30 pm.
Irish Traditional Music Archive
  (☎ 661 9699) 63 South Merrion Square; collects, preserves and catalogues traditional Irish music; officially open to the public during weekday office hours, but phone first for an appointment.
Museum of Childhood
  (☎ 497 3223) The Palms, 20 Palmerston Park, Rathmines, Dublin 6; the main display is a collection of dolls, some nearly 300 years old; only open from 2 to 5.30 pm on Sunday, but you may be able to make an appointment to visit at other times; entry is IR£1/75p.

OTHER GALLERIES

Apart from the major galleries mentioned earlier in this chapter, Dublin boasts many private galleries, arts centres and corporate exhibition areas.

The **Douglas Hyde Gallery** (☎ 608 1116) is in the Arts Building in Trinity College (Map 6); the entrance is on Nassau St. The **City Arts Centre** (Map 6, ☎ 677 0643), 23-25 Moss St, has changing exhibitions in its two galleries, which are open Monday to Saturday from 11 am to 5 pm. Entry is free. In the **Bank of Ireland Arts Centre** (Map 7) in Foster Place, behind the actual bank, there are usually changing displays of contemporary Irish art. Other Dublin galleries include the following:

Andrew's Lane Theatre Gallery
(Map 7, ☎ 679 5720) 9-17 Andrew's Lane, Ex-
chequer St, Dublin 2
Arts Council
(Map 6, ☎ 661 1840) 70 South Merrion
Square, Dublin 2
Crypt Art Centre
(Map 7, ☎ 671 3383) Royal Chapel, Dublin
Castle, Dublin 2
Designyard
(Map 7, ☎ 677 8453) Applied Arts Centre, 12
East Essex St, Dublin 2
Gallery of Photography
(Map 7, ☎ 671 4654) Meeting House Square,
Temple Bar, Dublin 2
Graphic Studio
(Map 7, ☎ 679 8021) Through the Arch, Cope
St, Temple Bar, Dublin 2
Kennedy Gallery
(Map 6, ☎ 475 1740) 12 Harcourt St, Dublin 2
Kerlin Gallery
(Map 7, ☎ 670 9093) Anne's Lane, Dublin 2
Oliver Dowling Gallery
(Map 6, ☎ 676 6573) 19 Kildare St, Dublin 2
Original Print Gallery
(Map 7, ☎ 677 3657) Black Church Studio, 4
Temple Bar, Dublin 2
Peppercanister Gallery
(Map 6, ☎ 475 7816) St Stephen's Church,
Upper Mount St, Dublin 2
Rubicon Gallery
(Map 7, ☎ 670 8055) 10 St Stephen's Green,
Dublin 2
Solomon Gallery
(Map 7, ☎ 679 4237) Top Floor, Powerscourt
Townhouse shopping centre, South William St,
Dublin 2
Taylor Galleries
(Map 6, ☎ 676 6055) 16 Kildare St, Dublin 2
Temple Bar Gallery & Studios
(Map 7, ☎ 671 0073, 679 9259) 5 Temple Bar,
Dublin 2
Tom Caldwell Gallery
(Map 6, ☎ 668 8629) 31 Upper Fitzwilliam St,
Dublin 2

Activities

Dublin offers plenty of sporting opportunities for visitors.

BEACHES & SWIMMING

Even a hot summer day is unlikely to raise
the water temperature much above freezing
but there are some pleasant beaches and

many Joyce fans feel compelled to follow in
Buck Mulligan's footsteps and take a dip in
the Forty Foot Pool at Dun Laoghaire as
Mulligan did in *Ulysses*. Sandy beaches
near the centre include Sutton (7km), Portmarnock (10km), Malahide (10km; this
beach holds a very popular Christmas Day
swim for the very brave), Claremont
(12km) and Donabate (15km). Although the
beach at Sandymount is nothing special, it's
only 5km south-east of central Dublin.
There are outdoor public pools at Blackrock, Clontarf and Dun Laoghaire.

SCUBA DIVING

Ireland has some of the best scuba diving in
Europe though most of it is off the west
coast. From Dun Laoghaire scuba divers
head for the waters around Dalkey Island.
The Irish Underwater Council (☎ 284
4601), 78A Patrick St in Dun Laoghaire,
publishes the quarterly magazine *Subsea*.
Oceantec (☎ 280 1083) is a dive shop in
Dun Laoghaire that organises local dives.
See Dun Laoghaire in the Seaside Suburbs
chapter for more details.

SAILING & WINDSURFING

The coastline north and south of Dublin is
popular for sailing. Howth, Malahide and
Dun Laoghaire are the most popular sailing
centres, but you can also go sailing at Clontarf, Kilbarrack, Rush, Skerries, Sutton and
Swords. See Dun Laoghaire in the Seaside
Suburbs chapter for details of sailing clubs
there. The Irish Sailing Association (☎ 280
0239) is at 3 Park Rd, Dun Laoghaire.

Dinghy sailing courses are offered by the
Irish National Sailing School (☎ 280 6654)
at 115 Lower George's St, Dun Laoghaire,
and by the Fingall Sailing School (☎ 845
1979), Upper Strand Rd, Broadmeadow
Estuary, Malahide.

Windsurfing enthusiasts should head for
Surfdock Centre (☎ 668 3945), which operates from a barge at Grand Canal Dock,
South Dock Rd, Ringsend. The centre runs
windsurfing courses costing from IR£25 for
a three hour 'taster' session to IR£90 for a

12 hour course. You can also rent sailboards from IR£10 an hour.

FISHING

Ireland is renowned for its fishing, and many visitors come to the country for no other reason. Bord Fáilte produces several information leaflets on fishing. Dublin's fishing-tackle shops can supply permits, equipment, bait and advice; check the classified phone directory under Fishing Gear & Tackle. Sea fishing is popular at Howth, Dun Laoghaire and Greystones. The River Liffey has salmon fishing (fair) and trout fishing (good). Brown trout are found between Celbridge and Millicent Bridge, near Clane, 20km from the centre. The Dublin Trout Anglers' Association has fishing rights along parts of this stretch of the Liffey and on the River Tolka.

GLIDING & HANG-GLIDING

Phone ☎ 831 4551 or 088-589245 for information on hang-gliding from the Great Sugar Loaf Mountain in County Wicklow. Contact the Dublin Gliding Club (☎ 298 3994), at Gowtan Grange near Punchestown, for general information on gliding in the Dublin area.

GOLF

Golf is enormously popular in Ireland. There are more than 20 private nine-hole and 18-hole club courses in and around Dublin and typical fees range from around IR£10 to IR£30 a day (more on weekends); fees are usually based on a per day rather than a per round basis. Public courses include Corballs (☎ 843 6583) at Donabate (15km) and Deer Park (☎ 832 2624) at Howth (10km).

Dublin also has many short 'pitch and putt' courses; for information contact the Pitch & Putt Union of Ireland (☎ 450 9299), House of Sport, Long Mile Rd, Dublin 12.

BOWLING

There are two kinds of bowling available in Dublin. Indoor ten-pin bowling is very popular and can be played at Leisureplex Coolock (☎ 848 5722), Malahide Road; Village Green Centre (☎ 459 9411), Tallaght; Stillorgan Bowl (☎ 288 1656), Stillorgan; Metro Bowl (☎ 855 0400), 149 North Strand Road; Superdome (☎ 626 0700), Palmerstown and Bray Bowl (☎ 286 4455), Quinsboro Road, Bray.

The more genteel outdoor game is played at Herbert Park in Ballsbridge (☎ 665 1875) and at Kenilworth Bowling Club (☎ 497 2305), Grosvenor Square.

CYCLING

Ireland has produced its fair share of cycling champions (such as former world champion Sean Kelly and 1988 Tour de France winner and world champion Stephen Roche), but competitive cycling is not nearly as popular as it is in continental Europe. In 1998, however, Ireland was given the honour of hosting the first two stages of the Tour de France, partly in recognition of the achievements of Kelly and Roche (the first stage began in the southern Dublin suburb of Dundrum, Roche's birthplace).

For full information about competitive cycling events, including the Tour of Ireland, contact the Federation of Irish Cyclists (☎ 855 1522) at 619 North Circular Rd, Dublin 9.

Bicycles can be rented for about IR£38 per week plus deposit. There are two dozen firms around the city that rent them; see Bicycle in the Getting Around chapter for details of rental outlets.

OTHER ACTIVITIES

The Dublin Ice Rink (☎ 453 4153), 37A Dolphin's Barn, Dublin 8, is open Monday to Friday from 2.30 to 5 pm and 7.30 to 10.30 pm. Squash and tennis courts can also be found in and around the city. For more information on these and other sports the best paper is *In Dublin*.

For bird-watching, see the Clontarf & North Bull Island section earlier in this chapter and Ireland's Eye under Howth in the Seaside Suburbs chapter.

Courses

ENGLISH-LANGUAGE COURSES

Dublin is a popular centre for learning English, particularly among people from other Catholic countries (mainly Spain, Italy, France and Portugal). Students come here in huge numbers every summer and are a colourful part of the city scene.

Bord Fáilte publishes a list of schools recognised by the Department of Education for the teaching of English as a foreign language. Some schools run summer courses or provide various specialised programmes, for business people for example.

The schools can arrange accommodation and organise sporting and cultural activities. Some of the approved schools in Dublin are:

Academy of English Studies Ireland
(☎ 279 6464, fax 279 6465) 33 Dawson St (Map 7), Dublin 2
Dublin School of English
(☎ 677 3322, fax 626 4692) 10-12 Westmoreland St (Map 7), Dublin 2
English Language Institute
(☎ 475 2965, fax 475 2967) 99 St Stephen's Green (Map 6), Dublin 2
Language Centre
(☎ 706 8520, fax 269 4409) University College Dublin, Belfield, Dublin 4

Dublin Walks

WALK 1: MOUNTJOY SQUARE
TO ST STEPHEN'S GREEN

Walking between Mountjoy Square and St Stephen's Green takes you from one part of the city's Georgian heritage to another. You start at one of Dublin's great Georgian squares, in the run-down northern part of the city, proceed down O'Connell St, the city's major thoroughfare, cross the Liffey and finish at another of the great Georgian squares, this time in the city's wealthiest area. Many of the attractions en route are described in greater detail in the Things to See & Do chapter of this book.

Mountjoy Square (1 on map) is one of Dublin's magnificent squares but it has fallen on hard times. The fine buildings are still there, just waiting for a north Dublin renaissance. From the north-western corner of the square walk up Upper Gardiner St and turn left along Lower Dorset St to **No 7 Eccles St** (2), the fictional home of Joyce's Leopold and Molly Bloom in *Ulysses*. Apart from a plaque and a relief of Joyce's face, there's nothing to see because the house was demolished to build a nursing home in 1982. Real-life residents of Eccles St included the architect Francis Johnston, whose home at **No 64** (3) has survived, though in a rather shabby state. At one time Johnston had his own private bell tower in the back garden until neighbours complained about the noise.

Turn around and cross Lower Dorset St on to North Temple St. On Hardwicke Place by Temple St is the fine but now disused **St George's Church** (4) designed by Francis Johnston, whose house we just left. And where did the church's bells come from? Why, from Johnston's back garden bell tower of course!

Turn right on to Denmark St and pass the **Jesuit College** at Belvedere House (5). James Joyce attended the school between 1893 and 1898 and went on to become its most famous graduate. The tall spire of the

Abbey Presbyterian Church (6) on the corner of North Parnell Square and Frederick St looms in front of you. Built in 1864, it is often referred to as Findlater's Church after the grocery magnate who financed the building's construction.

The northern slice of Parnell Square is the **Garden of Remembrance** (7), opened in 1966 to commemorate the 50th anniversary of the Easter Rising. The sculpture (8) here illustrates the legend of the **Children of Lir**, who were transformed into swans by their wicked stepmother. Outside the garden is a small **monument** (9) to the victims of a Loyalist paramilitary terrorist bomb campaign in Dublin on 17 May 1974. The writer Oliver St John Gogarty (1878-1957) was born at **5 East Parnell Square** (10).

On the northern side of the square, facing the park, are the **Dublin Writers' Museum** (11) and the **Hugh Lane Municipal Gallery of Modern Art** (12). Walk around the square, noting more fine but dilapidated Georgian buildings on the western side of the square, one of them housing the **Sinn Féin Bookshop** (13). The southern part of Parnell Square is occupied by the **Rotunda Hospital** (14), built in 1757. As you walk along the southern side of the square look for the **Patrick Conway** pub (15), which opened in 1745. In the south-eastern corner of the square is the old Rotunda, now occupied by the **Gate Theatre** (16).

O'Connell St, Dublin's major boulevard, begins at this corner of the square and sweeps south to O'Connell Bridge and the Liffey. Unfortunately, the street has had a hard time of it this century. One side was burnt out in the 1916 Easter Rising, the other during the Civil War, and whatever remained was ripped out by short-sighted property developers in the 1960s and 70s.

Despite this, O'Connell St has numerous points of interest, including a varied collection of statues down the centre, the first of which is a grandiose **statue of Charles**

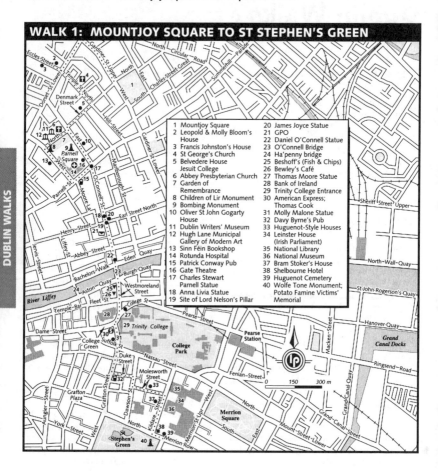

WALK 1: MOUNTJOY SQUARE TO ST STEPHEN'S GREEN

1 Mountjoy Square
2 Leopold & Molly Bloom's House
3 Francis Johnston's House
4 St George's Church
5 Belvedere House Jesuit College
6 Abbey Presbyterian Church
7 Garden of Remembrance
8 Children of Lir Monument
9 Bombing Monument
10 Oliver St John Gogarty House
11 Dublin Writers' Museum
12 Hugh Lane Municipal Gallery of Modern Art
13 Sinn Féin Bookshop
14 Rotunda Hospital
15 Patrick Conway Pub
16 Gate Theatre
17 Charles Stewart Parnell Statue
18 Anna Livia Statue
19 Site of Lord Nelson's Pillar

20 James Joyce Statue
21 GPO
22 Daniel O'Connell Statue
23 O'Connell Bridge
24 Ha'penny bridge
25 Beshoff's (Fish & Chips)
26 Bewley's Café
27 Thomas Moore Statue
28 Bank of Ireland
29 Trinity College Entrance
30 American Express; Thomas Cook
31 Molly Malone Statue
32 Davy Byrne's Pub
33 Huguenot-Style Houses
34 Leinster House (Irish Parliament)
35 National Library
36 National Museum
37 Bram Stoker's House
38 Shelbourne Hotel
39 Huguenot Cemetery
40 Wolfe Tone Monument; Potato Famine Victims' Memorial

Stewart Parnell (17). Continue walking down O'Connell St, passing the fountain **statue of Anna Livia** (based on the Irish name for the Liffey), referred to by locals as 'the floozy in the Jacuzzi' among other names (18). The Henry St-Earl St crossing was the former position of **Nelson's Pillar** (19), blown up by the IRA in 1966. There's a notable **statue of James Joyce** (20) at the O'Connell St end of pedestrianised Earl St. His bemused look perhaps reflects the irony that a writer whose masterpiece was banned in his own country throughout his life should be so honoured.

On the other side of O'Connell St, the **GPO** (21) towers over the street. Its role as the starting point for the 1916 Easter Rising makes this an important site in Ireland's recent history. At the river end of the street the **statue of Daniel O'Connell** (22) looks squarely up the street that bears his name.

Cross the Liffey on **O'Connell Bridge** (23), the most important bridge in the city. If you look to the right you can see the pedestrian **Ha'penny Bridge** (24). Across the bridge you join Westmoreland St and pass two of Dublin's best-known restaurants, **Beshoff's** (25) and **Bewley's** (26). At the bottom of Westmoreland St, on the left, is a **statue of Thomas Moore** (27), the poet, eloquently plonked by a public toilet.

To the right is the long, curving, windowless façade of the **Bank of Ireland** (28), which started life as the Irish Houses of Parliament. When the Act of Union subsumed the Irish Parliament into the British one, the building became a bank. Perhaps surprisingly it did not become the parliament building for independent Ireland. On the left is the main entrance to **Trinity College** (29), flanked by statues of Edmund Burke and Oliver Goldsmith looking out over College Green, once a real green but now

filled with buildings, including those popular tourist destinations, the offices of **American Express** and **Thomas Cook** (30).

Your steps now take you into Grafton St, passing the statue of the fictional **Molly Malone** (31). In the song named after her she 'wheeled her wheelbarrow, through streets broad and narrow', which is what she's doing here, although Dubliners will tell you that she belongs on the less fashionable north side, on or near Moore St. In typical Dublin fashion the notably well-endowed statue has been dubbed 'the tart with the cart'. In summer, pavement artists are often busy producing chalk pictures on the pavement here.

Road traffic has to turn into Nassau St but you can enter the pedestrianised area of **Grafton St**, Dublin's fanciest shopping

DUBLIN WALKS

Statues You Won't See

The Irish tendency to make political statements by blowing things up has had disastrous consequences for many statues of British dignitaries, most notably the Lord Nelson Pillar on O'Connell St, which was felled in 1966.

Equestrian statues have had a particularly bad time of it, perhaps because anyone regally riding a horse was likely to be some oppressive Englishman and so fully deserved to be unseated. For example, William of Orange and his horse were commemorated on College Green in front of Trinity College in 1701. Unfortunately he was portrayed riding away from the college and for this slight (quite apart from any general Irish dislike for King Billy) the statue suffered numerous indignities over the years. Consequently, in 1765 it was raised to a much higher pedestal. This new elevated position did not prevent it from being bombed in 1836, but a new head, leg and arm put the king to rights until a more serious explosion resulted in his complete removal in 1929.

King George I was honoured with an equestrian statue on Essex Bridge in 1722, but it was moved to Aungier St in 1753 when the bridge was rebuilt and then moved again to Mansion House in 1798. In 1937 it was sold to a British professor and left Ireland. King George II was also honoured with an equestrian statue in St Stephen's Green in 1758 but it was demolished by a bomb in 1937. An equestrian statue of Field Marshal Gough was erected in Phoenix Park in 1880. In 1944 the head and sword were removed, but with a saw rather than explosives. The high explosives followed in 1956 and, with more effect, in 1957, thus eliminating the city's last equestrian statue.

Riding a horse was not, however, the sole prerequisite for explosive destruction; pedestrian statues have had the same treatment. Among these were the earl of Carlisle (1869, Phoenix Park, blown up in 1958) and the earl of Eglington and Winton (1866, St Stephen's Green, also blown up in 1958).

street. At the next corner, turn left off Grafton St into Duke St, where the famous pub, **Davy Byrne's** (32), is situated. At the bottom of Duke St turn right on to Dawson St and left into Molesworth St, looking for the gabled **Huguenot-style houses** (33) built between 1736 and 1755.

Molesworth St brings you out on to Kildare St, facing the back of **Leinster House** (34), the Irish parliament. It is flanked on either side by the similarly designed **National Library** (35) and **National Museum** (36). Turn right down Kildare St, looking for the sign at **No 30** (37) announcing that Bram Stoker, the author of *Dracula*, used to live there. At the bottom of the street the **Shelbourne Hotel** (38) stands on the corner, facing **St Stephen's Green**. The Shelbourne, Dublin's premier hotel, opened for business in 1824, though the present building only dates back to 1867. At the front of the hotel, note the statues of Nubian princesses and their slave girls with fettered ankles. Past the Shelbourne is a **Huguenot Cemetery** (39), a reminder of the French Huguenots who came to Ireland from the late 17th century. Opposite the Shelbourne, on the northwestern corner of St Stephen's Green, is the **Wolfe Tone Monument** (40) dedicated to the leader of the failed 1796 invasion. You'll also find a monument to the victims of the mid 19th century Potato Famine.

Back on the other side of the road, the Shelbourne is a good place to end this stroll, because if you've timed it right you can drop in for afternoon tea and scones.

WALK 2: CUSTOM HOUSE TO THE FOUR COURTS

Modern Dublin's architecture is a mixed bag. Although nothing wonderful has been torn down and replaced with something colossal and awful, a few buildings have been torn down and replaced with something mediocre. Dublin's erratic skyline is an indication that architecture is not modern Ireland's greatest skill. When the city was in its prime, its most important architect was James Gandon, and this walk takes you

by a convoluted route between his two riverside masterpieces.

The **Custom House** (1 on map), built between 1781 and 1791, dominates Custom House Quay. It's a building that rewards both a distant view and closer inspection, so start by walking along the front to see the heads that represent the gods of Ireland's greatest rivers. The only goddess is that of the River Liffey, over the main entrance. The building, burnt out during the 1921 Civil War then totally rebuilt, now houses government offices.

From the Custom House walk along Eden Quay past **Liberty Hall** (2), the headquarters of the Irish Transport & General Workers' Union. Although it reaches 61m, making it Dublin's only real skyscraper, it's simply a boring 17 storey building.

Turn up Marlborough St to the **Abbey Theatre** (3) on the corner of Lower Abbey St. Despite the 15 year delay in rebuilding it, this replacement for the original Abbey Theatre, which was destroyed by fire in 1951, is a disappointing place to carry such a famous name.

Walk along Lower Abbey St under the elevated DART railway line to Beresford Place behind the Custom House. There you'll find the **Busáras** (4), the main Dublin bus station. The huge **International Financial Services Centre** (5), also on Beresford Place, houses the Allied Irish Bank, the Bank of Ireland and other such institutions.

Cross the river by the **Talbot Memorial Bridge** (6) and stand on George's Quay to admire the view of the Custom House across the Liffey. This is the best view of the building because farther upriver the railway **Loop Line Bridge** (7) slashes right across the front. Walk up Moss St from the river and turn left into Townsend St, then immediately right past **St Mark's Church** (8) on the corner of Pearse St. Built in 1758, the church is no longer used for worship.

Turn left along Pearse St, then right at Westland Row behind Trinity College. **Pearse station** (9), originally known as Westland Row station, was the city-centre terminal for the Dublin to Kingstown (Dun

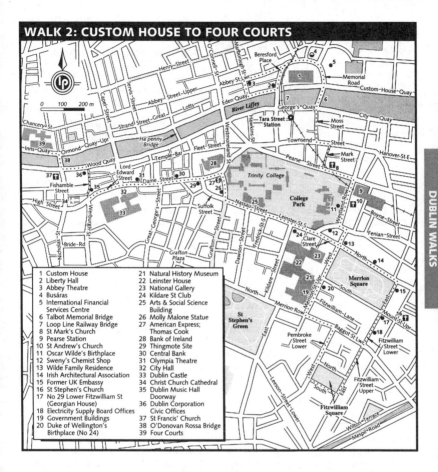

WALK 2: CUSTOM HOUSE TO FOUR COURTS

1 Custom House
2 Liberty Hall
3 Abbey Theatre
4 Busáras
5 International Financial Services Centre
6 Talbot Memorial Bridge
7 Loop Line Railway Bridge
8 St Mark's Church
9 Pearse Station
10 St Andrew's Church
11 Oscar Wilde's Birthplace
12 Sweny's Chemist Shop
13 Wilde Family Residence
14 Irish Architectural Association
15 Former UK Embassy
16 St Stephen's Church
17 No 29 Lower Fitzwilliam St (Georgian House)
18 Electricity Supply Board Offices
19 Government Buildings
20 Duke of Wellington's Birthplace (No 24)

21 Natural History Museum
22 Leinster House
23 National Gallery
24 Kildare St Club
25 Arts & Social Science Building
26 Molly Malone Statue
27 American Express; Thomas Cook
28 Bank of Ireland
29 Thingmote Site
30 Central Bank
31 Olympia Theatre
32 City Hall
33 Dublin Castle
34 Christ Church Cathedral
35 Dublin Music Hall Doorway
36 Dublin Corporation Civic Offices
37 St Francis' Church
38 O'Donovan Rossa Bridge
39 Four Courts

DUBLIN WALKS

Laoghaire) line, which began operation in 1834 as the first commuter-train service in the world. It was built by the railway engineer William Dargan, who also organised the 1853 Dublin Industrial Exhibition.

Next to the station is the Catholic **St Andrew's Church** (10), built between 1832 and 1837. As you proceed down Westland Row you'll pass **Oscar Wilde's birthplace** (11) at No 21.

Taking a left and then a right turn brings you to the north-western corner of **Merrion Square**, but as you make that first left turn look on your right for **Sweny's Chemist Shop** (12) at 1 Lincoln Place. This is where Bloom pauses in *Ulysses* to buy a bar of lemon soap. Walk along the northern side of the square, passing some of Dublin's finest Georgian houses, though few of them are private homes today. The Wildes lived at **No 1** (13) and the **Irish Architectural Association** has its headquarters at No 8 (14). On the eastern side at No 39 (15) is the site of the **former UK embassy**.

Look down Upper Mount St to **St Stephen's Church** (16), built in 1824 and a popular landmark affectionately known as the 'Peppercanister Church'. On the corner of Upper Mount St at **No 29 Lower Fitzwilliam St** (17) is a beautifully restored old Georgian house now open to the public. Until 1965 East Merrion Square and its continuation, Lower Fitzwilliam St, made up the longest unbroken stretch of Georgian architecture in Europe. Then the Electricity Supply Board demolished 16 of the buildings to construct a new **office block** (18). Loud protests were to no avail. No 29 is, no doubt, a belated act of contrition.

Head south, across Lower Baggot St to **Fitzwilliam Square**, the last of Dublin's great Georgian squares and one of the finest. The central park is still reserved for local residents. Make a circuit of the square and then head north up Lower Pembroke St to rejoin Lower Baggot St. Turn left and then right up Upper Merrion St, glancing at the imposing **Government Buildings** (19) on the left and passing **No 24** (20), where Arthur Wellesley, the Duke of Wellington, may have been born, on the right. This is now one of four townhouses that make up the Merrion Hotel. On the left you pass the **Natural History Museum** (21), **Leinster House** (22), the seat of the Irish government, and the **National Gallery** (23). You're now back on Merrion Square. At the top corner turn left along Clare St, which becomes Leinster St.

On the corner of Kildare and Leinster Sts, the Kildare St Club (24) is now home to the **Heraldic Museum**, the **Genealogical Office** and the **Alliance Française**, but at its peak the club was the bastion of Dublin conservatism. Across Leinster St are the grounds of **Trinity College**. It's said that in a College Park cricket match the great Victorian batsman WG Grace (1848-1915) once hit a magnificent six (the cricketing equivalent of a baseball home run) that soared right over Leinster St and smashed a window of the Kildare St Club. The club was founded in 1782 and moved into these Venetian-style premises in 1861. Note the fading carved animals that decorate the window ledges.

Continue along Nassau St with the grounds of Trinity College on your right. The **Arts & Social Science Building** (25) is one of the newer buildings on the campus and houses the Douglas Hyde Gallery of Modern Art. Rounding the end of the campus you turn into Grafton St, passing the statue of **Molly Malone** (26) and the offices of **American Express** and **Thomas Cook** (27), then into College Green with the columned sweep of the **Bank of Ireland** (28), the original Irish parliament, on the other side of the road.

Near the junction of Suffolk and Dame Sts is the site of a **Viking ceremonial mound** (29). It was levelled in 1685. On the right is the hideous modern **Central Bank** (30), completed in 1978. When it was almost finished, the building was found to be nearly 10m higher than shown on the plans and completely out of scale with its surroundings. An inquiry was held and the copper roof was removed to reduce the intrusion (simultaneously lessening the building's aesthetic appeal).

Continuing along Dame St you come to the ageing **Olympia Theatre** (31) on the right and the **City Hall** (32) on the left. Behind the City Hall is **Dublin Castle** (33), an architectural conglomeration of styles that has been built and rebuilt over the centuries. Dame St becomes Lord Edward St before you turn right down Fishamble St, the oldest street in Dublin, beside **Christ Church Cathedral** (34). The **Dublin Music Hall** (35) once stood on Fishamble St but only its doorway remains.

On the other side of Fishamble St are the **Dublin Corporation Civic Offices** (36), probably the most controversial modern constructions in Dublin. There was outrage at the city council's lack of taste and judgement when these large buildings were planned because they would clearly overshadow the cathedral. Anger turned to fury when excavations of the Wood Quay site revealed numerous remains of Dublin's earliest Viking settlement. Despite a huge protest march in 1978, the excavations were completed and the new offices built. In the 1990s two more blocks were added and, while they cannot entirely make up for the damage done, they have certainly improved the overall appearance of the offices.

Turn left on to **Wood Quay**; originally built in wood in the 13th century, then rebuilt in stone in 1676, this is the oldest quay on the Liffey. On the far side of Winetavern St is **St Francis' Church** (37), usually known as Adam and Eve's Church after the pub that once stood in front of it.

Finally, cross the **O'Donovan Rossa Bridge** (38) to James Gandon's second riverside masterpiece, the **Four Courts** (39). Originally begun by Thomas Cooley in 1776, it was integrated into Gandon's grand plan and completed between 1786 and 1801. Its copper dome mirrors the dome of Adam and Eve's Church across the river.

WALK 3: FROM THE CATHEDRALS THROUGH THE LIBERTIES

This walk takes you from Dublin's two Church of Ireland cathedrals through the area known as the Liberties west of Temple Bar, ending at Heuston station.

This area of Dublin includes Christ Church and St Patrick's cathedrals and extends to the St James's Gate Guinness Brewery. Medieval Dublin had a number of 'liberties' – areas outside the city jurisdiction where local courts were at liberty to administer the law. During the 17th century Protestants, including large numbers of French Huguenots, flocked here from the Continent to escape religious persecution at home. The weaving industries they established flourished until British trading restrictions brought about their collapse in the 18th century.

The area degenerated into a squalid slum and much recent redevelopment has concentrated on providing modern public housing, some of it impressive, some of it depressing. Although this is the oldest area of Dublin, settled by the Vikings 1000 years ago, in medieval times it was the area

'without', the part of the town outside the city walls that once enclosed Dublin Castle.

In that era Christ Church was the cathedral 'within' and St Patrick's was the cathedral 'without'. The Liberties has a number of twin Catholic and Protestant churches: two St Audoen's, two St Nicholas Withouts and two St Catherine's.

The walk starts at **St Patrick's Cathedral** (1 on map), inextricably connected with author, poet and satirist Jonathan Swift (see the boxed text 'Jonathan Swift' in the St Patrick's Cathedral section of the Things to See & Do chapter). Turn into St Patrick's Close beside the cathedral and the **Deanery** (2) is on your right. Swift once lived here but the present building is a more recent replacement. Just beyond the bend in the close is **Marsh's Library** (3) on the left.

At the junction head north up Bride St, passing red-brick Iveagh Trust housing put up around the end of the 19th century to accommodate Guinness workers. Although they're little more than slums now, these were fine buildings in their heyday. In a sign of the times the old **public baths** (4) in Bride Rd have been turned into a fitness club! Bride St eventually becomes Werburgh St and passes **St Werburgh's Church** (5) on the right. This fine old church is rarely used nowadays. Just before the church turn right down Little Ship St. Steps on the left at the end lead to **7 Hoey's Court** (6), birthplace of Jonathan Swift in 1687. An arch at the end of Little Ship St leads to the back of Dublin Castle. The striking powder-blue tower on the left is **Bermingham Tower** (7), built in the 13th century and used to detain state prisoners. It was badly damaged by a gunpowder blast in 1775 and rebuilt in an astonishing Strawberry Gothic style. Opposite the Bermingham Tower, the Old Barracks are being restored; at the time of writing the Chester Beatty Library was scheduled to open in the **Clock Tower Building** (8) in June 1999.

At the top of Werburgh St stands **Christ Church Cathedral** (9) on Christchurch Place. Between here and Wood Quay, excavations for the **Dublin Corporation Civic**

DUBLIN WALKS

Offices (10) revealed extensive traces of the city's 9th to 11th century Viking origins. Despite protests the corporation went ahead with the building. Fishamble St, running down to the river beside the corporation offices, has followed the same curving route and rejoiced in the same name for 1000 years. Follow the alley that runs behind the cathedral and links Fishamble St and Winetavern St and you'll find a **pebble mosaic** marking out the site of a Viking settlement (11), a late consolation for those who had campaigned against the construction.

Turn south into Winetavern St and continue past Christ Church Cathedral into Nicholas St; then turn right up Back Lane, past **Tailor's Hall** (12), built between 1703 and 1707, though 1770 is the date on the front door. This is Dublin's oldest surviving guild hall and dates from the time when the local weaving industry provided the material for the Liberties' tailors. Tailor's Hall was due to be demolished in the 1960s but An Taisce (National Trust for Ireland) stepped in and restored it as their headquarters. Across the road is **Mother Redcap's**

Market (13), a colourful collection of stalls selling everything from antiques to records, open Friday to Sunday. Back Lane emerges where High St changes into Cornmarket, and across the road is the **Catholic St Audoen's Church** (14). Behind this newer Catholic St Audoen's is the medieval **Church of Ireland St Audoen's Church** (15) and one of the few remaining fragments of the old city wall.

The Cornmarket was the grain market of medieval Dublin, but if you turn left from this street into Francis St you'll find the more modern **Iveagh Market** (16) on the left-hand side. It was established in 1907 by Lord Iveagh of the Guinness family and there are wonderfully expressive stone faces over the arches; round the corner, the face giving a broad wink is said to be modelled on Lord Iveagh himself. The market operates from Tuesday to Saturday but it's a pretty wretched affair. Opposite the market is the **Tivoli Theatre** (17).

Continue down Francis St, a centre for antique shops, past the Catholic church of **St Nicholas Without** (18), built in 1832 and

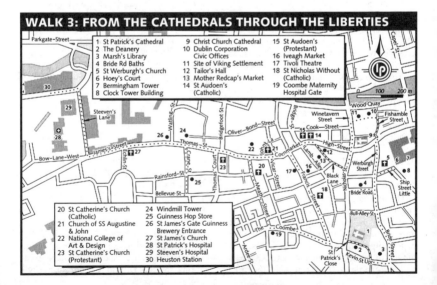

WALK 3: FROM THE CATHEDRALS THROUGH THE LIBERTIES

1 St Patrick's Cathedral	9 Christ Church Cathedral
2 The Deanery	10 Dublin Corporation Civic Offices
3 Marsh's Library	11 Site of Viking Settlement
4 Bride Rd Baths	12 Tailor's Hall
5 St Werburgh's Church	13 Mother Redcap's Market
6 Hoey's Court	14 St Audoen's (Catholic)
7 Bermingham Tower	15 St Audoen's (Protestant)
8 Clock Tower Building	16 Iveagh Market
	17 Tivoli Theatre
	18 St Nicholas Without (Catholic)
	19 Coombe Maternity Hospital Gate

20 St Catherine's Church (Catholic)	24 Windmill Tower
21 Church of SS Augustine & John	25 Guinness Hop Store
22 National College of Art & Design	26 St James's Gate Guinness Brewery Entrance
23 St Catherine's Church (Protestant)	27 St James's Church
	28 St Patrick's Hospital
	29 Steeven's Hospital
	30 Heuston Station

This sculpture above Iveagh Market is said to have been modelled on Lord Iveagh himself.

better known as St Nicholas of Myra. At the bottom of Francis St turn right into The Coombe, so called because it was once the 'coomb' or river valley of the Poddle. At its eastern end The Coombe becomes Dean St, named after the deanery of St Patrick's Cathedral, but it was previously known as Crosspoddle St because it used to cross the Poddle at this point.

West along The Coombe is the gateway of the now relocated **Coombe Maternity Hospital** (19). A plaque on the gate tells the sad story of the hospital's foundation in 1826, after two poor women and their newborn babies died during a snowstorm while making a dash for the Rotunda Hospital in north Dublin. The hospital was relocated to Cork St in 1967 and the portico is all that remains. Behind the gate a curious list of names is displayed; just who were The Grindstone Man, Johnny Wet Bread, Johnny Forty Coats, Stab the Rasher, The Umbrella Man, Damn the Weather, Nancy Needle Balls, Bang Bang, The Tuggers and Rags, Bottles and Bones?

Turn right into Meath St and walk up past the **Catholic St Catherine's Church** (20) to the junction of Thomas St. Turn right into Thomas St to the Church of SS Augustine and John (21). Completed in 1874, this Gothic-style Augustinian church was built on the site of a medieval priory to a design by Edward Welby Pugin, son of the famous architect Augustus Welby Pugin, who played a large part in Britain's Gothic revival. Known locally as John's Lane, it has Dublin's loftiest church spire. To the west of the church is the building that once housed John Power's distillery. When the Power's company was taken over, production of the well-known Power's Whiskey was moved to County Cork. The building (22), constructed in 1791, now houses the **National College of Art & Design** (NCAD).

Turn back along Thomas St and continue to the **Protestant St Catherine's Church** (23), built in 1769 but now deconsecrated and looking decidedly tatty and unused. A plaque records that Irish patriot Robert Emmet was beheaded outside the church in 1803 and another states that 16 of his supporters were hanged. His followers killed the Lord Chief Justice Kilwarden nearby.

Continue along Thomas St, passing the older parts of the St James's Gate Guinness Brewery on the left, to Crane St. Across the road you can see a 50m-high **windmill tower** (24) topped by a weather vane featuring St Patrick. Turn left down Crane St to the **Guinness Hop Store** (25), where you can learn about the history of the noble black brew and sample it too. Continue past Rainsford St to Bellevue St where you turn right, and walk past some ancient-looking brewery buildings. Near here was James's St harbour, the original terminus of the Grand Canal, where Guinness barges used to load up with stout. However, the harbour has been filled in and nothing of it remains. Retrace your steps up Crane St to Thomas St, turn left and walk along James's St. Continue past the imposing **brewery gate** (26) with 1759, the year of its founding, emblazoned above. **St James's Church** (27) is on the corner of Echlin St.

DUBLIN WALKS

Keep going along James's St, past the brewery, and bear right at a restored obelisk with four sundials, built in 1790. Turn right up Steeven's Lane, passing **St Patrick's Hospital** (28). Founded with money from Jonathan Swift's will, this psychiatric hospital is also known as Swift's Hospital. Naturally, Swift penned a witty poem to explain his philanthropic act:

He gave the little wealth he had,
To build a house for fools and mad:
And shew'd by one satiric touch,
No nation wanted it so much.

Just north of St Patrick's Hospital is **Steeven's Hospital** (29). Built from 1721 to 1733, it was the oldest public hospital in Ireland but is now closed. Swift was a director of the hospital and Stella Johnson, his long-term friend, left a large legacy for the hospital after her death in 1728. From here it's only a little further to **Heuston station** (30), built between 1845 and 1846 and originally known as Kingsbridge station. From here you can continue west to the Irish Museum of Modern Art (IMMA) nearby in the Royal Hospital Kilmainham or walk back to central Dublin along the Liffey.

Detail of Edward Smyth sculpture, King's Inns

The Dome of James Gandon's Custom House

Charles Stewart Parnell memorial, O'Connell St

Preserving the city's heritage, Parnell Square

The River Liffey – not only does its east-west course split Dublin geographically, it also divides the city psychologically into very distinct north and south sides.

Places to Stay

Dublin's accommodation map seems to be changing radically all the time. The city's increased popularity as a tourist destination has seen a massive increase in the number of new hotels and plans are afoot to build even more over the next few years. At the lower end of the accommodation scale the number of hostels and cheaper hotels has increased, but the real change has been in the number of top-grade hotels: there used to be only a handful of hotels that could claim to be 'the most luxurious place to stay' but now there are at least a dozen – for a small city such as Dublin this represents a massive increase. Many mid-range hotels that for many years offered plain and simple rooms at affordable prices have undergone major refurbishment and reinvented themselves to cater for the growing demand for high-quality service. They offer a more intimate and personalised service than the larger hotels, and have done extremely well too. Consequently, prices have soared. In some cases, they now rank alongside prices in some of the world's most expensive cities. It seems that the days of cheap accommodation are gone.

Another consequence of Dublin's popularity is that finding a bed can be tricky in any price range, especially between April and September. If you can plan ahead and book your room, it will make life easier. The alternative is to go to one of the Dublin Tourism offices and ask them to book you a room. For IR£1 plus a 10% deposit on the cost of the first night, they'll find you somewhere to stay, and will do so efficiently and with a smile. Sometimes this may require a great deal of phoning around so it can be a pound well spent. There are two tourist offices in the city, at Dublin airport and in the ferry terminal at Dun Laoghaire (see Tourist Offices in the Facts for the Visitor chapter).

The Backpackers Centre in Store St gives advice on the hostels run by Independent Holiday Hostels (IHH). See Useful Organisations in the Facts for the Visitor chapter for more information.

Accommodation options in central Dublin can be neatly divided into the areas north and south of the Liffey. The south is generally neater, tidier and more expensive. In compensation northside prices are often lower for equivalent standards. Prices drop as you move away from the centre so you can go farther out for cheaper prices or for better standards at the same price.

Accommodation prices vary according to season, reaching a peak during the main holiday periods or over public holidays. Prices quoted are those for the high season. You can usually get a bed in a hostel for IR£10 to IR£15. In a typical B&B the cost per person will be around IR£15 to IR£20. More expensive B&Bs or mid-range hotels cost around IR£20 to IR£60 per person. Dublin's top hotels cost upwards of IR£60 per person. Then there are the deluxe hotels, which can cost over IR£100 per person.

Places listed in this chapter are in central Dublin or the nearby suburbs. The suburbs of Dun Laoghaire and Howth are within easy commuting distance of the centre by car or Dublin Area Rapid Transit (DART); accommodation there is covered in the Seaside Suburbs chapter.

PLACES TO STAY – BUDGET
Camping

There's no convenient central camping ground in Dublin. Do *not* try to camp in Phoenix Park. Not only is it illegal, but it has proved to be dangerous – a German cyclist camping there was murdered in 1991. The **Shankill Caravan & Camping Park** (☎ 282 0011) is 16km south of the centre on the N11 Wexford Rd. A site for two costs IR£6 between June and August. You can get there on bus Nos 45 or 46 from Eden Quay. Another site is **Donabate Caravan Park** (☎ 843 6008) near Swords,

145

16km north of Dublin. Sites are IR£4 per person (IR£6 with a car); bus No 33B runs there from Eden Quay.

Hostels

Since there are no central camping grounds, budget travellers usually head for one of Dublin's many hostels, one of which is run by An Óige, the national youth hostel association. Others are run independently. Hostels offer the cheapest accommodation and are also great centres for meeting other travellers and exchanging information. You usually get a bunk in a crowded and often dilapidated dormitory, but some also offer smaller rooms or even singles and doubles if you're prepared to pay a bit more. A bunk room for four or more can be ideal for a budget-minded family.

Despite the number of hostels, they can all get booked up at the height of the summer rush (late June to early October).

North of the Liffey All of the hostels in the following section appear on Map 4.

The An Óige **Dublin International Youth Hostel** (☎ 830 1766, 61 Mountjoy St) is a well-equipped, 460 bed hostel in a restored and converted old building. It's open to members of Hostelling International (HI) and An Óige for IR£9, non-members IR£9.50. Overseas visitors who are not members can stay at the hostel and may join by obtaining a guest card and paying IR£1 for a stamp on top of the nightly charge. If they buy six stamps (total IR£7.50) they become a HI member. To stay here, you must have or hire a sleeping sheet.

The hostel is in the run-down northern area of the city centre, and grilles on the side windows reflect the fact that this isn't the most salubrious part of town. From Dublin Airport, bus No 41A drops you in Upper Dorset St, a few minutes walk from the hostel. It's a longer but clearly signposted walk from the bus and train stations.

Near the An Óige hostel is the mid-sized **Young Traveller Hostel** (☎ 830 5000) on St Mary's Place just off Upper Dorset St. All rooms accommodate four people and have

a shower and washbasin, but there are no kitchen facilities. The nightly cost is IR£10 including breakfast. You are advised not to walk alone in the streets round here at night.

Just next to the pro-Cathedral is the **Marlborough Hostel** (☎ 874 7629, 81-82 Marlborough St). It has four to 10-bed dorms from IR£7.50 per person and doubles from IR£13 per person. Facilities include a TV room, hot showers, lockers and a pleasant garden at the back. There is also a good information board in the lobby.

The IHH **Cardijn House Hostel** (☎ 878 8091, 'Goin' My Way', 15 Talbot St), not far from O'Connell St, is a smaller, older, central hostel. The nightly cost in slightly shabby four to 10-bed dorms is IR£8, including breakfast; showers are 50p. There are good, clean cooking facilities.

For convenience you can't beat the new **Abbey Hostel** (☎ 878 0700, 29 Bachelor's Walk) just next to O'Connell Bridge. Prices range from IR£14 per person in a 12 bed dorm to IR£30 for a bed in a double (less in low season). Breakfast is included. All rooms are furnished handsomely, and there are secure lockers throughout. Its excellent facilities include a dining hall, a conservatory and a barbecue area. Not surprisingly, this is a popular option for travellers and advance booking is advised.

Also convenient is the big IHH **Isaac's Hostel & Hotel** (☎ 836 3877, 2-5 Frenchman's Lane) near the Busáras and Connolly station and not far from popular restaurants and pubs on either side of the Liffey. This hostel, in a converted 18th century wine warehouse, has cooking facilities and a small café, but is run along lines that make some old-fashioned An Óige hostels look laid back: dorms are closed between 11 am and 5 pm, and baggage in the basement locker room can only be retrieved exactly on the hour and half-hour. Trains also pass close to some of the rooms. Dorm beds cost from IR£6 to IR£7.50. (In the adjoining Isaac's Hotel singles cost IR£14 and doubles IR£17.50 per person.)

Nearby is the more relaxed and welcoming IHH **Globetrotter's Tourist Hostel**

(☎ 873 5893, 46-48 Lower Gardiner St), where dorm beds cost IR£10 including continental breakfast. With 10 people to some dorms there's bound to be a bit of disturbance, but this is a clean, modern place with good security. The breakfasts, in a pleasant dining room overlooking a small garden, consist of a wide choice of cereals, juices and pastries. If you arrive midweek out of season a three-nights-for-the-price-of-two offer may eliminate even the small price difference between this and other hostels.

At IHH **Abraham House** (☎ 855 0600, 82-83 Lower Gardiner St) dorm beds cost IR£7.50/9.50 in the low/high season.

South of the Liffey IHH **Kinlay House** (Map 7, ☎ 679 6644, 2-12 Lord Edward St) is central, beside Christ Church Cathedral and Dublin Castle, but some rooms can suffer from traffic noise. Kinlay House is big and well equipped and costs from IR£11 per person in four-bed dorms, IR£11.50 to IR£13 for the better rooms (some with en suite bathrooms) and IR£17 for a single. The price includes a continental breakfast and cooking facilities are available. Bus Nos 54A, 68A, 78A and 123 stop outside.

IHH **Avalon House** (Map 7, ☎ 475 0001, 55 Aungier St), in a renovated old building, is just west of St Stephen's Green. It's well equipped and some of the cleverly designed rooms have mezzanine levels, which are great for families. The basic nightly cost in 12-bed dorms is IR£10.50 including a continental breakfast. A bed in a four bed room with attached bathroom costs IR£11.50; in a two bed room it's IR£13.50. Take bus Nos 16, 16A, 19 or 22 right to the door or Nos 11, 13 or 46A to nearby St Stephen's Green. From the Dun Laoghaire ferry terminal take bus No 46A to St Stephen's Green or the DART to Pearse station.

In the lively (and noisy) Temple Bar area is **Strollers Budget Accommodation** (Map 7, ☎ 677 5614/5422, 29 Eustace St), with prices including breakfast ranging from IR£10.50 to IR£14.50 a head. The hostel has no cooking facilities but guests get discounts in the adjoining café. Nearby is the

newish **Temple Bar House** (Map 7, ☎ 671 6277, 1 Cecilia St), with prices ranging from IR£10 for a bed in a dorm to IR£18 in a double. The more expensive rooms have en suite bathrooms; self-catering facilities are available. The hostel has a discount deal with a nearby covered car park.

Further out but with a good range of accommodation is **Morehampton House** (☎ 668 8866, 78 Morehampton Rd, Donnybrook). The cheapest beds, at IR£7.95, are in eight and 10-bed basement dorms. In bigger, lighter eight and four-bedded rooms you pay IR£9.95; in twins IR£12.50; and in triples IR£11. Breakfast is IR£1, but there are clean, spacious cooking facilities and a garden for picnics. Bus Nos 10, 46A and 46B pass the hostel.

Student Accommodation

South of the Liffey From June to September you can stay at Trinity College or University College Dublin (UCD). **Trinity College** (Map 7, ☎ 608 1177) sometimes has wonderfully positioned accommodation on campus in the city, but it's expensive at IR£28 per person for B&B. At **Trinity Hall** (☎ 497 1772, Dartry Rd, Rathmines) rates are IR£15 to IR£25 for singles or IR£14 to IR£25 per person in twin-bed rooms. If you're under 25 years of age and have a student card, you may be able to get a reduction on the price. There are some family rooms where children aged under 10 can stay free with two adults. To get there, take bus Nos 14 or 14A from D'Olier St beside the O'Connell Bridge.

UCD Village (☎ 706 7777) is 6km south of the centre, on the way to Dun Laoghaire. Accommodation here is in apartments, with three single rooms sharing a bathroom and a kitchen/dining/living area. It's modern and well appointed but a little far out and, at IR£24 (IR£118 a week), rather expensive. For a family, a three room apartment at IR£350 per week (minimum stay) may be good value. If you have a car, the ease of parking may compensate for the distance and the soulless surroundings, bus No 10 departs every 10 minutes from O'Connell

St/St Stephen's Green and goes direct to the campus. The fare is IR£1.10.

Bed & Breakfasts

In Dublin, as throughout Ireland, B&Bs are the backbone of cheap accommodation. Most Dublin B&Bs are small, consisting of a handful of rooms in a private house, though some are increasing the standard of their amenities and service and becoming guesthouses. They often present opportunities to meet the Irish less formally than in a regular hotel. The staff at tourist offices can make bookings and will direct you to a suitable choice of accommodation.

Dublin B&Bs generally cost between IR£15 to IR£25 per person per night. The cheaper ones don't always have private bathrooms, but where they do the cost is usually just IR£2 more. Dublin also has some more luxuriously equipped B&Bs costing from IR£25 per person, a price category that overlaps with the smaller hotels and guesthouses. Most places levy a supplement for single occupancy.

Since most B&Bs are small (between two and four rooms), they can quickly fill up, and with Dublin's increased popularity as a tourist destination, that can happen pretty much year-round. Your best bet is to book as far in advance of your arrival as possible, otherwise you might find yourself making dozens of phone calls in an effort to find a bed for the night. There's bound to be someone with a spare room, but you may find yourself some distance from the centre. If you arrive when accommodation is tight and don't like the location offered, the best advice is to take it and then try to book something better for subsequent nights.

Breakfast at a B&B almost invariably consists of cereal followed by a 'fry', which means fried eggs, bacon, sausages and bread. A week of B&B breakfasts exceeds every international guideline for cholesterol intake, but if you decline fried food you're left with cereal and toast, though some places offer bread as well. If your bloodstream can take it, you'll have enough food to last till dinner time, but it's a shame more

places don't offer alternatives such as fruit or delicious Irish bread and scones. More expensive B&Bs usually offer a better choice at breakfast.

Dublin has several areas with good B&Bs. For something cheap but close to the city, Gardiner St north of the Liffey is the place to look, though the street is rather run-down and is not the safest part of town, especially at the northern end. Still, the proper exercise of caution, particularly at night, should be enough to guarantee a trouble-free stay.

Further out, you can find a better price and quality combination north of the centre at Clontarf or in the seaside suburbs of Dun Laoghaire or Howth. The Ballsbridge area, just south-east of the centre, offers quality and convenience, but you pay more for the combination. Other suburbs to try are Sandymount (immediately east of Ballsbridge) and Drumcondra (north of the centre toward the airport).

North of the Liffey All of the B&Bs in the following section appear on Map 4.

There is a collection of places on Lower Gardiner St, near the bus and train stations, and another group on Upper Gardiner St, farther north near Mountjoy Square. This is not Dublin's prettiest or safest area but the B&Bs are respectable if rather basic.

The plain *Harvey's Guesthouse* (☎ 874 8384, 11 Upper Gardiner St) and *Stella Maris* (☎ 874 0835, 13 Upper Gardiner St) are just north of Mountjoy Square. Singles cost IR£16 per person (IR£18 with bathroom). There are several more B&Bs in the next few buildings on Upper Gardiner St, such as *Flynn's B&B* (☎ 874 1702) at No 15, *Carmel House* (☎ 874 1639) at No 16 and *Fatima House* (☎ 874 5410) at No 17. The cheapest is *Marian Guest House* (☎ 874 4129) at No 21, with rooms from IR£15 per person. Just off Upper Gardiner St from Mountjoy Square is the *Dergvale Hotel* (☎ 874 4753/3361, 4 Gardiner Place). Regular rooms are slightly more expensive here: singles/doubles with attached bathroom cost IR£26/50.

Hardwicke St is only a short walk from these Upper Gardiner St places and has a number of popular B&Bs, such as *Waverley House* (☎ 874 6132) at No 4 and *Sinclair House* (☎ 874 6132) at No 3. At these places singles cost from IR£20 to IR£22 and doubles cost from IR£30 to IR£34.

Clontarf There are numerous B&Bs along Clontarf Rd, about 5km north-east of the centre, but this is a busy, noisy road and the views are as much of oil terminals as of the sea. One of these B&Bs is the friendly and welcoming *Ferryview* (☎ 833 5893) at No 96. Further along there's the slightly more expensive *White House* (☎ 833 6798) at No 125, *San Vista* (☎ 833 9582) at No 237, *Bayview* (☎ 833 9870) at No 265 and *Sea Breeze* (☎ 833 2787) at No 312. B&Bs on Clontarf Rd typically cost from IR£15 to IR£20 for singles and between IR£25 and IR£35 for doubles. Bus No 30 from Abbey St will get you there for IR£1.

South of the Liffey Ballsbridge is not only the embassy quarter and the site for a number of upper-bracket hotels but is also the locale for a number of better quality B&Bs, such as *Morehampton Townhouse* (☎ 660 8630, 46 Morehampton Rd), directly opposite the Sachs Hotel. Singles/doubles are IR£40/55. All rooms are centrally heated and have bathrooms, and the excellent breakfast proves that there's more to life in the morning than bacon and eggs.

Mrs O'Donoghue's (☎ 660 0941, 41 Northumberland Rd), which has no sign, is convivial and costs IR£24/44. Despite its imposing Victorian presence there are only eight rooms in this fine, traditional B&B.

PLACES TO STAY – MID-RANGE

The line dividing the better B&Bs from guesthouses and cheaper hotels is often hazy. Places in this mid-range bracket usually cost from IR£25 to IR£60 per person per night. Some of the small, central hotels in this category are among the most enjoyable places to stay in Dublin. Add 12.5% tax to all prices.

The mid-range places are a big jump up from the cheaper B&Bs in facilities and price but still cost a lot less than Dublin's expensive hotels. Another advantage is that breakfast is usually provided (it generally isn't in the top-notch hotels) and it's a good breakfast (unlike those in the cheapest B&Bs), with fruit, a choice of cereals, croissants, scones and other delights to supplement the bacon and eggs.

North of the Liffey

Unless otherwise noted, all hotels in the following section appear on Map 4.

Just off O'Connell St is *Wynn's Hotel* (☎ 874 5131, fax 874 1556, 35-36 Lower Abbey St). Only a few steps away from the Abbey Theatre, this older hotel has 70 rooms, all with en suite bathroom, that cost IR£60/90 for singles/doubles, with reductions at weekends. Beside the river the *Ormond Hotel (Map 7, ☎ 872 1811, fax 872 1909, Upper Ormond Quay)* has 55 rooms with bathroom for IR£50/100. If you are staying midweek the prices are substantially lower. A plaque outside notes its role in the sirens episode of *Ulysses*.

The Townhouse (☎ 878 8808, fax 878 8787, 47-48 Lower Gardiner St), next to the Globetrotters Tourist Hotel and sharing a dining room with it, has singles/doubles for IR£37.50/60, with en suite facilities and a good breakfast included. This place is pleasingly decorated (the 'Rip van Winkle' honeymoon suite is particularly memorable) and safety-conscious, and has a small Japanese garden and car park. *Maple Guest House* (☎ 874 0225/5239, 75 Lower Gardiner St) has singles/doubles with bathroom for IR£40/60.

North of O'Connell St is *Caulfields Hotel* (☎ 878 0643, fax 878 1650, 18-19 Dorset St), a small hotel with 20 rooms costing IR£35/60. Weekend rates are slightly more expensive but are still a bargain. A full Irish breakfast is included.

Slightly closer to the centre is the *Castle Hotel* (☎ 874 6949, fax 872 7674, 34 Gardiner Row), with 35 rooms. It's just off Parnell Square, a few minutes walk from

PLACES TO STAY

O'Connell St but on the edge of the better part of north Dublin, before the decline sets in. Singles/doubles/triples cost IR£45/82/105. Nearby is **Barry's Hotel** (☎ 874 9407, fax 874 6508, 1-2 Great Denmark St). The hotel's 29 rooms, all with bathroom, cost IR£37/70.

South of the Liffey

Unless otherwise noted, all hotels in the following section appear on Map 6.

Just off O'Connell Bridge, the **Aston Hotel** (Map 7, ☎ 677 9300, fax 677 9007, 7-9 Aston Quay) is a comfortable new hotel with 27 rooms and all modern facilities, including cable TV and en suite bathrooms. For its location, prices are reasonable at IR£50/70 for single/double rooms. **The Fitzwilliam** (☎ 660 0448, fax 676 7488, 41 Upper Fitzwilliam St), on the corner of Lower Baggot St, is central but is nevertheless quiet at night. There are 12 rooms in this small hotel, all with en suite bathroom, for IR£45/70.

Staunton's on the Green (☎ 478 2133, fax 478 2263, 83 St Stephen's Green) is in a Georgian house in an excellent position. Single/double rooms cost IR£53/88, which includes breakfast.

Close to St Stephen's Green, in a magnificent Georgian building, is the **Russell Court Hotel** (☎ 478 4991, fax 478 4066, 21-25 Harcourt St), with 42 rooms with bathroom costing IR£65/87 a night. Across the road at No 84, **Albany House** (☎ 475 1092, fax 475 1093) has singles/doubles for IR£60/100. Further down at No 60, in a Georgian building where George Bernard Shaw lived from 1874 to 1876, is the **Harcourt Hotel** (☎ 478 3677, fax 475 2013), with 40 rooms costing IR£35/60 or IR£56/100 with bathroom.

Another place off St Stephen's Green is the **Leeson Court Hotel** (☎ 676 3380, fax 661 8273, 26-27 Lower Leeson St). The 20 rooms all have bathrooms and cost between IR£45 and IR£55 for singles and from IR£75 to IR£85 for doubles.

Latchfords (☎ 676 0784, 99-100 Lower Baggot St) offers serviced rooms with self-catering facilities in an impressive Georgian house. Prices are IR£52/79, with reductions for week-long stays. There's an excellent bistro attached.

Immediately opposite Christ Church Cathedral in Christ Church Place the big **Jurys Christ Church Inn** (☎ 455 0000, fax 454 0012) has rooms for IR£59 each.

Overlooking the Liffey and backing onto Temple Bar, the renovated **Wellington Hotel** (Map 7, ☎ 677 9315, fax 677 9387, 21-22 Wellington Quay) charges from IR£35 to IR£45 for a single and IR£68 to IR£80 for a double. Nearby, **Bloom's Hotel** (Map 7, ☎ 671 5622, fax 671 5997), on Anglesea St behind the Bank of Ireland, has 86 single/double rooms costing IR£65/75.

A short distance from Dublin Castle is the renovated **Central Hotel** (Map 7, ☎ 679 7302, fax 679 7303, 1-5 Exchequer St), which has 70 rooms for IR£95/140 without breakfast. The rooms are rather small but it's well located.

Elsewhere in Dublin

The friendly **Ariel House** (☎ 668 5512, fax 668 5845, 52 Lansdowne Rd) 2km southeast of the centre in Ballsbridge, is close to Lansdowne Rd station and near the big Berkeley Court Hotel. There are 28 beautifully decorated rooms, each with en suite bathroom; the nightly cost is IR£50/100 for single/double rooms, with breakfast extra. Out of peak season you may be able to negotiate a discount.

Further down, Lansdowne Rd changes its name to Herbert Rd, where you find the **Mt Herbert** (☎ 668 4321, fax 660 7077, 7 Herbert Rd), about 3km from the centre. There are 155 rooms with bathroom for IR£43.50/63 including breakfast. This hotel is also close to Lansdowne Rd station.

The well-equipped **Ashling Hotel** (Map 3, ☎ 677 2324, Parkgate St) 2.5km from the city centre and directly across the river from Heuston station, has 54 rooms costing IR£56.50/86 for a single/double room. The Austrian-born British philosopher Ludwig Wittgenstein stayed here in 1940 en route to the Aran Islands.

PLACES TO STAY – TOP END
North of the Liffey (Map 4)

The long-established **Gresham Hotel** (☎ 874 6881, fax 878 7175, 20-22 Upper O'Connell St) has elegant rooms for IR£140/160. The bar is a great place to go for a drink, even if you're not staying here. Across the street from the Gresham at No 40 is the **Royal Dublin Hotel** (☎ 873 3666, fax 873 3120), with 117 rooms at IR£99/126 for singles/doubles.

South of the Liffey

Unless otherwise noted, all hotels in the following section appear on Map 6.

Close to the National Museum, **Buswell's Hotel** (☎ 676 4013, 661 3888, fax 676 2090, 23-27 Molesworth St) has singles/doubles for IR£60/100 without breakfast. The small **Longfield's** (☎ 676 1367, fax 676 1542, 9-10 Lower Fitzwilliam St), between Merrion and Fitzwilliam squares, has 26 rooms at IR£90/140 for singles/doubles.

Brooks Hotel (Map 7, ☎ 670 4000, fax 670 4455, 59-62 Drury St) has 75 comfortable and modern rooms. Prices start at IR£110/150 without breakfast.

Stephen's Hall (☎ 661 0585, fax 661 0606, 14-17 Lower Leeson St) is near the south-eastern corner of St Stephen's Green. The 37 rooms, all with bathroom, cost IR£95/134 without breakfast.

The **Grafton Plaza** (Map 7, ☎ 475 0888, fax 475 0908), in Johnsons Place behind the St Stephen's Green shopping centre, has singles/doubles costing IR£110/135; continental breakfast is IR£6. It's expensive, but the location is hard to beat.

Also central is the **Georgian House** (☎ 661 8832, fax 661 8834, 20-21 Lower Baggot St), equally close to St Stephen's Green and Merrion Square. Once again this is a fine old Georgian building in excellent condition. Its 47 rooms all have attached bathrooms and cost IR£95/137. The breakfast is excellent and the restaurant is noted for its seafood. There's also a car park. At the time of writing the hotel was about to undergo renovations but it should be open again by the summer of 1999.

The elegant **Mont Clare Hotel** (☎ 661 6799, fax 661 5663, Clare St, just off Merrion Square) has 74 rooms costing IR£140 (without breakfast) for both single and double occupancy. Across the street, the **Davenport Hotel** (☎ 661 6800, fax 661 5663, Lower Merrion St) has 120 rooms in what was once Merrion Hall, built in 1863 for the Plymouth Brethren (a Puritan religious sect). All rooms cost IR£200, not including breakfast.

Ireland's largest hotel, the modern **Burlington** (☎ 660 5222, fax 660 8496, Upper Leeson St) is 2.5km south of the centre, over the Grand Canal. Rates start at IR£123/139 without breakfast.

In Ballsbridge, **Jury's Hotel & Towers** (☎ 660 5000, fax 660 5540, Pembroke Rd) is a large modern hotel. Rates start at IR£129 for a single, IR£150 for a double without breakfast. In summer the Irish cabaret here is a popular attraction.

In the same area is **Sachs Hotel** (☎ 668 0995, fax 668 6147, 19-29 Morehampton Rd). This small but elegant and expensive place has 20 rooms, all with bathroom, costing IR£85/120 for singles/doubles.

Airport Hotels

There are several hotels near Dublin airport, including the large **Forte Crest Hotel** (☎ 844 4211, fax 842 5874), off the M1 motorway beside the airport. It has 188 rooms costing IR£89/105 for singles/doubles. Airport hotels are subject to a 15% tax on top of the price.

PLACES TO STAY – DELUXE

Even more expensive than any top-end hotel are the deluxe hotels, which are truly in a league of their own. Temple Bar's most '-est' (nicest, trendiest, chicest and dearest) hotel is the newly refurbished **Clarence** (Map 7, ☎ 670 9000, fax 670 7800, 6-8 Wellington Quay). Bought by the band U2 in 1992, it underwent a three year facelift that turned it into a luxury hotel with few rivals in the city. Prices range from IR£185 for a simple single to more than IR£500 for a double suite. The penthouse is a nifty IR£1500 per night, not including breakfast.

The city's best-known hotel is the elegant **Shelbourne** *(Map 6, ☎ 676 6471, fax 661 6006, 27 St Stephen's Green)*. This is indubitably the best address at which to meet in Dublin. Despite the prices (singles start at IR£170) the rooms are a little cramped, but afternoon tea (IR£7.50 a head) at the Shelbourne is something all Dublin visitors should experience.

In time, the **Merrion** *(Map 6, ☎ 603 0600, fax 603 0700, Upper Merrion St)* may come to rival the Shelbourne as the city's most famous hotel. Occupying four Georgian houses (one of which is the reputed birthplace of Arthur Wellesley, the Duke of Wellington), this hotel is strictly for those who can afford the best. Singles start at IR£200, doubles at IR£220 and doubles in the main house start at IR£265.

The **Conrad** *(Map 6, ☎ 676 5555, fax 676 5424)*, a popular business hotel run by the Hilton group, is on Earlsfort Terrace, south of St Stephen's Green. The Conrad offers 'corporate rates' to both businesspeople and tourists; rooms start at IR£160, for a single or double.

Also close to St Stephen's Green, the grand, modern **Westbury** *(Map 6, ☎ 679 1122, fax 679 7078)* is in a small lane just off Grafton St, south Dublin's pedestrianised main shopping street. Singles start at IR£200. Rooms on the upper floors offer views of the Dublin Hills.

The **Berkeley Court** *(☎ 660 1711, fax 661 7238, Lansdowne Rd)*, south-east of the centre in a quiet and relaxed location in Ballsbridge, offers spacious rooms starting at IR£200. The penthouse suite is popular with visiting dignitaries.

LONG-TERM RENTALS

Finding long-term accommodation in Dublin is difficult for Dubliners, never mind visitors from abroad. Bord Fáilte runs a service called Ireland's Reservation (☎ 1800 668 668) that specialises in reserving accommodation. However, while it can find places for up to six months or even a year, it charges a non-refundable deposit of 10% of the total price.

There are several lettings agencies in Dublin. Matthews Letting & Management (☎ 679 2434, fax 679 2453, 40 Dame St, Map 7) specialises in long and short-term lets of apartments and houses, furnished or unfurnished. Home Locators (☎ 679 5233, fax 679 2715, 35 Dawson St, Map 6) has a wide selection of properties on its books. It charges a IR£5 registration fee and then helps you locate suitable accommodation.

A number of British newspapers, notably the *Daily Telegraph*, carry advertisements for long-term rentals in Ireland.

Places to Eat

FOOD

Whatever may be the case elsewhere in Ireland, no one need fear overcooked vegetables and shrivelled fish in Dublin. Indeed you'd have to be trying pretty hard not to eat well here.

The last decade has seen a huge increase in the number of restaurants of every type and price range, and the result has been a revolutionary change in Dubliners' attitudes to eating out. What was regarded as a luxury, experienced only on special occasions, has become almost a daily habit. This is reflected not only in the number of restaurants but in the crowds drawn to them virtually every night. During the day, an array of affordable set menus offers a wider variety of options than the usual takeaway sandwich or traditional pub lunch.

There is no shortage of fast-food joints, offering everything from traditional fish and chips to burgers, pizzas, kebabs and tacos. There are many branches of the usual suspects, from McDonald's (the Grafton St branch was once reputed to be the busiest in the world) to Burger King, plus the local pizza chain La Pizza and the vaguely Middle Eastern Abrakebabra.

Pubs are often good places in which to eat, particularly at lunch time, when a bowl of soup (usually vegetable) and some good bread can make a fine, economical meal. Seafood restaurants, long neglected in Ireland, are often good, and there are some superb vegetarian places.

Irish bread has a wonderful reputation and is indeed very good, but there's a tendency to fall back on the infamous sliced white bread *(pan* in Irish). B&Bs in particular are often guilty of this. Irish scones are a delight, however, and tea and scones make a great snack at any time of day. Even some pubs can rise to tea and scones these days. See Bed & Breakfasts in the Places to Stay chapter for information about the famous Irish fried breakfast.

DRINKS

In Ireland a drink means a beer – either lager or stout. Stout usually means Guinness, the world-famous black beer of Dublin, though other brands – Murphy's and Beamish – are available. If you don't develop a taste for stout (and you should at least try while you're in Dublin), a wide variety of lager beers are available, including Irish Harp or the usual imported varieties such as Budweiser, Foster's or Carlsberg, which are brewed in Dublin under licence. Smithwicks (the 'w' isn't pronounced) is the only locally brewed ale. Simply asking for a Guinness or a Harp will get you a pint (570mL, IR£2.40 to IR£2.80 in a pub). If you want a half-pint (IR£1.20 to IR£1.50) ask for a 'glass' or a 'half'. Children are usually allowed in pubs until about 7 or 8 pm.

Another traditionally Irish drink, though actually of relatively recent origin, is Irish coffee: a strong, hot, creamed coffee with a healthy shot of Irish whiskey, served in a heated glass.

When ordering a whiskey Irish people never ask for a Scotch (though it is available); they use the brand name of an Irish whiskey instead: Bushmills, Jameson's, Paddy's, Powers or whatever. Whiskey may seem expensive but the Irish measure is generous, by law.

Nonalcoholic drinks in pubs and hotels are restricted to the predictable brand-named fizzy ones, and to judge by the prices charged for them, you might think that customers are deliberately being discouraged from drinking them.

Coffee is available in nearly all pubs, and usually costs from 80p to IR£1.20, but don't expect a smile if you order one at 10.30 on a busy night. If you ask for cream with your coffee, cream is what you'll get, a big dollop of it. The Irish drink lots of tea and this is usually served black, in a small teapot, with milk in a separate jug.

Specialities & Special Hours

If you're looking for certain types of food (Irish, seafood, vegetarian) or for meals at certain hours (an early breakfast or a late-night snack) here are some suggestions.

Irish Dishes

There are various traditional Irish dishes and several restaurants in Dublin where you can find them – *Gallagher's Boxty House* and *Paddy's Place*, for example. Irish dishes and specialities you might like to try include:

Bacon & Cabbage	a stew consisting of just bacon and cabbage
Barm Brack	an Irish cake-like bread
Boxty	rather like a filled pancake
Dublin Coddle	a semi-thick stew made with sausages, bacon, onions and potatoes
Guinness Cake	a popular fruitcake flavoured with Guinness
Irish Stew	a quintessential Irish stew of mutton, potatoes and onions, flavoured with parsley and thyme and simmered slowly
Soda Bread	Belfast is probably the best place in Ireland for bread, but soda bread in particular, white or brown, is found throughout the country

Seafood

The curious Irish aversion to seafood probably has, like so many other Irish curiosities, a religious connection. Until fairly recently the Catholic Friday fasting restrictions were strictly adhered to and fish was something you were forced to have on Friday. Like long-suffering schoolchildren, if you're forced to eat it you don't like it. Fish is only slowly overcoming this resistance. Irish trout and salmon are delicious, however.

Seafood specialists include *The Ante Room* on Lower Baggot St and *King Sitric's*, looking out over the harbour at Howth (see the Seaside Suburbs chapter). The *Periwinkle Seafood Bar* in the Powerscourt Townhouse shopping centre also has some good seafood dishes at lunch time. The *Lobster Pot* in Ballsbridge is solidly old-fashioned and rather expensive.

For pub food with a nautical flavour try the *Lord Edward Seafood Restaurant* in the Lord Edward Pub on Christ Church Place. For Dublin's best fish and chips turn the corner to *Leo Burdock's* on Werburgh St.

Vegetarian

Despite the locals' carnivorous tendencies (a meal isn't a meal without meat) there are some excellent places for vegetarian food in Dublin, particularly at lunch time. Places to try include the *Well Fed Café* in Temple Bar, *Cornucopia* in Wicklow St just off Grafton St, *Blazing Salads*

PLACES TO EAT

For the sake of clarity, places to eat are divided into four areas: north of the Liffey; Temple Bar; the Grafton St area; and Merrion Row, Baggot St and beyond. Dining north of the river essentially involves fast food, cheap eats or chains. You won't eat badly here, but the choice of restaurants is better to the south. Temple Bar is the area with the highest concentration of restaurants. It's bounded by the river to the north, Westmoreland St to the east in the Powerscourt Townhouse shopping centre and *Capers* on Nassau St opposite Trinity College. Cornucopia also offers a choice of hot and cold vegetarian breakfasts. There are many restaurants offering international cuisine with a strong vegetarian influence (Mexican, Lebanese or Italian for example) and a great many other restaurants have at least some vegetarian dishes on their menu.

Late Night

There are cafés and restaurants where you can get coffee or a meal until late into the night.

On South Anne St the *Coffee Inn* is a good place for a late-night coffee and you can sit outside, which is very pleasant on a mild summer evening. Also on South Anne St the US-style diner *Eddie Rocket's* will serve you a good burger until 1 am on weeknights, until 3 am on Thursday and right through to 4 am on Friday and Saturday. If you're looking for real restaurant food until reasonably late (past midnight), you could certainly do worse than try *QV-2* on St Andrew's St.

The *Coffee Dock* is open 22½ hours a day (it closes from 4.30 to 6 am) in Jury's Hotel & Towers, Pembroke Rd, south of the Grand Canal. *Break for the Border*, on Lower Stephen St, west of Grafton St, has food and entertainment until 2 am daily.

Breakfast

Bed and breakfast is such an Irish institution that it's hardly surprising that Dublin is not the best place for breakfast. The problem is compounded by the fact that the Irish are a long way from being early risers, so even those places that do turn out a good breakfast may not do so until a discouragingly late hour. The Irish are likely to reply that holiday-makers shouldn't be concerned about being up early in any case!

A glowing exception is *Eddie Rocket's*, which not only manages to stay open late but also manages to reopen at 8 am. The various *Bewley's* cafés are also excellent places for breakfast; the Grafton St branch opens at 7.15 am.

Cornucopia, a wholefood specialist on Wicklow St, opens from 8 am Monday to Friday, from 9 am Saturday. In Temple Bar the *Elephant & Castle* will rustle up a hearty breakfast from 8 am on weekdays, 10 am at weekends. *Fitzer's* on Dawson St also opens at 8 am on weekdays, and at 9 am on Saturday. Round the corner on Nassau St *The Kilkenny Kitchen* is open from 9 am Monday to Saturday.

Other early morning possibilities include *Pasta Fresca*, on Chatham St, open from 8 am Monday to Saturday, and *Munchies*, on the corner of Exchequer St and South William St, open from 7 am Monday to Saturday. There are other branches of *Munchies* on Lower Baggot St and Lower Pembroke St.

and Christ Church Cathedral to the west. The southern edge is formed by Dame St and Lord Edward St, but restaurants on both the northern and southern side of Dame St are listed in this section. Grafton St, from Trinity College to St Stephen's Green, is the heart of the city, and while there aren't many restaurants on the street itself, the area around it has a wide variety of places. Merrion Row, leading south-east from St Stephen's Green, and Baggot St have an eclectic selection of restaurants.

euro currency converter IR£1 = €1.27

PLACES TO EAT – BUDGET

Despite the influx of trendy restaurants that seem to charge as much for décor and ambience as they do for food, it is still possible to eat well without denting your budget too much. Aside from the ubiquitous fast food outlets, Dublin is rich with cafés and small restaurants catering for those on a tight budget, especially students.

North of the Liffey (Map 4)

Fast Food O'Connell St is the fast food centre not just of north Dublin but of the whole city, with a branch of *Abrakebabra*, a *Burger King*, a *KFC*, two branches of *La Pizza* and two of *McDonald's*. On Monday (except for Bank Holidays), Tuesday and Wednesday *La Pizza* features a deep-pan pizza feast for IR£3.99 a head. *Hamburger Heaven* (☎ 855 2424, 5 Beresford Place) is especially handy for residents of the Gardiner St hostels and B&Bs. The price tags on the 25 varieties of burger are somewhat higher than at McDonald's.

Cafés The *Dublin International Youth Hostel* and *Isaac's Hostel* (see Hostels in the Places to Stay chapter) both have good cafeteria-style facilities. Isaac's is pretty small though. For sizeable sandwiches there's a branch of *O'Briens* at 54 Mary St.

Kylemore Café (1-2 O'Connell St) is a big and somewhat impersonal self-service café that is good for a cup of tea or coffee at any time of day. Alternatively, in stylish surroundings on the 1st floor of the *Clery & Co* department store on O'Connell St you can have afternoon tea complete with cucumber sandwiches for IR£4.25.

At 5-7 O'Connell St there's the International Food Court, which has a variety of counters, including *Beshoff's* for fish and chips. There's a *Bewley's Café* north of the Liffey at 40 Mary St. Bewley's is a Dublin institution offering good food at reasonable prices. See the boxed text opposite for more details.

Close to the Corporation Fruit Market, between Chancery St and Mary's Lane, is *Paddy's Place (☎ 873 5130)* where the food is as staunchly Irish as the name. It's open from 7.30 am to 3 pm Monday to Friday so you can have an early breakfast or a filling lunch-time Irish stew or Dublin coddle.

Temple Bar (Map 7)

Fast Food *Abrakebabra* has a branch at 19 Westmoreland St and another in Merchant's Arch, just south of the Ha'penny Bridge. The Westmoreland St branch is fine during the day but has a reputation for attracting drunken brawlers late at night. *Iskander's (31 Dame St)* has better-quality kebabs but late-night queues are ridiculously long. An excellent purveyor of fish and chips (from IR£2.95) is *Beshoff's (☎ 677 8026, 14 Westmoreland St)*. Round the corner from Dublin Castle and next to the Lord Edward Pub, *Leo Burdock's (☎ 454 0306, 2 Werburgh St)* is open until 11 pm from Monday to Saturday and is said to serve the best fish and chips in Ireland. You can eat them down the road in the park beside St Patrick's Cathedral.

Cafés Just beyond Dublin Castle and directly opposite Christ Church Cathedral on Lord Edward St, the *Refectory* in Kinlay House is a good place for lunch-time sandwiches or a quick snack at any time of day. Backpackers staying at *Avalon House* on Aungier St (see Hostels in the Places to Stay chapter) will find the most stylish hostel café in town. The *Well Fed Café (☎ 677 2234, 6 Crow St)* is a big, busy alternative place with big portions of food and delicious desserts. It's great for lunch or a snack and caters well to vegetarians. Main dishes start at IR£3. It's open from noon to 8 pm Monday to Saturday.

There are two branches of *Bewley's* on the edges of Temple Bar. These cafeteria-style places offer good-quality food, especially the all-day special of bacon, egg, sausages, beans and chips for IR£3.50, including coffee, tea or a soft drink. They're equally good for a quick cup of tea or coffee and offer a variety of teas, a pleasant surprise in a country where tea often comes strong and stewed. Watch the cake prices

Bewley's & Beshoff's

In a city of institutions, Bewley's is an institution many visitors will be grateful for. At one of *Bewley's Oriental Cafés* you can be sure of getting a good meal at a reasonable price or simply a good cup of tea or coffee (neither of which is necessarily easy to find in Ireland) and a place to rest your weary feet. The Bewley family, Quakers from England, established their first tea shop in Dublin in around 1840, close to where the Olympia Theatre now stands.

The Bewley business went through numerous changes in the following century before a shop was opened in Westmoreland St in 1916. The vogue for the Oriental style also arrived with this coffee shop, and it became a fashionable and stylish venue complete with a door attendant to help guests from their carriages or cars. The Grafton St café followed in 1927 and today there are other branches of Bewley's on South Great George's St and Mary St in Dublin as well as in a number of other towns in Ireland and Northern Ireland.

In 1971, when the cafés were still family owned, Bewley Community Ltd was established as a pioneering example of employee ownership. Unhappily, it almost became the company's death knell when inefficient methods and a bloated workforce led to near bankruptcy. In 1986 the business was bought out and now runs profitably. Despite the introduction of self-service, Bewley's still manages to exude Dublin's easy-going charm at its best, and you can still admire the stained-glass windows at the Grafton St branch or sit in the old wooden pews at Westmoreland St. At the Grafton St branch there's even a Bewley's museum and theatre!

At *Beshoff's* the main attraction is fish and chips rather than coffee, but there's the same old-fashioned style to the establishment. Founded by Ivan Beshoff, a survivor of the mutiny on the Russian battleship *Potemkin* in 1905, the Victorian-looking Beshoff's is on Westmoreland St near Bewley's. There's another branch on O'Connell St, with fine views of the 'floozy in the Jacuzzi' from the upstairs windows.

Wherever you are in Dublin, you're never far from a Bewley's or a Beshoff's.

PLACES TO EAT

though. The branch at 11-12 Westmoreland St is open from 7.30 am to 9 pm Monday to Saturday and 8.30 am to 9 pm on Sunday. There's another branch at 13 South Great George's St, open from 7.45 am to 6 pm Monday to Saturday.

Café Irie (12 Upper Fownes St) isn't – as the name suggests – even vaguely Jamaican, but the sandwiches, served on a variety of breads (the *ciabatta* is particularly nice), are excellent, filling and cheap, starting at IR£1.95.

The café in the *Irish Film Centre (6 Eustace St)* is a lovely place for a lunchtime snack – mostly sandwiches and bar food – or a full evening meal, including plenty of vegetarian choices.

For an excellent lunch try *Marks Bros Café (☎ 677 0185, 7 South Great George's St)*, which turns out big, filling sandwiches, tasty, wholesome soups and absolutely scrumptious carrot cakes.

Restaurants There are almost no cheap restaurants in Temple Bar. *Da Pino (☎ 671 9308, 38-40 Parliament St)* is the exception. The IR£4.40 lunch menu – offering a selection of delicious pizzas or a minute steak – is hard to beat.

Grafton St Area (Map 7)

Fast Food Grafton St is the fast food centre south of the Liffey, with a *McDonald's* at No 9, a *Burger King* at No 39 and *La Pizza* just round the corner at 1 St Stephen's Green North. *Subway*, on South Anne St just off Grafton St, turns out filling sandwiches, baps (a soft Irish version of a bread roll) and rolls for IR£1.80 to IR£3.90. Eat there or if it's a sunny day have a picnic in nearby St Stephen's Green.

Cafés *The Coffee Inn (☎ 671 9302, 6 South Anne St)* has good coffee, outdoor tables (weather permitting) and stays open till late every night (until 3 am on Friday and Saturday). There are pizzas and pasta dishes to go with the coffee. *Café Java (☎ 670 7239, 5 South Anne St)* serves excellent lunches for around IR£3.50; the set

weekday lunch menu costing IR£3.95 offers soup, a sandwich and tea or coffee. There's a second branch (☎ 660 0675) at 145 Upper Leeson St.

Munchies, on the corner of Exchequer St and South William St, west of Grafton St, claims to produce the best sandwiches in Ireland. For IR£2 (sandwiches) or IR£2.40 (baps) you can check out how good they are. Further along Exchequer St is the *Wed Wose Café*, at No 18, which serves sandwiches, burgers and breakfasts all day, the latter a perfect hangover cure!

The newly refurbished Powerscourt Townhouse shopping centre, between South William St and Clarendon St, has many dining outlets and is a great location for lunch. Options include *Blazing Salads II (☎ 671 9552)*, a popular vegetarian restaurant on the top level with a variety of salads for 80p each. It's open Monday to Saturday

NEIL BEER

Time to relax – Dubliners have embraced European-style café culture enthusiastically.

from 9 am to 6 pm. *La Piazza* next door does pizzas. On the 1st floor of the centre *Chompys'* (☎ 679 4552) boasts bagels, pancakes and sandwiches for less than IR£5. On the ground floor are the *Whistlestop Café* and *Fair City Sandwich Bar*, serving everything from soups to burgers.

A café that has been entirely unaffected by Dublin's dining revolution is the *Alpha* (☎ 677 0213, 37 Wicklow St). For nearly 35 years this place has been serving solid lunches and dinners to Dublin's working community at prices that you won't see beaten anywhere in the city. The clientele is a mix of regulars (some of whom have eaten here since the day it opened) and students, all of whom love the friendly ambience that pervades the place.

St Stephen's Green shopping centre has branches of *O'Brien's*, the sandwich shop, and *Café Kylemore* on the 1st floor and the *Pavlova Pantry* on the 2nd floor, serving some delectable pavlovas. Beside the centre is a branch of *Chicago Pizza Pie Factory* (☎ 478 1233) on the site of the former dandelion market where U2 played some of their early gigs. Nearby the *Café des Artistes (Clarendon Market)* has great breakfasts and lunch-time baguettes.

Right opposite Trinity College, the large *Kilkenny Kitchen* (☎ 677 7066) on the 1st floor of the Kilkenny Shop at 6 Nassau St serves generally excellent cafeteria-style food but at times the queues can be discouragingly long. There's a snack counter which, at peak times, can be somewhat faster. Also opposite Trinity College, *Capers* (☎ 679 7140), at 4 Nassau St above the Runner Bean greengrocer's, is popular with college students. From the upstairs room you can gaze across the college grounds. The food comes in healthy quantities, in healthy style (there are plenty of vegetarian dishes available) and with lots of salads. The café opens during the day on weekdays and in the evening on Thursday, Friday and Saturday.

Fitzer's outlets, which have meals from around IR£5, make a great place for lunch or an early evening meal on weekdays.

There's a branch at 52 Dawson St towards the Trinity College end.

Restaurants *Cornucopia* (☎ 677 7583, 19 Wicklow St) is a popular wholefood café turning out healthy goodies for those escaping the Irish cholesterol habit. There's even a hot vegetarian breakfast for IR£2.25 as an alternative to muesli. It's open for lunch Monday to Saturday and until 8 pm on weekdays (9 pm on Thursday). *Captain America's Cookhouse & Bar* (☎ 671 5266, 44 Grafton St) serves burgers until midnight every night of the week. It claims Chris de Burgh used to busk in a corner before he hit the big time.

Merrion Row, Baggot St & Beyond (Map 6)

Fast Food & Cafés Aside from the usual selection of fast food chains, there are some interesting budget options outside of the immediate city centre. Merrion Square, connected to Merrion Row by Merrion St, has one café well worth a detour, particularly at lunch time. The National Gallery *Fitzer's* (☎ 661 4496), the best of the chain, is rather hidden away – you have to go through the gallery (entry is free) to find it – but the artistic interlude makes a pleasant introduction to this popular, if slightly pricier, restaurant. It has the same opening hours as the gallery and offers hot dishes for IR£5 to IR£6.50, as well as salads, cakes and wine. There's a *Fitzer's Take-Out* (☎ 660 0644) at 24 Upper Baggot St.

Galligan's Café (☎ 676 5955, 6 Merrion Row) is a great place for breakfast from 7.30 am weekdays or from 9 am on Saturday and for lunch or afternoon snacks. The basement bistro is open from 5 to 11 pm too. Across the road a branch of *Pierre Victoire* (☎ 678 5412) does set lunches for IR£5.90 and set dinners for IR£6.90. Further along, *Georgian Fare* (☎ 676 7736, 14 Lower Baggot St) has good sandwiches, while *Miller's Pizza Kitchen* (☎ 676 6098, 9-10 Lower Baggot St) has a full range of pizzas and pasta. There's a branch of *Abrakebabra* next door.

PLACES TO EAT

PLACES TO EAT – MID-RANGE

There is a surprising number of affordable restaurants in Dublin, largely on the south-side, and with new ones opening all the time the competition is fairly stiff, keeping prices at similar levels across the board.

North of the Liffey (Map 4)

Close to the river upstairs at 100-102 Talbot St is *101 Talbot* (☎ *874 5011)*, open for lunch Monday to Saturday and dinner Tuesday to Saturday in a brave attempt to bring good food north of the river. The prices are reasonable and the food moderately adventurous and well prepared. The pasta dishes from IR£4.95 are filling and affordable. Close to the Gate Theatre, the *Bangkok Café* (☎ *878 6618, 106 Parnell St)* may look a little rough around the edges but inside you'll find good Thai cuisine with main dishes for about IR£7.

Temple Bar (Map 7)

The popular *Bad Ass Café* (☎ *671 2596, 9-11 Crown Alley)* is a cheerful, bright warehouse-style place south of Ha'penny Bridge. It offers reasonable pizzas for about IR£7.50 in a convivial atmosphere and has pulleys to whip orders to the kitchen at busy times. It doesn't open for breakfast. Sinéad O'Connor once worked here as a waitress. Two doors down, *Paddy Garibaldi's (☎ 671 7288, 15-16 Crown Alley)* does burgers and steaks to complement the pizza and pasta. *Nico's* (☎ *677 3062, 53 Dame St)* on the corner of Temple Lane offers conservative Italian food with a strong Irish influence. It's popular, has a piano player and is open for dinner Monday to Saturday, as well as for lunch on weekdays. Main dishes cost IR£7 to IR£10.

At the south-eastern corner of Meeting House Square (known as Diceman's Corner after a mime artist who used to perform on Grafton St) is *Il Baccaro* (☎ *671 4597)*, an Italian trattoria whose rustic cuisine is very popular with Dublin's Italian community. It's only open in the evenings. For a truly excellent Italian meal for less than IR£15, *Ar Vicoletto* (☎ *670 8662, 5 Crow St)* is

hard to beat. The warm gorgonzola salad is sublime and the spaghetti carbonara is as authentic as it gets. Just down the street at No 1 is *Tante Zoé's* (☎ *679 4407)*. It's open Monday to Saturday for lunch and Monday to Sunday for dinner, and is further proof of how cosmopolitan Dublin dining is: Cajun and Creole food are the specialities, with starters costing IR£2.75 and main dishes from IR£7.

Il Pasticcio (☎ *677 6111, 12 Fownes St)* does wood-baked pizzas and good pasta in a rather cramped setting with paintings by up-and-coming artists on the walls. Pasta main dishes range from IR£4.50 to IR£6.95, pizzas from IR£4.50 to IR£5.95. At 3-4 Bedford Row, hidden down a side turning and therefore likely to have tables when other, more obvious, places are full, *Café Gertrude* (☎ *677 9043)* does sandwiches, salads and pizzas at realistic prices.

At the idiosyncratically named *Eamonn Doran Imbibing Emporium* (☎ *679 9773, 3A Crown Alley)* opposite the Bad Ass Café you can get burgers or fish for IR£5 and a four course meal for IR£15. Omelettes are a speciality at the popular, bustling but overpriced *Elephant & Castle* (☎ *679 3121, 18 Temple Bar)*; how 'free' are coffee fill-ups when the first cup is IR£1.50? It stays open until midnight on Friday and Saturday, until 11.30 pm on other days. Next door at 20-21 Temple Bar is the even more popular *Gallagher's Boxty House* (☎ *677 2762)*. A *boxty* resembles a stuffed pancake and tastes like a bland Indian *masala dosa*. Real Irish food is not something that's widely available in Dublin so it's worth trying. Main dishes cost from IR£6 to IR£7. Beside Gallagher's is the *Alamo* (☎ *677 6546)*, where you can get good and reasonably priced Mexican dishes. *La Med* (☎ *670 7358, 22 East Essex St)* has a choice of Mediterranean dishes for about IR£7. There is live jazz during Sunday brunch.

On the corner of Wellington Quay and Asdills Row is *Omar Khayyam* (☎ *677 5758)*, a good restaurant offering Lebanese-style dishes. Excellent vegetarian: kebabs start at IR£9.75.

The interior of Bewley's, one of Dublin's venerable dining institutions ...

... and the exterior of the other.

Taking a moment away from it all.

NEIL BEER

NEIL BEER

The new in the old: Arthouse in Temple Bar ...

... and The Globe in South Great George's St.

NEIL BEER

NEIL BEER

An old faithful, the Olympia theatre ...

... and one of Dublin's many new hopefuls.

Poco Loco (☎ 679 1950, 32 Parliament St) serves straightforward Tex-Mex interpretations of Mexican food; its combination plates (from IR£6) are great value. It's open weekdays for lunch and daily for dinner.

Dame St's international mix of restaurants includes Chinese joints such as *Fans Cantonese Restaurant* (☎ 679 4263/4273) at No 60. The best Chinese food in the area is at the *Good World Restaurant* (☎ 677 5373, 18 South Great George's St). It is popular with the Chinese community, who choose their dishes from a Chinese menu rather than the one presented to locals. Needless to say, the former has more exciting dishes than the latter. Across the street at No 71, *Yamamori Noodles* (☎ 475 5001) is one of the most popular and trendiest restaurants in the city centre. The large sushi platter is IR£11 but you can eat well for about IR£8; try the chicken, beef or salmon teriyaki. The IR£5 lunch special is an absolute bargain, even if it just covers noodle dishes, but it is only available until 5.30 pm. Just down the street in Castle House is *Juice* (☎ 475 7856), a super-trendy vegetarian restaurant that puts an imaginative, California-type spin on all kinds of dishes. The real treat is the selection of fruit smoothies, a delicious and healthy alternative to soft drinks.

For an unpretentious French restaurant try *Chez Jules* (☎ 677 0499), tucked away on D'Olier St just outside the eastern end of Temple Bar, where you eat at long benches covered with red-and-white checked tablecloths. The food is well cooked and fairly reasonably priced.

Pub Grub For a good pub lunch, try the *Stag's Head* (☎ 679 3701, 1 Dame Court). Apart from being a popular drinking spot during the summer months (see the Entertainment chapter), this place turns out simple, well-prepared, filling meals. For seafood try the *Lord Edward Seafood Restaurant* (☎ 454 2420, 23 Christ Church Place) upstairs in the Lord Edward Pub, opposite Christ Church Cathedral. It's open Monday to Friday for lunch and Monday to Saturday for dinner. Further west *The Brazen Head* (Map 5) in Bridge St is always packed at lunch time. It has a variety of menus offering everything from sandwiches to a carvery.

Grafton St Area (Map 7)

Apart from fast-food joints, the only place in which to eat on Grafton St proper is *Bewley's* (☎ 677 6761), about halfway up at No 78. This is the flagship branch of the chain, and a recent renovation has converted it from an old-style café to a restaurant, with table service and fancier dishes than the other branches, though you can still get a lovely cup of coffee and a bun. It is open from 7.15 am to 11.30 pm Monday to Saturday and 8.30 am to 10.30 pm on Sunday.

The *Cedar Tree* (☎ 677 2121, 11A St Andrew's St) is a Lebanese restaurant with a good selection of vegetarian dishes.

Café Mao (☎ 670 4899, 2-3 Chatham Row) serves up interesting and varied Asian dishes starting at less than IR£8. This is a popular lunch-time spot.

The excellent *La Taverna* (☎ 677 3665, 33 Wicklow St) is open daily for lunch and dinner and combines sunny Greek food with an equally sunny atmosphere. A three course meal costs about IR£15. The *Imperial Chinese Restaurant* (☎ 677 2580, 12A Wicklow St), open daily, is noted for its lunch-time dim sum. These Chinese snacks are popular on Sunday, when the Imperial serves brunch Chinese-style in what is known as *yum cha*, or 'drink tea', the traditional accompaniment to dim sum.

The modern, cheerful *Pasta Fresca* (☎ 679 2402, 3-4 Chatham St) off Grafton St's southern end proves once again that the Irish like their Italian food. It has authentic pasta dishes for IR£4.95 to IR£8.50 and is open from 8 am until reasonably late Monday to Saturday. On Sunday it opens from noon to 8.30 pm. Just off Exchequer St is *The Odessa* (☎ 670 7634, 13 Dame St), a super-trendy restaurant where you can eat well in comfort and style for between IR£10 and IR£15; Sunday brunch is a favourite with the city's hip young things.

PLACES TO EAT

For a taste of Mexico, head to *Judge Roy Bean's (☎ 679 7539, 45-47 Nassau St)* on the corner of Grafton St for popular tacos and an equally popular bar; it's open noon to midnight daily.

Eddie Rocket's (☎ 679 7340, 7 South Anne St) is a 1950s-style US diner dishing out anything from breakfast at 7.30 am to an excellent late-night burger for IR£2.95. On Friday and Saturday nights it's open to 4 am. Right next door is the trendy and popular *Gotham Café (☎ 679 5266, 8 South Anne St)* where you'll get pizzas prepared with some pizzazz.

If you can stand the inevitable fishy smell, the *Periwinkle Seafood Bar (☎ 679 4203)* in the Powerscourt Townhouse shopping centre serves economical seafood lunches with the accent on shellfish.

Visitors to India may remember Rajdoot as a popular brand of Indian motorcycle. Those in search of Indian food in Dublin can scoot to *Rajdoot Tandoori (☎ 679 4274/4280, 26-28 Clarendon St)* in the Westbury Centre behind the Westbury Hotel for superb North Indian tandoori dishes. Set lunches cost IR£7.50.

La Mère Zou (☎ 661 6669, 22 St Stephen's Green) is a Belgian restaurant that serves solid, Continental dishes at lunch and more sophisticated entrées in the evening. It's open for lunch and dinner during the week, but for dinner only on Saturday and Sunday.

Pub Grub Several pubs close to Grafton St have good food. At 37 Exchequer St on the corner of St Andrew's St the *Old Stand* is a popular pub with meals at around IR£5. *Davy Byrne's (21 Duke St)* has been famous for its food ever since Joyce's Leopold Bloom dropped in for a Gorgonzola cheese sandwich and a Burgundy in *Ulysses*. It's now a swish watering hole, but you can still get food there.

Merrion Row, Baggot St & Beyond

There's an international line-up of restaurants mixing with the colourful Baggot St pubs, one of which is *Ayumi-ya (Map 6, ☎ 662 0233)*, in the basement at 132 Lower Baggot St. This is a westernised Japanese steakhouse offering the best noodles in town and good-value set meals: a starter, soup, main course, dessert and tea or coffee costs IR£13.95. Across the road at no 17A is *Cibo's (Map 6, ☎ 676 2050)*, which does pizzas and pasta as well as more expensive Italian dishes.

The Ante Room (Map 6, ☎ 660 4716), 20 Lower Baggot St underneath the Georgian House guesthouse, is a seafood specialist with main courses from about IR£10 and traditional Irish music on most summer nights. *Langkawi (☎ 668 2760, 46 Upper Baggot St)* has reasonable, affordable Pacific Rim cuisine.

Beyond Baggot St *Marrakesh (☎ 660 5539, 11 Ballsbridge Terrace)* serves Moroccan cuisine cooked in authentic clay *tagines* (stew pots). The couscous royale is worth the trip alone. This place is only open in the evenings.

PLACES TO EAT – TOP END
North of the Liffey (Map 4)

As far as pricey restaurants go, there is only one to speak of on the northside, at least for now. *Chapter One (☎ 873 2266/2281)*, in the basement of the Dublin Writers' Museum on Parnell Square North, is worth trying because the food, though resolutely conservative, is delicious. It serves lunch (weekdays only) and dinner and features menus for those who wish to eat before or after attending a performance at the Gate Theatre on the other side of the square.

Temple Bar (Map 7)

In Temple Bar the trick is to find a restaurant where the food justifies the expense.

The Tea Rooms (☎ 670 7766, Clarence Hotel, 6-8 Wellington Quay) is one of the trendiest restaurants in Dublin. It is pricey, but the food is very good. It's open daily for dinner but only from Monday to Friday for lunch. On Meeting House Square, *Eden (☎ 670 5372)* is the epitome of Temple Bar chic, with good, solid dishes served in minimalist surroundings. You can eat for less than IR£20 but it'll cost you more to eat well. It's very popular so book in advance. It's closed on Monday.

The Mermaid Café (☎ 670 8236, 22 Dame St) is fast earning a reputation as one of the better restaurants in the city. The seafood is particularly good. It's open daily for lunch, Tuesday to Saturday for dinner. The French *Les Frères Jacques (☎ 679 4555, 74 Dame St)* is one of Temple Bar's fancier places, with set meals for IR£22. The mood is slightly serious and the bill can make a bit of a dent in your credit-card limit. It's open Monday to Friday for lunch, Monday to Saturday for dinner.

Grafton St Area (Map 7)

La Stampa (☎ 677 8611, 35 Dawson St) is Dublin's upmarket Italian restaurant, with a large, attractive Georgian dining area and bright modern paintings. It's open daily from lunch time until late and main courses are in the IR£9 to IR£14 range, including vegetables. A set lunch costs IR£11.50.

St Andrew's St is full of good restaurants. The excellent *Trocadero (☎ 677 5545, 679 9772, 3 St Andrew's St)* offers no culinary surprises, which is one reason why it's so popular. Simple food, straightforward preparation, large portions and late opening hours are its selling points. Main courses are around IR£10. The Troc, as it's known, is open past midnight every night except Sunday, when it closes at 11.30 pm. On the other side of the street, the stylish *QV-2 (☎ 677 3363/2246, 14-15 St Andrew's St)* looks more expensive than it is. There are good pasta dishes for IR£5.95 to IR£7.95 and main courses for IR£7.25 to IR£12.50, but vegetables cost extra. It offers good, mildly adventurous food and pleasant surroundings. It's open daily for lunch and dinner, closing after midnight.

Just beside the Powerscourt Townhouse is *The Rhino Room (☎ 670 5260, 14 South William St)* a trendy-cum-casual spot where you can eat extremely well for less than IR£20, excluding wine (and there are plenty to choose from). The fresh raspberry dessert

is divine. It is open for lunch and dinner Monday to Saturday. Downstairs, *Cooke's Café (☎ 679 0536)* is more fashionable and expensive than its sister restaurant above but the food isn't really good enough to justify the extra expense. Reservations are essential for dinner.

On St Stephen's Green, the Fitzwilliam Hotel at No 109 is home to *Peacock Alley (☎ 478 7015)* owned by super-chef Conrad Gallagher, whose speciality is French provincial cuisine. A dinner will set you back about IR£40 but you can have lunch for about half that amount. At No 85-86, in the basement of Newman House, is *The Commons (Map 6, ☎ 475 2597)*, where the food is exquisite but pricey. The six course 'tasting menu' costs IR£45. It's as well to book ahead, especially for weekends.

Merrion Row, Baggot St & Beyond

The best restaurant in Ireland is *Restaurant Patrick Guilbaud (Map 6, ☎ 676 4192)* in the Merrion Hotel, Upper Merrion St. The eponymous owner-chef does his best to ensure that it stays that way. If you eat here your stomach and credit card will know all about it. There's nothing overpoweringly fancy about anything; it's just good food, beautifully prepared and elegantly presented. There's a set lunch menu for IR£20 but dinner is à la carte. It's open for lunch and dinner Monday to Saturday. Needless to say, reservations are essential. Also in the Merrion Hotel is *Lloyd's (Map 6, ☎ 662 7240)*, a large French brasserie owned by the Peacock Alley's Conrad Gallagher.

For especially good fish, head for *McGrattans in the Lane (Map 6, ☎ 661 8808)* in Fitzwilliam Lane just down from the National Gallery. A three course lunch here costs IR£12.95 but the à la carte menu will set you back about IR£25.

You can slide backwards in time by continuing along Baggot St, across the Grand Canal and on to Pembroke Rd to *Le Coq Hardi (☎ 668 9070)* at No 35. This is the older counterpart of Patrick Guilbaud, with heavier, traditional French dishes and a

PLACES TO EAT

superb wine list. The bill is likely to be heavy too. It's open for lunch Monday to Friday and for dinner Monday to Saturday.

Also out from the centre is the **Lobster Pot Restaurant** (*☎ 668 0025, 9 Ballsbridge Terrace*). It's an old-fashioned place which offers substantial dishes in an equally substantial atmosphere; seafood is the house speciality and prices are reasonably high. Next door, **Roly's Bistro** (*☎ 668 2611*) at No

7 receives rave reviews for its adventurous food; advance booking is advisable. On the same street, **Kites Chinese Restaurant** (*☎ 660 7415, 15-17 Ballsbridge Terrace*) serves Chinese food with style at moderate to high prices. The **Old Dublin** (*Map 5, ☎ 454 2028, 90 Francis St*) specialises in Russian and Scandinavian food. It costs around IR£20 a head but is worth the splash.

Entertainment

Dublin is undoubtedly one of Europe's most vibrant entertainment capitals, with a wide variety of options to satisfy (nearly) every desire. It has theatres, cinemas, nightclubs and concert halls; stadiums, racecourses and dog tracks; but the real centre of activity is still the pub, and in Dublin there are about 700 of them to suit every taste and trend. There's little doubt that Dublin now has something for everyone – a far cry from the days when the most you could hope for was a few drinks in an old-fashioned pub and a bit of a dance in one of the basement clubs on Lower Leeson St. Today a thriving nightlife, with bars, cafés and clubs packed virtually every night of the week, has made the city one of the most popular getaway destinations in Europe.

Where to play? The most obvious and most popular area is Temple Bar, which transforms itself nightly into a party district with few rivals in Europe. It is extremely popular with groups of English on a stag or hen weekend – although in November 1998 many of Temple Bar's publicans announced that they would no longer cater to these often loud and raucous groups because they alienated local trade. But with one or two exceptions the best, most authentic bars and clubs are outside Temple Bar's narrow, cobbled streets, albeit not too far away. While much of the city's nightlife is concentrated on the south side, 'in' Dubliners have begun conquering the north side of the Liffey, where a number of very trendy bars have opened to great success. Although it's still a nascent scene, word is that the area immediately north of the river, from the Grattan Bridge in the west to Butt Bridge in the east, is *the* new place to see and be seen.

For entertainment information, pick up a copy of the weekly music review *Hot Press* (IR£1.95), the *Event Guide*, a bimonthly freebie available at many locations, including bars, cafés and hostels or the fortnightly magazine *In Dublin* (IR£1.95). The *Evening Herald* (IR65p), a city tabloid, also has a weekend pull-out on Thursday listing all events throughout the weekend. During the peak season, Dublin Tourism publishes *Events of the Week*, a free leaflet listing all kinds of activities.

PUBS & BARS

For information on the city's many and varied drinking establishments see the special section 'Dublin's Pubs & Bars' on pages 171 to 181.

IRISH CABARET

Although strictly aimed at tourists, there are several places in Dublin where you can go for an evening of Irish entertainment with Irish songs, Irish dancing and probably a few jokes thrown in along the way.

Jury's Irish Cabaret (☎ 660 5000, Jury's Hotel, Pembroke Rd, Ballsbridge) puts on 2½ hours of Irish music, song and dance in the evening. This has been a tourist favourite for more than 30 years. You can either come for dinner and the show from 7.30 pm (IR£36.50) or just for the show from 8 pm (IR£22, including two drinks). It operates nightly except Monday from early May to mid-October.

Similar performances are staged at the *Burlington Hotel* (☎ 660 5222, Leeson St). The two-hour performances take place nightly from 8 pm May to October. Dinner starts an hour earlier and the cost for a four course dinner and the show is IR£36.50. The mock medieval *Clontarf Castle* (☎ 833 2321, Castle Ave, Clontarf, Dublin 3) also has shows from 7.30 pm Monday to Saturday costing IR£22 (IR£36 with dinner). Bus No 44A stops nearby.

DISCOS & NIGHTCLUBS

Perhaps the most manifest example of Dublin's entertainment revolution is the nightclub scene. Once confined to a grim strip of basement clubs along Lower Leeson

St, late-night venues have sprouted up all over the city, both north and south of the Liffey. They cater to virtually every taste, whether your thing is live salsa played by a 14 piece brass ensemble or hardcore drum-and-bass spun by some of the city's best young DJs. Most club nights are run by in-dependent promoters hired by the owner to provide a particular theme, so if there's a live soul band on Tuesday night, Saturday night may feature the latest in house music or a 70s disco party.

The seemingly endless list of 'what's on' is constantly changing, so check out the listings in *In Dublin* and the *Event Guide* to keep abreast of the scene. Most clubs open just after pubs close (11 to 11.30 pm) and close at 2 or 2.30 am. Entry to most is between IR£4 and IR£6 on weekdays, rising to IR£8 at weekends.

Dublin's most renowned nightclub is still *The PoD*, short for 'Place of Dance' *(Map 6, ☎ 478 0166, 35 Harcourt St)*, a futuristic, metal-gothic cathedral of dance that attracts a large weekend crowd of twentysome-things. It's not nearly as popular as it used to be, which may have less to do with fickle trends and more to do with the somewhat negative reputation of its bouncers, who are notoriously difficult to get past.

In Temple Bar, the U2-owned *Kitchen (Map 7, ☎ 677 6635, The Clarence Hotel, 6-8 Wellington Quay)* is surprisingly laid back, considering its widespread fame. The music is hard and fast and the back bar is usually patronised by celebrities and those eager to see and be seen. Formerly the Mission, *Club Zazu (Map 7, Eustace St)* is a little hard to handle unless your idea of a good time is drinking yourself into a near-coma. Monday night's Freedom is one of Dublin's better gay nights, however. *Club M (Map 7, ☎ 671 5485, Anglesea St)* offers a mix of 90s Ibiza-style dance music and 80s tunes to a dance floor of kids convinced that an 80s revival is a long way overdue. *Eamonn Doran's Imbibing Emporium (Map 7, ☎ 679 9773, 3A Crown Alley)* is a large place with food, drink and music (mostly rock) every night.

Rí Rá (Map 7, ☎ 677 4835, Dame Court) is one of the friendlier clubs in the city centre and is full nearly seven nights a week. Doors open at 11.30 pm.

Lillie's Bordello (Map 7, ☎ 679 9204, Adam Court, off Grafton St) is strictly for the well-heeled, except on Sunday nights when the atmosphere is more relaxed for Lost in Music, which has live soul and salsa as well as some excellent DJs. Like Lillie's, *Renard's (Map 6, ☎ 677 5876, South Frederick St)* is upmarket and more than a little snobby. Strictly for the 'wannabe' set.

The Gaiety Theatre (Map 7, ☎ 677 1717, South King St) is no longer home to Mambo! and Velure, but their replacements, Salsa Palace on Friday and Soul Stage on Saturday, offer the same mix of soul and salsa that made their predecessors the most successful Friday and Saturday nights in Dublin. Doors open at 11.30 pm.

Break for the Border (Map 7, ☎ 478 0300, Lower Stephen St) is a huge country and western style eatery that reverts to a nightclub once pubs close. It's good fun, if a little cheesy, and is renowned in Dublin as one of the biggest pick-up joints around.

Columbia Mills (☎ 677 8466, Sir John Rogerson's Quay) is a great club with a good mix of music from techno to 80s chart hits. It's open from Thursday to Saturday.

Copper Face Jack's (Map 6, ☎ 475 8777, Harcourt St) is popular with an older crowd and lacks much of the pizzazz found in other nightclubs. This may have something to do with its popularity with off-duty police officers!

Across the road is *The Vatican (Map 6, ☎ 478 4066),* in the basement of the Russell Court Hotel, offering precious little in terms of décor, although that doesn't seem to stop the droves of young people who flock here from Tuesday to Saturday nights. It's very popular with British weekenders.

If none of the above is to your satisfaction, you'll hardly console yourself with the basement clubs along Lower Leeson St, formerly Dublin's only strip of nightclubs. They are more or less all the same, and the only advantage they have over other clubs in the city is that for some bizarre reason they are allowed to keep their doors open until 4 am. There are no admission charges, but the price of drinks certainly makes up for that; count on paying at least IR£18 for an unremarkable bottle of wine.

Shaft (22 Ely Place) and *Beatroot (34 O'Connell St)* are currently the 'in' gay clubs. For more details look out for the monthly *Gay Community News*, which is available through the Temple Bar Information Centre *(Map 7, Eustace St)* or at Condom Power *(Map 7, Dame St)*.

CONCERTS

Classical concerts are performed at the *National Concert Hall (Map 6, ☎ 671 1533/ 1888, Earlsfort Terrace)*. In summer there are usually lunchtime concerts (from 1.05 to 2 pm) on Tuesday and Friday with entry prices of around IR£4. Classical performances may also take place at the *Bank of Ireland Arts Centre (Map 7, Foster Place)*, the *Hugh Lane Municipal Gallery of Modern Art (Map 4, Parnell Square)* or the *Royal Dublin Showground Concert Hall*.

There are also programmes of lunch-time concerts in some churches; *St Stephen's Church (Map 6, Upper Mount St)*, for example. Even the *Powerscourt Townhouse shopping centre* (Map 7) offers free lunch-time live music on Wednesday.

Big rock concerts are held at the *Point Depot (☎ 836 3633, East Link Bridge, North Wall Quay)*. Originally constructed as a rail terminus in 1878, it is the premier venue for all local and visiting pop and rock bands. *Slane Castle*, 46km north-west of Dublin, is home to the yearly Slane Festival, a one day extravaganza featuring top names in international pop and rock. The Rolling Stones, Bob Dylan, Bruce Springsteen and REM have all played here over the years to crowds in excess of 60,000; in 1998 the bill was headlined by new boys The Verve. The *Lansdowne Rd stadium*, a mecca for rugby and soccer enthusiasts, is also used for the occasional big rock performances (U2 played the Irish dates of

their PopMart tour there), as is *Croke Park Stadium* (Map 4).

Smaller performances take place at the new all-seater *Vicar Street (Map 5, ☎ 454 5533)* Thomas St, near Christ Church Cathedral. This venue has a capacity of 750 and offers a varied programme of performers, such as 70s singer-songwriter Don McLean and jazz giant Dave Brubeck. The *Red Box (Map 6, ☎ 478 0166, Harcourt St)* in the old Harcourt St station is the best venue for dance gigs, with top European dance bands and DJs strutting their stuff to crowds of groovy movers. The *Temple Bar Music Centre (Map 7, ☎ 670 0533, Curved St)* hosts all kinds of gigs from Irish traditional to drum-and-bass. *Whelan's (Map 6, ☎ 478 0766, Wexford St)* features mostly rock and folk gigs. The pleasantly tatty *Olympia Theatre (Map 7, ☎ 677 7744, Dame St)* puts on Midnight at the Olympia every Friday night from 12 to 2 am, featuring everything from disco to country.

Bookings can be made either directly at the concert venue or through HMV (Map 7, ☎ 679 5334; 24-hour credit-card bookings ☎ 456 9569), 65 Grafton St, Dublin 2. HMV has another branch (Map 4, ☎ 873 2899) at 18 Henry St, Dublin 1. Ticketron (☎ 459 0315, 842 2494) also sells tickets for many Dublin gigs, both large and small.

CINEMAS

Many of Dublin's city-centre cinemas, which were mostly spread out across the north side of the Liffey, have been forced out of business by large suburban multiplex cinemas. Nevertheless, a number of older cinemas remain, with commercial features shown on the northside and independent movies more popular on the south side.

The multiscreen first-run cinemas are the twelve screen *Virgin Multiplex (Map 4, ☎ 872 8400, Parnell Centre, Parnell St)*, which has replaced many smaller cinemas, and the four screen *Savoy (Map 4, ☎ 01874 6000, Upper O'Connell St)*. Next door to the Virgin Multiplex is the new *IMAX Cinema (Map 4, ☎ 817 4222)* with its giant 24m-wide screen showing documentaries made with special IMAX cameras. The *Ambassador (Map 4, ☎ 872 7000, Parnell St)* is the city's most elegant single-screen cinema and features new releases.

The *Irish Film Centre (Map 7, ☎ 679 5744, 6 Eustace St, Temple Bar)* has a couple of screens and shows classics and new independent films. The complex also has a bar, a café and a bookshop. The *Screen (Map 6, ☎ 671 4988, 2 Townsend St)*, between Trinity College and O'Connell Bridge, shows fairly good art-house films on its three screens.

Entry prices are generally IR£3.50 for all afternoon shows, rising to IR£5 for evening shows. The IMAX is more expensive, with prices between IR£5 and IR£7.50 depending on the feature. The Savoy has late-night shows at weekends.

THEATRE

Dublin's theatre scene is small but busy. See the Things to See & Do chapter for more information about the histories of some of Dublin's best known theatres. Theatre bookings can usually be made by quoting a credit-card number over the phone; you can collect your tickets just before the performance.

The famous *Abbey Theatre (Map 4, ☎ 878 7222, Lower Abbey St)* near the river is Ireland's national theatre. It puts on new Irish works as well as revivals of classic Irish works by writers such as WB Yeats, JM Synge, Sean O'Casey, Brendan Behan and Samuel Beckett. Performances are at 8 pm, with Saturday matinees at 2.30 pm. Tickets cost IR£10 and IR£12.50, but student discounts are available and all seats are IR£8 on Monday. The smaller and less expensive *Peacock Theatre* is part of the same complex.

Also to the north of the Liffey is the *Gate Theatre (Map 4, ☎ 874 4045, eastern corner of Parnell Square)*. It specialises in international classics and older Irish works with a touch of comedy by playwrights such as Oscar Wilde, George Bernard Shaw and Oliver Goldsmith, although newer plays are sometimes staged too.

The *Olympia Theatre (Map 7, ☎ 677 7744, Dame St)* often has rock concerts as well as plays. The *Gaiety Theatre (Map 7, ☎ 677 1717, King St South)* opened in 1871 and is used for modern plays and TV shows as well as musical comedies and revues. Experimental and less commercial performances take place at the *Tivoli Theatre (Map 5, ☎ 454 4472, Francis St)*. The *Andrew's Lane Theatre (☎ 679 5720, 9-17 St Andrew's Lane)* is a well-established fringe theatre. The *Project Arts Centre (Map 4, ☎ 671 2321, Henry Place)* puts on excellent productions of experimental plays by up-and-coming Irish and foreign writers.

The Trinity College *Players' Theatre (☎ 677 2941, ext 1239)*, at the eastern end of the campus, hosts student productions throughout the academic year as well as the most prestigious plays from the Dublin Theatre Festival in October.

Several pubs host theatrical performances. These include the *International (☎ 677 9250, 23 Wicklow St)*. Puppet performances are put on at the *Lambert Puppet Theatre & Museum (☎ 280 0974, Clifton Lane, Monkstown)*.

The following venues also stage theatrical performances:

City Arts Centre
  (Map 6, ☎ 677 0643) 23-25 Moss St, Dublin 2
Eblana Theatre
  (Map 4, ☎ 679 8404) Busáras, Dublin 1
Focus Theatre
  (Map 6, ☎ 676 3071) 6 Pembroke Place, Dublin 2
Riverbank Theatre
  (Map 5, ☎ 677 3370) 10 Merchant's Quay, Dublin 8

BUSKERS

Dublin has a good deal of free entertainment in the form of buskers, but donations are always gratefully accepted. The best work busy Grafton St, where they are occasionally hassled by shopkeepers (for blocking access to their establishments) and by the police but are mainly left alone. At the Trinity College end of Grafton St you'll usually trip over pavement artists, most of whom are students at the various art colleges, busily chalking their pictures around the statue of Molly Malone. Farther along the street you're likely to come across crooning folk singers, raucous rock bands, classical string quartets and oddities such as the poet who breaks into verse only when paid cash in advance.

SPECTATOR SPORTS

Dublin offers plenty of sporting opportunities for the spectator.

Hurling & Gaelic Football

According to legend, hurling, that most Irish of sports, began with Sétanta, the five-year-old hurling genius and nephew of King Conor of Ulaid (Ulster) who later became known as Cuchulainn. Hurling has elements of hockey and lacrosse; players can hit the ball along the ground or through the air or even carry it on the end of their hurley or *camán*. Dublin itself is not, however, a great power in hurling. The best teams are more likely to be from Kilkenny or Cork.

Ireland's most popular sport, Gaelic football, is a high-speed, aggressive activity too. It features a round ball that can be kicked along the ground as in soccer or passed between players as in rugby. Australian Rules football has many similarities with Gaelic football, as evidenced by the Compromise Rules Series that took place in October 1998 between Ireland and Australia, with the Irish team featuring players who had become major stars in Australia. (Ireland won, and Australia will have to wait until the year 2000 to take their revenge on home soil.)

The All Ireland Hurling Final takes place on the first Sunday in September and attracts a crowd of more than 80,000 spectators. The All Ireland Football Final takes place on the third Sunday in September. Games are played at Dublin's Croke Park. For information call ☎ 836 3222.

Football & Rugby

The truly Gaelic sports, hurling and Gaelic football, have their greatest following in rural Ireland and it's probably true to say that football (soccer) and rugby are more popular in Dublin itself. Support for British teams is huge here; in fact the most popular football teams in Ireland are probably Manchester United, Liverpool and Glasgow Celtic! Although popular interest in the Republic of Ireland national team is no longer at the frenzied level it was from 1986 to 1996, when, under the management of Jack Charlton (who played for England when they won the World Cup in 1966), it was considered one of the more difficult sides to beat in Europe, the current team still attracts full houses to every game. For details of international matches, contact the Football Association of Ireland (☎ 676 6864).

Ireland is also a power in world rugby and great attention is paid to the annual Five Nations Championship, which pits Ireland against England, Wales, Scotland and France. Even more passion is likely to be roused when the national team plays Australia. International soccer and rugby matches take place at Lansdowne Rd Stadium in Ballsbridge. For information call ☎ 668 4601.

Horse & Greyhound Racing

The Irish love of horse racing can be seen at Leopardstown (☎ 289 3607) in Foxrock, home of the prestigious Hennessey Gold Cup, which is run in February. On race days buses run to the course from Eden Quay.

There are several other racecourses within an hour's drive. The Irish Grand National is held on Easter Monday at Fairyhouse (☎ 825 6167), 25km north of Dublin. The Curragh (☎ 045-441 205), 50km to the west in County Kildare, hosts five classic flat races between May and September. The popular April Steeplechase Festival is held 40km south-west of Dublin at Punchestown (☎ 045-897 704) near Naas. (Horses of less exalted breeds can be seen for sale at the Smithfield horse trading market behind the Four Courts in central Dublin on the first Sunday of each month.)

Greyhound racing takes place at Harold's Cross Park (☎ 497 1081) near Rathmines, a

ENTERTAINMENT

short hop from the city centre on the No 16 bus, and the more comfortable Shelbourne Park (☎ 668 3502) in Ringsend, only ten minutes from the centre on the No 3 bus. Races are held two or three times a week from February to early December; call to check days and starting times (they usually begin at about 7.30 pm).

Golf

The popularity of Ireland's fastest-growing sport is due in part to the success of Irish golfers such as Darren Clarke, Padraig Harrington and Paul McGinley, who can be seen driving, chipping and putting against the best players in Europe in the Smurfit European Open, which takes place in late July/early August at the K Club (Straffan, County Kildare), which was designed by Arnold Palmer. Call ☎ 676 6650 for ticket and date information.

Other Sports

Polo matches can be viewed for free in Phoenix Park on Wednesday, Saturday and Sunday. Car and motorcycle races are held at Mondello Park, although they have also been held in Phoenix Park. Ireland is not a major player in the cricket world but there is an Irish national team, which can be seen playing on the green at College Park in Trinity College.

DUBLIN'S PUBS & BARS

Since Irish life is so tied up with pub culture, a visit to one of the many pubs spread throughout the city is an absolute must. Despite the challenges of 'Europeanisation' – cafés, clubs and restaurants – the pub is still the hub of much of the social activity in the city, a meeting point for friends and strangers alike, the place where Dubliners are at their friendly and convivial best (and, it must be said, sometimes their drunken and incoherent worst!). Although there are about 700 pubs across the city (an average of one per 1119 people), many of those in the city centre are packed to the rafters most nights. This applies particularly to Temple Bar, which may officially be Dublin's 'cultural quarter' but is better termed as the 'party zone' or, as one wag dubbed it, 'Ibiza in the rain'. In the summer months the cobbled streets are filled with thousands of Dubliners and foreigners, all out for a good time. A revealing statistic is that 15% of Dublin pubs have a turnover in excess of IR£1 million per year. And Dubliners are not yet satisfied. At the time of writing, a raging debate over pub licences was under way, and it appears that the strict restrictions on the awarding of licences are to be relaxed, allowing for a proliferation of new pubs in the coming years.

Dublin's pub-going tradition has a long history. Even in medieval times the city had many drinking establishments, and in the late 17th century a survey revealed that one in every five houses in the city was involved in selling alcohol. A century later another survey counted 52 public houses along Thomas St in the Liberties alone. There may not be quite so many pubs today but Dublin still has a huge selection, so there's no possibility of not finding a Guinness should you develop a terrible thirst.

Apart from imbibing large quantities of alcohol, the Irish have also been responsible for some important developments in the field of drink production. They were pioneers in the development of distilling whiskey (distilled three times and spelt with an 'e', as opposed to the twice-distilled Scotch whisky). The Irish adopted the dark British beer that had become known as porter due to its popularity with the porters at London's Covent Garden market. Promoted by the Guinness family, it soon gained an enduring stranglehold on the Irish taste for beer.

Yet you may be disappointed at the apparent disappearance of the traditional pub and the modernisation of the city's historic pubs, especially in Temple Bar, where this is most evident. Alas, it is becoming more and more difficult to find a pub whose décor has been untouched for 50 years and whose main feature isn't a 250-watt stereo system but a *snug*, a partitioned-off section where you can meet friends in privacy under low lighting. Some snugs have their own serving hatches, so drinks can be passed in discreetly should the drinkers not want to be seen ordering 'just the one'. In a rush to cash in on the tourist renaissance, tacky 'überbars' have sprung up around the city,

Previous Page: One of the many pubs where you can still hear traditional Irish music in Dublin (photograph by Doug McKinlay).

Inset: Time, ladies and gentlemen, please! (photograph by Fionn Davenport).

serving bland beer (even in Dublin you can find a terrible pint of Guinness) in equally bland surroundings. But a few places have opened in recent years that can proudly hold their own as fine examples of modern Dublin pubs, offering a new home to the finer traditions that have made Dublin perhaps the finest pub capital in the world.

Dublin pubs also have a long and proud tradition of live music, from rock bands to the more traditional *seisúns* – semi-improvised jam sessions that are at the heart of all Irish traditional music. See the Walking Tours section in the Getting Around chapter for information on the highly recommended Literary and Musical Pub Crawls, which offer a fine introduction to some of Dublin's pubs on balmy summer nights. Be sure to check ahead as schedules can be wildly erratic; telephone numbers are provided for all pubs offering music.

Most pubs close by 11.30 pm (11 pm from October to April) but many now have late licences, which permit them to serve until 1.30 am on Thursday and Friday and until midnight on Saturday. See the Dublin's Pubs & Bars map on the next page for all pubs mentioned in this section.

North of the Liffey

Traditional Just off O'Connell St on Middle Abbey St, *The Oval* is a popular journalists' hangout. Across O'Connell St on Lower Abbey St, the *Abbey Mooney* is a large pub with a warm, convivial atmosphere. Farther north is *Patrick Conway (70 Parnell St)*, just across from the Virgin cinema complex. Although slightly out of the way, this is a true gem of a pub. It has been operating since 1745, and no doubt new fathers have been stopping in here for a celebratory pint since the day the Rotunda Maternity Hospital opened across the road in 1757. *Joxer Daly's (103-104 Upper Dorset St)* is a Victorian-style pub that is conveniently close to the Young Traveller and An Óige hostels. A word of warning, however; if you're in this area late at night, you should be

Right: What's your poison?

FIONN DAVENPORT

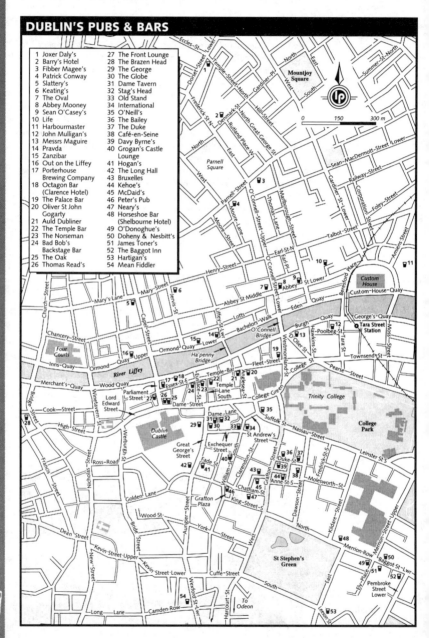

DUBLIN'S PUBS & BARS

1 Joxer Daly's
2 Barry's Hotel
3 Fibber Magee's
4 Patrick Conway
5 Slattery's
6 Keating's
7 The Oval
8 Abbey Mooney
9 Sean O'Casey's
10 Life
11 Harbourmaster
12 John Mulligan's
13 Messrs Maguire
14 Pravda
15 Zanzibar
16 Out on the Liffey
17 Porterhouse
   Brewing Company
18 Octagon Bar
   (Clarence Hotel)
19 The Palace Bar
20 Oliver St John
   Gogarty
21 Auld Dubliner
22 The Temple Bar
23 The Norseman
24 Bad Bob's
   Backstage Bar
25 The Oak
26 Thomas Read's

27 The Front Lounge
28 The Brazen Head
29 The George
30 The Globe
31 Dame Tavern
32 Stag's Head
33 Old Stand
34 International
35 O'Neill's
36 The Bailey
37 The Duke
38 Café-en-Seine
39 Davy Byrne's
40 Grogan's Castle
   Lounge
41 Hogan's
42 The Long Hall
43 Bruxelles
44 Kehoe's
45 McDaid's
46 Peter's Pub
47 Neary's
48 Horseshoe Bar
   (Shelbourne Hotel)
49 O'Donoghue's
50 Doheny & Nesbitt's
51 James Toner's
52 The Baggot Inn
53 Hartigan's
54 Mean Fiddler

particularly vigilant because the streets around here have been plagued by crime and a certain amount of violence due to a heroin epidemic.

Music Slattery's *(☎ 872 7971, 129 Capel St)* on the corner of Mary's Lane is considered by many to be the home of Dublin pub rock. Brian Downey, the former drummer with the 70s group Thin Lizzy, plays a regular weekly session here with his band. Sean O'Casey's *(☎ 874 8675, 105 Marlborough St)* on the corner of Lower Abbey St has a weekly menu of live rock and Irish traditional sessions. Keating's *(☎ 873 1567, 10 Jervis St)* is a modern bar with a nightly traditional seisún. Fibber Magee's *(☎ 874 5253)* at the Gate Hotel on Parnell St is a bit of a dive but has nightly music from DJs and live rock bands. The bar in Barry's Hotel *(☎ 874 6943, Great Denmark St)* is home to a time-honoured country music session.

Other Pubs The new northside scene is best exemplified by three bars, all recently opened and all within walking distance of each other. *Pravda (Lower Liffey St)* near the Ha'penny Bridge is Russian in name only. It's a big place but you're better off coming during the week and avoiding the weekend queues that can keep you waiting for up to half an hour to get in. Around the corner, *Zanzibar (Lower Ormond Quay)* is an enormous bar that actually seems to pride itself on keeping you waiting before allowing you in. It's trendy and, once you get in, a lot of fun. Easily the best of the new northside bars, however, is **Life** *(Irish Life Mall)* off Lower Abbey St. This elegant, well-designed bar serves delicious cocktails and, on Friday, hosts **The Good Life**, a free club-within-a-pub that is chic and trendy without a hint of pretentiousness.

Nearby, in the Financial Services Centre, the **Harbourmaster** is a favourite with Dublin's financial services employees. The northside's only gay bar is **Out on the Liffey** *(27 Upper Ormond Quay)*, which is popular with both men and women.

Temple Bar

Traditional The refurbishment of Temple Bar has sadly left its cobbled streets virtually devoid of old-style, traditional pubs; with one exception the pubs that have retained their old-world charm and nicotine-stained walls are outside the area's boundaries. Within Temple Bar the **Palace Bar** *(Fleet St)*, with its mirrors and wooden niches, is often said to be the perfect example of an old Dublin pub. It's popular with journalists from the nearby *Irish Times*. Just off Fleet St, outside the eastern boundary of Temple Bar, **John Mulligan's** *(Poolbeg St)* is another pub that has scarcely changed over the years. It featured as the local in the film *My Left Foot* and is also popular with journalists from the nearby newspaper offices. Mulligan's was established in 1782 and has long been reputed to have the best Guinness in Ireland as well as a wonderfully varied collection of regulars.

The Perfect Guinness

In Irish pubs, talk is just as important as the beer and the talk will often turn to the perfect Guinness. But just what is the perfect pint? Proximity to the St James's Gate Guinness Brewery is one requirement, for although a Guinness in Kuala Lumpur can still be a fine thing, it's frequently asserted that Guinness at its best can only be found in Ireland.

Up to the early 70s, when Guinness introduced gases and other agents to its brewing process to give the drink longer life and a more marketable taste, the pint looked less than appetising. The syrupy liquid was topped with a thin yellowy head and served at room temperature. Today Guinness is served cold and its head is thicker and almost perfectly white.

Long-time drinkers of Guinness have a million and one ideas of what the perfect pint is, but a good test of quality is the following. When you're about halfway through drinking, look at the sides of the glass; if there are rings of white foam around the inside edges (the thicker the better), then you can be sure that the pint was a pretty good one.

Personnel is also important. Older bars still employ bartenders who have served an apprenticeship in the trade (unlike some newer, trendier bars, who employ people with varied amounts of experience). An expert bartender not only knows how to serve a pint properly but is also conscientious about ensuring that the pipes are kept clean and free-flowing; after all, there is nothing worse than drinking a pint that has passed through dirty pipes.

The perfect Guinness requires expertise in its 'pulling'. If you want a perfect pint you certainly do not simply hold the glass under the tap and slosh it in. It isn't difficult, but a certain precision is required. The glass must be tilted to about 45 degrees, then the tap is pulled forward so that the liquid is poured against the back of the glass. When it is about three-quarters full, the glass is left to 'settle', which means that the heavier black liquid settles underneath the lighter, creamy head. After a couple of minutes, the pint is topped up by pushing the tap backwards, allowing only the black beer into the glass. When the pint is full, it is left to settle a second time, and then the pint is ready for serving.

There's a new system known as 'coldflow', designed to standardise the taste of Guinness and to allow the pint to be poured in one go. You're unlikely to find this in Dublin, however, as time-honoured traditions are as important to Dubliners as the quality of their pint.

Now that you know what to look out for, where should you go to find the perfect pint of plain, or 'the black stuff' as it is referred to in Dublin? Most Dubliners agree that the pint served in the Guinness Hop Store is among the best served anywhere. Guinness denies that there is any difference between the Hop Store and anywhere else, but a glass there is colder, smoother and more delicious. As for pubs, only a handful of city-centre establishments serve a pint that is a cut above the rest. Few will argue with the quality of the pint in John Mulligan's of Poolbeg St, where the assorted regulars are considered experts on the subject (practice makes perfect). Grogan's Castle Lounge on South William St also has an excellent pint, served by an experienced, apprenticed staff. Kehoe's of South Anne St is another place to go for a great pint; if you can, sit in the snug, where you can enjoy a truly traditional ambience. Hartigan's of Lower Leeson St doesn't look like much but its Guinness is top quality. Just outside the city centre, Guinness aficionados will enjoy the pint in Kavanagh's, at the back of Glasnevin cemetery, just off De Courcey Square. This is strictly an 'old school' bar – there isn't even a phone on the premises. The pub is commonly referred to as 'the Gravediggers' because it is the traditional drinking hole of the cemetery employees. The pint is absolutely perfect, with not a hint of new-fangled inventions such as 'cold flow'.

DOUG McKINLAY

DOUG McKINLAY

Top: The Brazen Head: allegedly haunted by the ghost of the great Irish patriot Robert Emmet.

Bottom: It's all a blur – pub life.

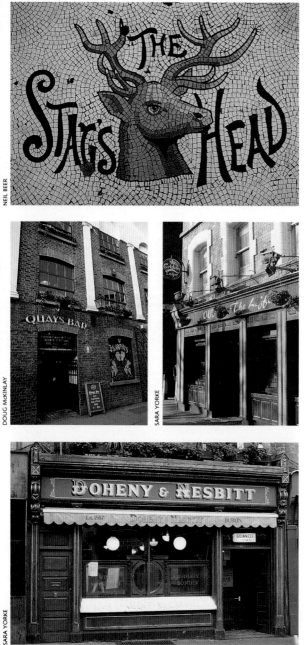

NEIL BEER

DOUG McKINLAY

SARA YORKE

SARA YORKE

Left & Facing Page:
On every street corner, and sometimes even in-between, you'll never have to look far for a pub in Dublin.

Left: Two's company, three's a band and all are welcome – what more could you ask for?

The *Dame Tavern* and the *Stag's Head* are diagonally opposite each other at the intersection of Dame Court and Dame Lane, just off Dame St. A street party takes place between the pubs on summer evenings. The Stag's Head was built in 1770 and remodelled in 1895, and is sufficiently picturesque to have featured in a postage stamp series of Irish pubs. *O'Neill's* (Suffolk St) is a fine old pub that serves an excellent and hearty pub lunch for around IR£6. It's near Trinity College, so it has long been a student haunt. A block over on Exchequer St is the *Old Stand*, furnished in hybrid Georgian-Victorian style and renowned for its rugby connections and pub food.

The Long Hall (51 South Great George's St) luxuriates in full Victorian splendour and is one of the city's most beautiful and best-loved pubs. Check out the ornate carvings in the woodwork behind the bar and the elegant chandeliers.

West of Temple Bar, on Bridge St just south of the Liffey, is *The Brazen Head*, Dublin's oldest pub, though its history is uncertain. The pub's sign proclaims that it was founded in 1198, but the earliest reference to it dates back to 1613 and licensing laws didn't come into effect until 1635. The present building is thought to date from 1754, and the sunken level of the entrance courtyard clearly indicates how much street levels have altered since its construction. In the 1790s it was the headquarters of the United Irishmen, who apparently talked too much after a few drinks, leading to numerous arrests being made here. At that time Robert Emmet was a regular visitor. James Joyce mentioned it in *Ulysses* with a somewhat half-hearted recommendation for the food: 'you get a decent enough do in the Brazen Head'.

Music The traditional music sessions at the *Oliver St John Gogarty* (☎ 671 1822) at the junction of Fleet and Anglesea Sts are extremely popular with tourists, most of whom don't mind that the music is less than authentic. *Bad Bob's Backstage Bar* (☎ 677 5482, East Essex St) features mostly country and western and is open late virtually every night of the week. *The Brazen Head* (☎ 677 9549) has the occasional traditional session.

Other Pubs Check out popular pubs such as *The Norseman* (27-28 East Essex St) and *The Temple Bar* (48 East Essex St) which, despite a major overhaul in the last few years, have maintained that genteel elegance for which they are renowned. Upstairs in The Norseman is *The Pendulum Club*, which hosts the occasional live music gig, from Irish traditional music to jazz. On the corner of Temple Bar and Anglesea St is the *Auld Dubliner*, whose unashamed pursuit of the tourist punt has led to it being jokingly referred to as the 'Auld Foreigner'. The trendiest bar in Temple Bar is easily the *Octagon Bar* (Clarence Hotel, 6-8 Wellington Quay). Drinks are marginally more expensive than elsewhere but judging by the clientele that have passed the bouncer's strict entry test this is hardly a concern.

The *Front Lounge* (*Parliament St*) is a sophisticated new bar popular with the cubs of the Celtic Tiger. It is also one of the only bars in Dublin where gays and lesbians mix freely and comfortably with the straight community. Just across the street is the *Porter House Brewing Company*, a microbrewery and pub that has dared challenge the legendary supremacy of Guinness. See the boxed text 'Rivals for Uncle Arthur' on the opposite page. Those who tell you that their Wrassler XXXX is the best stout in the city wouldn't be far wrong. Nearby is *Thomas Read's* (*1 Parliament St*), a spacious, airy bar spread across two levels, where the clientele seems to favour a selection of wine and coffee over beer. Next door, and linked to Thomas Read's by stairs, is *The Oak*, a more traditional bar where beer is still king.

Just up from Dame St is *The Globe* (*11 South Great George's St*), one of the first of the new breed of trendy pubs to open in the city. It doesn't seem to have suffered from the increasing competition because it is still packed with cool kids most nights. Further on up the street at No 35 is *Hogan's*, once an old-style, traditional bar, now a gigantic boozer spread across two floors. A popular hangout for young professionals, it gets very full at weekends with folks eager to take advantage of its late licence.

You can't miss the pink neon lettering of Temple Bar's only overtly gay bar, *The George* (*89 South Great George's St*) directly opposite The Globe. This huge bar is full virtually every night, and at weekends is constantly in the throes of a gigantic party that goes on until late.

DOUG McKINLAY

Left: The oldest bar in Europe? There's been a tavern on this site since Viking days.

Grafton St Area

Traditional Just off Grafton St, be sure to pop your head into *Kehoe's* *(9 South Anne St)*, one of the only city-centre bars to have recently passed into new ownership without losing any of its traditional appeal. Its snug is still intact, while upstairs drinks are served in what was once the publican's living room. And it looks it!

Also off Grafton St, you'll find *McDaid's* *(3 Harry St)*, Brendan Behan's 'local' and a bit of a tourist trap. *Neary's* (1 Chatham St) is a showy Victorian-era pub with a particularly fine frontage and is popular with actors from the nearby Gaiety Theatre.

Grogan's Castle Lounge *(South William St)*, known simply as Grogan's (after the original owner), is a city-centre institution. It has long been a favourite haunt of Dublin's writers and painters as well as others from the bohemian, alternative set, most of whom seem to be waiting for the 'inevitable' moment when they are finally recognised as geniuses. An odd quirk of the pub is that drinks are marginally cheaper in the stone-floor bar than the carpeted lounge, even though they are served by the same bar!

Rivals for Uncle Arthur

The unquenchable thirst of Dubliners has created opportunities for the bravest of local breweries. Arthur Guinness, founder of the brewing empire, set quite a precedent, but others are not being intimidated and the challenge is being met.

The award-winning Porter House, on Parliament St, not only claims to stock Ireland's largest selection of beers from around the world but also brews its own beers on the premises. The company's most conventional brew, Plain Porter, won a gold medal for best stout at the 1998 Brewing Industry International Awards. The more intrepid drinker can choose from, among others, the Weissbier, a favourite of those who relish a hint of clove, banana and bubble-gum in their pint, the fruity An Brainblásta or the non-vegetarian option, Oyster Stout, which really is brewed with fresh oysters. Aficionados will tell you that their Wrassler XXXX, brewed from a recipe dating back to the early 20th century, is the best stout in the city and this particular pint is reputed to have been Michael Collins' favourite tipple.

Another establishment providing an alternative to the more traditional Irish pint is Messrs Maguire on Burgh Quay. This micro-brewery offers five of its own beers ranging from a creamy Porter to Haus, a German style lager.

Claire Hornshaw

Music The *International* (☎ 677 9250, 23 Wicklow St) has live jazz and blues most nights except Wednesday, when it hosts a comedy night. *Bruxelles* (☎ 677 5362, Harry St) has weekly live rock music, perhaps the only link the now-trendy pub has to its heavy metal past.

Other Pubs Facing each other on Duke St are two pubs made famous by James Joyce in *Ulysses*, the *Bailey* at No 2 and *Davy Byrne's* at No 21. Neither pub bears any resemblance to its Joycean predecessor, but it is the Bailey that has come out best. Davy Byrne's was Bloom's 'moral pub' in *Ulysses* and he stopped there for a Gorgonzola cheese sandwich with mustard washed down with a glass of Burgundy. Today it is a bland (but popular) upwardly mobile watering hole. The Bailey only recently reopened its doors after a two year revamp that has turned it into a stylish, ultra-modern pub replete with light-boxes and comfortable seating. On Sunday night a DJ plays jazz, funk and other music, which is in keeping with the urbane tone of the place. Just down the street is *The Duke*, a fairly bland bar where the business crowd congregates. A short walk from Grafton St is *Café-en-Seine* (40 Dawson St), which looks more like a giant Parisian bistro than an Irish pub. Its super-hip clientele may have moved on to fresher pastures but it is still a big hit with the 'in' crowd. *Peter's Pub* (1 Johnston Place) at the top of South William St is a quiet, pleasant bar that is great for early evening drinks.

A joke in Dublin is that the major political decisions of the day aren't made in the Dáil but on Stephen's Green, in the Shelbourne Hotel's *Horseshoe Bar*. Politicians of every hue rub shoulders with journalists and businessfolk in a fairly relaxed atmosphere – the perfect ambience for Irish politicking!

Merrion Row, Baggot St & Beyond

Traditional Facing each other across Lower Baggot St are two traditional pubs, *James Toner's* (No 139) and *Doheny & Nesbitt's* (No 5). Toner's, with its stone floor, is almost a country pub in the heart of the city and the shelves and drawers are reminders that it once doubled as a grocery store. Doheny & Nesbitt's is equipped with antique snugs and is a favourite place for political gossip among politicians and journalists; Leinster House is only a short stroll away.

Hartigan's (100 Lower Leeson St) is about as spartan a bar as you'll find in the city and the daytime home to some serious drinkers, who appreciate the quiet, no-frills surroundings. In the evening it's popular with students from the medical faculty of University College Dublin.

Music The most renowned traditional music bar in all Dublin is *O'Donoghue's* (☎ 661 4303, Merrion Row), where world-famous folk group the Dubliners started out in the 1960s. On summer evenings a young, international crowd spills out into the courtyard beside the pub.

The ***Baggot Inn*** (☎ *676 1430*), close to Toner's on Lower Baggot St, is a popular pub for rock music. The ***Mean Fiddler*** (☎ *478 0391, Wexford St*), which is part of the UK-based chain, is one of the bigger venues in Dublin. It's spread over two floors and the décor is all futuristic neon lights and metal, befitting the techno and house acts that provide the musical entertainment.

Serious aficionados of traditional music should make the trip to ***Comhaltas Ceoltóiri Éireann*** (☎ *280 0295, 35 Belgrave Square, Monkstown*). The name, pronounced 'keol-tas quail-tori Erin', means 'Fraternity of Traditional Musicians of Ireland', and it is here that you'll find the best Irish music and dancing in all of Dublin, featuring some of the country's top players. To get there, take bus Nos 7, 7A or 8 from Trinity College, get off before Monkstown village and follow the blue signs. Alternatively, you can take the DART; the venue is a five minute walk from Seapoint station.

Other Pubs *Odeon*, in the old Harcourt St Station at the top of the street of the same name, is a trendy new spot with a 50m-long bar and ample space for the hundreds of punters who flock there to show off their designer gear.

Right: A taste of Europe: Paris comes to Dublin.

SARA YORKE

Shopping

WHAT TO BUY

If it's made in Ireland, you can probably buy it in Dublin. Popular buys include fine Irish knitwear, such as the renowned Aran sweaters; jewellery with a Celtic influence, including Claddagh rings with two hands clasping a heart; books on Irish topics; crystal from Waterford, Galway, Tyrone and Tipperary; Irish coats of arms; china from Belleek; and Royal Tara chinaware or linen from Donegal. *Dublin Style: An Insider's Guide* by Deirdre McQuillan is a handy guide to shopping in the city.

Dublin's new-found economic wealth has resulted in an increase in the number of top fashion outlets, previously the preserve of the select few. Today you can find every major label on display in the shops along and around Grafton St and it is no longer unusual to overhear the city's trendsetters discuss where the best deals on Diesel gear are or where to find a nice Prada shirt.

There are all sorts of weird and wonderful small shops in Temple Bar, including a number of interesting record shops, an equally varied collection of small bookshops, some of Dublin's most eclectic clothes shops and a variety of other unusual outlets. Among the latter is Rory's Fishing Tackle (Map 7, ☎ 677 2351) at 17A Temple Bar – just the place for fishing enthusiasts.

See Taxes and Refunds under Money in the Facts for the Visitor chapter for information on claiming back sales tax (called value-added tax or VAT).

WHERE TO SHOP
Shopping Centres & Department Stores

In the city centre, the flash St Stephen's Green shopping centre (Map 7), with its white wrought-iron balconies, overlooks the north-western corner of St Stephen's Green at the top of Grafton St. Inside you'll find a diverse mixture of chain stores and individual shops (including a Levi's shop and a Benetton outlet), plus an outlet of the Dunne's Stores department store, which also has a supermarket in the basement. The centre is also home to a restaurant and a couple of cafés. It is open daily from 9 am to 6 pm (8 pm on Thursday).

The wonderful Powerscourt Townhouse shopping centre (Map 7) between South William St and Clarendon St, just to the west of Grafton St, is a big, modern shopping centre in a fine old 1774 building (see the boxed text opposite). The main arcade underwent a substantial renovation in 1998 but should be back to its pristine best by the time you read this. The centre is worth visiting just for the architecture. Among its top class outlets are an antique market, several high-fashion stores and the Crafts Council Gallery.

The Royal Hibernian Way centre (Map 7) off Dawson St is also a relatively exclusive shopping centre with a collection of small shops on the site of the old Royal Hibernian Hotel. Other shopping centres include the Irish Life shopping mall (Map 4), with entrances on Lower Abbey St and Talbot St, and the Westbury shopping arcade (Map 7) off Grafton St.

On the north side of the Liffey, two shopping centres are worth checking out. The Jervis St shopping centre (Map 4), just north of Grattan Bridge, is an ultramodern mall with dozens of outlets, including Penney's, the cheapest department store in Ireland. In contrast, the Ilac Centre (Map 4), off Moore St near O'Connell St, is a little dilapidated but still has some interesting outlets with goods at affordable prices.

Dublin's two best-known department stores, the long-running Brown Thomas (Map 7, ☎ 679 5666) and Switzers, have finally teamed up in Grafton St/Wicklow St. The site across the road previously occupied by Brown Thomas is now a new branch of the British chain Marks & Spencer (Map 7, ☎ 679 7855).

The Powerscourt Townhouse Shopping Centre

Of all Dublin's shopping centres, none is more original or impressive than the Powerscourt Townhouse between William St South and Clarendon St, just off Grafton St. Unlike most shopping centres, this was not built from scratch but was laboriously created out of a wonderful 18th century mansion that had been taken over by a firm of wholesale drapers in 1832 and robbed of all its grandeur.

Powerscourt Townhouse was built between 1771 and 1774 for Richard Wingfield, the third Viscount Powerscourt and a one-time MP for County Wicklow. It was designed by Robert Mack (who also designed the Essex Bridge over the Liffey), built using granite taken from the Powerscourt Estate in County Wicklow and cost UK£8000.

After the Act of Union, Powerscourt House, like so many grand Dublin mansions, became redundant and was bought by the government in 1807 for UK£15,000. The architect Francis Johnson was then commissioned to add on three other buildings to create a central courtyard at a cost of a further UK£15,000. In 1811 the building was occupied by the Commissioner for Stamp Duty. When that department moved into the Custom House in 1832, Powerscourt House was sold to Messrs Ferrier Pollock, a firm of wholesale drapers, for UK£7500. Within three weeks, fire broke out and the house was only saved from destruction by the fact that it happened during the daytime, when the flames could be quickly extinguished. In 1977 Power Securities Ltd bought the house from Ferrier Pollock and turned it into a shopping centre that opened to the public in 1981.

Externally, Powerscourt Townhouse has a central stairway to the door, with gates at each end that look like extra wings. A Doric entablature runs along the main building and over the gates to unify the façade. On the roof a curious square stone box may have been intended as an observatory. Internally, the house is decorated in a style midway between rococo and neo-classical, with fine plasterwork by James McCullagh and Michael Reynolds. Their bill for decorating the hall came to one hundred and six pounds, two shillings and six pence, and for the stairway two hundred and fifty pounds, seven shillings and eight pence. Michael Stapleton was responsible for the main reception rooms, now the grandest shop interiors; in particular try to visit the Solomon Gallery on the top floor, as well as KH Interiors (once the dining room) and Mary's Gift Shop, both on the 1st floor of the original building. Among other features that it's still possible to appreciate are the black, grey and white marble hall floor and the fine mahogany staircase with acanthus-leaf balustrade by Ignatius McDonagh. Powerscourt Townhouse appears in one of James Malton's prints of Dublin, dated 1796, although in it Clarendon St has been opened out to make viewing easier. Malton wrote that it was 'furnished with elegance and taste, particularly the Ball and Drawing Rooms: in the latter are two slabs made of the lava of Mt Vesuvius which are mounted on rich gilt frames and placed as Pier Tables between the windows'. Sadly, these are now lost.

The centre is open from 9 am to 6 pm Monday to Saturday (to 7pm on Thursday). Free lunch-time concerts take place every Wednesday at 1.15 pm.

SHOPPING

The other Dublin department store is Clery & Co (Map 4, ☎ 878 6000), a graceful shop on O'Connell St that – like so many buildings on the north side of the city – has seen better days.

Markets

Dublin has some colourful markets, such as the open-air Moore St Market (Map 4) which has flowers, fruit, vegetables and fish, and people hawking cheap cigarettes, tobacco and chocolate. Moore St runs from Henry St to Parnell St, parallel to O'Connell St in north Dublin. The market operates from Monday to Saturday.

The Iveagh Market (Map 5, ☎ 454 2090), on Francis St in the area known as the Liberties, operates from Tuesday to Saturday, selling mainly second-hand clothes and furniture. To the west of the Iveagh Market is Mother Redcap's Market (Map 5, ☎ 454 0652), tucked away on Back Lane near Christ Church Cathedral and the two St Audoen's churches. It has a colourful collection of stalls selling everything from antiques to records and is open Friday to Sunday from 10 am to 5.30 pm.

There's another small flea market (☎ 475 0941) in Mercer St behind the St Stephen's Green shopping centre. It's open daily from 11 am to 6 pm and has the usual mix of clothes, jewellery, books and records.

The George's St Arcade (Map 7) is one of the nicest arcades in Dublin. It has a mixture of shops and selling everything from olives to drums, jewellery to dresses. Look out for Bygone Days, selling second-hand books, postcards, prints and other ephemera, and Jenny Vander, whose selection of second-hand clothes is pretty wild. You can get your tarot cards read here too. Stalls are usually open from 10 am to 6 pm Monday to Saturday.

The Dublin Corporation fruit and vegetable market runs along both sides of St Michan's St (Map 4), between Chancery St and Mary's Lane near the Four Courts.

Irish Crafts & Souvenirs

There is a common misconception about Irish crafts. The 'traditional' crafts, which include everything from hawthorn walking sticks to anything with a shamrock on it, are not all necessarily traditional. Much of it is mass-produced, factory-made junk that is strictly for tourists, hence its presence at the airport and in tacky shops all over town. However, in the last decade or so the crafts market has benefited from a new generation of artisans who have introduced modern

concepts and ideas to traditional work with great success.

The Trinity College Library Shop, in the Colonnades building at Trinity College, has a wide variety of books and other Irish souvenirs, but, of course, it's best known for reproductions from the Book of Kells.

The Kilkenny Shop (Map 6, ☎ 677 7066), 6 Nassau St, has a wonderful selection of finely made Irish crafts, featuring clothing, glassware, pottery, jewellery, crystal and silver from some of Ireland's best designers. The House of Ireland (Map 7, ☎ 671 4543), 38 Nassau St, is another all-purpose shop with all types of Irish crafts.

The Tower Design Centre (Map 6, ☎ 677 5655), housed in a 19th century warehouse in Pearse St that was Dublin's first iron-structured building, has studios for local craftspeople. They produce jewellery in both contemporary and Celtic-inspired designs, Irish pewter, ceramics, silk and other fabrics, pottery, rugs and wall hangings, cards, leather bags and various other handcrafted items. It's immediately opposite the Waterways Visitors' Centre, off Lower Grand Canal St.

Various smaller shops specialise in Irish crafts, among them the Irish Celtic Craftshop (☎ 667 9912) at 10-12 Lord Edward St, near Christ Church Cathedral. Whichcraft (Map 7, ☎ 670 9371), nearby at 5 Castle Gate, sells wonderful pieces, both old and new, at reasonable prices. The Crafts Council Gallery (☎ 679 7368) and other individual shops selling craft items are in the Powerscourt Townhouse shopping centre on South William St.

Clothing

Clothing, particularly woollen sweaters, is probably the most authentically Irish buy. The Irish also make some high-quality outdoor-activity gear, perhaps because they have plenty of wet weather.

Irish knitwear is justly famous, though the demand for those superb heavy Aran sweaters is so great that even the most genuine is unlikely to have been knitted on the islands. One of the major wool outlets in

Dublin is the Dublin Woollen Company (Map 7, ☎ 677 5014), 41 Lower Ormond Quay near the Ha'penny Bridge. It has a large collection of sweaters, cardigans, scarves, rugs, shawls and other woollen goods and runs a tax-free shopping scheme.

Traditional and exciting contemporary designs in knitwear can be found at The Sweater Shop (☎ 671 3270), 9 Wicklow St, just off Grafton St and near Trinity College. Blarney Woollen Mills (Map 7, ☎ 671 0068) is at 21-23 Nassau St.

For less conventional clothing head for Temple Bar and its diverse collection of unusual outlets: China Blue in Merchant's Arch, Damascus and Eager Beaver, both on Crown Alley, and Sé Sí in Crow St are just some of the possibilities. Flip at 4 Upper Fownes St specialises in 'vintage' US clothing and DV8 on Crown Alley has unusual footwear.

For high fashion your best bet is the area around Grafton St. In the Powerscourt Townhouse shopping centre you'll find custom-made shoes, exotic wedding dresses and wonderful one-off pieces of jewellery. Alias Tom (Map 7, ☎ 671 7200) on the corner of Lemon St and Duke Lane has the latest designer wear for men, stocking most of Europe's top designers (and a couple of Irish ones as well). The prices are steep though. Acquiesce (Map 7, ☎ 671 9433), at 31 South Anne St, is one of the better fashion shops for women, with a good selection of top designer brands.

Camping & Backpacking Equipment

There are plenty of places with good-quality camping, walking and backpacking equipment. The Scout Shop (Map 7, ☎ 671 2055) is at 14 Fownes St in Temple Bar. A number of outlets, including surplus specialists, are to be found north of the river along Talbot St off Marlborough St and Mary's Lane off Capel St.

Records & Musical Instruments

Music plays an important role in Ireland, whether it's traditional Irish music or the contemporary music that has given Ireland a position on the cutting edge of modern rock. Dublin's biggest record store is the riverside Virgin Megastore (Map 7, ☎ 677 7361), 14 Aston Quay. Nearby in Temple Bar, but far more intimate in size, is the knowledgeably staffed Claddagh Records (Map 7, ☎ 677 0262), 2 Cecilia St, which specialises in traditional music. Also in Temple Bar is Comet Records (Map 7, ☎ 671 8592), 5 Cope St, which specialises in independent label releases – metal, indie, ska and techno. Borderline Records (Map 7, ☎ 679 9097), 17 Temple Bar, is another possibility. At 16 Fade St, between South Great George's St and Drury St, are two record stores, Road Records (Map 7, ☎ 671 7340) and (in its basement) Big Brother Records (☎ 672 9355). Vinyl junkies and indie fans will get a kick out of the selection in Big Brother, a good mix of hip-hop, deep house, jazzy beats and drum-and-bass, as well as jazz and soul. Upstairs you'll find the latest in indie music.

The Golden Disc Group has an outlet in the Grafton Arcade on Grafton St (Map 7, ☎ 677 1025) and five others throughout the city centre. Music giant HMV (Map 7, ☎ 679 5334) is at the top of Grafton St.

Waltons (☎ 874 7805), 2 North Frederick St, has traditional Irish records and music as well as bodhráns and other traditional musical instruments. It has another branch (Map 7, ☎ 475 0661) at 69-70 South Great George's St and one in the George's St Shopping Centre in Dun Laoghaire.

Antiques

For antiques try the antique market at the Powerscourt Townhouse shopping centre or head for Francis St in the Liberties area, Dublin's premier antique shopping street. Odeon (Map 5, ☎ 473 2384), 69-70 Francis St, is great for jewellery, fashion antiques and other curios.

An antiques and collectibles fair takes place every second Sunday at Newman House (Map 6, 85-86 St Stephen's Green). Check the Irish Times on Sunday for information on antiques sales and auctions.

SHOPPING

Bookshops

Most of the bookshops in Dublin offer an extensive choice of books on Ireland and subjects of Irish interest, as well as Irish literature and more.

Directly opposite Trinity College is the excellent Fred Hanna's (Map 6, ☎ 677 1255), 27-29 Nassau St. Round the corner is the large, well-stocked Hodges Figgis (Map 7, ☎ 677 4754), 57 Dawson St. Directly opposite, Waterstone's (Map 7, ☎ 679 1415) at 7 Dawson St carries a wide range of books. Another branch of Waterstone's (☎ 878 1311) can be found in the Jervis St shopping centre (Map 4). In the Stephen's Green shopping centre (Map 7) is Hughes & Hughes (☎ 478 3060).

If you're looking for a large range of phrasebooks and an extensive language section, try International Books (☎ 679 9375) at 18 South Frederick St (Map 7).

The Dublin Bookshop (Map 7, ☎ 677 5568), 24 Grafton St, has a particularly good selection of books of Irish interest. North of the Liffey, Eason's (Map 4, ☎ 873 3811), 40 Upper O'Connell St near the GPO, has a wide range of books and one of the biggest selections of magazines in Ireland. The Winding Stair (Map 7, ☎ 873 3292), 40 Lower Ormond Quay, has new and second-hand books and a café upstairs. All these bookshops have an extensive choice of books on Ireland.

A number of bookshops cater for special interests. Forbidden Planet (Map 7, ☎ 671 0688), 5-6 Crampton Quay, is a wonderful science fiction and comic-book specialist. Sub-City (Map 7, ☎ 677 1902), 2 Exchequer St, is similar. The Sinn Féin Bookshop (Map 4, ☎ 872 7096) is at 44 Parnell Square West. An Siopa Leabhar (Map 6, ☎ 478 3814), in Harcourt St just off St Stephen's Green, has books in Irish. For official publications and maps there's the Dúchas bookshop (Map 6, ☎ 671 0309), Sun Alliance House, Molesworth St.

The Dublin Writers' Museum (Map 4) on Parnell Square has an excellent bookshop. The IMMA at the Royal Hospital Kilmainham and the National Gallery (Map 6) in Merrion Square both have bookshops offering a good range of art books. The Library Book Shop at Trinity College has a wide selection of Irish-interest books, including, of course, various titles on the Book of Kells.

George Webb (Map 7, ☎ 677 7489), at 5 Crampton Quay, has books of Irish interest, as does Greene's Bookshop (Map 6, ☎ 873 3149), just off Merrion Square, and Cathach Books (Map 7, ☎ 671 8676), at 10 Duke St.

Jewellery & Crystal

There are several jewellery shops in the Powerscourt Townhouse shopping centre. Sleaters (Map 7, ☎ 677 7532), 9 Johnsons Court, and Lawrences (☎ 873 1493), 27 Henry St, specialise in Irish and Celtic-style jewellery. John Brereton has a number of outlets in Dublin, including in the Powerscourt Townhouse shopping centre, at 29 Lower O'Connell St, at 2 Chatham St and at 108 Capel St.

A number of places stock an extensive range of world-famous Waterford crystal, particularly the Brown Thomas department store. Although Waterford is the best-known Irish crystal, there are other companies that cut good-quality crystal glass, such as Tyrone and Tipperary.

Designer Goods & Oddities

If you've admired those wonderful brass door knockers on fine Dublin Georgian doors, then Knobs & Knockers (Map 6, ☎ 671 0288), 19 Nassau St, has plenty.

Dublin's oldest shop (1670), Thomas Read & Co (Map 7, ☎ 677 1487) at 4 Parliament St in Temple Bar, sells cutlery.

Belying Dublin's squeaky clean image is Condom Power (Map 7, ☎ 677 8963), a sex shop in the basement of 57 Dame St.

Art

Dublin has a large number of galleries which exhibit and sell the works of contemporary Irish artists. For a list of these galleries and where to find them, see the Other Galleries section in the Things to See & Do chapter.

Seaside Suburbs

There are a number of seaside suburbs around the curve of Dublin Bay that make worthwhile trips from the city centre. Dun Laoghaire to the south and Howth to the north are historic ports; the former also has pleasant beach walks and a vibrant town centre with a fascinating museum, while the latter is one of the most beautiful spots in all of County Dublin. Accessible on the DART rail service, both are interesting alternatives to staying in the city.

DUN LAOGHAIRE

Dun Laoghaire (pronounced 'dun leary'), 13km south of central Dublin, is a busy harbour with ferry connections to Britain. It was once also a popular resort. After a visit to Ireland in 1821 King George IV departed from Dun Laoghaire, and from then until Irish independence in 1922 the port was known as Kingstown. The suburb may have lost some of its 19th century charm but it's still worth visiting, if only for its location on the sea, which affords some pleasant walks and some beautiful views.

Dun Laoghaire's B&Bs are numerous and a bit cheaper than those in central Dublin, and fast, frequent DART rail connections make it easy to use as a base.

History

There was a coastal settlement at the site of Dun Laoghaire more than 1000 years ago but it was little more than a small fishing village until 1767, when the first pier was built. Dun Laoghaire grew rapidly after that time. The Sandycove Martello Tower (see the boxed text 'Martello Towers' under Sandycove in this section) was erected in the early 19th century out of fear of an invasion from Napoleonic France.

Construction of a harbour was proposed in 1815 to provide refuge for ships unable to reach the safety of Dublin Harbour in bad weather. The original plan was for a single pier, but engineer John Rennie proposed two massive piers enclosing a 100 hectare artificial harbour. Work began in 1817 and by 1823 the workforce comprised 1000 men. Despite huge expenditure the harbour wasn't actually completed until 1842. Carlisle Pier was only added in 1859 and parts of the West Pier stonework have never been finished. The total cost approached UK£1 million, an astronomical figure in the mid-19th century.

The commencement of shipping services to and from Liverpool and Holyhead, and the completion in 1834 of a train line from Dublin, the first anywhere in Ireland, made this a state-of-the-art transport centre.

From Dun Laoghaire to Holyhead is a distance of just over 100km and a ferry service has operated across the Irish Sea on this route since the mid-19th century. The first mail steamers took nearly six hours to make the crossing but by 1860 the time was less than four hours and on one occasion in 1887 the paddle steamer *The Ireland* made the crossing in less than three hours. In 1918 RMS *Leinster* was torpedoed by a German U-boat 25km from Dun Laoghaire and more than 500 lives were lost.

Car ferries to Dun Laoghaire were introduced in the early 1960s.

Orientation

Dun Laoghaire is fairly small with one main street, George's St, which runs parallel to the coast. The most prominent landmark is the ferry terminal. The huge harbour is sheltered by the the East and West piers. Sandycove, with the James Joyce Museum and the Forty Foot Pool, is about 1km south-east of central Dun Laoghaire.

Information

The tourist office (☎ 284 4768) is in Carlisle Terminal. A new ferry terminal and berthing facilities have been built nearby.

The local branch of Pembrey's Bookshop is at 78 Lower George's St. Across the road is Eason's, a newsagency and bookshop chain. The Star Laundrette (☎ 280 5074) is at 47 Upper George's St.

The Harbour

The 1290m East and 1548m West piers, each ending in a lighthouse built in the 1850s, are popular for walking (especially the East Pier), bird-watching and fishing (particularly from the end of the West Pier). You can also ride a bicycle out along the piers (bottom level only).

The East Pier has an 1890s bandstand and a memorial to Captain Boyd and the crew of a Dun Laoghaire lifeboat who were drowned in a rescue attempt. Near the end of the pier is an anemometer (1852), one of the first of these wind-speed measuring devices to be installed anywhere in the world. The East Pier ends with a lighthouse and the East Pier Battery, from which VIPs arriving by sea may receive a gun salute.

The harbour has long been a popular yachting centre and the Royal Irish Yacht Club's building, dating from around 1850, was Ireland's first purpose-built yacht club. The Royal St George Yacht Club's building dates from 1863 and that of the National Yacht Club from 1876. The world's first single-design sailing boat class started life at Dun Laoghaire, a dinghy known as the Water Wag. A variety of specifically Dublin Bay classes still race here, as do Mirrors and other popular small sailing boats.

St Michael's Pier, also known as the Car Ferry Pier, was added in 1969. Carlisle Pier, also known as Mailboat Pier, was modified to take car ferries in 1970. On the West Pier side of the harbour are two anchored lightships whose jobs are now done by automatic buoys.

National Maritime Museum

The National Maritime Museum is in the former Mariners' Church in Adelaide St, built in 1837 'for the benefit of sailors in men-of-war, merchant ships, fishing boats and yachts'. The beautiful window in the chancel is a replica of the 'Five Sisters' window at York Minster in England. Ex-

hibits include a French ship's longboat captured at Bantry in 1796 from Wolfe Tone's abortive French-backed invasion.

The huge clockwork-driven Great Baily Light Optic came from the Baily Lighthouse on Howth Peninsula (see Howth later in this chapter). Its herringbone patterned lens reflected light across the bay from 1902 until 1972, when it was replaced with an electrically driven lens.

There's a model of the *Great Eastern* (1858), an early steam-powered vessel built by English engineer Isambard Kingdom Brunel. Although it proved a commercial failure as a passenger ship, it successfully laid the first transatlantic telegraph cable. There are also various items from the German submarine U19, which landed Sir Roger Casement in Kerry in 1916 (see the Sandycove section). These were donated 50 years after the event by the U-boat's captain, Raimund Weisbach.

The museum is open from 1 to 5 pm Tuesday to Sunday, from May to September; entry is IR£1.50/75p.

Around the Town

Nothing remains of the *dún* or fort that gave Dun Laoghaire its name because it was destroyed during the construction of the train line. The train line from Dun Laoghaire to Dalkey was built along the route of an earlier line known as The Metals, which was used to bring stone for the harbour construction from the quarries at Dalkey Hill. By means of a pulley system, the laden trucks trundling down to the harbour pulled the empty ones back up to the quarry.

On the waterfront is a curious monument commemorating George IV's visit in 1821. It consists of an obelisk balanced on four stone balls, one of which is missing as the result of an IRA bomb attack. On the other side of the coast road is the Christ the King sculpture, created in Paris in 1926 by Andrew O'Connor as a memorial to the dead of WWI. It was bought in 1949 but kept in storage until 1978 because the local Church authorities expressed reservations about its 'appropriateness'.

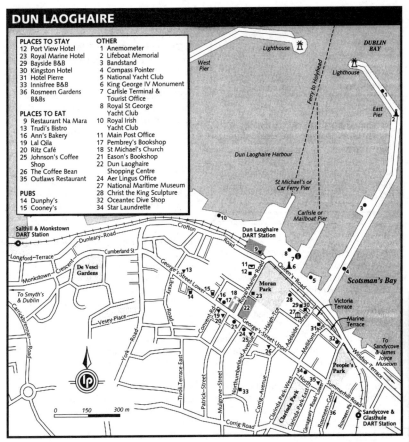

DUN LAOGHAIRE

PLACES TO STAY
12 Port View Hotel
23 Royal Marine Hotel
29 Bayside B&B
30 Kingston Hotel
31 Hotel Pierre
33 Innisfree B&B
36 Rosmeen Gardens
    B&Bs

PLACES TO EAT
9 Restaurant Na Mara
13 Trudi's Bistro
16 Ann's Bakery
19 Lal Qila
20 Ritz Café
25 Johnson's Coffee
   Shop
26 The Coffee Bean
35 Outlaws Restaurant

PUBS
14 Dunphy's
15 Cooney's

OTHER
1 Anemometer
2 Lifeboat Memorial
3 Bandstand
4 Compass Pointer
5 National Yacht Club
6 King George IV Monument
7 Carlisle Terminal &
  Tourist Office
8 Royal St George
  Yacht Club
10 Royal Irish
   Yacht Club
11 Main Post Office
17 Pembrey's Bookshop
18 St Michael's Church
21 Eason's Bookshop
22 Dun Laoghaire
   Shopping Centre
24 Aer Lingus Office
27 National Maritime Museum
28 Christ the King Sculpture
32 Oceantec Dive Shop
34 Star Laundrette

Sandycove

One kilometre south-east of Dun Laoghaire is Sandycove, with a pretty little beach and a Martello Tower (see the boxed text on the next page) which is home to a James Joyce Museum. Sir Roger Casement, who attempted to organise a German-backed Irish opposition force during WWI, was born here in 1864. He was captured after being landed in County Kerry from a German U-boat and was executed by the British as a traitor in 1916.

James Joyce Museum The Martello Tower at Sandycove is where the action begins in James Joyce's epic novel *Ulysses*. Originally, the entrance led straight into what is now the 'upstairs'. The tower now houses a James Joyce Museum, which has photographs, letters, documents, various editions of Joyce's work and two death masks of Joyce on display. The museum was opened in 1962 by Sylvia Beach, the Paris-based publisher who first dared to put *Ulysses* into print.

euro currency converter IR£1 = €1.27

SEASIDE SUBURBS

Martello Towers

Thirty-four Martello towers were built around the coast of Ireland between 1804 and 1815 to counter a feared invasion by Napoleon's forces. A typical Martello Tower stands about 12m high with 2.5m-thick walls. Originally, the entrance to the tower led straight into what is now the 'upstairs'. These towers were copied from one at Cape Mortella in Corsica. Among other sites near Dun Laoghaire, towers can be found at Sandycove, Dalkey Island, Killiney and Bray to the south, and Howth and Ireland's Eye (the island off Howth) to the north.

In 1904 Oliver St John Gogarty, upon whom the 'stately, plump' Buck Mulligan in *Ulysses* is based, rented the tower from the army for the princely sum of £8 a year. Joyce stayed there for a few days, though not for as long as he had planned. Another guest, Samuel Chenevix Trench (who is portrayed in *Ulysses* as the Englishman Haines), had a nightmare one night and dealt with it by drawing his revolver and taking a shot at the fireplace. Gogarty took the gun from him, yelled 'Leave him to me' and fired at the saucepans on the shelf above Joyce's bed. Relations between Gogarty and Joyce were already uneasy after Joyce had accused Gogarty of snobbery, so Joyce took this incident as a hint that he was not welcome and left the next morning. He was soon to leave Ireland as well, eloping to the Continent with Nora Barnacle in 1904. Trench's aim did not improve – just five years later he shot himself, fatally, in the head.

There are fine views from the tower. To the south-east you can see Dalkey Island with its signal tower and Killiney Hill with its obelisk. Howth Head is visible on the northern side of Dublin Bay. Next to the tower is the house of architect Michael Scott, who owned the tower from 1950 until

it was turned into a museum. There's another Martello Tower not far to the south near Bullock Harbour.

The tower (☎ 280 9265/8571) is open from 10 am to 1 pm and 2 to 5 pm Monday to Saturday and from 2 to 6 pm Sunday, from April to October. Entry is IR£2.50/1.50 (students IR£1.80). At other times of the year the tower is only open on weekdays and then only to groups, for a flat fee of IR£55. Call Dublin Tourism (☎ 605 7700) for more details.

You can get to the tower by a 30 minute walk along the seafront from the harbour at Dun Laoghaire, a 15 minute walk from the Sandycove & Glasthule DART station or a five minute walk from West Sandycove Ave, which is served by bus No 8.

Forty Foot Pool Just below the Martello Tower is the Forty Foot Pool, an open-air, sea-water bathing pool that probably took its name from the army's 40th Foot Regiment, which was stationed at the tower until the regiment was disbanded in 1904. At the close of the first chapter of *Ulysses,* Buck Mulligan heads to the Forty Foot Pool for a morning swim.

A morning wake-up here is still a Dun Laoghaire tradition, winter or summer, though a winter dip isn't much braver than a summer one because the water temperature is only about 5°C lower then than in summer. Basically, it's bloody cold any time of year.

When it was suggested that in these enlightened times a public stretch of water like this should be open to both sexes, the 'forty foot gentlemen' put up strong opposition. A compromise eventually saved the day; it was agreed that a 'togs must be worn' ruling would apply after 9 am. Prior to that hour, however, nudity prevails and the swimmers are still predominantly 'forty foot gentlemen'.

Activities

A series of walks in the area make up the signposted Dun Laoghaire Way. The *Heritage Map of Dun Laoghaire*, available from the tourist office and from bookshops, includes a map and notes on the seven separate walks.

Scuba divers head for the waters around Dalkey Island. Oceantec (☎ 280 1083, fax 284 3885) is a dive shop at 10-11 Marine Terrace in Dun Laoghaire. It hires out diving equipment at IR£12.50 for half a day; a one hour local dive costs IR£22.50.

Places to Stay

Staying in Dun Laoghaire is a popular (and often cheaper) alternative to staying in Dublin city. Although the suburb is quite a distance from the centre, the DART makes it easy to get to and from town.

B&Bs Rosmeen Gardens is packed with B&Bs. *Mrs Callanan (☎ 280 6083)* at No 1, *Rathoe (☎ 280 8070)* at No 12, *Rosmeen House (☎ 280 7613)* at No 13, *Mrs McGloughlin (☎ 280 4333)* at No 27, *Annesgrove (☎ 280 9801)* at No 28 and *Mrs Dunne (☎ 280 3360)* at No 30 have rooms from IR£22 to IR£30 for singles and IR£30 to IR£45 for doubles.

There are also some B&Bs on Northumberland Ave, such as *Innisfree (☎ 280 5598)* at No 31. Close to the harbour is *Bayside B&B (☎ 280 4660, Seafront, 5 Haddington Terrace)*, with singles for IR£27 and doubles from IR£40. Other B&Bs can be found on nearby Mellifont and Corrig avenues.

Hotels Pleasantly located on Royal Marine Rd is the small *Port View Hotel (☎ 280 1663, fax 280 0447)*. About half of the 20 rooms have en suite facilities; these cost IR£40/60 for singles/doubles. Also close to the waterfront is the larger *Hotel Pierre (☎ 280 0291, fax 284 3332, 3 Victoria Terrace)* whose 36 rooms, most with en suite facilities, cost IR£50/65. Close by is the *Kingston Hotel (☎ 280 1810, fax 280 1237, Haddington Terrace)* with 24 rooms, all with bathroom, costing IR£35/55.

Dun Laoghaire also has a number of attractively situated seaside hotels. The premier hotel is the A-rated *Royal Marine Hotel (☎ 280 1911, fax 280 1089, Royal Marine Rd)*, two minutes walk from the Carlisle Pier car-ferry terminal. All 104 rooms have en suite bathrooms and cost from IR£70/89.

Places to Eat

There's no shortage of places to eat in Dun Laoghaire; you'll find everything from the ubiquitous fast-food joints and small cafés to charming restaurants with menus to suit all price ranges.

Fast Food & Cafés Branches of *McDonald's*, *La Pizza* and *Abrakebabra* are all on George's St. The *Ritz Café (Patrick St)* offers traditional fish and chips. *Ann's Bakery (Lower George's St)* has good tea, coffee and snacks during the day, as does *Johnson's Coffee Shop*. *The Coffee Bean (21 Upper George's St)* is popular at lunch time, with good coffee and snacks, such as baked potatoes and quiches, from IR£3.

Restaurants *Outlaws Restaurant (☎ 284 2817, 62 Upper George's St)* has steak, burgers (including vegeburgers) and other 'Wild West' fare. It's open from 5.30 pm in the evening.

The town has several Indian restaurants. *Lal Qila (☎ 280 5623, Convent Rd)*, just off Lower George's St, has standard Indian fare; the vegetarian dishes cost IR£5 and the meat ones IR£7. *Dilshad Tandoori Restaurant (☎ 284 4604, Convent Rd)* has a similar menu; the tandoori dishes have a good reputation. Alternatively, there's the *Krishna Indian Restaurant (☎ 280 1855)* on the 1st floor at 47 George's St.

Near the harbour and next to the DART station, *Brasserie Na Mara (☎ 280 6787)* offers more expensive dishes (around IR£20) with an emphasis on seafood. *Trudi's Bistro (☎ 280 5318, 107 Lower George's St)* is another fancier restaurant with excellent and slightly adventurous food (such as stuffed parsnips). Count on paying around IR£22 to IR£28 per person, including drinks. It's open in the evening from Tuesday to Saturday.

Entertainment

Popular pubs include *Cooney's (88 Lower George's St)* and *Dunphy's (41 Lower George's St)* across the road. *Smyth's*, with its nautical interior, is towards Dublin along the extension of Lower George's St. The *Hotel Pierre* (see Places to Stay) is noted for its jazz performances, and the *Purty Kitchen & Bar (Old Dunleary Rd)* often has traditional Irish music or rock.

Getting There & Away

See the Getting There & Away chapter for details of the ferry services between Dun Laoghaire and Holyhead in the UK.

Bus Nos 7, 7A and 8 from next to Trinity College cost IR£1.10 one way to Dun Laoghaire. The trip can take anywhere from 25 minutes to one hour depending on the traffic. The DART rail service takes you from Dublin to Dun Laoghaire in 15 to 20 minutes and also costs IR£1.10 one way.

DALKEY

Dalkey, just over 1km south-east of Sandycove and smaller and prettier than Dun Laoghaire, has the remains of a number of old castles. **Bulloch Castle** overlooking Bullock Harbour was built by the monks of St Mary's Abbey in Dublin in the 12th century. On Castle St are two castles – **Goat Castle** and **Archibold's Castle**. On the same street is the ancient **St Begnet's Church**, dating from the 9th century.

Dalkey Quarry, now a popular site for rock climbers, originally provided most of the stone for the gigantic piers at Dun Laoghaire Harbour.

Dalkey has several holy wells, including **St Begnet's Holy Well**, reputed to cure rheumatism, on the nine hectare Dalkey Island, which lies a few hundred metres offshore. The waters around the island are popular with local scuba divers. A number of rocky swimming pools are also along the coast at Dalkey.

Getting There & Away

Dalkey is on the DART suburban line. Alternatively you can catch bus No 8 from Burgh Quay in the city centre. Both cost IR£1.10, but you're probably better off using the DART as the bus may get caught in traffic.

BRAY

The arrival of the railway in the 1850s turned Bray, 19km south of Dublin, into another popular and easily accessible seaside destination for Dubliners. Its central position between the city and the Wicklow Mountains is a draw, but it's not a very attractive seaside town, with a long seafront parade of fast food places and amusement arcades. The young James Joyce lived here from 1888 to 1891.

Like Sandycove, Bray has a **Martello Tower**. From Bray Head there are fine views southward to the Great Sugar Loaf Mountain, a prominent peak in the Wicklow Mountains. There's an 8km **cliff walk** around Bray Head to the pleasant coastal resort of Greystones further south.

The **National Aquarium** (☎ 286 4688) is on the seafront in Bray but it isn't particularly spectacular. Entry costs IR£2.50/2. **Kilruddery House & Gardens** (☎ 286 3405), about 3km south of Bray, has one of the oldest gardens in Ireland. It's open daily from 1 to 5 pm in May, June and September. Entry to the house and gardens costs IR£4, or IR£2 to the gardens only.

Places to Eat

One attraction for which it's worth making the foray from Dublin is *The Tree of Idleness (☎ 286 3498/8183, The Strand)*, a seafront restaurant with delicious Greek-Cypriot food; main courses start at IR£2.50. The *Porter House* pub nearby claims to have Ireland's largest selection of beers from around the world.

Getting There & Away

Bray is on the DART suburban line from Dublin, or you can catch bus No 45 (from Hawkins St) or No 84 (from Burgh Quay). Both the DART and the buses cost IR£1.10 one way; the DART has the advantage that it can't get stuck in traffic.

Dun Laoghaire's ever-popular yachting centre

NEIL SETCHFIELD

Sculpture on the ferry deck, Dun Laoghaire

DOUG McKINLAY

In training for the Tour de France, Bray

DOUG McKINLAY

Bray, home to James Joyce from 1888 to 1891

DOUG McKINLAY

The Martello tower overlooking Sandycove

DOUG McKINLAY

For business or pleasure: the waters of Howth Harbour are used by both fishing boats and yachts.

HOWTH

The bulbous Howth Peninsula delineates the northern end of Dublin Bay. Howth town, 15km north-east of central Dublin, is a popular destination for an excursion and has also developed as a residential suburb. There's a pleasant little port replete with boats of all shapes and sizes; looming above it is the Hill of Howth, wonderful for walking and with some splendid views of Dublin city and the bay. A night in Howth makes an agreeable seaside escape and, like Dun Laoghaire to the south, it's within easy commuting distance.

Howth is easily reached by DART train or by simply following the Clontarf Rd around the northern bay shoreline. En route you pass Clontarf, site of the pivotal clash between Irish and Viking forces at the Battle of Clontarf in 1014 (see History in the Facts about Dublin chapter). Further along is North Bull Island, a wildlife sanctuary where many migratory birds pause in winter.

History

Howth has Viking origins and its name (which rhymes with both) comes from the Viking word *hoved* or head. Howth Harbour, dating from 1807 to 1809, was Dublin's main harbour for packet boats from England. Howth Rd was built to ensure the rapid transfer of incoming mail and dispatches into Dublin. The replacement of sailing packets with steam packets in 1818 reduced the transit time from Holyhead to seven hours. But by 1813 the harbour had already started to silt up and Howth was superseded by Dun Laoghaire in 1833.

Howth's most famous arrival was King George IV, who visited Ireland in 1821 and is chiefly remembered for staggering drunk off the boat. He left his footprint at the point where he stepped ashore on West Pier.

In 1914 Robert Erskine Childers' yacht *Asgard* brought a cargo of 900 rifles into the port to arm the nationalists. During the Civil War Childers, who was on the IRA side, was court-martialled and executed by a firing squad for the illegal possession of a revolver (given to him by Michael Collins). The *Asgard* is now on display at Kilmainham Gaol in Dublin.

Howth's popularity as a seaside escape from Dublin made the Howth electric trams famous. They were withdrawn in the late 1950s, and all that remains of them is an exhibit in the National Transport Museum.

Howth Town

Howth is a pretty little town built on steep streets running down to the waterfront. Although the harbour's role as a shipping port has long gone, Howth is now a major fishing centre and yachting harbour.

St Mary's Abbey stands in ruins near the town centre. It was originally founded in 1042, supposedly by the Viking king Sitric, who also founded the original church on the site of Christ Church Cathedral in Dublin. St Mary's Abbey was amalgamated with the monastery on Ireland's Eye (see the section later in this chapter) in 1235. Some parts of the ruins date from that time but most are from the 15th and 16th centuries. The tomb of Christopher St Lawrence (Lord Howth) in the south-eastern corner dates from around 1470. You can walk around the grounds but to enter the abbey you need to obtain the key from the caretaker; see the instructions on the gate.

Howth Castle & Demesne

Howth Castle's *demesne* (an Irish term meaning 'grounds') was acquired by the Norman noble Sir Almeric Tristram in 1177 and has remained in the family ever since, though the unbroken chain of male succession finally came to an end in 2009. The family name was changed to St Lawrence when Sir Almeric won a battle at the behest (so he believed) of St Lawrence.

Originally built in 1564, Howth Castle itself, which also belongs to the family, has been much restored and rebuilt over the years, most recently in 1910 by the British architect Sir Edwin Lutyens.

An Irish legend relates that in 1575 Grace O'Malley, the 'Queen' of western Ireland,

SEASIDE SUBURBS

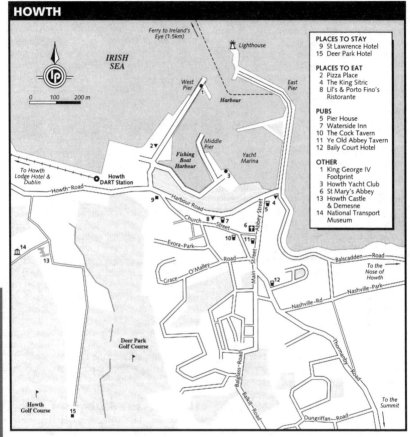

HOWTH

PLACES TO STAY
9   St Lawrence Hotel
15 Deer Park Hotel

PLACES TO EAT
2   Pizza Place
4   The King Sitric
8   Lil's & Porto Fino's
    Ristorante

PUBS
5   Pier House
7   Waterside Inn
10 The Cock Tavern
11 Ye Old Abbey Tavern
12 Baily Court Hotel

OTHER
1   King George IV
    Footprint
3   Howth Yacht Club
6   St Mary's Abbey
13 Howth Castle
    & Demesne
14 National Transport
    Museum

Map labels: Ferry to Ireland's Eye (1.5km); Lighthouse; IRISH SEA; West Pier; East Pier; Harbour; Middle Pier; Fishing Boat Harbour; Yacht Marina; To Howth Lodge Hotel & Dublin; Howth Road; Howth DART Station; Harbour Road; Church Street; Abbey Street; Evora Park; Balscadden Road; To the Nose of Howth; Grace O'Malley Road; Main Street; Nashville Park; Nashville Rd; Deer Park Golf Course; Balglass Road; Balkill Road; Thormanby Road; Howth Golf Course; Dungriffan Road; To the Summit; 0 100 200 m

visited the castle on her way back from a visit to England's Queen Elizabeth I. When the family refused her entry because they were busy having dinner she kidnapped the son and only returned him when Lord Howth promised that his doors would always be open at meal times. It is claimed that for many years the castle extended an open invitation to hungry passers-by.

Despite Grace's demand, the castle is no longer open, but you can visit the castle gardens, noted for their rhododendrons, which bloom in May and June, for their azaleas and for a long, 10m-high beech hedge planted in 1710. Entry is free.

Also in the grounds are the ruins of the 16th century **Corr Castle** and an ancient *dolmen* (a Neolithic grave memorial, built of vertical stones topped by a table stone) known as Aideen's Grave. It's said that Aideen died of a broken heart after her husband was killed at the Battle of Gavra near Tara in 184 AD, though the dolmen is much older than that.

The castle is a short walk from the centre of Howth and there's a popular golf course in the castle grounds.

National Transport Museum

The somewhat ramshackle National Transport Museum (☎ 848 0831) has a range of exhibits, including double-decker buses, a bakery van, fire engines and trams, including a Hill of Howth electric tram that operated from 1901 to 1959. The museum is open daily from 10 am to 5.30 pm from Easter to September, on weekends from 2 to 5 pm October to Easter. Entry is IR£1.50/1. To reach the museum go through the castle gates and turn right just before the castle.

Around the Peninsula

The 171m-high **Summit**, about 5km up the hill to the south-east of town, offers views across Dublin Bay to the Wicklow Mountains. From the Summit you can walk to the top of the Ben of Howth, which has a cairn said to mark a 2000-year-old Celtic royal grave. The 1814 **Baily Lighthouse** at the south-eastern corner is on the site of an old stone fort or 'bailey' and can be reached from the town by a dramatic 3km clifftop walk. There was an earlier hilltop beacon here by 1670.

Ireland's Eye

About 1.5km offshore from Howth is Ireland's Eye, a rocky sea-bird sanctuary with the ruins of a 6th century monastery. A Martello Tower (see the boxed text under Dun Laoghaire earlier in this chapter) is at the north-western end of the island, where boats from Howth land, while at the eastern end a spectacular rock face plummets into the sea. In addition to the sea birds wheeling overhead, you can see young birds on the ground during the nesting season. Seals can also be spotted around the island.

Doyle & Sons (☎ 831 4200) take boats out to the island from the East Pier of Howth Harbour during the summer, usually on weekend afternoons. The cost is IR£4/2 return. Don't wear shorts if you're planning to visit the monastery ruins because they're surrounded by a thicket of stinging nettles. And bring your rubbish back with you – far too many island visitors don't.

North of Ireland's Eye is Lambay Island, a larger, more remote sea-bird sanctuary.

Places to Stay

B&Bs along Thormanby and Nashville Rds costing from IR£15 to IR£16 per person per night include *Gleann-na-Smol* (☎ 832 2936, Nashville Rd), *Hazelwood* (☎ 839 1391, Thormanby Rd) and *Highfield* (☎ 832 3936, Thormanby Rd). The *St Lawrence Hotel* (☎ 832 2643, Harbour Rd), directly overlooking the harbour, has 11 rooms with bathroom. Singles/doubles cost IR£30/60 including breakfast.

On the Dublin side of Howth town there are good views of Ireland's Eye from *Howth Lodge Hotel* (☎ 832 1010), where rooms with bathroom cost IR£70 per person. By the golf course in the grounds of Howth Castle is the larger *Deer Park Hotel* (☎ 832 2624), where single/double rooms cost IR£62/90.

Places to Eat

Howth has fine seafood that self-caterers can buy fresh from the trawler at the string of seafood shops along West Pier.

Pizza Place (☎ 832 2255, 12 West Pier) has reasonably priced pizzas and pasta dishes from IR£3.50, along with a great selection of Italian ice-creams. *Lil's (Harbour Rd)* serves good snacks such as ploughman's sandwiches (IR£3) during the day, while upstairs *Porto Fino's Ristorante* (☎ 839 3054, Harbour Rd) has Italian food in the evening. The *St Lawrence Hotel* (see Places to Stay earlier in this section) has a carvery restaurant open daily. Alternatively, Howth's many pubs provide economic dining options (see Entertainment later in this section).

The King Sitric (☎ 832 5235), near East Pier, is well known for its fine seafood and is open for lunch and dinner from Monday to Saturday. Try the excellent crab. Main dinner courses cost from IR£18 to IR£25; a set dinner menu is IR£27.50.

SEASIDE SUBURBS

Entertainment

Howth's pubs are noted for their jazz performances. You can try *The Cock Tavern* near the entrance to the abbey grounds, the *Baily Court Hotel* *(Thormanby Rd)*, the *Waterside Inn* *(Harbour Rd)*, the *Pier House* *(☎ 832 4510, Harbour Rd)*, and others; all are likely to have something on and all are in the centre. *Ye Old Abbey Tavern* *(☎ 839 0307, Main St)* opposite St Mary's Abbey also has occasional traditional Irish entertainment in the evenings and is open from 7.30 pm to 12.30 am.

Getting There & Away

The easiest and quickest way to get to Howth from Dublin is on the DART train, which whisks you there in just over 20 minutes for a fare of IR£1.10. For the same fare, bus Nos 31 and 31A from Lower Abbey St in the city centre run as far as the Summit, 5km to the south-east of Howth.

Excursions

Ireland is so small that almost anywhere is within day-trip distance of Dublin – it's no problem to zip up to Belfast for the day, for example. Bus Éireann has day tours from Dublin as far as Kilkenny, Waterford and even Lough Erne in Northern Ireland. The places described in this chapter, however, are all easy and popular day trips from the capital, by car or public transport, and feature on many day-tour itineraries. For details on tour operators, see Organised Tours in the Getting Around chapter.

A trio of attractions immediately south of Dublin must surely earn top honours in their respective categories. Just outside the County Wicklow town of Enniskerry are the exquisite Italianate gardens of Powerscourt House. Further south, the medieval monastic site of Glendalough nestles in a wonderful forested valley. Completing the threesome is the Wicklow Way, a superb eight to 10 day walk through what is known as 'the garden of Ireland', a superb landscape of meadows, forests, dramatic cliffs and mountains. This is perhaps the most popular long walk in Ireland (shorter sections can also be tackled). For more information on the Wicklow Way see Lonely Planet's *Walking in Ireland*.

About 20km west of the city centre, near Maynooth in County Kildare, is Castletown, with a fine stately home from the days of the Anglo-Irish Ascendancy, plus two unusual follies. In Tully, just outside Kildare Town, is the National Stud, a centre for the breeding of race horses. Next door are the Japanese Gardens, considered by experts to be among the finest in Europe. Malahide Castle, one of the most interesting old homes in Ireland, is only a bus ride north of Dublin.

The Boyne Valley makes an excellent day excursion from Dublin. Apart from sites associated with the 1690 Battle of the Boyne (see The Protestant Ascendancy in the History section of the Facts about Dublin chapter), the valley has a number of prehistoric remains, including magnificent Newgrange, Europe's largest Neolithic passage grave (a burial place with a passageway leading to one or more chambers). North of Newgrange are another fine monastic site at Mellifont and some of Ireland's most magnificent high crosses (crosses carved in stone, combining engraved Celtic swirls with scenes from the Gospels) at Monasterboice. The town of Drogheda makes a good base for touring the Boyne Valley and has some interesting points of interest in its own right.

In the upper valleys of the River Boyne and its tributaries are the ancient site of Tara, the ruins of Trim Castle and various medieval ruins at Kells, the original home of the Book of Kells (see The Book of Kells in the Things to See & Do chapter).

POWERSCOURT ESTATE

About 1km from the picturesque village of Enniskerry and about 22km south of Dublin is **Powerscourt House** (1731), designed by Richard Castle (who was also the architect of Russborough House and the obelisk at Castletown House, both described later in this chapter). Much of the house accidentally burnt down in 1974, just after a major renovation had been completed. Plans to restore the house have been abandoned, though the main hall has an exhibition with a film on the history of the site from 1200 to the present day. The only other parts of the house presently open to the public are the ballroom and the Garden Room, which are also used for private functions. But it's the magnificent 20 hectare **garden** that attracts the crowds. The owners now live in one wing of the house.

Even with modern equipment, it takes a small army of gardeners to keep the vegetation neat and tidy. The terraced gardens descending the hill in front of the house are backed by the peak of the 506m-high Great

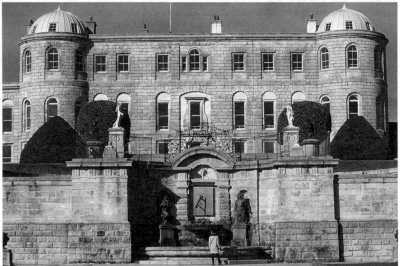

DOUG McKINLAY

Powerscourt House was restored after a serious fire in 1974 just after a previous renovation.

Sugar Loaf Mountain on the horizon. The Japanese call this 'borrowed scenery'. Powerscourt also has its own small Japanese garden, as well as curiosities such as a pets' cemetery. The original owners of Powerscourt had a townhouse in Dublin, now the Powerscourt Townhouse shopping centre.

Powerscourt Estate (☎ 286 7676) is open daily from 9.30 am to 5.30 pm (4.30 pm from November to January). Admission is IR£1.50/1.30 for the house and IR£2/1.70 for the garden. Free guided tours are available. There is a teashop, a garden centre and an outlet of the popular Avoca Handweavers shop, which has a range of fine Irish clothing. The nearest place to stay is Glendalough.

Powerscourt Waterfall

A 6km walk to a separate part of the estate takes you to this 130m waterfall, the highest in Britain and Ireland. It's most impressive after heavy rain. You can also get to the falls by road, following the signs from the estate.

It's open daily from 10.30 am to 7 pm (to dusk in winter). Entry is IR£1.50/1.

Places to Eat

The best place to eat in Enniskerry is *Poppies Country Cooking*, on the main square, with solid lunches (including several vegetarian options) for less than IR£7 and great buns and cakes, all in a rustic atmosphere.

Getting There & Away

Enniskerry is 3km west of the N11, the main road to Dublin to Wicklow, Arklow and Wexford. A Bus Éireann (☎ 836 6111) express bus from the Busáras in Dublin drops you at the turnoff for Enniskerry. Dublin area bus No 44 goes to Enniskerry from Hawkins St in Dublin, or you can take the DART train to Bray and get bus No 85 from the station.

Bus Éireann runs a tour to Powerscourt on Tuesday from June to mid-September. It departs from Busáras in Dublin at 10 am and returns at 5 pm. The tour costs IR£17 (admission to Powerscourt is included).

EXCURSIONS

GLENDALOUGH

Glendalough (pronounced 'glendalock'), 'glen of the two lakes', is a magical place – an ancient monastic settlement beside a pair of dark lakes, overshadowed by the sheer sides of a deep valley. Its setting in the Wicklow Mountains is one of Ireland's most picturesque, and the monastery is one of the country's most important historical sites. It's 54km south of Dublin – close enough to attract big crowds in summer.

Things to See & Do

The monastery, founded by St Kevin (see the boxed text) in the 6th century, grew to be one of the most important in Ireland, surviving Viking raids in the 9th and 10th centuries and an English incursion in 1398 before final supression in the 16th century.

The site is entered through Ireland's only surviving monastic gateway. The ruins include a round tower, the cathedral, a fine high cross and the curious St Kevin's Church. The latter is sometimes referred to as St Kevin's Kitchen because of its chimney-like tower. Entry is free.

Just under 1km beyond the monastic site is Upper Lake, with a cave known as St Kevin's Bed, to which the saint is said to have retreated. On the southern shore of the lake and accessible only by boat is Teampall na Scellig, an oratory or small church-like building used for private prayer. There are other reminders of St Kevin dotted around the lake.

The on-site Glendalough Visitor Centre (☎ 0404-45325/45352) is open daily from 9.30 am to 6 pm (4.30 pm from November to February); entry costs IR£2/1. The centre has some interesting displays, including a model of the monastery in its prime. A high-quality 20 minute audiovisual display is shown regularly.

Places to Stay & Eat

A dorm bed at the fine An Óige *Glendalough Hostel* (☎ 0404-45143/45342) near the round tower costs IR£7. At the village of Laragh, 3km east of the monastic site, the *Wicklow Way Hostel* (☎ 0404-45398) beside Lynham's Bar also charges IR£7; 1km south of Laragh, the *Old Mill Hostel* (☎ 0404-45156) charges IR£8 for a bed in a dorm or IR£22 for a double room. Laragh also has plenty of B&Bs, and the *Glendalough Hotel* (☎ 0404-45135) next to the monastic ruins has singles/doubles for IR£44/66, with breakfast.

About the best place for a substantial meal is the *Wicklow Heather Restaurant* (☎ 0404-45157), beside the post office in Laragh, where a set lunch costs IR£9.95. In summer several other places are open for tea, coffee, sandwiches and cakes.

St Kevin

St Kevin was born in around 498 AD into the royal house of Leinster. His name is derived from Ceomghan (or Coemhghein), meaning the 'fair one' or 'well featured'. As a child he studied under the charge of three holy men – Éanna, Eoghan and Lochan. While under their tutelage he went to Glendalough where, it is said, he lived in a tree. He left and later returned to spend his days as a hermit in the cave that became known as St Kevin's Bed. He couldn't completely escape the world, however; knowledge of his piety spread and many people came to Glendalough to share his isolated existence. They were not always welcome and he is reputed to have pushed one of his followers (who disturbed his isolation) over a cliff edge into one of the lakes.

His monastic settlement eventually spread from the Upper Lake to the site of the remains we see today. St Kevin became abbot of the monastery in 570 and is said to have died in 617 or 618, which would have made him about 120 years old.

euro currency converter IR£1 = €1.27

Getting There & Away

St Kevin's Bus Service (☎ 281 8119) departs for Glendalough daily at 11.30 am from outside the Royal College of Surgeons on West St Stephen's Green in Dublin. Departures from Glendalough are at 4.15 pm (5.30 pm on Sunday). Tickets cost IR£6/10 one way/return.

Bus Éireann has a daily tour to Glendalough and Wicklow from April to October (on Wednesday, Saturday and Sunday only between January and March). The tour departs from Busáras at 10.30 am and returns at 5.45 pm (4 pm in winter), and costs IR£17 (IR£14 in winter). You can also pick up the tour at Dun Laoghaire's tourist office at 11 am.

Bus Éireann also has a tour to Glendalough, Avondale Forest Park and Charles Stewart Parnell's home, and to the Wicklow Mountains on Friday only, from June to mid-September. The tour departs at 9.30 am and returns at 4.30 pm, and costs IR£17.

WICKLOW WAY

Running for 132km from County Dublin through County Wicklow to County Carlow, this is the oldest and one of the most popular of Ireland's long-distance scenic walks. It's well documented in leaflets, which can be picked up at the beginning of the walk or in the Dublin Tourism office in the city. For more detail on the Wicklow Way and other walks in the Dublin area and the rest of Ireland see Lonely Planet's *Walking in Ireland*. Much of the trail traverses country above 500m in altitude, so be prepared for rapid changes in the weather. If you don't feel up to tackling the whole eight to 10 day walk, the three day section from Knockree (near Enniskerry) to Glendalough is the most attractive and has easy transport connections at both ends. At the Dublin end the walk starts at Marlay Park in Rathfarnham.

Places to Stay

There are An Óige hostels along the route at *Glencree* (☎ 01-286 4037), *Knockree* (☎ 01-286 4036), *Glendalough* (☎ 0404-45143/45342), *Glenmalure* (no phone) and *Aghavannagh* (☎ 0402-36366), as well as numerous B&Bs.

RUSSBOROUGH HOUSE

Russborough House (☎ 045-865239), 5km south of Blessington in County Wicklow, was designed by the architect Richard Castle and built between 1740 and 1751. The house is a magnificent example of Palladian architecture, with a façade that extends more than 200m between two semicircular loggias. Inside the style is exuberantly Baroque, especially in the ornate plasterwork created by the LaFranchini brothers, who also worked on Castletown House (see the section on the next page).

In 1952 the house was bought by Sir Alfred Beit, the co-founder (with Cecil Rhodes) of the De Beers Mining Co in South Africa. He brought with him one of Europe's finest private art collections, with work by Goya, Gainsborough, Rubens and Vermeer.

Two robberies orchestrated by Martin Cahill, the notorious 'General' of Dublin's criminal underworld (and the subject of a film, *The General*, by director John Boorman), resulted in the majority of the collection being donated to the National Gallery in 1988. Most of the stolen paintings were recovered, though some have been permanently ruined by mishandling. Works still on display at Russborough House include paintings by Gainsborough, Rubens and Murillo.

The house is open daily from 10.30 am to 5.30 pm from June to August. In May and September it opens from 9.30 am to 2.30 pm Monday to Saturday. In April and October it opens on Sunday and bank holidays only. Admission is IR£3/1.50 (students IR£2) for the main 45 minute tour of the house, which includes all the important works of art.

Getting There & Away

There are regular services to the Blessington area, about 35km south-west of Dublin, on bus No 65 from Eden Quay.

KILDARE TOWN

Kildare is a lovely, picturesque town featuring a pleasant triangular square with pubs on each side.

Things to See & Do

In Kildare the grounds of **St Brigid's Cathedral** contain the remains of an ancient fire temple, where a perpetual fire was kept burning until the dissolution of the monasteries in 1537. The cathedral has a fine stained-glass window facing west that depicts the three main saints of Ireland: Patrick, Brigid and Columba. In the graveyard is a **round tower** which, at 32.9m, is the second-highest in the country. The tower is open from 10 am to 1 pm and 2 to 5 pm (2 to 5 pm only on Sunday) from April to September; admission costs IR£1/50p. The views of the surrounding countryside are terrific.

National Stud & Japanese Gardens

Three kilometres south of Kildare, in the small village of Tully, is the National Stud (☎ 045-521251), the only government-sponsored horse stud farm in Ireland. Founded in 1900 by Colonel William Hall-Walker (of the Johnnie Walker distilling family) and handed over to the state in 1943, it is the home of some of Ireland's top breeding stallions. Its most famous tenant is 19-year-old Indian Ridge, who covers 75 mares a season for IR£30,000 *each*. Not surprisingly, he's insured for IR£10 million. Another favourite is Vintage Crop, winner of the Melbourne Cup in 1995. There is also a museum with the impressively large skeleton of champion racehorse Arkle, winner of many races in the 1960s. You don't have to be a racing aficionado to appreciate a visit here; the setting is beautiful and makes for a great afternoon walk if the weather is fine.

Next door are the Japanese Gardens (☎ 045-521617), founded by Colonel Hall-Walker in 1906 and laid out by master gardener Tasso Eida and his son Minoru. The gardens chart the symbolic journey from birth to death through a series of landmarks, including a Tunnel of Ignorance, a Hill of Ambition and bridges signifying engagement and marriage. Although not entirely oriental in style (they include western trees such as Scots pine), these are considered to be among the finest Japanese gardens in Europe.

The National Stud and Japanese Gardens are open daily from 9.30 am to 6 pm, from February to November. Entry is with a combined ticket costing IR£5/3.

Places to Eat

Kildare has numerous pubs serving meals. The popular *Silken Thomas pub* (☎ 045 522252), partly converted from a cinema, in the town square has reasonable food for around IR£8, in an old-world atmosphere.

Getting There & Away

Bus Éireann services from Dublin (IR£5/ 2.75) take about an hour to reach Kildare. One service a day (two on Sunday) stops at the National Stud and Japanese Gardens.

Trains run about every 40 minutes from Heuston station (IR£7.50) and take about 30 minutes for the 55km trip.

CASTLETOWN HOUSE

Castletown House near Maynooth, built between 1722 and 1732 for William Conolly, speaker of the Irish House of Commons and at that time Ireland's richest man, is another fine example of an imposing Anglo-Irish home. The design of the house was begun by Alessandro Galilei and finished by Edward Lovett Pearce, architect of the Bank of Ireland. The adjacent village of Celbridge, which has a tree-lined avenue leading directly to the house, was built as an adjunct to the house. Descendants of Conolly continued to live at Castletown House until 1965. At the time of writing, the house was being restored by Dúchas and was due to reopen in April 1999.

Lady Louisa Conolly commissioned the stucco work and the unusual print room, but she also had a passion for building follies. A curious tower known to locals as the

EXCURSIONS

Obelisk, designed by Richard Castle, can be seen to the north from the Long Gallery at the back of the house. To the east, on private property just outside Leixlip, is the even more curious conical **Wonderful Barn**.

Castletown House (☎ 628 8252) is open from 10 am to 6 pm daily (from 1 pm on weekends) June to September, from 10 am to 5 pm Monday to Friday and from 1 to 5 pm on Sunday in October, from 2 to 5 pm on Sunday only from November to March and from 1 to 6 pm on Sunday only in April and May. Admission is IR£2.50/1. At the time of writing Wonderful Barn was undergoing a major restoration, but it should be open by the time you read this.

Getting There & Away

Castletown is 21km west of Dublin on the N4. Bus Nos 67 and 67A leave D'Olier St in Dublin about every hour for Celbridge and take a little over an hour to get there; the fare is IR£2.50. The bus stops at the gates of Castletown House.

MALAHIDE

Though Malahide has been virtually swallowed up by Dublin's northward expansion, it remains a pretty place with a small marina, a cluster of B&Bs, several coffee shops and a choice of ethnic restaurants. The well-tended, 101 hectare Malahide Demesne (castle grounds) incorporates Malahide Castle, the town's principal attraction, as well as Talbot Botanic Gardens and the extensive Fry Model Railway.

Malahide Castle

Despite the vicissitudes of Irish history, the Talbot family managed to keep Malahide Castle (☎ 846 2184) under its control from 1185 to 1976, apart from when Cromwell was in power (1649-60). It's now owned by Dublin County Council. The castle is the usual hotchpotch of additions and renovations. The oldest part is a three storey, 12th century tower house. The façade is flanked by circular towers, tacked on in 1765.

The castle is packed with furniture and paintings. Highlights include a 16th century oak room with decorative carvings and the medieval Great Hall with family portraits, a minstrel's gallery and a painting of the Battle of the Boyne (see under The Protestant Ascendancy in the History section of the Facts about Dublin chapter). Puck, the Talbot family ghost, is said to have last appeared in the castle in 1975.

The castle is open year-round, from 10 am to 12.45 pm and 2 to 5 pm Monday to Friday and from 11.30 am to 6 pm (2 to 5 pm from November to March) on weekends and holidays. Entry is IR£3/1.65 (students IR£2.50, family ticket IR£8.25). Combined tickets are available for the castle and Fry Model Railway (see the next section), and for the castle and Newbridge House (see the section later in this chapter).

The parkland around the castle is a good place for a picnic. It can be visited daily from 10 am to 9 pm (to 5 pm from November to March).

Fry Model Railway

Ireland's biggest model railway (240 sq metres) authentically displays much of Ireland's rail and public transport system, including the DART line and Irish Sea ferry services, in O-gauge (32mm track width). A separate room features model trains and other memorabilia. Unfortunately the operators suffer from the over-seriousness of some grown men with complicated toys; rather than let you simply look and admire, they herd you into the control room in groups for demonstrations.

The railway is open from 10 am to 1 pm and 2 to 6 pm Monday to Thursday (also on Friday in June, July and August), 11 am to 1 pm and 2 to 6 pm on Saturday, and 2 to 6 pm on Sunday and holidays, from April to September; and from 2 to 5 pm on weekends and holidays only during the rest of the year. Entry costs IR£2.75/1.60 (students IR£2.10). A combined ticket for the model railway and Malahide Castle costs IR£4.65/2.60 (students IR£3.60). You don't have to use all parts of the combined ticket on the same day. Family tickets for two adults and up to four children cost IR£7.50 for the railway, or IR£11.95 for both the railway and the castle.

Getting There & Away
Malahide is 13km north of Dublin. Bus No 42 from Talbot St takes about 45 minutes. Alternatively, take a Drogheda train as far as the Malahide town station, which is 10 minutes walk from the castle.

SWORDS
The village of Swords is 16km north of Dublin and 5km west of Malahide. The Archbishop of Dublin built a fortified **palace** here in the 12th century, though the castellated walls date from the 15th century and numerous other modifications were made over the centuries. The windows to the right of the main entrance date from around 1250. It's open from 9.30 am until dusk year-round; there's no admission fee.

Swords also had an ancient monastery but today only its 23m-high **round tower** remains and even that was rebuilt several times between 1400 and 1700. It stands in grounds owned by the Church of Ireland. The body of Brian Ború was kept overnight in the monastery after his death in 1014 at the Battle of Clontarf, when his forces defeated the Vikings (see Viking & Norman Invasions in the History section of the Facts about Dublin chapter).

Getting There & Away
Bus Nos 33 and 33B leave Dublin's Eden Quay every 30 minutes or so and take less than an hour. The fare is IR£1.10 one way.

NEWBRIDGE HOUSE
North of Malahide at Donabate is Newbridge House (☎ 843 6534), an historic Georgian mansion with fine plasterwork, a private museum, an impressive kitchen and a large traditional farm with cows, pigs and chickens. In the stables is an astonishingly elaborate coach, built in 1790 for the Lord Chancellor. It was painted black for Queen Victoria's funeral and it wasn't until 1982 that the paint was scraped off to reveal the glittering masterpiece beneath. The size of the coach is almost as impressive as the decoration: the back wheels alone stand 1.65m high.

Newbridge House is open daily from 10 am to 1 pm and 2 to 5 pm (to 6 pm Sunday and public holidays) from April to September. During the rest of the year it's open only on weekends and holidays from 2 to 5 pm. Admission costs IR£2.95/1.60 (students IR£2.55, family IR£7.95). A ticket for the farm costs IR£1/80p (family IR£2). There is also a combined ticket for the house and Malahide Castle, which costs IR£4.85/2.45 (students IR£3.30, family IR£12.25). You don't have to use all parts of the combined ticket on the same day.

The 144 hectares of Newbridge Demesne (grounds) surrounding the house are open from 10 am to 9 pm from April to September (to 5 pm the rest of the year); admission is IR£2.75.

Getting There & Away
Donabate is 19km north of Dublin. Bus No 33B runs from Eden Quay to Donabate village. You can also get there on the Suburban Rail service from either Connolly or Pearse station in the city centre.

LUSK
On the way to Skerries you'll spot the dominating turrets of Lusk church, now a heritage centre, where a 10th century round tower stands beside and joined to a medieval tower.

On the medieval tower's various floors are displays of medieval and later stone effigies from various churches in County Dublin. The much less impressive 19th century nave houses Willie Monks' dusty, somewhat forlorn collection of household and other items.

The heritage centre is open between 2 and 5 pm on Wednesday and Sunday only, from mid-June to mid-September. Admission is IR£1.50/60p.

Getting There & Away
Bus No 33 from Eden Quay takes about an hour to get to Lusk (IR£2.50).

SKERRIES

The sleepy seaside resort of Skerries is 30km north of Dublin. St Patrick is said to have made his arrival in Ireland here at Red Island, now joined to the mainland. There's a good cliff walk south from Skerries to the bay of Loughshinny. At low tide you can walk to Shenick's, a small island off Skerries. Colt and St Patrick's are two other small islands, the latter with an old church ruin. Farther offshore is Rockabill with its lighthouse. The 7th century oratory and holy well of St Moibhi and the ruins of Baldongan Castle are all near the town.

Getting There & Away

Bus No 33 departs from Eden Quay about every hour and takes approximately an hour to reach Skerries. Trains from Connolly station are less frequent but slightly faster.

DROGHEDA

Drogheda, on the River Boyne about 5km inland, was captured by the Danes in 911 and later fortified by the Normans under the command of Hugh de Lacy. By the 14th century it was one of Ireland's four major towns; parts of the medieval walls and early monastic buildings lie scattered around the town.

In 1649 Drogheda was the scene of Cromwell's most notorious Irish slaughter. He met stiff resistance and when his forces eventually overran the town the defenders were shown no mercy. Nearly 3000 people were massacred, including innocent civilians and children. When 100 of the town's inhabitants hid in the steeple of St Peter's Church, Cromwell's men simply burnt the church down. Many of the women and children who survived the barbarity were shipped off to the West Indies and sold into slavery. Drogheda was also on the losing side at the Battle of the Boyne in 1690, but quickly surrendered the day after James II was defeated.

It took many years for the town to recover from these events. In the 19th century a number of Catholic churches were built. The massive train viaduct and the string of quayside buildings hint at the town's brief Victorian-era industrial boom, when it was a centre for brewing and the manufacture of cotton and linen.

Orientation & Information

Drogheda's attractions are all in or near the centre of town. The town straddles the River Boyne, with the main shopping area on the northern bank along West and Laurence Sts. The area south of the river is dominated by the mysterious Millmount mound, which supposedly covers a passage grave (see the later Boyne Valley section for more on passage graves). The tourist office (☎ 041-37070), near the junction of West and George's Sts, only opens in July and August. The main post office and most of the banks are on West St.

Things to See & Do

Dominating the centre of town is **St Peter's Roman Catholic Church** (1791) on West St. In an ornate glass case on the left side of the church is the head of St Oliver Plunkett (1629-81), who was executed by the perfidious English after being wrongly accused of taking part in the 1678 Popish Plot (a supposed Catholic conspiracy to murder Charles II and massacre Protestants).

At the corner of West and Shop sts is the **Tholsel**, an imposing 18th century granite building that was once the town hall. Today it is a bank.

Straddling Laurence St, the eastward extension of West St, is **St Laurence Gate**, the finest surviving portion of the city walls. The only other remaining city gate is the 13th century **Butter Gate**, north-west of the Millmount Museum.

On top of the hill is the 14th century **Magdalene Tower**. Originally part of a Dominican friary founded in 1224, it played a dramatic role in fierce fighting during the 1922 Civil War. Anti-Treaty soldiers occupied the tower and fired on pro-Treaty forces from this vantage point until it was bombarded by the pro-Treaty troops. But for the finest views over the town you must go to **Millmount**, across the river. **Mill-**

mount Museum (☎ 041-33097) has interesting displays on the town and its history; curiously, however, there is very little on Cromwell's 1649 atrocities. The museum is open from 10 am to 6 pm daily except Sunday, from April to October (to 5.30 pm on Wednesday and weekends during the rest of the year). Entry is IR£1.50/1. You can drive up to the hilltop or climb the steps from St Mary's Bridge, to the north-west of the bus terminal and to the north-east of the train station.

Places to Stay & Eat

The *Harpur House* hostel (☎ *041-32736, William St)* has dorm beds for IR£7. There are also quite a few B&Bs in and around the town. In addition to pubs and cafés, try the reasonably priced *Snackmaster Restaurant* on Dominic St off West St, run by a friendly Egyptian.

Getting There & Away

Drogheda is 48km north of Dublin, on the main N1 route to Belfast. Buses depart hourly from the Busáras in Dublin and take about an hour (IR£4.50 one way). In Drogheda the Bus Éireann station (☎ 041-35023) is on the corner of New St and Donore Rd, south of the river.

Trains leave Dublin's Connolly Station about every two hours and take less than an hour. Drogheda's train station is south of the river and east of the centre, off the Dublin road.

Drogheda is the central jumping-off point for a visit to the Boyne Valley sites (see the following section). A Bus Éireann tour visits Newgrange, Mellifont, Monasterboice, Tara and Slane. It operates on Sunday, Tuesday and Thursday from May to October. The tour departs from Dublin's Busáras at 10 am and returns at 5.45 pm. A ticket costs IR£15/8.

Getting Around

If you want to visit the sights of Drogheda and don't have your own transport, you can hire a taxi on Laurence St or a bike in Trinity St.

BOYNE VALLEY

Many historic markers along the Boyne Valley are sites of the Battle of the Boyne, the epic struggle between the forces of Catholic James II and Protestant William of Orange. The defeat of the Catholic forces was to have long-running and tragic consequences for Ireland. In spite of their significance, the sites are of limited interest unless you're a student of Irish history, though the fertile valley has other worthwhile attractions.

Brugh na Bóinne

The prehistoric passage tombs of the Boyne Valley are collectively known as Brugh na Bóinne or Boyne Palace. At first it was surmised that they were the grave sites of the kings of Tara (who ruled in the first few centuries AD), but it's now known that they predate that period of Irish history by many centuries. At that time this fertile valley sheltered some of Ireland's earliest farming communities. As well as the site at Newgrange, there are two lesser, but still impressive, sites at Dowth and Knowth.

These ancient passage tombs were the largest constructions in Ireland until Norman castles were erected, and the country between the three major tombs is littered with countless other ancient mounds and standing stones. Over the centuries the tombs have been plundered by everybody from Vikings to Victorian treasure hunters and the mounds have decayed and been covered by grass and trees.

Newgrange, Knowth and Dowth are all well signposted. There are no buses to any of the sites, but a couple of buses between Slane and Drogheda on Monday, Wednesday and Friday will drop you on the main road about 3km from Newgrange.

Newgrange The finest Celtic passage tomb in Ireland is a huge flattened mound just north of the River Boyne about 13km west of Drogheda. It's believed to date from around 3200 BC, making it older than Stonehenge or the Egyptian pyramids. The site was restored in the 1970s and you can walk down a narrow passage to the tomb chamber, about a third of the way across the colossal mound. At dawn on five mornings surrounding the winter solstice (19 to 23 December) the rising sun's rays shine directly down the long passage and illuminate the tomb chamber for about 15 minutes. This is truly one of the most spectacular sights in all of Ireland but most visitors will have to settle for a simulated version; there is a 10 year waiting list for the 20 or so places available on each of the five days.

The grass-covered mound is about 80m in diameter and 13m high. It's faced by a pebbled wall, which in turn is encircled by huge horizontal stones, many finely decorated with curious designs. Farther out from the mound is a circle of standing stones, many of which have been broken off or removed. From the entrance, with its extravagantly incised entrance stone, the passage leads 19m into the mound to the cross-shaped central chamber. This has huge standing stones and dished stones in which burnt bones of the bodies buried here were originally found. Above the chamber massive stones form a ceiling.

Overlooking the graves is an award-winning interpretive centre (☎ 041-24488) with excellent audio-visual exhibits and displays on the people who built them. The site is open from 9.30 am to 7 pm from June to mid-September, 10 am to 5 pm from then to the end of October, 10 am to 4.30 pm from November to February, 10 am to 5 pm in March and April and 9.30 am to 6.30 pm in May. The entry fee of IR£3/1.25 includes a good guided tour; the last one leaves about half an hour before closing time.

In summer, particularly on Sunday, Newgrange gets fairly crowded so try to come early – or late.

Dowth The circular mound at Dowth, between Newgrange and Drogheda, is several hundred years younger than the one at Newgrange. It's smaller – at about 63m in diameter – but slightly higher, at 14m. An 8m-long passage leads into a cross-shaped central chamber similar to Newgrange's.

Dowth was excavated by archaeologists from the Royal Irish Academy in 1847 and for a time it even had a teahouse on top. Unfortunately the site is closed to visitors for the foreseeable future because it's still being excavated.

Knowth The third major burial mound is between Newgrange and Slane. Modern excavations began at Knowth in 1962 and a 35m-long passage to the central chamber was soon cleared. This passage is much longer than the one at Newgrange. In 1968 an extraordinary discovery was made when a second passage was unearthed. There are 18 smaller passage graves around the main mound. The site is famous for its artwork, which includes ornate kerbstones.

Knowth is open from 9.30 am to 6.30 pm from June to mid-September and from 10 am to 5 pm from mid-September to May. Entry costs IR£2/1.50. The last tour starts about 45 minutes before closing time.

DONORE & DULEEK

In 1429 Henry VI offered a UK£10 grant to anybody who would build a castle within the area known as the Pale, which essentially meant the counties of Dublin, Kildare, Meath and Louth. To ensure that there was no cheating, minimum dimensions were stipulated. The result is here at Donore: a miniature castle barely big enough to claim the UK£10.

Duleek claims to have had Ireland's first stone church, founded by St Patrick; the town's name itself comes from *An Damh Liag*, meaning 'stone church'. Duleek's 12th century abbey ruins contain a number of excellent effigies and tombstones. Outside the ruins is a 10th or 11th century high cross.

There are buses to Donore and Duleek from Drogheda.

MELLIFONT ABBEY

Mellifont Abbey (☎ 041-26459), about 8km north-west of Drogheda, was Ireland's original Cistercian monastery and in its prime was the most magnificent and important centre of this monastic sect. The abbey was founded in 1142 by the Archbishop of Armagh, who, dismayed by local corruption in the order, brought in a troupe of monks from France. They were deliberately placed in this remote location, far from any distracting influences. The French and Irish monks failed to get on and the visitors soon returned to the Continent, but within 10 years nine more Cistercian monasteries followed and Mellifont eventually became the mother house for 21 lesser monasteries.

Only fragments of the settlement remain but the plan of the monastery can be easily traced. The buildings are clustered around an open garth (courtyard surrounded by a cloister). Other buildings include a cross-shaped church, a chapterhouse, an east range that once had the monks' dormitories above it, and a south range that had the refectory or dining area, the kitchen and the warming room. The most recognisable building is the lavabo, the monks' octagonal washing house. Near the car park is a small but interesting architectural museum.

Entry is IR£1.50/60p. The grounds are open from 9.30 am to 6.30 pm from mid-June to mid-September, 10 am to 5 pm from May to mid-June and from mid-September to the end of October. The visitor centre keeps shorter hours.

Mellifont can be easily reached by bus from Drogheda.

MONASTERBOICE

Off the N1 road about 10km north of Drogheda is Monasterboice, with an intriguing little enclosure containing a cemetery, two ancient though unimportant church ruins, a fine though topless round tower and two of the best high crosses in Ireland. Monasterboice is signposted from Mellifont. Entry is free.

The **high crosses**, depicting biblical scenes, are superb examples of Celtic art with an important didactic use for an often illiterate populace. Like Greek statuary, they may once have been brightly painted, though there is no trace of colour now. Muiredach's Cross is the older, dating from

the early 10th century, and is also in better condition. The newer West Cross stands 6.5m high, making it one of the highest high crosses, but it's much more worn, with only a dozen or so of its 50 panels still legible.

The original monastic settlement is said to have been founded by St Buithe, a follower of St Patrick, in the 5th century. Over the centuries his name somehow mutated into Boyne, hence the river's name. Though a little-known saint, he is said to have ascended directly to heaven on a ladder lowered from above.

Buses run to the site from Drogheda.

SLANE

At the junction of the N2 and N51, 15km west of Drogheda, Slane is perched on a hillside overlooking the River Boyne. It's a picturesque town with a curious quartet of identical houses facing each other at the junction. A local tale relates that they were built for four sisters who had developed an intense mutual dislike and kept watch on each other from their doorways.

It's said St Patrick announced the arrival of Christianity from the top of Slane Hill. The ruins of a 16th century church occupy the site of St Patrick's original church. On the Slane Castle estate is St Eric's Hermitage, a ruined Gothic church on the site where the saint is said to have spent his last days some time between 512 and 514 AD. At the time of writing it was undergoing restoration and was closed to the public.

Getting There & Away

There are buses to Slane several times a day from Dublin (a one hour trip) and from Drogheda (less than half an hour).

KELLS

Almost every visitor to Ireland visits the Book of Kells exhibition in Dublin's Trinity College (see The Book of Kells in the Things to See & Do chapter), but fewer pause to see the town where it came from. Little remains of the ancient monastic site, but there are some fine high crosses, a 1000-year-old round tower, the equally ancient St Columba's Oratory and an interesting exhibit in the gallery of the church.

St Columba established a monastic settlement here in the 6th century, and in 807 it was augmented by monks from a sister monastery on the remote Scottish island of Iona, retreating from a Viking onslaught. They probably brought the Book of Kells with them. Kells proved little safer, for Viking raids soon spread to Ireland, and the town was plundered on several occasions.

Things to See & Do

The comparatively modern **St Columba's Church** stands in the grounds of the old monastic settlement. In the church's gallery is an exhibit (open from 10 am to 5 pm Monday to Friday and 10 am to 1 pm on Saturday from April to September) about the settlement and its famous book. In the churchyard the 30m-high round tower lacks its original roof but is known to date back to at least 1076, because a murder was recorded to have taken place there in that year. Best preserved of the several high crosses in the churchyard is the 9th century **South Cross** or **Cross of SS Patrick & Columba**. A medieval **church tower** stands beside the modern church and has a number of interesting tombstones set into its walls.

Round the corner from the church is **St Columba's Oratory**, a squat, thick-walled survivor from the old monastic settlement. The original entrance door to this 1000-year-old building was more than 2m above ground level in order to make entry difficult for raiders. Inside, a ladder leads to a low attic room under the roofline. If it's locked you can get the keys from the brown house near the stop sign at the bottom of the hill.

The **Market High Cross** was placed in Cross St by Jonathan Swift, and in 1798 the British garrison executed rebels by hanging them from the crosspiece.

Getting There & Away

Kells is 63km north-west of Dublin. Buses leave almost hourly between 7 am and 10 pm daily from the Busáras. The trip takes about an hour and costs IR£6 one way.

HILL OF TARA

Tara, near the Dublin-Navan N3 road, was already a place of legend 1000 years ago, when it was held to be the palace and fort of Ireland's original high kings, priest-kings who ruled the many over-kings and kings but had no law-making powers. Only mounds and depressions in the grass mark where an Iron Age hill fort and surrounding ringforts once stood. The rather romantic names attached to the various features have no obvious basis in fact. Behind St Patrick's Church, the **Rath of the Synods** has four concentric ditches and banks. South of this is the large **Royal Enclosure**, which was once a hill fort and contains a passage tomb, similar to the tombs of Newgrange (see Newgrange in the Boyne Valley section of this chapter). It has been dubbed the Mound of the Hostages. The **Royal Seat**, an ancient ringfort, and **Cormac's House** are also within the Royal Enclosure. The **Stone of Destiny** in Cormac's House is claimed to be the inauguration stone of the kings of Tara. Another hill fort stands south of the Royal Enclosure. To the north of the site is the **Banquet Hall**, which was probably the entranceway to the Hill of Tara. To the north-west of this feature are three smaller circular enclosures.

In 1843 Daniel O'Connell held one of his 'monster meetings' protesting against the 1801 Act of Union here (see Disasters of the 19th Century in the History section of the Facts about Dublin chapter).

There's an interpretive centre in a church on the site; it's open from 9.30 am to 6.30 pm daily from mid-June to mid-September and from 10 am to 5 pm daily between May and mid-June and from mid-September to October. Admission is IR£1/40p. The site itself is open and free at all times.

Getting There & Away

Buses linking Dublin and Navan pass within 1km of the site. Services run from the Busáras every hour from 7.30 am to 10.45 pm. The journey takes about an hour and costs IR£4.20 one way; ask the driver to drop you off at the Tara Cross.

TRIM

A pleasant little town on the River Boyne, Trim has several interesting ruins including those of Ireland's largest Anglo-Norman castle, a sprawling construction with a huge keep. The original Trim Castle was completed in the late 12th century but was destroyed a year later. Its successors had a dramatic history. The town surrendered to Cromwell's forces in 1649, but not before the town walls, parts of the castle walls and the Yellow Steeple were severely damaged.

According to locals, Elizabeth I considered Trim as a possible site for Trinity College, though the latter ended up in Dublin. *Truim* means 'ford of the elder trees'; there was an ancient ford over the river at this point.

The tourist office (☎ 046-37111) in Mill St sells a handy *Trim Tourist Trail* walking-tour booklet.

Things to See & Do

The ruins of **Trim Castle** are reached both by a riverside path and through the Town Gate. King John visited Trim in 1210, giving the castle its alternative name of King John's Castle. Geoffrey de Greneville, who was responsible for the second stage of the keep's construction between 1220 and 1225, was a keen crusader and later became a monk at the Dominican Abbey just outside the town's northern wall.

The open grassy area at the heart of the castle is dominated by de Greneville's massive stone keep. Outside the central keep are the remains of an earlier wall and moat. The main outer wall, still standing, dates from around 1250. The finest stretch of the outer wall is from the Dublin Gate to the River Boyne. The outer wall has five towers and a number of sally gates from which sorties could 'sally' out to meet the enemy. The ruins are open daily between 9 am and 6 pm.

Across the river from the castle are the ruins of the Augustinian **St Mary's Abbey**, originally built in the 12th century but rebuilt after a fire in 1368. Part of the abbey cloister was converted into a manor house known as Talbot Castle in 1415 and the Talbot coat of arms is on the northern wall. The building was later used as a school whose pupils included Arthur Wellesley (later the Duke of Wellington), Jonathan Swift and his friend Stella Johnson. North of the abbey building is the **Yellow Steeple**, dating from the restoration of 1368 but damaged in the 1649 Cromwell takeover.

East of town is an interesting group of ruins around **Newtown Cathedral** in Newtown Cemetery. The 13th century **Chapel of the Victorines** encloses the 16th century tomb effigies of Sir Lucas Dillon and his wife, Lady Jane Bathe, known locally as 'the jealous man and woman'. The other buildings here are the **Cathedral of SS Peter & Paul**, which was founded in 1206 by Simon Rochfort, and **Newtown Abbey**, also known as the Abbey of the Canons Regular of St Victor.

Over the river from these ruins is the **Crutched Friary**, built as a hospital after the crusades by the Knights of St John of Jerusalem. There are ruins of the keep and traces of a watchtower and other buildings. The bridge beside the friary is thought to be the second-oldest bridge in Ireland, and Marcy Regan's Pub, beside the bridge, claims to be the second-oldest pub.

Getting There & Away

Trim is about 45km north-west of Dublin. Buses depart from the Busáras in Dublin six times daily; the journey takes just over an hour and costs IR£5 one way.

Glossary

An tUachtaran (pronounced 'an ukta-rawn') – Irish president

bodhrán (pronounced 'bore-run') – hand-held goatskin drum

ceilidh (pronounced 'kaylee') – communal dance

Dáil Éireann – house of representatives, or lower house, of the Irish parliament; usually shortened to Dáil (pronounced 'doyle')
demesne – castle grounds
dolmen – Neolithic grave memorial, built of vertical stones and topped by a table stone
Dúchas – institution responsible for administering state-owned properties such as parks, museums and gardens (formerly the Office of Public Works)
dún – fort

Fianna Fáil (pronounced 'fianna foyle') – 'Warriors of Ireland', political party
Fine Gael (pronounced 'fina gael') – 'Gaelic Nation', political party

Gaeltacht area – area where Irish is the predominant language
garth – courtyard surrounded by a cloister

high cross – Celtic ringed cross, decorated with geometrical motifs and, later, scenes from the Bible

Oireachtas (pronounced 'orawk-tas') – parliament

passage tomb – Neolithic subterranean burial place with a passegeway leading to one or more chambers

Senead Éireann (pronounced 'shanad erin') – senate, or upper house, of the Irish parliament; usually shortened to Senead
Sinn Féin (pronounced 'shin fain') – 'We ourselves', Republican political party

Taoiseach (pronounced 'teashok') – Irish prime minister
teachta Dála (pronounced 'tchawkta dawla') – members of the lower house of parliament, commonly referred to as TDs

Common Phrases & Signs

Irish	Pronunciation	English
An lár	*an laah*	city centre
Céad míle fáilte	*kade meala fawlcha*	a hundred thousand welcomes
Fir	*fear*	men
Gardaí	*gardee*	police
Mná	*me-naw*	women
Oifig an phoist		post office
Ná caitear tobac		no smoking
Sláinte	*slawncha*	cheers

LONELY PLANET

Phrasebooks

onely Planet phrasebooks are packed with essential words and phrases to help travellers communicate with the locals. With colour tabs for quick reference, an extensive vocabulary and use of script, these handy pocket-sized language guides cover day-to-day travel situations.

- handy pocket-sized books
- easy to understand Pronunciation chapter
- clear & comprehensive Grammar chapter
- romanisation alongside script to allow ease of pronunciation
- script throughout so users can point to phrases for every situation
- full of cultural information and tips for the traveller

'...vital for a real DIY spirit and attitude in language learning'
— *Backpacker*

'the phrasebooks have good cultural backgrounders and offer solid advice for challenging situations in remote locations'
— *San Francisco Examiner*

Arabic (Egyptian) • Arabic (Moroccan) • Australian *(Australian English, Aboriginal and Torres Strait languages)* • Baltic States *(Estonian, Latvian, Lithuanian)* • Bengali • Brazilian • Burmese • Cantonese • Central Asia • Central Europe *(Czech, French, German, Hungarian, Italian, Slovak)* • Eastern Europe *(Bulgarian, Czech, Hungarian, Polish, Romanian, Slovak)* • Ethiopian (Amharic) • Fijian • French • German • Greek • Hill Tribes • Hindi/Urdu • Indonesian • Italian • Japanese • Korean • Lao • Latin American Spanish • Malay • Mandarin • Mediterranean Europe *(Albanian, Croatian, Greek, Italian, Macedonian, Maltese, Serbian, Slovene)* • Mongolian • Nepali • Papua New Guinea • Pilipino (Tagalog) • Quechua • Russian • Scandinavian Europe *(Danish, Finnish, Icelandic, Norwegian, Swedish)* • South-East Asia *(Burmese, Indonesian, Khmer, Lao, Malay, Tagalog Pilipino, Thai, Vietnamese)* • Spanish (Castilian) *(also includes Catalan, Galician and Basque)* • Sri Lanka • Swahili • Thai • Tibetan • Turkish • Ukrainian • USA *(US English, Vernacular Talk, Native American languages, Hawaiian)* • Vietnamese • Western Europe *(Basque, Catalan, Dutch, French, German, Greek, Irish)*

LONELY PLANET

Lonely Planet Journeys

JOURNEYS is a unique collection of travel writing – published by the company that understands travel better than anyone else. It is a series for anyone who has ever experienced – or dreamed of – the magical moment when they encountered a strange culture or saw a place for the first time. They are tales to read while you're planning a trip, while you're on the road or while you're in an armchair, in front of a fire.

These outstanding titles explore our planet through the eyes of a diverse group of international writers. JOURNEYS books catch the spirit of a place, illuminate a culture, recount a crazy adventure, or introduce a fascinating way of life. They always entertain, and always enrich the experience of travel.

MALI BLUES
Traveling to an African Beat
Lieve Joris (translated by Sam Garrett)
Drought, rebel uprisings, ethnic conflict: these are the predominant images of West Africa. But as Lieve Joris travels in Senegal, Mauritania and Mali, she meets survivors, fascinating individuals charting new ways of living between tradition and modernity. With her remarkable gift for drawing out people's stories, Joris brilliantly captures the rhythms of a world that refuses to give in.

THE GATES OF DAMASCUS
Lieve Joris (translated by Sam Garrett)
This best-selling book is a beautifully drawn portrait of day-to-day life in modern Syria. Through her intimate contact with local people, Lieve Joris draws us into the fascinating world that lies behind the gates of Damascus. Hala's husband is a political prisoner, jailed for his opposition to the Assad regime; through the author's friendship with Hala we see how Syrian politics impacts on the lives of ordinary people.

THE OLIVE GROVE
Travels in Greece
Katherine Kizilos
Katherine Kizilos travels to fabled islands, troubled border zones and her family's village deep in the mountains. She vividly evokes breathtaking landscapes, generous people and passionate politics, capturing the complexities of a country she loves.

'beautifully captures the real tensions of Greece' – *Sunday Times*

KINGDOM OF THE FILM STARS
Journey into Jordan
Annie Caulfield
Kingdom of the Film Stars is a travel book and a love story. With honesty and humour, Annie Caulfield writes of travelling in Jordan and falling in love with a Bedouin with film-star looks.

She offers fascinating insights into the country – from the tent life of traditional women to the hustle of downtown Amman – and unpicks tight-woven Western myths about the Arab world.

Lonely Planet Travel Atlases

L onely Planet has long been famous for the number and quality of its guidebook maps. Now we've gone one step further and produced a handy companion series: Lonely Planet travel atlases – maps of a country produced in book form.

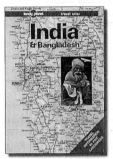

Unlike other maps, which look good but lead travellers astray, our travel atlases have been researched on the road by Lonely Planet's experienced team of writers. All details are carefully checked to ensure the atlas corresponds with the equivalent Lonely Planet guidebook.

- full-colour throughout
- maps researched and checked by Lonely Planet authors
- place names correspond with Lonely Planet guidebooks
- no confusing spelling differences
- legend and travelling information in English, French, German, Japanese and Spanish
- size: 230 x 160 mm

Available now: Chile & Easter Island • Egypt • India & Bangladesh • Israel & the Palestinian Territories • Jordan, Syria & Lebanon • Kenya • Laos • Portugal • South Africa, Lesotho & Swaziland • Thailand • Turkey • Vietnam • Zimbabwe, Botswana & Namibia

Lonely Planet TV Series & Videos

L onely Planet travel guides have been brought to life on television screens around the world. Like our guides, the programs are based on the joy of independent travel, and look honestly at some of the most exciting, picturesque and frustrating places in the world. Each show is presented by one of three travellers from Australia, England or the USA and combines an innovative mixture of video, Super-8 film, atmospheric soundscapes and original music.

Videos of each episode – containing additional footage not shown on television – are available from good book and video shops, but the availability of individual videos varies with regional screening schedules.

Video destinations include: Alaska • American Rockies • Australia – The South-East • Baja California & the Copper Canyon • Brazil • Central Asia • Chile & Easter Island • Corsica, Sicily & Sardinia – The Mediterranean Islands • East Africa (Tanzania & Zanzibar) • Ecuador & the Galapagos Islands • Greenland & Iceland • Indonesia • Israel & the Sinai Desert • Jamaica • Japan • La Ruta Maya • Morocco • New York • North India • Pacific Islands (Fiji, Solomon Islands & Vanuatu) • South India • South West China • Turkey • Vietnam • West Africa • Zimbabwe, Botswana & Namibia

The Lonely Planet TV series is produced by: Pilot Productions
The Old Studio
18 Middle Row
London W10 5AT, UK

LONELY PLANET

Guides by Region

L onely Planet is known worldwide for publishing practical, reliable and no-nonsense travel information in our guides and on our Web site. The Lonely Planet list covers just about every accessible part of the world. Currently there are nine series: travel guides, shoestring guides, walking guides, city guides, phrasebooks, audio packs, travel atlases, diving and snorkeling guides and travel literature.

AFRICA Africa – the South • Africa on a shoestring • Arabic (Egyptian) phrasebook • Arabic (Moroccan) phrasebook • Cairo • Cape Town • Central Africa • East Africa • Egypt • Egypt travel atlas • Ethiopian (Amharic) phrasebook • The Gambia & Senegal • Kenya • Kenya travel atlas • Malawi, Mozambique & Zambia • Morocco • North Africa • South Africa, Lesotho & Swaziland • South Africa, Lesotho & Swaziland travel atlas • Swahili phrasebook • Trekking in East Africa • Tunisia • West Africa • Zimbabwe, Botswana & Namibia • Zimbabwe, Botswana & Namibia travel atlas
Travel Literature: The Rainbird: A Central African Journey • Songs to an African Sunset: A Zimbabwean Story • Mali Blues: Traveling to an African Beat

AUSTRALIA & THE PACIFIC Australia • Australian phrasebook • Bushwalking in Australia • Bushwalking in Papua New Guinea • Fiji • Fijian phrasebook • Islands of Australia's Great Barrier Reef • Melbourne • Micronesia • New Caledonia • New South Wales & the ACT • New Zealand • Northern Territory • Outback Australia • Papua New Guinea • Papua New Guinea (Pidgin) phrasebook • Queensland • Rarotonga & the Cook Islands • Samoa • Solomon Islands • South Australia • Sydney • Tahiti & French Polynesia • Tasmania • Tonga • Tramping in New Zealand • Vanuatu • Victoria • Western Australia
Travel Literature: Islands in the Clouds • Sean & David's Long Drive

CENTRAL AMERICA & THE CARIBBEAN Bahamas and Turks & Caicos • Bermuda • Central America on a shoestring • Costa Rica • Cuba • Eastern Caribbean • Guatemala, Belize & Yucatán: La Ruta Maya • Jamaica • Mexico • Mexico City • Panama
Travel Literature: Green Dreams: Travels in Central America

EUROPE Amsterdam • Andalucia • Austria • Baltic States phrasebook • Berlin • Britain • Central Europe • Central Europe phrasebook • Czech & Slovak Republics • Denmark • Dublin • Eastern Europe • Eastern Europe phrasebook • Estonia, Latvia & Lithuania • Finland • France • French phrasebook • Germany • German phrasebook • Greece • Greek phrasebook • Hungary • Iceland, Greenland & the Faroe Islands • Ireland • Italian phrasebook • Italy • Lisbon • London • Mediterranean Europe • Mediterranean Europe phrasebook • Paris • Poland • Portugal • Portugal travel atlas • Prague • Romania & Moldova • Russia, Ukraine & Belarus • Russian phrasebook • Scandinavian & Baltic Europe • Scandinavian Europe phrasebook • Slovenia • Spain • Spanish phrasebook • St Petersburg • Switzerland • Trekking in Spain • Ukrainian phrasebook • Vienna • Walking in Britain • Walking in Italy • Walking in Switzerland • Western Europe • Western Europe phrasebook
Travel Literature: The Olive Grove: Travels in Greece

INDIAN SUBCONTINENT Bangladesh • Bengali phrasebook • Bhutan • Delhi • Goa • Hindi/Urdu phrasebook • India • India & Bangladesh travel atlas • Indian Himalaya • Karakoram Highway • Nepal • Nepali phrasebook • Pakistan • Rajasthan • South India • Sri Lanka • Sri Lanka phrasebook • Trekking in the Indian Himalaya • Trekking in the Karakoram & Hindukush • Trekking in the Nepal Himalaya
Travel Literature: In Rajasthan • Shopping for Buddhas

LONELY PLANET

Mail Order

Lonely Planet products are distributed worldwide.They are also available by mail order from Lonely Planet, so if you have difficulty finding a title please write to us. North and South American residents should write to 150 Linden St, Oakland, CA 94607, USA; European and African residents should write to 10a Spring Place, London NW5 3BH, UK; and residents of other countries to PO Box 617, Hawthorn, Victoria 3122, Australia.

ISLANDS OF THE INDIAN OCEAN Madagascar & Comoros • Maldives • Mauritius, Réunion & Seychelles

MIDDLE EAST & CENTRAL ASIA Arab Gulf States • Central Asia • Central Asia phrasebook • Iran • Israel & the Palestinian Territories • Israel & the Palestinian Territories travel atlas • Istanbul • Jerusalem • Jordan & Syria • Jordan, Syria & Lebanon travel atlas • Lebanon • Middle East on a shoestring • Turkey • Turkish phrasebook • Turkey travel atlas • Yemen
Travel Literature: The Gates of Damascus • Kingdom of the Film Stars: Journey into Jordan

NORTH AMERICA Alaska • Backpacking in Alaska • Baja California • California & Nevada • Canada • Florida • Hawaii • Honolulu • Los Angeles • Miami • New England USA • New Orleans • New York City • New York, New Jersey & Pennsylvania • Pacific Northwest USA • Rocky Mountain States • San Francisco • Seattle • Southwest USA • USA phrasebook • Washington, DC & the Capital Region
Travel Literature: Drive Thru America

NORTH-EAST ASIA Beijing • Cantonese phrasebook • China • Hong Kong • Hong Kong, Macau & Guangzhou • Japan • Japanese phrasebook • Japanese audio pack • Korea • Korean phrasebook • Kyoto • Mandarin phrasebook • Mongolia • Mongolian phrasebook • North-East Asia on a shoestring • Seoul • South-West China • Taiwan • Tibet • Tibetan phrasebook • Tokyo
Travel Literature: Lost Japan

SOUTH AMERICA Argentina, Uruguay & Paraguay • Bolivia • Brazil • Brazilian phrasebook • Buenos Aires • Chile & Easter Island • Chile & Easter Island travel atlas • Colombia • Ecuador & the Galapagos Islands • Latin American Spanish phrasebook • Peru • Quechua phrasebook • Rio de Janeiro • South America on a shoestring • Trekking in the Patagonian Andes • Venezuela
Travel Literature: Full Circle: A South American Journey

SOUTH-EAST ASIA Bali & Lombok • Bangkok • Burmese phrasebook • Cambodia • Hill Tribes phrasebook • Ho Chi Minh City • Indonesia • Indonesian phrasebook • Indonesian audio pack • Jakarta • Java • Laos • Lao phrasebook • Laos travel atlas • Malay phrasebook • Malaysia, Singapore & Brunei • Myanmar (Burma) • Philippines • Pilipino (Tagalog) phrasebook • Singapore • South-East Asia on a shoestring • South-East Asia phrasebook • Thailand • Thailand's Islands & Beaches • Thailand travel atlas • Thai phrasebook • Thai audio pack • Vietnam • Vietnamese phrasebook • Vietnam travel atlas

ALSO AVAILABLE: Antarctica • Brief Encounters: Stories of Love, Sex & Travel • Chasing Rickshaws • Not the Only Planet: Travel Stories from Science Fiction • Travel with Children • Traveller's Tales

LONELY PLANET

Lonely Planet Online
www.lonelyplanet.com *or* AOL keyword: lp

Whether you've just begun planning your next trip, or you're chasing down specific info on currency regulations or visa requirements, check out Lonely Planet Online for up-to-the-minute travel information.

As well as mini guides to more than 250 destinations, you'll find maps, photos, travel news, health and visa updates, travel advisories, and discussion of the ecological and political issues you need to be aware of as you travel. You'll also find timely upgrades to popular guidebooks which you can print out and stick in the back of your book.

There's also an online travellers' forum where you can share your experience of life on the road, meet travel companions and ask other travellers for their recommendations and advice.

And of course we have a complete and up-to-date list of all Lonely Planet travel products including travel guides, diving and snorkelling guides, phrasebooks, atlases, travel literature and videos, and a simple online ordering facility if you can't find the book you want elsewhere.

Lonely Planet Diving & Snorkelling Guides

Known for indispensible guidebooks to destinations all over the world, Lonely Planet's Pisces Books are the most popular series of diving and snorkelling titles available.

There are three series: **Diving & Snorkelling Guides**, **Shipwreck Diving** series, and **Dive Into History**. Full colour throughout, the **Diving & Snorkelling Guides** combine quality photographs with detailed descriptions of the best dive sites for each location, giving divers a glimpse of what they can expect both on land and in water. The **Dive Into History** series is perfect for the adventure diver or armchair traveller. The **Shipwreck Diving** series provides all the details for exploring the most interesting wrecks in the Atlantic and Pacific oceans. The list also includes underwater nature and technical guides.

FREE Lonely Planet Newsletters

We love hearing from you and think you'd like to hear from us.

Planet Talk

Our FREE quarterly printed newsletter is full of tips from travellers and anecdotes from Lonely Planet guidebook authors. Every issue is packed with up-to-date travel news and advice, and includes:

- a postcard from Lonely Planet co-founder Tony Wheeler
- a swag of mail from travellers
- a look at life on the road through the eyes of a Lonely Planet author
- topical health advice
- prizes for the best travel yarn
- news about forthcoming Lonely Planet events
- a complete list of Lonely Planet books and other titles

To join our mailing list, residents of the UK, Europe and Africa can email us at go@lonelyplanet.co.uk; residents of North and South America can email us at info@lonelyplanet.com; the rest of the world can email us at talk2us@lonelyplanet.com.au, or contact any Lonely Planet office.

Comet

Our FREE monthly email newsletter brings you all the latest travel news, features, interviews, competitions, destination ideas, travellers' tips & tales, Q&As, raging debates and related links. Find out what's new on the Lonely Planet Web site and which books are about to hit the shelves.

Subscribe from your desktop: www.lonelyplanet.com/comet

Index

Text

A

Abbey Theatre 114
abbeys, *see* churches & cathedrals
accommodation 145-52
  bed & breakfasts 148-9
  camping grounds 145-6
  Dun Laoghaire 191
  guesthouses 149-50
  hostels 146-7
  hotels 149-52
  Howth 195
  renting 152
  student accommodation 147-8
activities, *see* individual entries
addresses 36
Ahern, Bertie 16
air travel 61-6
  airline offices 65-6
  Australia 65
  buying tickets 61
  Canada 65
  departure tax 61
  Europe 64-5
  glossary 62-3
  New Zealand 65
  travellers with special needs 61
  UK 64
  USA 65
  within Ireland 61-4
airport 70
Anglo-Irish Treaty 14-15
Áras an Uachtaráin 126
Arbour Hill Cemetery 121
architecture 30-5
  Georgian 30-2
  modern 32-3
  Norman 30
  Viking 30
Ark, the 52
arts, *see* individual entries
Ashtown Castle 126

B

Baily Lighthouse 195
Ballsbridge 130-1
Bank of Ireland 87-8
Battle of Clontarf 11
Battle of the Boyne 11, 205
Beckett, Samuel 23
Bedford Tower 92
Behan, Brendan 23
Beshoff's *157*
Bewley's *157*
bicycle travel 73-4
  rental 73-4
Bloomsday 58-9
Book of Kells 85
books 47, *see also* literature
Ború, Brian 11
bowling 133
Boyne Valley, *see* Brugh na Bóinne
Bray 192
Brugh na Bóinne (Boyne Valley) 205-6
  Dowth 206
  Knowth 206
  Newgrange 205-6
Bulloch Castle 192
bus travel 66, 68
  discounts 67
business hours 56-7

C

car & motorcycle travel 71-3
  drinking & driving 56
car rental 72-3
casino at Marino 127-8
Castle, Richard 34
Castletown House 201-2
Chester Beatty Library 92-3
children of Lir *115*
children, travel with 51-4
Children's Cultural Centre, *see* the Ark
Christ Church Cathedral 52, 93-5, **94**
churches & cathedrals
  Abbey Presbyterian Church 119
  Christ Church Cathedral 52, 93-5, **94**

Church of the Holy Trinity (Royal Chapel) 92
Mellifont Abbey 206-7
Newman University Church 108
St Andrew's Church 110
St Audoen's Church (Catholic) 95
St Audoen's Church (Protestant) 95
St Columba's Church (Kells) 208
St George's Church 120
St Mary's Abbey (Dublin) 120
St Mary's Abbey (Howth) 193
St Mary's Abbey (Trim) 209
St Mary's Church 120
St Mary's Pro-Cathedral 114-15
St Michan's Church 121
St Patrick's Cathedral 96-9, **96**
St Stephen's Church 111-26
St Werburgh's Church 93
Trinity College Chapel 84
Unitarian Church 106
Whitefriars Carmelite Church 110-11
cinema 24-6
City Hall 93
Civil War 14-15
climate 17
Clontarf 128-9
Collins, Michael 14, 15
conduct, *see* cultural considerations
Connolly, James 13
consulates, *see* embassies & consulates
Corr Castle 194
costs, *see* money
courses 134
  language 134
credit cards, *see* money
cricket 170
Cromwell, Oliver 11, 204
cultural centres 54-5

cultural considerations 26-7
Custom House 114
customs regulations 39
cybercafés 46
cycling 133

D
Dalkey 192
dance 20
de Valera, Eamon 14-15
disabled travellers 51
Donore 206
Doyle, Roddy 22
drinks 153, 172, 176, 179
Drogheda 204-5
drugs *55*, 56
Dublin Castle 90-3, **91**
Dublin Experience 86
Dublin Harbour 82
Dublin Music Hall 89
Dublin Zoo 52-3, 126
Dublinia 95
Duleek 206
Dun Laoghaire 187-92, **189**
   Forty Foot Pool 190
   Harbour 188
   James Joyce Museum
      189-90
   Sandycove 189-90

E
Easter Rising 13
ecology, *see* environmental
   considerations
economy 18-19
education 19
electricity 48
Ely Place 110
email 45-6
embassies & consulates
   38-9
emergencies 56
Emmet, Robert 12
entertainment 165-81
   buskers 168-9
   cinemas 167-8
   concerts 167
   discos & nightclubs 165-7
   Dun Laoghaire 192
   Howth 196
   Irish cabaret 165
   pubs & bars 171-81
   spectator sports 169-70
   theatre 168
environmental considerations
   17

euro *40-1*
excursions 197-210

F
ferry travel 67-8
   France 68
   UK 67-8
festivals, *see* special events
Fianna Fáil 15, 18
Fine Gael 15, 18
fishing 133
food 153-64
   breakfast *155*
   budget 156-9
   Dun Laoghaire 191
   Grafton St area 158-9,
      161-2, 163
   Howth 195
   Irish dishes *154*
   late night opening *155*
   Merrion Row, Baggot St &
      beyond 159, 162, 163-4
   mid-range 160-2
   north of the Liffey 156, 160,
      162
   seafood *154*
   specialities & special hours
      154-5
   Temple Bar 156-8, 160-1,
      162-3
   top end 162-4
   vegetarian *154-5*
football 169
Fort Lucan 53
Four Courts 122
Fry Model Railway Exhibition
   53, 202-3
Fusiliers' Arch 106

G
Gaelic football 169
Gaiety Theatre 111
galleries
   Bank of Ireland Arts Centre
      131
   City Arts Centre 131
   Douglas Hyde Gallery of
      Modern Art 86, 131
   Hugh Lane Municipal
      Gallery of Modern Art
      116-17
   Irish Museum of Modern Art
      (IMMA) 123-4
   National Gallery 103
   other galleries 132
   RHA Gallagher Gallery 109

Gallows Hill 130
Gandon, James 33
Gate Theatre 116
gay & lesbian travellers 51
Genealogical Office 104-5
genealogy *105*
gentlemen's clubs *108*
geography 16
Glasnevin Cemetery 127
Glendalough 199-200
gliding 133
golf 133, 170
government 17-18
Government Buildings 104
GPO 113-14
Grafton St 100-1
Grand Canal 129-30
Great Denmark St 119
greyhound racing 169
Guerin, Veronica *55*
Guinness *176*
Guinness brewery 122-3
Guinness Hop Store 123

H
hang-gliding 133
Haughey, Charles 18
health 49-50
   insurance 49
   medical services 49-50
Henrietta St 122
highlights 77
Hill of Tara 208
history 11-16
   Act of Union 12
   Anglo-Irish Treaty 14-15
   Bloody Sunday (1920) 14
   Civil War 14-15
   Easter Rising 13
   IRA 14
   Irish Free State 14-15
   Irish Republic 15
   Normans 11
   Northern Ireland 16, 18
   Potato Famine 12
   Vikings 11
holidays, *see* public holidays
horse racing 169
Howth 193-6, **194**
   castle 193-5
Hugh Lane Municipal Gallery
   of Modern Art 116-17
hurling 169

I
ice skating 133-4

Internet
    access 45-6
    resources 46
Internet cafés, see cybercafés
IRA (Irish Republican Army) 14
Ireland's Eye (Howth) 195
Irish Free State 14-15
Irish Museum of Modern Art
    (IMMA) 123-4
Irish Parliament 103-4
Irish Republic 15
Irish Writers' Centre 118
itineraries 77-9
Iveagh House 107

J
James Joyce Cultural Centre
    120-1
Japanese Gardens 201
Joyce, James *21*, *58-9*

K
karting 54
Kells 207-8
Kildare 201
    Japanese Gardens 201
    National Stud 201
Kilmainham Gaol 124-6
Kilmainham Gate 124
Kilruddery House & Gardens
    192
King's Inns 121-2

L
Labour Party 18
Lane, Hugh *117*
language 27-8
    courses 134
Leinster House 103-4
libraries 54
Liffey 79
    Liffey bridges *80-1*
    Liffey quays 79-82
literature 20, 21, *22-3*, see also
    books
Lusk 203

M
Magazine Fort 126

Bold indicates maps.
Italics indicates boxed text.

Malahide 202-3
    castle 202
Malton, James *118-19*
Mansion House 101
maps 37
Marsh's Library 99-100
Martello towers *190*
McAleese, Mary 16
Mellifont Abbey 206-7
Merrion Square 109-10
microbreweries 179
Misery Hill 130
Monasterboice 207
money 39-44
    costs 42
    credit cards 42
    taxes 43-4
    tipping 43
motor sport 170
Mountjoy Square 119-20
Municipal Buildings 93
museums
    Dublin Civic Museum 100
    Dublin Writers' Museum 52,
        117-18
    free museums *43*
    Fry Model Railway
        Exhibition 53, 202-3
    Geological Museum 86
    George Bernard Shaw House
        131
    Heraldic Museum 104-5
    Irish Jewish Museum 131
    Irish Traditional Music
        Archive 131
    James Joyce Museum
        189-90
    Museum of Childhood 53,
        131
    National Maritime Museum
        188
    National Museum 53, 101-3
    National Transport Museum
        (Howth) 195
    Natural History Museum
        105
    Pearse Museum 131
    World of Wax 54, 118-19
music 20-4

N
National Aquarium 192
National Botanic Gardens 127
National Gallery 103
National Library 104
National Museum 53, 101-3

National Stud 201
Newbridge Demesne
    Traditional Farm 53
Newbridge House 203
Newman House 107-8
newspapers & magazines 47-8
North Bull Wall 129

O
O'Connell, Daniel 12
O'Connell St 111-13
Old Jameson Distillery 121
Olympia Theatre 111
organised tours
    to Dublin 68
    within Dublin 74-6

P
painting 24
parks & squares
    Fitzwilliam Square 110
    Iveagh Gardens 109
    Merrion Square 109-10
    Mountjoy Square 119-20
    National Botanic Gardens
        127
    Parnell Square 115-16
    Phoenix Park 53-4, 124-6,
        125
    St Stephen's Green 105-9
Parnell Square 115-16
Parnell, Charles Stewart 12-13
passage tombs, see Brugh na
    Bóinne
Pearse, Patrick 13
people 19
Phoenix Park 53-4, 124-6,
    125
    Visitors' Centre 53-4, 126
photography & video 48
politics 17-18
postal services 44
Potato Famine 12
Powerscourt Estate 197-8
    Powerscourt House 197
    Powerscourt Waterfall 198
Powerscourt Townhouse
    shopping centre 100, *183*
public holidays 57
public transport
    bus 71
    taxi 73
    to/from the airport 70
    to/from the ferry terminals
        70
    train 71

pubs & bars 171-81, **174**
  Grafton St area 179-80
  Merrion Row, Baggot St &
    beyond 180-1
  north of the Liffey 173-5
  Temple Bar 175-8

R

radio 48
Record Tower 92
religion 27
rhyming names *112*
Robinson, Mary 16
Rotunda Hospital 116
Royal Canal 126
Royal College of Surgeons 106
Royal Dublin Society
  Showground 131
Royal Hospital Kilmainham
  123-4
Royal Irish Academy 101
rugby 169
Russborough House 200

S

safety 42, 55-6
sailing 132
Sandycove 189-90
scuba diving 132
seaside suburbs 187-96
senior travellers 51
Shaw, George Bernard 23
shopping 182-6
  antiques 185
  books 186
  camping & backpacking
    equipment 185
  clothing 184-5

crystal 186
department stores 182-3
Irish crafts 184
jewellery 186
markets 183-4
records 185
shopping centres 182
souvenirs 184
Sinn Féin 13
Skerries 204
Slane 207
special events 57
  Bloomsday 58-9
  St Patrick's Day 57
squares, *see* parks & squares
St Begnet's Holy Well 192
St James's Gate Guinness
  Brewery 122-3
St Kevin *199*
St Mary's Pro-Cathedral
  114-15
St Patrick's Cathedral 96-9, **96**
St Patrick's Day 57
St Patrick's Tower 123
St Stephen's Green 105-9
street names 36
Swift, Jonathan 22, *98-9*
swimming 132
Swords 203

T

taxes, *see* money
telephone services 44-5
television 48
Temple Bar 88-90
theatre 26
time 48
tipping, *see* money

toilets 49
tourist offices 37
train travel 66
  discounts 67
Trim 209-10
  castle 209
Trinity College 83-7, **83**

U

Ulysses 21, 58-9
Upper Merrion St 110

V

video systems 48
Vikings 11
visas & documents 37-8

W

walking 74, 200
walking tours 135-44
Waterways Visitors' Centre 130
Web sites, *see* Internet
  resources
weights 48
Wicklow Way 200
Wilde, Oscar 22
William of Orange 11
windsurfing 132-3
Wolfe Tone 12
women travellers 50-1
work 60

Y

Yeats, John Butler 24
Yeats, WB 22

Boxed Text

Bewley's & Beshoff's 157
Bloomsday 58
Children of Lir, The 115
Dealing with Drugs 55
Dublin Clubs 108
Dublin Driving 72
Dublin Writers 22
He's 'Armless 97
Hugh Lane 117

James Joyce & Ulysses 21
James Malton & 18th Century
  Dublin 118
Jonathan Swift 98
Liffey Bridges 80
Martello Towers 190
Name's the Game, The 112
Powerscourt Townhouse
  Shopping Centre, The 183

Perfect Guiness, The 176
Rivals for Uncle Arthur
  179
Specialities & Special Hours
  154
St Kevin 199
Statues You Won't See 137
Tracing Your Ancestors 105
What's Free 43

A vision of tranquillity, broken every September by brave contestants undertaking the Liffey swim.

Never a dull moment – Grafton St has Dublin's widest selection of shops and street entertainers.

The extraordinary 1980s architectural extravaganza of the St Stephen's Green shopping centre.

MAP 2 DART & Suburban Rail Plan

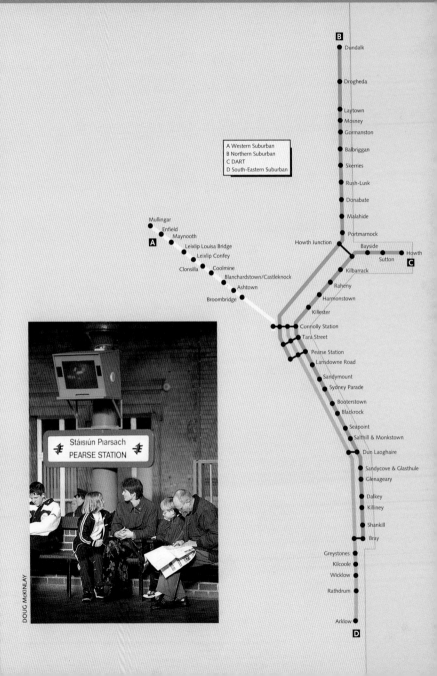

A Western Suburban
B Northern Suburban
C DART
D South-Eastern Suburban

B

Dundalk

Drogheda

Laytown
Mosney
Gormanston

Balbriggan

Skerries

Rush-Lusk

Donabate

Malahide

Portmarnock

Howth Junction

Bayside

Howth

Sutton

C

Kilbarrack

Raheny

Harmonstown

Killester

Connolly Station

Tara Street

Pearse Station

Lansdowne Road

Sandymount

Sydney Parade

Booterstown

Blackrock

Seapoint

Salthill & Monkstown

Dun Laoghaire

Sandycove & Glasthule

Glenageary

Dalkey

Killiney

Shankill

Bray

Greystones
Kilcoole
Wicklow

Rathdrum

Arklow

D

Mullingar
Enfield
Maynooth
Leixlip Louisa Bridge
Leixlip Confey
Coolmine
Clonsilla
Blanchardstown/Castleknock
Ashtown
Broombridge

A

Stáisiún Piarsach
PEARSE STATION

DOUG McKINLAY

MAP 3

To Glasnevin Cemetery & Botanic Gardens

Dunard Ave.
Dunard Walk
Dunard Drive
Dunard Park
Dunard Road
Dunard Court
Earls Court
Old Cabra Road
Caragh Road
Park View
Glenbeigh Park
McKee Park
McKee Drive
Glenbeigh Road
Annamoe Road
Cabra Drive
Ellesmere Avenue
Blackhorse Grove
Drumalee Road
Drumalee Park
Aughrim Street
Aisbury Walk

North Road

Dublin Zoo

McKee Barracks

Blackhorse Avenue

Marlborough Road
Marlborough Mews

North Circular Road

Garda Headquarters

Aughrim Place
Cowper Place
Carnew Street
Arklow Street
Ross Street
Ashford Street
O'Devaney Gardens
Cowper Street
Oxmantown Road
Finn Street
Thor Place
Swords Street
Ben Edar Road
Niall St.

Zoo Road

The Hollow

Fountain Road

People's Garden

Findlater Street
Aberdeen Street
Kinahan Street
O'Devaney Gardens
O'Devaney Gardens

Montpelier Gardens
Montpelier Park
St Bricin's Park

St Bricin's Hospital

Wellington Road

PHOENIX PARK

Chesterfield Avenue

Department of Defence

Infirmary Road

Montpelier Drive
Montpelier Hill
Arbour Hill
Temple Street West

2

1

MAP 5

Conyngham Road
Parkgate Street

3

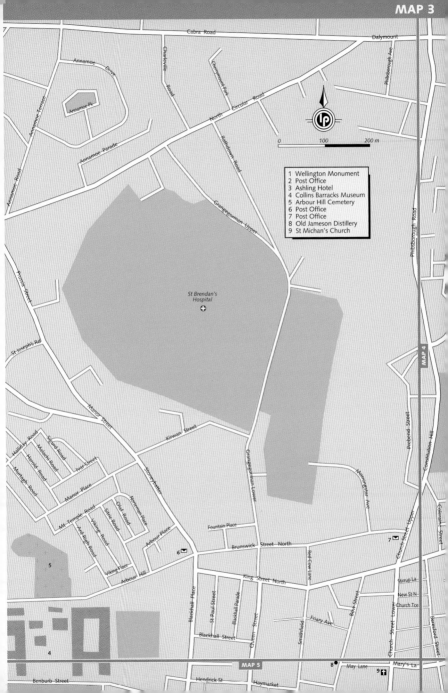

MAP 3

1 Wellington Monument
2 Post Office
3 Ashling Hotel
4 Collins Barracks Museum
5 Arbour Hill Cemetery
6 Post Office
7 Post Office
8 Old Jameson Distillery
9 St Michan's Church

MAP 4

North Circular Road

Mater
Misericordiae
Hospital

Eccles Street

0   100   200 m

St Joseph's Parade

Blessington pl

Primrose Ave

Wellington Street Upper

Blessington Lane

Fontenoy Street

Western Way

Mountjoy St Mid

Temple Cottages

Dominick Street Upper

Henrietta Lane

17

Henrietta Street

Henrietta Place

King's Inn Street

King Street North

Loftus Lane

Green Street

36

37   Parnell Street

Byrnes Row

Wolfe Tone Street

Jervis Lane Upper

Chapel Lane

Cuckoo Lane

Mary Street

38

Anglesea Row

Capel Street

Mary's Lane

64

Fruit
Market

65

Arran St E.

63

Abbey Street Upper

North Circular Road

Synnott Place

Dorset Lane

Gardiner Street Upper

Sherrard Street Upper

Eccles Place

Kelly's Row   2

Temple Street North   3

Nerney's Court

4

Hardwicke Street

7

6

Frederick Street North

Dorset Street

Great Denmark Street

10

North Great George's Street

11

St Mary's Pl   16   15

Granby Row

14

Parnell Sq North   13   12

Gardiner Place

8

Cardiff Place

9

Hill Street

Grenville Street

Rutland Place West

Parnell Square East

Garden of
Remembrance

21

Parnell Square West

Dominick Lane

Dominick Place

Granby Pl

18   Parnell Square West

19

20

23

24

22   Britain Place

Sean MacDermott

Parnell Street

Esther Brugha Street

25

26

Thomas Lane

Marlborough Street

27

Moore Lane

35   31

34   33   32

O'Connell St Upper

30

Cathedral Street

Moore Street

39

Henry Place

41

42

43   Earl Street North

40

Sampson's Lane

Henry Street

44

45   46   Sackville Place

Earl Place

Prince's St North

Liffey Street Upper

60   59

61

Abbey Street Middle

MAP 6

Bachelors
Walk   62

Royal Canal Bank

Goldsmith Street

Berkeley Road

Killarney Pde

Dunmanus Rd

Victoria Parade

Lynott Row

Innisfallen Pde

William's Place

Belvidere Road

Glenarm Road

Belvidere Place

Belvidere Court

North

MAP 3

Auburn Street

Berkeley Street

Wellington St Lower

5

Blessington Lane

Primrose Place

Broadstone Place

St Mary's Pl

N'Tenace

Long Lane

Dominick Street Lower

Bethan Street

Anne St North

Halston Street

Beresford St

George's Hill

Hammond Lane

St Michan's Street

Leo Street

Wellington Street

Dorset Street Upper

Dorset Street

Primrose Street

Blessington Street

MAP 4

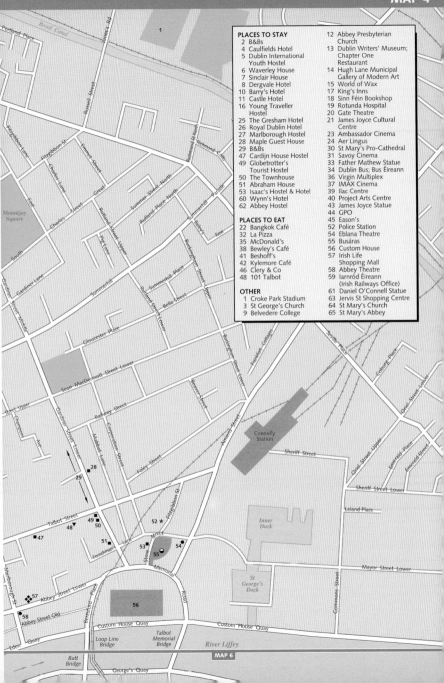

PLACES TO STAY
2 B&Bs
4 Caulfields Hotel
5 Dublin International
  Youth Hostel
6 Waverley House
7 Sinclair House
8 Dergvale Hotel
10 Barry's Hotel
11 Castle Hotel
12 Young Traveller
   Hostel
25 The Gresham Hotel
26 Royal Dublin Hotel
27 Marlborough Hostel
28 Maple Guest House
29 B&Bs
47 Cardijn House Hostel
49 Globetrotter's
   Tourist Hostel
50 The Townhouse
51 Abraham House
53 Isaac's Hostel & Hotel
60 Wynn's Hotel
62 Abbey Hostel

PLACES TO EAT
22 Bangkok Café
32 La Pizza
35 McDonald's
38 Bewley's Café
41 Beshoff's
42 Kylemore Café
46 Clery & Co
48 101 Talbot

OTHER
1 Croke Park Stadium
3 St George's Church
9 Belvedere College

12 Abbey Presbyterian
   Church
13 Dublin Writers' Museum;
   Chapter One
   Restaurant
14 Hugh Lane Municipal
   Gallery of Modern Art
15 World of Wax
17 King's Inns
18 Sinn Féin Bookshop
19 Rotunda Hospital
20 Gate Theatre
21 James Joyce Cultural
   Centre
23 Ambassador Cinema
24 Aer Lingus
30 St Mary's Pro-Cathedral
31 Savoy Cinema
33 Father Mathew Statue
34 Dublin Bus; Bus Éireann
36 Virgin Multiplex
37 IMAX Cinema
39 Ilac Centre
40 Project Arts Centre
43 James Joyce Statue
44 GPO
45 Eason's
52 Police Station
54 Eblana Theatre
55 Busáras
56 Custom House
57 Irish Life
   Shopping Mall
58 Abbey Theatre
59 Iarnród Éireann
   (Irish Railways Office)
61 Daniel O'Connell Statue
63 Jervis St Shopping Centre
64 St Mary's Church
65 St Mary's Abbey

MAP 5

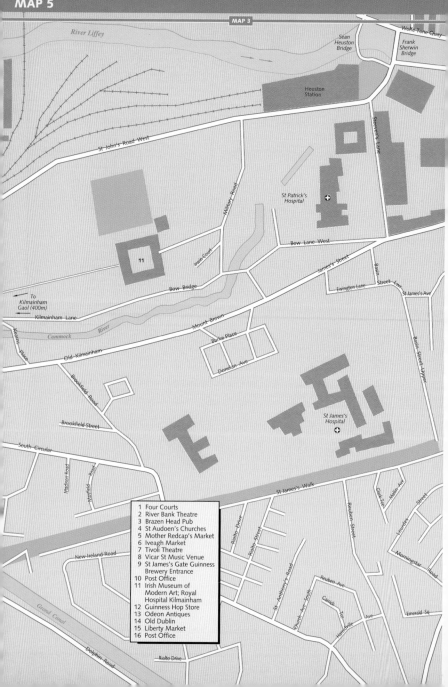

MAP 3

River Liffey

Wolfe Tone Quay

Sean Heuston Bridge

Frank Sherwin Bridge

Heuston Station

Sheverin's Lane

St John's Road West

Military Road

St Patrick's Hospital

Bow Lane West

James's Street

Basin Street Lwr

11

Irwin Court

Ewington Lane

St James's Ave

Bow Bridge

To Kilmainham Gaol (400m)

Kilmainham Lane

Mount Brown

Cammock River

Burke Place

Kearns Place

Old Kilmainham

Donelan Ave

Basin Street Upper

Brookfield Road

St James's Hospital

Brookfield Street

South Circular

Madison Road

Mayfield Road

St James's Walk

Clark Tce

Mallin Ave

Reuben Street

Lourdes Street

Morningstar Road

New Ireland Road

Rialto Drive

Rialto Street

St Anthony's Road

Church Ave South

Reuben Ave

Carrick Tce

Hamsville

Ave

Emerald Sq

Grand Canal

Dolphin Road

Rialto Drive

1 Four Courts
2 River Bank Theatre
3 Brazen Head Pub
4 St Audoen's Churches
5 Mother Redcap's Market
6 Iveagh Market
7 Tivoli Theatre
8 Vicar St Music Venue
9 St James's Gate Guinness
   Brewery Entrance
10 Post Office
11 Irish Museum of
   Modern Art; Royal
   Hospital Kilmainham
12 Guinness Hop Store
13 Odeon Antiques
14 Old Dublin
15 Liberty Market
16 Post Office

MAP 5

MAP 3

MAP 6

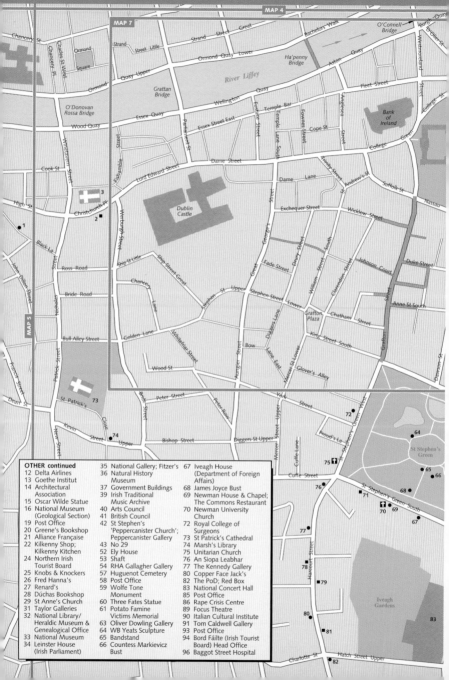

MAP 6

MAP 4

MAP 7

O'Connell Bridge

River Liffey

Strand
Strand Street Little
Ormond Quay Lower
Ha'penny Bridge
Aston Quay
Bachelors Walk
Westmoreland St

Chancery St
Charles St West
Chancery Pl
Ormond
Square
Quay Upper
Ormond

Grattan Bridge

Essex Quay
Wellington Quay
Temple Bar
Fleet Street
College St

O'Donovan Rossa Bridge
Wood Quay

Essex Street East
Parliament Street
Essex Street East
Fownes Street
Cope St
College Green
Bank of Ireland

Cook St

Dame Street
Dame Lane
Trinity Street
St Andrew's St
Suffolk St
Nassau

High St
Christchurch Pl

3

2

Lord Edward Street
Werburgh Street

Dublin Castle

Exchequer Street
George's Street
Wicklow Street

1

Black La
John Dillon Street
Nicholas Street

Ross Road

Ship St Little
Ship Street Great
Fade Street
Drury Street
George's Street South
Johnson Court
Duke Street

Bride Road

Chancery Lane
Stephen St Upper
William Street South
Clarendon Street
Anne St South

MAP 5

Golden Lane
Whitefriar Street
Stephen Street Lower
Drury Lane
King Street South
Grafton Plaza
Chatham Street
Grafton Street

Bull Alley Street

Bow
Mercer Street
Glover's Alley

Wood St

St Patrick's
73

Peter Street
Bride Street
Peter Row
York Street
St Stephen's Green West
72

St Stephen's Green

Dean St
Francis Street
New Street
Kevin Street Upper
74
Bishop Street
Diggers St Upper
Mercer Street Upper
Cuffe Lane
Proud's La
64

75
Cuffe Street

76
St Stephen's Green South
65
66
68

71
70
69
67

77

78

79

80
81

82

Charlotte St
Hatch Street Upper

Harcourt Street

Iveagh Gardens
83

OTHER continued

12 Delta Airlines
13 Goethe Institut
14 Architectural Association
15 Oscar Wilde Statue
16 National Museum (Geological Section)
19 Post Office
20 Greene's Bookshop
21 Alliance Française
22 Kilkenny Shop; Kilkenny Kitchen
24 Northern Irish Tourist Board
25 Knobs & Knockers
26 Fred Hanna's
27 Renard's
28 Dúchas Bookshop
29 St Anne's Church
31 Taylor Galleries
32 National Library/ Heraldic Museum & Genealogical Office
33 National Museum
34 Leinster House (Irish Parliament)

35 National Gallery; Fitzer's
36 Natural History Museum
37 Government Buildings
39 Irish Traditional Music Archive
40 Arts Council
41 British Council
42 St Stephen's 'Peppercanister Church'; Peppercanister Gallery
43 No 29
52 Ely House
53 Shaft
54 RHA Gallagher Gallery
57 Huguenot Cemetery
58 Post Office
59 Wolfe Tone Monument
60 Three Fates Statue
61 Potato Famine Victims Memorial
63 Oliver Dowling Gallery
64 WB Yeats Sculpture
65 Bandstand
66 Countess Markievicz Bust

67 Iveagh House (Department of Foreign Affairs)
68 James Joyce Bust
69 Newman House & Chapel; The Commons Restaurant
70 Newman University Church
72 Royal College of Surgeons
73 St Patrick's Cathedral
74 Marsh's Library
75 Unitarian Church
76 An Siopa Leabhar
77 The Kennedy Gallery
80 Copper Face Jack's
82 The PoD; Red Box
83 National Concert Hall
85 Post Office
86 Rape Crisis Centre
89 Focus Theatre
90 Italian Cultural Institute
91 Tom Caldwell Gallery
93 Post Office
94 Bord Fáilte (Irish Tourist Board) Head Office
96 Baggot Street Hospital

MAP 6

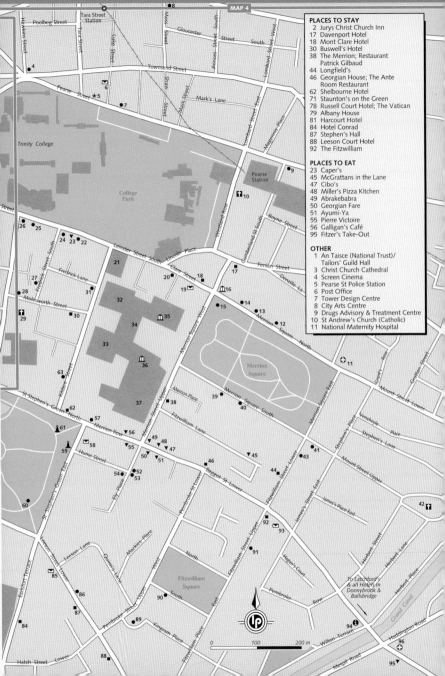

MAP 4

PLACES TO STAY
2 Jurys Christ Church Inn
17 Davenport Hotel
18 Mont Clare Hotel
30 Buswell's Hotel
38 The Merrion; Restaurant
    Patrick Gilbaud
44 Longfield's
46 Georgian House; The Ante
    Room Restaurant
62 Shelbourne Hotel
71 Staunton's on the Green
78 Russell Court Hotel; The Vatican
79 Albany House
81 Harcourt Hotel
84 Hotel Conrad
87 Stephen's Hall
88 Leeson Court Hotel
92 The Fitzwilliam

PLACES TO EAT
23 Caper's
45 McGrattans in the Lane
47 Cibo's
48 Miller's Pizza Kitchen
49 Abrakebabra
50 Georgian Fare
51 Ayumi-Ya
55 Pierre Victoire
56 Galligan's Café
95 Fitzer's Take-Out

OTHER
1 An Taisce (National Trust)/
   Tailors' Guild Hall
3 Christ Church Cathedral
4 Screen Cinema
5 Pearse St Police Station
6 Post Office
7 Tower Design Centre
8 City Arts Centre
9 Drugs Advisory & Treatment Centre
10 St Andrew's Church (Catholic)
11 National Maternity Hospital

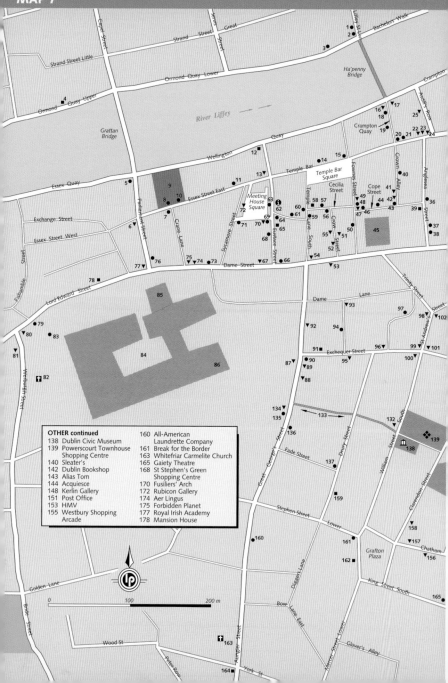

MAP 7

OTHER continued

138 Dublin Civic Museum
139 Powerscourt Townhouse
    Shopping Centre
140 Sleater's
142 Dublin Bookshop
143 Alias Tom
144 Acquiesce
148 Kerlin Gallery
151 Post Office
153 HMV
155 Westbury Shopping
    Arcade

160 All-American
    Laundrette Company
161 Break for the Border
163 Whitefriar Carmelite Church
165 Gaiety Theatre
168 St Stephen's Green
    Shopping Centre
170 Fusiliers' Arch
172 Rubicon Gallery
174 Aer Lingus
175 Forbidden Planet
177 Royal Irish Academy
178 Mansion House

0   100   200 m

MAP 7

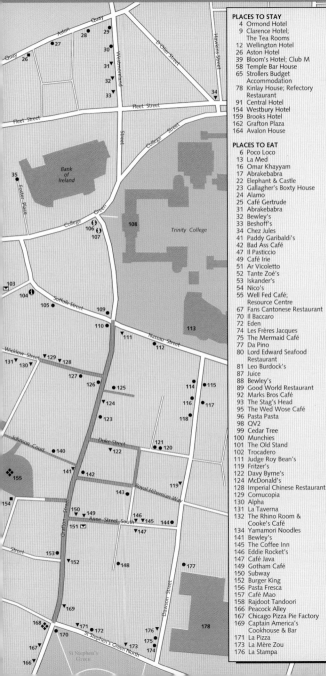

PLACES TO STAY
4 Ormond Hotel
9 Clarence Hotel;
The Tea Rooms
12 Wellington Hotel
26 Aston Hotel
39 Bloom's Hotel; Club M
58 Temple Bar House
65 Strollers Budget
Accommodation
78 Kinlay House; Refectory
Restaurant
91 Central Hotel
154 Westbury Hotel
159 Brooks Hotel
162 Grafton Plaza
164 Avalon House

PLACES TO EAT
6 Poco Loco
13 La Med
16 Omar Khayyam
17 Abrakebabra
22 Elephant & Castle
23 Gallagher's Boxty House
24 Alamo
25 Café Gertrude
26 Abrakebabra
32 Bewley's
33 Beshoff's
34 Chez Jules
41 Paddy Garibaldi's
42 Bad Ass Café
47 Il Pasticcio
49 Café Irie
51 Ar Vicoletto
52 Tante Zoé's
53 Iskander's
54 Nico's
55 Well Fed Café;
Resource Centre
67 Fans Cantonese Restaurant
70 Il Baccaro
72 Eden
74 Les Frères Jacques
75 The Mermaid Café
77 Da Pino
80 Lord Edward Seafood
Restaurant
81 Leo Burdock's
87 Juice
88 Bewley's
89 Good World Restaurant
92 Marks Bros Café
93 The Stag's Head
95 The Wed Wose Café
96 Pasta Pasta
98 QV2
99 Cedar Tree
100 Munchies
101 The Old Stand
102 Trocadero
111 Judge Roy Bean's
119 Fritzer's
122 Davy Byrne's
124 McDonald's
128 Imperial Chinese Restaurant
129 Cornucopia
130 Alpha
131 La Taverna
132 The Rhino Room &
Cooke's Café
134 Yamamori Noodles
141 Bewley's
145 The Coffee Inn
146 Eddie Rocket's
147 Café Java
149 Gotham Café
150 Subway
152 Burger King
156 Pasta Fresca
157 Café Mao
158 Rajdoot Tandoori
166 Peacock Alley
167 Chicago Pizza Pie Factory
169 Captain America's
Cookhouse & Bar
171 La Pizza
173 La Mère Zou
176 La Stampa

OTHER
1 Dublin Woollen Company
2 Hags with the Bags
3 Winding Stair
5 Sunlight Chambers
7 Bad Bob's
8 Octagon Bar
10 Kitchen
11 Applied Arts Centre;
Designyard
14 Original Print Gallery
15 Temple Bar Gallery
& Studios
18 China Blue
19 George Webb
20 Borderline Records
21 Rory's Fishing Tackle
27 Virgin Records Megastore
28 USIT Student Travel
29 Irish Ferries
30 Stena Sealink
35 Bank of Ireland
Arts Centre
36 Stock Exchange
37 DV8
38 Damascus
40 Eamon Doran's Imbibing
Emporium
43 Eager Beaver
44 Through the Arch;
Graphic Studio
45 Central Bank
46 Comet Records
48 Boy Scout Shop
50 Flip
56 Sé Sí
57 Claddagh Records
59 Cyberia
60 Betacafé
61 Temple Bar Music Centre
62 Temple Bar Information
Centre
63 The Ark
64 Club Zazu
66 Condom Power
68 'Friends' Meeting House
69 Irish Film Centre (IFC)
71 Gallery of Photography
73 Olympia Theatre
76 Thomas Read & Co
79 Irish Celtic Craftshop
82 St Werburgh's Church
83 Whichcraft
84 Dublin Castle
85 City Hall
86 Crypt Art Centre
(Dublin Castle)
90 Sub-City
94 Rí Rá
97 Andrew's Lane Theatre
& Gallery
103 Post Office
104 Dublin Tourism Office
(St Andrew's Church)
105 Automobile Association
of Ireland
106 Thomas Cook
107 American Express
108 Trinity College
109 Molly Malone Statue
110 House of Ireland
112 Blarney Woollen Mills
113 Douglas Hyde Gallery
114 Alitalia Office
115 Ryanair Office
116 Hodges Figgis
117 Waterstone's
118 Air Portugal (TAP);
Iberia; Swissair
120 Cathach Books
121 Cathach Records
123 Marks & Spencers
125 Lillie's Bordello
126 Brown Thomas
127 Sweater Shop
133 George's St Arcade
135 Walton's
136 Planet Cyber Café
137 Road Records &
Big Brother Records

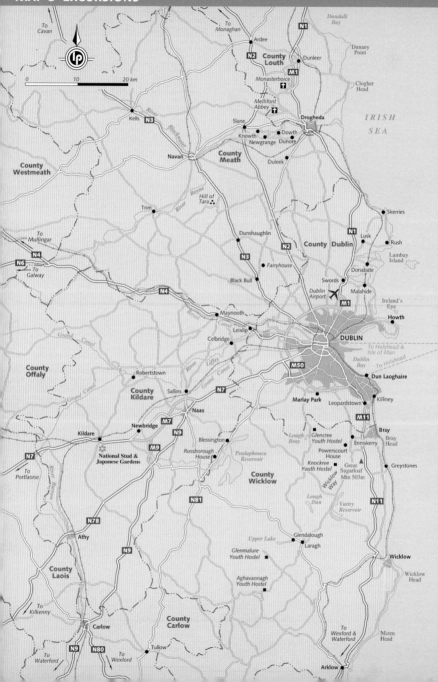

MAP 8 EXCURSIONS

The Perron, the superb Italian-style stairway at Powerscourt House, leads to the Triton Lake. Two statues of Pegasus, the immortal winged horse of Greek mythology, overlook the lake.

MAP LEGEND

BOUNDARIES

............................International
............................State
............................Disputed

HYDROGRAPHY

............................Coastline
............................River, Creek
............................Lake
............................Intermittent Lake
............................Salt Lake
............................Canal
............................Spring, Rapids
............................Waterfalls
............................Swamp

ROUTES & TRANSPORT

............................Freeway
............................Highway
............................Major Road
............................Minor Road
............................Unsealed Road
............................City Freeway
............................City Highway
............................City Road
............................City Street, Lane

............................Pedestrian Mall
............................Tunnel
............................Train Route & Station
............................Metro & Station
............................Tramway
............................Cable Car or Chairlift
............................Walking Track
............................Walking Tour
............................Ferry Route

AREA FEATURES

............................Building, Hotel
............................Park, Gardens
............................Cemetery

............................Market
............................Beach, Desert
............................Urban Area

MAP SYMBOLS

○ **CAPITAL**............National Capital
◉ **CAPITAL**............State Capital
● **CITY**............City
● **Town**............Town
● Village............Village
○............Point of Interest

■............Place to Stay
⚐............Camping Ground
⊡............Caravan Park
⌂............Hut or Chalet

▼............Place to Eat
🍺............Pub or Bar

✈............Airport
............Ancient or City Wall
⁙............Archaeological Site
⊖............Bank
🏛............Castle
🏛............Cathedral or Church
............Cliff or Escarpment
◐............Embassy
✿............Garden
⛳............Golf Course
⊕............Hospital
🗼............Lighthouse
🗿............Monument
▲............Mountain or Hill

🏛............Museum
←............One Way Street
🅿............Parking
)(............Pass
★............Police Station
✉............Post Office
❖............Shopping Centre
............Swimming Pool
............Synagogue
☎............Telephone
............Temple
❶............Tourist Information
............Transport
............Zoo

Note: not all symbols displayed above appear in this book

LONELY PLANET OFFICES

Australia
PO Box 617, Hawthorn, Victoria 3122
☎ (03) 9819 1877 fax (03) 9819 6459
email: talk2us@lonelyplanet.com.au

USA
150 Linden St, Oakland, CA 94607
☎ (510) 893 8555 TOLL FREE: 800 275 8555
fax (510) 893 8572
email: info@lonelyplanet.com

UK
10a Spring Place, London NW5 3BH
☎ (0171) 428 4800 fax (0171) 428 4828
email: go@lonelyplanet.co.uk

France
1 rue du Dahomey, 75011 Paris
☎ 01 55 25 33 00 fax 01 55 25 33 01
email: bip@lonelyplanet.fr
minitel: 3615 lonelyplanet *(1,29 F TTC/min)*

World Wide Web: www.lonelyplanet.com *or* AOL keyword: lp
Lonely Planet Images: lpi@lonelyplanet.com.au